DISCOVERING MANCHESTER

A walking guide to Manchester and Salford – plus suburban strolls and visits to surrounding attractions

Barry Worthington

With photographs by Graham Beech

Reprinted with revisions 2005

Published by Sigma Leisure – an imprint of
Sigma Press, 5 Alton Road, Wilmslow, Cheshire SK9 5DY, England.

British Library Cataloguing in Publication Data
A CIP record for this book is available from the British Library.

ISBN: 1-85058-774-4

Typesetting and Design by: Sigma Press, Wilmslow, Cheshire.

Cover: Manchester Town Hall, © manchesterimages.com. The two smaller photographs are of: the Marks and Spencer flagship store in Manchester; the lifting bridge across the canal to the Lowry Centre, Salford Quays *(both by Graham Beech)*

Photographs within the book: all by Graham Beech, except where stated otherwise.

Maps: Gelder Design & Mapping, using a base map kindly provided by Marketing Manchester.

Printed by: Interprint Ltd, Malta.

Preface

This guidebook is intended to answer a definite need. Surprisingly enough, there is no other genuinely descriptive guide to the city centre, let alone the Greater Manchester area. The major attractions are perhaps mentioned in a few pages in British and American guides to Britain. As to the city itself, there are a few formats consisting of compilations of information. The best of the 'encyclopaedia-style' guidebooks is published by City Life. If you want information about cafés, pubs, clubs, music, shopping or performance venues, you can do no better than obtaining a copy of their publication.

In contrast, this guide does not supply encyclopaedic information for the visitor. Instead, it notes that you are an intelligent person with a great deal of curiosity about Manchester as a place. Assuming that you need a personal guide, preferably a knowledgeable local inhabitant, it will take you on a series of walks. Each walk will describe the surroundings, interesting or important buildings, visitable interiors, and the highlights of the main museum and gallery collections. It will try to set things in an historical or current context, usually illustrated with anecdotes about people – some famous, and others not so well known, but just as interesting. It will entertain, perhaps will be controversial, but never boring.

The walks are arranged in a particular order, but the guide is intended to be flexible. They can be combined with other walks, or extended into a number of excursions. (Notes in the text will indicate where such a choice can be made.) On average, each walk should take about one and a half hours, but if the visitor lingers in a museum or other attraction, this will be longer. An indication of the minimum time required for the major attractions will be given. Whatever the case, there will be found a convenient way of occupying a morning or an afternoon.

An accompanying map illustrates each walk, except for the chapters on the Museum of Science and Industry and Excursions and Environs. Numbered sites on the maps refer to numbers in the text. Businesses and commercial sites, such as shops or pubs, are indicated in *italics*. **Bold** letters denote objects of particular interest or important locations within a building. Opening times and free admission (where known) are recorded. The majority of the walks are suitable for wheelchairs (Castlefield being a notable exception) and most museums and attractions have lifts or ramps. Marks of commendation are, of course, based on the author's experience and tastes!

The information contained was correct upon going to press, but such things as opening times are always subject to alteration, so it would be best to check them if there is something you particularly wish to see.

Author's note to this update

Manchester is changing at an almost alarming rate. Consequently, the original text has been updated and descriptions of new developments and attractions are included. Large parts of the Ancoats walk have been rewritten to take account of the rapid gentrification of the district.

The first printing of this book had to anticipate a number of interiors of attractions that had not yet opened. It is now possible to give an accurate account of the galleries in Urbis and the Imperial War Museum North, together with new galleries in the City Art Gallery, Manchester Museum, and the Museum of Science and Industry.

Lastly, a number of omissions in the original guide have been remedied. However, like painting the Forth Bridge, a work of this nature is never complete. Updates will continue to be posted upon the Sigma website as required, and the author would be grateful for any suggestions, comments, or corrections from his readers, forwarded courtesy of the publisher.

Barry Worthington

Acknowledgements

This book could not have been written without the assistance of a great number of people, whether they were associated with the libraries, attractions, and developments that I visited, or the planners and council staff who tried to visualise for me things that were not yet in existence. Everyone, without exception, went out of their way to assist.

A vast number of sources of information were used in researching the walks, but the author found the following publications particularly useful.

Philip Atkins: *Guide Across Manchester* (1983)

Ian Beesley and Peter de Figuarido: *Victorian Manchester and Salford* (1988)

L.D. Bradshaw: *Origins of Street Names in the City of Manchester* (1985)

Derek Brumhead and Terry Wyke: *A Walk Round Manchester Statues* (1990)

John Parkinson Bailey: *Manchester – An Architectural History* (2000)

Jonathan Schofield: *City Life Guide to Manchester* (2000)

T. Swindells: *Manchester Streets and Manchester Men* (1910)

Victoria History of the County of Lancaster (1907-1914)

I must also place on record a debt of gratitude to Sigma Leisure, whose advice was invaluable. Your suggestions and comments may be sent to me, care of Sigma.

This book is for:

Granny Stew, Mr Harrington, Stanley Swift, Mark Friedman, Miss Eccles (and her dogs), Jessie the postmistress, Janet the snuff seller, Alderman Leslie Lever, and, above all …
Harold Thomas Worthington and Mary Florence Davies, my late and dearly beloved parents
… Manchester Men (and women) all.

Contents

Free Internet Update Service

Manchester and Salford are dynamic, fast-moving cities – new buildings appear, old ones are refurbished and a few may even disappear in the name of progress. Opening hours and facilities may also change. This book will be updated whenever it is reprinted, but check our website for updates and corrections in the meantime. This service is completely free of charge: just go to the 'updates' section at **www.sigmapress.co.uk** for further information.

We welcome input from our readers to this service.You can send your suggestions by post (see back cover) or by e-mail to:

info@sigmapress.co.uk

Thanks in advance for your help!

A Little History

Mancunians have always thought that they are special in some way, a trait that outsiders either find comical or infuriating. As to why they should consider themselves so different to the rest of the English is a moot question. The answer partly lies in geography, partly in historical circumstance.

Manchester, indeed, the whole north of England, lies in an area considered unimportant for the greater part of English history. It was once a wild unsettled region of scattered and far-flung habitations, a region of forest, hills, and 'waste'. Isolation, together with a largely pastoral economy, bred a sturdy independence of spirit – the feudal system was never properly established, the social structure always remained fluid. The English 'class structure' never thrived in these parts.

Again, Manchester has always been in the borderlands, between the Midlands and the North. Mancunians were, for many centuries, a frontier people – a melting pot of contrasting cultures and ways of life. This important trait later appears at the time of the industrial revolution, producing a truly cosmopolitan city and, perhaps, a new type of Englishman. In short, at various times in history, Manchester has been 'neither one thing nor the other'.

Moreover, such confusion does not make for accurate history. Who were the first inhabitants of Manchester? No one knows. Where was the first settlement, destined to grow into a great city? No one is exactly sure. The origins of Manchester are shrouded in mystery and legend. All that we know for sure is that the Romans built a fort here, at the fringe of the tribal confederation headed by the Brigantes, and called it 'Mamucium'. The reconstructed remains may be found in Castlefield. The fort soon attracted a 'vicus', a civilian settlement catering to the needs of travellers and the garrison, and it appears to have been an early centre of Christianity. But the Romans left, and Manchester once again was lost from view.

The limited evidence of the 'Dark Ages' suggest that the North West, at the fringes of Celtic England, was one of the last areas to be absorbed into the Anglo-Saxon world. Hence the locally based myths of Sir Lancelot and 'Sir Gawain and the Green Knight'. The new frontier, defined by the Mersey, now represented the borderland between the Saxon kingdoms of Mercia and Northumbria. The latter became part of the Danelaw when the Norsemen conquered it. This is why the city has a Deansgate and the local dialect has so many Scandinavian words and speech patterns. But the town was reoccupied by Edward the Elder, and garrisoned as an important strategic point. The Mersey is still an important 'cultural' frontier to this day – at least as far as some people are concerned – for beyond its waters lie the 'Cheshire set' who are considered (rather unfairly) as the antithesis of all that a true Mancunian should be.

Manchester was part of the royal manor of Salford in the reign of Edward the Confessor, and it is possible that Saxon kings and important nobility may have come to the area to hunt. But whatever existed was no doubt destroyed in the 'Harrowing of the North' by William the Conqueror. Manchester later appears, along with its church, in the famous Domesday Book, but the entry raises more questions than it answers. At some stage, the principal settlement moved from Castlefield to the area around the present cathedral, and a fortified manor house was established.

The parish church may have been here, but it is more likely that it was sited somewhere around Parsonage Gardens.

The manorial lords were absentees for the most part, but charters were issued, granting rights to the inhabitants (and a mistake by a clerk resulted in Manchester becoming a separate township from Salford). The little place prospered as a market centre for the region. A fine collegiate church, with an associated College of Priests, was endowed in the reign of Henry V.

A textile town

However, profounder changes were afoot. The Pennine hills became sheep pasture, and the rural inhabitants utilised idle hours in their cottages to spin the wool into yarn. Tradition suggests that Flemish weavers established themselves in Manchester in the reign of Edward III, but weaving certainly developed locally from the 14th century onwards. There were no trade guilds (or few that had any power) to regulate the trade, few concerns about experimentation, and plenty of cheap yarn to be had. In this liberal environment, the cloth industry thrived, and Manchester thrived with it. By the late-15th century, Manchester had enough wealthy men to endow chantry chapels in the collegiate church, hoping to buy their way into heaven.

The Reformation exerted a profound impact on Manchester. The place became a noted centre for Puritanism, a godly place for godly men. On the whole, the puritans have had a bad press – the name is now a synonym for 'prude', 'killjoy', or even 'hypocrite'. But the puritan frame of mind had another side to it. It gave birth to the individual sense of identity, the concept of equality of opportunity, religious tolerance, the desire for individual and intellectual self-improvement, and even paved the way for equality of the sexes. Many of these concepts later became enshrined in the phenomenon of the 'Manchester Man'.

Consequently, it comes as no surprise to learn that Manchester was a parliamentarian stronghold. Indeed the English Civil War is said to have begun here. This war released a pent-up outburst of religious and creative feeling. Nonconformity was the inheritance of the puritan revolution, and Manchester, like many other parts of the north of England, harboured nonconformists of every hue – Quakers, Baptists, Independents, and later, goodness knows how many varieties of Methodists. Even the established Anglican Church sometimes had to trim its sails to accommodate a no-nonsense independent religious frame of mind in the area.

How, then, to explain the curious episode of the Jacobites, the supporters of Charles Edward Stuart, who occupied Manchester without opposition in 1745? It must be remembered that Manchester then had no town corporation to rally opposition. The local magistrates were mainly landed gentry of conservative views. And it should be remembered that impoverished Tory gentry families had started to set their younger sons 'to trade', apprenticing them to merchants, becoming, in turn, Manchester merchants themselves. But it was the last throw of the dice, for the future lay with political radicalism.

By this time, Manchester was a phenomenon. It was "the greatest mere village" in the country, larger than some towns, but without local government and certainly without parliamentary representation. The 'village' was further transformed by the industrial revolution, which started to make its presence felt in the last quarter of the 18th century. This is not the place to detail what happened. Suffice it to say that residents saw Manchester transformed from a market town to a great industrial city within their lifetimes. The pace of change was incredible – and frightening.

Manchester became a tourist attraction, visited by all manner of people as a harbinger of what the future might hold. They were repelled, horrified, fascinated, and inspired, sometimes at the same time. Anything seemed to happen in Manchester – the creation of new manufacturing techniques, new forms of transport, new ways of living, new religious institutions, new educational institutions, new workers organisations, and an organised working class. Here was a new industrial society in the making, with a new culture, new values, perhaps epitomising a new civilisation. In terms of historical significance, in 1844 Benjamin Disraeli, in his novel 'Conningsby', went so far as to say:

"... the age of ruins is past. Have you seen Manchester? Manchester is as great a human exploit as Athens."

The new middle class, sometimes in alliance with the new working class, espoused the cause of political radicalism. They obtained municipal incorporation, and went on to obtain the repeal of the Corn Laws. Their thinking crystallised as the so-called 'Manchester School', linked to the twin lodestars of 'laissez-faire' and 'free trade'. This was more than economic theory. It was a belief in a form of economic progress that would create unimagined wealth, cause poverty to disappear, and promote an era of universal peace.

Victorian times

The 'Manchester Man' became a well-known English type, a strange contradiction. Wealthy, but usually self-made. Patriotic, but nonconformist in religion, and radical in politics, something of an outsider. He was patrician in outlook, but disliking snobbery, affectation, or the pretensions of class. An advocate of strict economy in public expenditure, but generous to a fault in the sphere of private charity, a public benefactor, and often a philanthropist.

But the population of Manchester was not completely English in origin. By the end of the 19th century, it contained communities of Irish, Germans, Levantines, Russian Jews, Italians, and goodness knows who else. Again, the interplay between the different cultures produced a rich social and cultural life, and a great flowering of the arts. Radicalism moved into other areas, for "what Manchester does today, the rest of the world does tomorrow". A new form of liberalism appeared, advocating a prototype welfare state. Manchester became a cradle of the modern Labour movement. And the Pankhurst family laid the foundations of female emancipation.

The great bubble of Victorian prosperity began to burst towards the end of the century. The Ship Canal project indicated a last attempt to reverse the tide in the period before the First World War. Manchester managed to weather the inter-war depression, but emerged a shadow of her former self. In any case, the structure of the British economy was changing. Textiles and heavy engineering were in a steady decline as Britain transformed itself into a tertiary economy. The Thatcher administration delivered the coup de grâce. In a parallel development, economic power shifted to the centre – the headquarters of major companies, newspapers, even trade unions, moved to London. Manchester appeared to be marginalised.

As a declining city in the 20th century, Manchester found itself beset by a host of problems – widespread unemployment, dereliction, drug abuse, and crime. The

Hulme development, in particular, achieved national notoriety. But Mancunians are nothing, if not resilient. Throughout this period, Manchester spearheaded moves to hold the identity of the region together. The growth of Manchester United to superstar status was just one side of the coin. Granada Television played an important role in keeping identities and aspirations to the fore, and a great deal was achieved by the former Greater Manchester Council in infrastructure improvement.

Modern Manchester

Hey presto! Manchester has now re-invented itself and is well on the way to becoming a European city of the first rank. It has the only category one 'gateway' airport outside Heathrow. It is unrivalled as a major centre of finance and commerce. It remains an important cultural centre. Recent years have seen a new concert hall, a new arts complex, and a blossoming of museums and galleries. Retail facilities now include 'names' once only found in the capital. Manchester has pioneered the introduction of light rail to British cities, with the introduction of the excellent Metrolink system.

Moreover, the city is now a byword for lifestyle – a 24-hour entertainment scene, a major international rock music centre, and a world of café society and studio or loft apartments. This has resulted in several television series being filmed in Manchester. In terms of subculture, one needs only to mention the Gay Village and the gay 'Mardi Gras' festival. Last, but not least, the centre of Manchester has been transformed, mainly because of the IRA bomb. Of course, Manchester still has its problems. But it is clear that Manchester people have pulled the rabbit out of the hat again.

These lines are being written in the year of the Commonwealth Games, intended to mark a decade of progress. The question is: where does Manchester go from here? The answer is clear. Manchester must, once more, become a cosmopolitan European City, loosening its ties with London, and forging its own links in a Europe of the Regions. To some extent, this is already starting to happen, and people are talking about regional devolution. And this would suit many Mancunians. After all, they are special!

The corner of the Marks & Spencer building on Exchange Square

1 The Mediaeval/Millennium Quarter

Start: Exchange Square

Estimated time of walk: 1½ hours

Interiors: Cathedral – 1 hour; Urbis – 1 hour; Chetham's – ½ hour

Highlights: Starting from the new square, a tour of the old quarter, taking in the oldest domestic building in the city, a mediaeval bridge, the historic cathedral, and a unique former college of mediaeval priests.

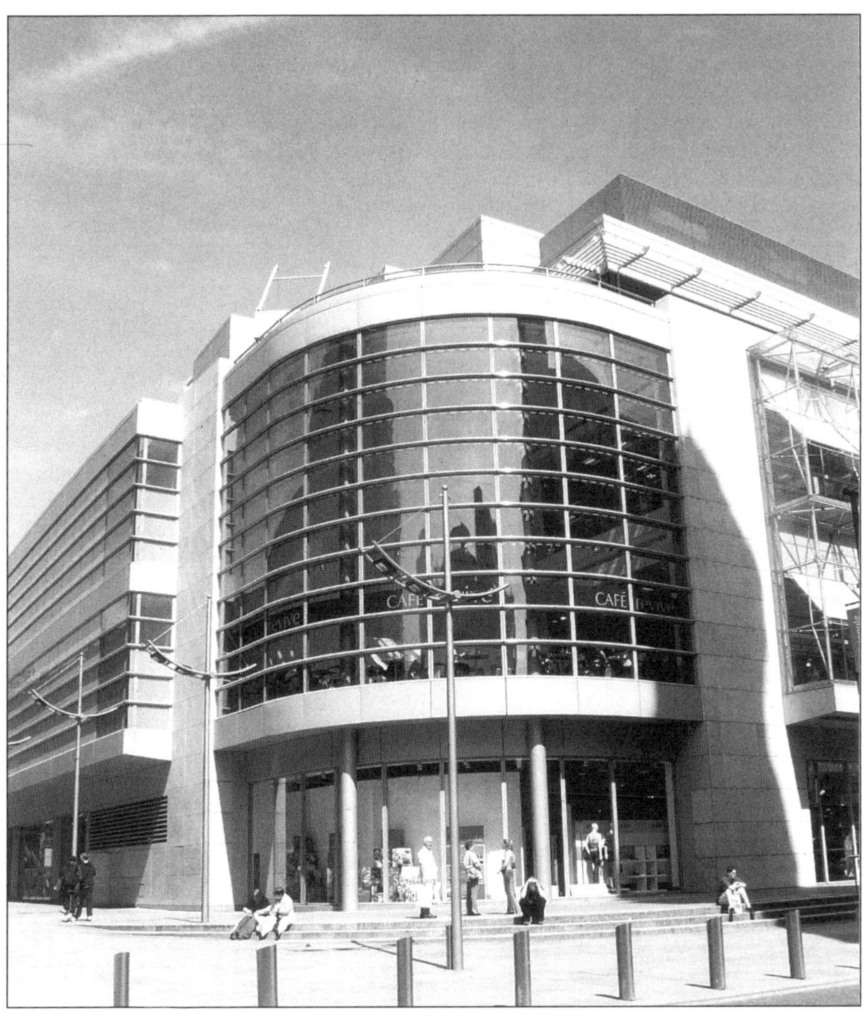

Where to begin? Piccadilly? Albert Square? The Roman Fort? None of these, for only one place encapsulates the current spirit of the city – Exchange Square, an affirmation of the process of renewal and reinvention, and a symbol of triumph over adversity. It is also the gateway to its historic heart. Thus, an exploration of the City of Manchester really ought to start at the flight of steps at the end of the city's latest street, and overlooking the newest civic square. New Cathedral Street steps *(1)* may be found by making for the unmissable landmark of *Marks and Spencer* at the top end of Market Street, and walking down New Cathedral Street on the north side of the building. The view from the steps over Exchange Square is quite spectacular. Directly ahead is a glimpse of the cathedral down a short alleyway rejoicing in the name of Cathedral Gates. Panning around in a clockwise direction, the picturesque Old Shambles lies to the right, and the great bulk of the Corn Exchange curves away towards Corporation Street. The 'Printworks' advertises itself by illuminated signs. The view continues along the Arndale Centre redevelopment, which includes a new *Next* store facing the Square and an impressive glass and steel entrance. This accesses New Canon Street, a former thoroughfare enclosed in the form of a winter garden. (The whole development is intended for completion by Christmas, 2005.) The eye then moves along the front of *Marks and Spencer's* department store – with its windmills! – to terminate beyond the West Shambles at the *Mitre Hotel,* completing the clockwise traverse. New Cathedral Street forms a line of sight linking the Old Shambles and St Ann's Church (p.37) behind us. This was an important feature of the redevelopment plan.

Exchange Square

Exchange Square (Martha Schwartz, 1999) is the net result of many years of street widening, wartime damage and, finally, the IRA bomb. It is a vibrant scene, particularly on a fine day, the perfect arena in which to watch people and the world go by. But notice an interesting attempt to solve the problem of different levels (the land slopes in a leftward direction, down towards the river). A flat paved area runs in front of *Marks and Spencer,* between Corporation Street and the steps. The low-level part of the square, which we overlook, is linked with the upper by a series of curved sloping **terraces**, that spring from a point near the end of the Corn Exchange like a gorgeous fan. The stone cladding is punctuated by rows of coloured lights that produce changing patterns in the evening. A **water feature** runs along the edge of the terracing, flat-surfaced rustic stones amid hidden fountains, the water gushing from tap-like dispensers at one end. Small (and not so small) children delight to walk along it.

Back to those **windmills**! The American designer, it is said, included palm trees in the original plan. She recommended artificial ones when told that they were not native to the city, and local opposition ensued. Fortunately, the day was saved. An art school lecturer, who was fascinated by the reflection of the Corn Exchange in the glass frontage of the new store, thought it reminded him of a sandcastle. All that was needed were windmills! So five giant versions were erected. They are powered by electric motors, by the way.

Marks and Spencer

Manchester boasts a flagship ***Marks and Spencer's*** store (Building Design Partnership). Michael Marks (a Polish Jew who arrived in England in 1884) met Thomas Spencer (an ambitious Yorkshireman) and opened a 'bazaar' in Leeds Market Hall.

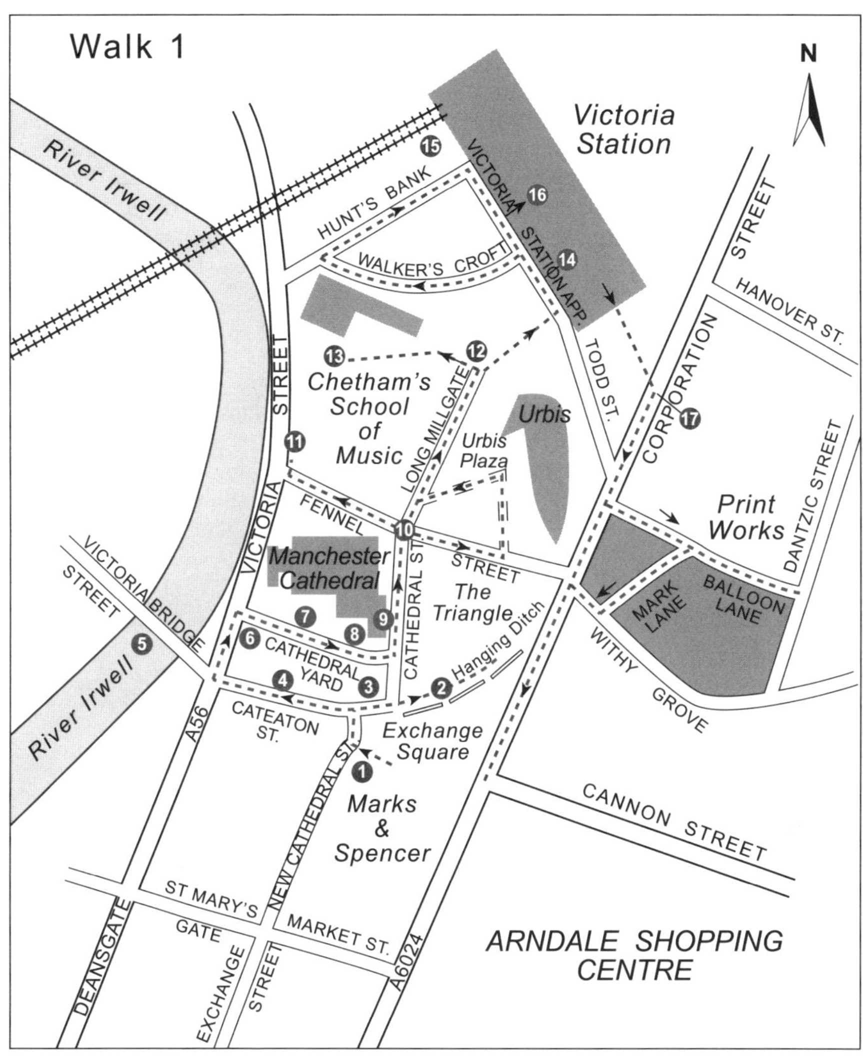

("Don't ask the price. It's a penny!") The rest, as they say, is history. Famous for the quality and value of their merchandise, *Marks and Spencer's* are still affectionately known as purveyors of women's knickers to the nation. The company is currently (2004) experiencing major difficulties and is tryng to reinvent itself.

The old store was badly damaged by the IRA bomb, and the decision to build a massive £85m replacement was seen as a vote of confidence in the city's future. The frontage is best viewed from the low-level portion of the square, and consists of an impressive but well-proportioned wall of glass, framed in Jura limestone. Shortly after opening, it was decided to sub-let a large part of the building to another retail undertaking. It now contains, in effect, two separate stores, each with its own network of escalators. (They are connected by passages on each floor.) A ground floor passage runs between Corporation Street and New Cathedral Street, bisecting an impressive central light well, complete with glass wall-climbing lifts. This passage divides *Marks and Spencer* (on the Market Street side) from *Selfridges* (on the Exchange Square side). The lifts on either side are incorporated into one or other of the stores. A visit to the café on the first floor of *Marks and Spencer* is recommended – there is a fine view of St. Ann's Square and Church. But take a detour to the basement, to contrast the everyday food hall with that of *Selfridges* next door. How the other half do live! The latter contains a very trendy Sushi Bar – complete with a revolving food conveyor! *Marks and Spencer* also has a bureau de change that boasts the best currency rates in the city, ATM's, a tax-free shopping desk, and baby-changing facilities.

The Corn Exchange and Hanging Ditch

After inspecting Mr Marks's emporium, proceed down the steps *(1)* to the lower level of the Square for a good view of the water feature. The double row of **posts** along the lower level marks the site of Hanging Ditch *(2)*. First mentioned in 1473, it ran alongside an old watercourse of the same name. Elements of the retreating Jacobite army came this way on 8th December 1745, a demoralised rabble shielding themselves from the stones of outraged citizens. This street once boasted a splendid coaching inn called the 'Spread Eagle'. The original mediaeval settlement was crowded beyond this thoroughfare and the defensive ditch, but eventually spread across the site of the Square. The old Market Place (p.72) lay somewhere under *Marks and Spencer*.

The former Corn Exchange

We follow this line of posts to the right, alongside the curving exterior of the **Corn Exchange.** Corn and other agricultural produce had long been traded in the streets around the cathedral, but the rapid growth of the town in the industrial revolution required some arena in which 'corn factors' and other merchants could deal with retailers and millers. The first Corn Exchange opened in 1837. This facility was soon too small for the volume of trading, and the present Exchange was built in stages between 1891 and 1904. The fine pedimented stone frontage, with an elaborate central entrance (a **datestone** of 1903 and heraldic beasts), does not seem to have any unifying theme, perhaps indicating the piecemeal nature of its construction. There were over 500 offices available to the produce trade in addition to the large trading floor. The building lost its importance as the trade altered, and it became a ghostly, somewhat shabby place, used for exhibitions and trade promotions. Older Mancunians remember the marvellous model railway exhibitions held every Christmas. Latterly, it became a much-loved 'alternative shopping' mecca (p.168). Its new incarnation, in the aftermath of the bomb, is as an upmarket shopping centre. Some marketing genius decided to call it *The Triangle*, but everyone still knows it as the Corn Exchange, and it is to be hoped that this grotesque aberration will be swiftly given a discrete burial. The shops include such names as *Jigsaw, Gant,* and *Muji.* The *Zinc Bar and Grill* is Sir Terence Conran's first venture outside the capital.

The shops fronting Hanging Ditch give access to the interior of the new shopping centre, but it is best to use the **new entrance.** The original entrance with its mahogany, glazed tiles, and marbling is suitably impressive, but is now used for offices. The old trading floor has been opened out to basement level to create a **performance area**. Arches have been constructed around the original pillars, the balcony now accesses shops instead of offices, and the three main walls (it was built on an irregular site) support an oval glazed roof, which culminates in a fine **dome**. The lift, encased in a circular stair, and the glass-framed escalators, are interesting design features.

The Shambles

Retrace your steps back along the Hanging Ditch side of the Square, and the quaint appearance of the **Old Shambles** *(3)* immediately demands attention. But all is not what it seems. This range of old buildings originally stood adjacent to the Market Place (p.72), and was the only part to escape destruction by the Luftwaffe in 1940. Town planners proved more deadly in the long run, and the structure was jacked up and placed in the middle of a hideous concrete shopping centre in the 1970s. The old 18th-century panelled rooms were ripped out at the same time. The new development came to the rescue. The Old Shambles was moved out of the way of *Marks and Spencer's* and placed on a suitable site near the cathedral. As this area was smaller, the dismantled building was re-erected in an 'L' shape around a little **courtyard** – ideal for outdoor eating and drinking. Whatever the rights and wrongs about the move, most people agree that the new setting is delightful.

A 'shambles' was a street of butchers where blood and offal flowed in the gutter. Thus stood the ***Old Wellington Inn***, which is the oldest part of the building. It dates from 1552, although some of the timbers may be older. Unseasoned wood was used during construction so that natural shrinkage would lock the parts together. This accounts for the warping in some of the beams. The appearance is more or less authentic, for the traditional black and white 'magpie' appearance of such buildings was an affectation of the Victorian 'restorers'. (However, the brick ground floor and the windows are modern reconstructions.) It was originally used for the receipt of market dues and tolls, though a passage led through to a cloth store, and there was accommodation on the first floor.

The *Old Wellington Inn* is forever associated with the Byrom family. Ralph Byrom came to Manchester from Lowton, near Leigh, in 1485, and became a prosperous wool merchant. His son Adam acquired property in Salford, Darcy Lever, Bolton, and Ardwick – and probably purchased this building in 1554, converting part of it into a draper's shop. (A third storey was added in the 17th century.) But

The Old Wellington Inn

things did not always go smoothly. After Adam's death, his daughter Margaret developed a form of mental illness that resulted in her execution as a 'witch' in 1597. So much for the charms of 'Merrie Englande'! The family split into a Salford and a Manchester branch, both cordially hating each other. They saw the outbreak of the Civil War as a way of prolonging the family quarrel by other means – Edward Byrom and his sons foiled a royalist plot (which presumably was supported by his Salford relatives) to seize the town (p.24).

John Byrom, the most famous family member, was born in this family property in 1691. His privileged background enabled him to take an M.A. at Cambridge and spend some time in France studying medicine. He is remembered chiefly as the inventor, in his student days, of a form of shorthand and as the author of the hymn 'Christians Awake' – first performed on Christmas Day, 1750 as a present for his daughter Dorothy. However, there is more to him than meets the eye. He was a member of the Royal Society and moved in some influential social and intellectual circles. Modern research has revealed him as 'The Queen's Chameleon', for he was deep in the councils of the Jacobite supporters of the deposed James II while also reporting to the secret service of Queen Ann and George I.

God bless the King! (I mean our faith's defender.)
God bless (no harm in blessing!) the Pretender
But who Pretender is, and who is King,
God bless us all! That's quite another thing!

The mystery deepens, for his private papers point to the membership of occult secret societies and prototype Masonic lodges. He has been claimed as a Rosicrucian, and even one of the 'illuminati'! He lived in a house that was somewhere near Hanging Ditch, so it might be said that his birthplace has migrated to join the site of his place of residence!

Sinclair's Oyster Bar

The premises are now used as a pub, with a restaurant upstairs. The interior, though tasteful, is a modern pastiche. Notice the **plaque** commemorating Byrom in the bar area – it should really be on the wall outside.

Sinclair's Oyster Bar is located in the other wing. When the building was adjacent to the Market Place, it housed an 18th-century Manchester institution – 'John Shaw's Punch House', founded by Shaw (p.38) in 1738, and presided over by him until his death in 1796. The strength of his punch was such that one pint was the rule if alone or a quart if in company, accompanied by the traditional innkeeper's warning "mind your pints and quarts, gentlemen!" (The origin of 'mind your p's and q's'!) Shaw was lord and master in his own establishment. Any lingerers after closing time, no matter who they were, were driven forth by the mop and bucket of Molly, his faithful servant. Shaw's was a meeting place of the High Tories, if not Jacobites, in the early years. Shaw and Molly are pictured on the **inn signs**. *Sinclair's,* the successor to Shaw's establishment, was more of a mid-day rendezvous for Victorian businessmen than a club. Oysters were introduced in 1845 and are still an important part of the menu. Legend has it that a customer known by everyone as 'Lady Spittlewick' consumed at least forty oysters a day here, until, in the twilight of her life, she was rushed to the infirmary and died. She had choked on a pearl! This part of the Shambles is an 18th-century brick extension covered with stucco.

The ***Mitre Hotel*** is situated to one side of the Old Shambles, on the corner of Cateaton Street. It is said that Charles Edward Stuart reviewed his army on this spot in November, 1745, before the advance to Derby. But, if all the traditions are true, the Bonny Prince spent all his time inspecting his troops in every street in Manchester! This part dates from 1815, but the Gothic style windows on the corner originate from the extensive reconstruction of 1867. John Whitehead, who was landlord in 1817, had been a circus acrobat. Given sufficient alcohol and an admiring audience, he was not averse to attempting a demonstration of his skills in the bar! The entrance to the hotel accommodation is round the back in Cathedral Yard (p.13).

The Cathedral Visitor Centre and Victoria Bridge

Leave Exchange Square by Cateaton Street (probably meaning a 'hollow way'). The

Crown and Anchor is adjacent to the *Mitre*. It acquired a modern exterior in the 1920s, and has since colonised the building next door. A pianist sometimes entertains the customers. On the other side of a narrow alleyway, the *Cathedral Shop* marks the **Cathedral Visitor Centre**, *(4)* located in a late Victorian office building. (The Cathedral Visitor Centre is open Tuesday to Saturday, 10.00 – 4.30, Sunday, 12.00 – 4.00, admission free.) Walk through the shop to the **exhibition area**, containing interactive displays relating to the Cathedral and the historical figures associated with it – not forgetting the life and work of the institution in the modern city. Notice the reproductions of the Roman Word Square (p.219) and the fragment of St. John's Gospel (p.56). The upstairs rooms are used for meetings, but do proceed to the **basement**. This contains a café in a most amazing setting – the **exposed arches of the mediaeval bridge!** (Description on p.13) We pass the attractive front of **Mynshull House**, a 'Jacobean revival' study in sandstone and terracotta of 1890. Mynshull, as the interesting inscriptions on the frontage state, made his fortune as a chemist and druggist in 17th-century Manchester. He bequeathed the income from two houses which formerly stood here for apprenticing local boys to a respectable trade. He was a puritan, and eventually moved in the highest circles of this group. (His niece married John Milton.) The subsequent fate of the family fortune probably had him revolving in his grave at a rate of knots! (p.140) A charming Edwardian folly of 1906 stands on the street corner. Although **Brittanic Buildings** is only one room wide, it makes the most of the narrow site by soaring above Mynshull house and terminating in some half-timbered gables.

This corner is the junction of Victoria Street (p.13) and Deansgate (p.52), so pause to take in the view of **Victoria Bridge** and its surroundings, directly ahead *(5)*. In the distant and misty past, Manchester was haunted by a 'boggart' (supernatural) dog, which was captured and buried under the bridge. This may be the folk memory of a 'building sacrifice'. Whatever the case, first a wooden and then a stone bridge replaced the ford over the river at this point in mediaeval times. The latter consisted of three arches, with angular pedestrian bays, as the roadway was only the width of a cart. Thomas de Bothe, a yeoman of Barton, left £30 for the maintenance of the bridge in 1368. He also paid for the construction of a chapel upon it, as travel was a dangerous undertaking in those days.

> Three times tell ane bead,
> And thrice a paternoster say,
> Then kiss me with the holy rood (cross),
> So shall we safely wend our way.

The chapel became a prison after the Reformation. It was a place of dread, as one prisoner had his toes gnawed off by rats and another poor fellow was drowned in a river flood.

The bridge witnessed stirring scenes in the English Civil War, said to have begun here after Manchester sided with Parliament. After failing to seize the militia magazine (p.24), Lord Strange besieged the town for a week in 1642, making several attempts to force the bridge from the Salford direction. Both sides were inexperienced at first, and a great deal of powder was shot off without result. (The first casualty was a rustic, who had seated himself on a stile between the opposing forces to get a good view!) Then rain stopped play. One of the Royalist officers stepped out of a doorway to respond, it is said, to a pretty girl's wave. And so Captain Standish was shot dead by a musketeer in the Collegiate Church (cathedral) tower, who had presumably been able to keep his powder dry. The Victorians placed a fine statue (by Noble) of Oliver Cromwell at this road junction near the bridge in 1875 (moved in 1968 to Wythenshawe Park), and it was said that no member of the royal family would ever arrive at Exchange Station (see below) as a result. The statue ought to be brought back to the area in honour of a man who hated all forms of bigotry. "I beseech ye, in the bowels of Christ ... think that ye may be mistaken."

The Manchester side of the bridge was widened in 1778, and the old relic survived as late as the 19th century. The **present bridge** opened on 20th June, 1839, the Queen herself actually using it in 1851. There are royal devices on the parapets and the remains of gas lamps. The view into Salford is dominated by the great tower of ***Premier Lodge*** (by Leach, Rhodes, and Walker, 1966), now converted into flats, but once (as Highland House) the tax offices. It had a reputation as one of the grimmest blocks in the city, with rather oddly shaped windows. The recent refurbishment is a great improvement.

A right-hand turn leads into Victoria Street. It was created in an improvement of 1837, which cut a way along the bank of the Irwell above the sloping ground. Consequently, the river side is supported on arches, and local myth states that the original pathway (with houses and shops!) lies preserved under the roadway. All that actually remains are some cobbles and a rusted street lamp. There were boat trips from a landing stage along the Ship Canal to Barton until the 1920s, and it is proposed to restore the staging and open up the arches as a riverside shopping arcade. The approach over the river leads to the site of Exchange Station, opened by the London and North Western Railway in 1884 on the Salford side, and now demolished. It was once linked to Victoria Station (p.26) by the longest railway platform in Britain. Housing has been proposed for the station area, but an impressive building is needed to set the scene off.

Pause to inspect the exterior of **Hanging Bridge**, within a small landscaped area to the right *(6)*. Mediaeval Manchester lay within the angle of the rivers Irk and Irwell, with the Hanging Ditch protecting the third side – comprising a natural ravine formed by a stream that had been improved and lengthened. The two-arched mediaeval stone bridge has been dated to around 1422, and was probably connected with the building work at the Church and College. However, some of the stonework on the left-hand side suggests the incorporation of a stone pier, which probably supported an earlier timber span. The visible portion forms part of the new Cathedral Visitor Centre (p.11). The ditch that it spanned was filled in by 1776.

Exit this area, and a right turn leads into Cathedral Yard. It was one of the narrow lanes around the large old churchyard. Graves had been used and re-used over many centuries, but by the end of the 18th century, enough was enough. The discovery that human remains were being disposed of in the Irwell was the final straw, and burials ceased in 1819.

The Cathedral

The great Gothic bulk of **Manchester Cathedral** dominates the scene. Nobody knows the location of the church in Manchester mentioned in the Domesday Book and no remains of an earlier church on this site have yet been discovered, resulting in speculation that the Saxon and Norman church may have been situated at Parsonage Gardens (p.68). Thomas de la Warre, Lord of the Manor of Manchester, obtained a charter from Henry V in 1421 to found a Church with an associated College of Priests in Manchester. (The State of Delaware is named after a later branch of his family.) Thomas, a priest himself, knew that a wild parish of sixty square miles of wood, moorland, and waste required urgent attention. His solution was a sort of spiritual corporation of priests, headed by a Warden and endowed with the income from property. This community would administer the sacraments, pray, and constitute the centre of an improved system of pastoral care.

King Henry, the victor of Agincourt, was heir presumptive to the throne of France. Obviously, St George and St Denys (the patron saints of England and France) had to be added to the original dedication to the Blessed Virgin. Alas, no sooner had work started on the new church, than Henry lay dying of dysentery at the Chateau of Vincennes. As he wrestled with his own inner demons, did he include the Collegiate Church charter in an imagined defence? "Thou liest ... thou liest ... a portion of me is with the Lord Jesus!" The church at Manchester is one of the few reminders of a fleeting time before all hopes and ambition turned to dust.

It remained as a Collegiate Church (though reincarnated as a Protestant institution) until 1847, when the Diocese of Manchester was created to serve the rapidly expanding industrial town. The first bishop placed his throne or 'cathedra' (p.17) in it, making the church a cathedral.

The original church was built of Collyhurst sandstone, which met its match in the pollution of the industrial revolution. Consequently, the Victorians encased it in Derbyshire grey stone, and did not pass up the opportunity to 'improve' the structure. The tower was rebuilt in the 1860s in a loftier form. The porches date from a restoration of the 1880s, and the impressive West End commemorates Queen Victoria's Jubilee in 1897 (including a statue of the Queen sculpted by no less a person than Princess Louise, one of her numerous offspring). The East End was reconstructed after wartime damage (p.20). Nevertheless, nobody can deny that the cathedral has an impressive and suitably historic appearance. The cathedral is open daily, and everyone is welcome to attend the services (some are choral) and musical recitals.

Entrance is usually by the **South Porch** from Cathedral Yard *(7)*. Before entering, notice the **cross** on the lawn (a monument to Dean McCormack) and the **figure** of Bishop Moorhouse (p.17) on the vestry wall to the right. Indeed, it is worth making a detour in this direction to seek the Dean's Door of the cathedral, beyond the sundial and the metal railings. Over it is a **sculpted panel by Eric Gill** *(8)*.

Back to the porch. This leads into the **Nave**, formerly the public part of the church, built by Ralph Langley (appointed Warden in 1465). The first impression of the interior of the building relates to size. It is quite small when compared to other cathedrals, being a squat rectangle, 220ft (67m) long by 116ft (35m) wide. However, one is impressed by the exceptional width of the church — Manchester is one of the widest cathedrals in Britain. A central double row of pillars support a **'clerestory' (upper row) of windows** beneath a flat **wooden roof** – 15th-century work, though much restored. Note the **angels playing musical instruments**. Lower level roofs cover the two side aisles, supported by outer rows of pillars. Chantry chapels formerly occupied the space beyond the side aisles, accounting for the unusual dimensions.

The Nave served two purposes in mediaeval times. It accommodated religious processions and was a public arena for hearing masses sung or said. Entertainment was provided in the form of plays and pageants, which were not necessarily religious in content and included "the play of Robin Hood". It also served as a communal hall for gossip, meetings, and for completing business transactions. A bargain on a market day might be sealed by shaking hands across the font.

The description of the interior starts at the east end of the Nave with the screen or **'pulpitum'** dating from the early 16th century, but much altered, dividing the public part of the church from the Chancel. Before the Reformation, it would have been surmounted by a 'rood' or large carving of the crucifixion, as a reminder of the redemptive sacrifice that had conquered sin and opened the way to heaven.

Woefully arrayed, woefully arrayed,
My body hung all black and blue.
My blood man, for thee ran.
Woefully arrayed, woefully arrayed.

To the left of the screen is mounted the **'Angel Stone'**. It was once thought to be part of a Saxon church that stood on this site, but, as re-used building material, it could have come from anywhere. Modern opinion suggests that it is a rather crude provincial production, and may be as late as the 12th century. The angel holds a scroll bearing the words "into thy hands I commend my spirit," and may have accompanied a crucifixion scene over a church door or altar.

Go to the left of the large screen or pulpitum. The **Chantry Chapel of St James** was situated here, in the north east corner of the Nave, beside the Regimental Chapel. Mediaeval man, unless either irredeemably wicked or a saint, could look forward to a period of punishment in purgatory to expiate earthly sin. However, unlike the pains of hell, this torment might be mitigated by prayers and masses for the dead. Anyone who could afford it would endow a chantry chapel with a resident priest, to ensure the spiritual health of family members and themselves in the next world. And in late mediaeval Manchester, the presence of families who had become wealthy in the developing cloth trade had led to a spate of chapel building. Consequently, the important Hulme family (p.166) endowed this chapel as a chantry in 1507. It originally contained a painting

Main entrance to Manchester Cathedral

of the general resurrection of the dead, with an inscription promising 26,026 days remission from purgatory in return for a daily recital of five 'paters', five 'aves' and the 'credo'.

Alas for such pious hopes! In the reign of Edward VI, in the course of the Reformation, the chantry chapels were abolished at the behest of the religious reformers who argued that purgatory was an invention. The chantry endowments were appropriated, though the families retained right of burial in their chapels.

The remains of a **piscina** (for washing sacred vessels) are visible in the south-east corner of the chapel area, near the aisle passage. The later **monuments of the Lever family** (on the north wall) contain a reflection upon infant mortality in the 17th century.

You see their age and years of grace,
I hope that heaven's their dwelling place.

Follow the north aisle towards the West End of the cathedral, passing the **North Porch** (1888). The **Holy Trinity Chapel** was formerly just beyond it, in the north-west corner of the Nave. It was endowed as a chantry by William Radcliffe, of Ordsall, (p.242) around 1498. It now contains a **statue of Humphrey Chetham** (p.24), the gift of an 'old boy' (by Theed, 1853). The child at the foot of the statue is dressed in the bluecoat uniform, worn until the last war. Do not miss the **Chetham family tombstones** on either side of the monument. The recent (1995) **stained glass** in this corner represents the revelation of St John.

Continue along the West End to the **modern area under the tower**, which is decorated with historical lists of important ecclesiastical and civil personages connected with the cathedral and Manchester. The **ceiling** is in the perpendicular style. This work dates from the rebuilding of the West End as a contribution to Queen Victoria's Jubilee celebrations (1897). In contrast, at the entrance to this area, the **tower arch** is mediaeval in origin – although disfigured by an attempt to plaster the walls in the 18th century. The **modern stained glass** at the West End is eye-catching. The Great West Window depicts the Virgin Mary (1980), that to the left St George (1973), and, to the right, St Denys (1976). The window in the south west corner of the Nave depicts the Creation (1991).

Now continue along the south aisle, passing the **South Porch**. The **Chapel of St George** lay in the area where the south wall forms a small bay, and contained an image of the national saint. It was endowed in 1508 by William Galey, a Manchester merchant, and was shared as a chantry with other families and the 'Guild of St George'. Notice the **statue of Thomas Fleming** (by Edward Hodges Baily, the sculptor of Nelson on the Trafalgar Square column), the 'uncrowned king of Manchester' (p.80). Fleming dominated town politics from 1810 until the advent of municipal incorporation. Although a despised Tory in the eyes of the political radicals, he was active in every town improvement, including (as the inscription states) the promotion of the first municipal gasworks in Britain. The profits defrayed most of the costs of widening and reconstructing streets. The institution of proper local government resulted in the victory of the Liberals and radicals. The political wounds went a little too deep, which probably accounts for the statue being in the cathedral and not in an outside street. In later times, the chapel passed into the possession of the Radcliffe family of Pool Fold (p.49), before being transferred (presumably by the deed of sale for the house) to the Brown family (p.49). The latter appear to have re-used the blank sides of the Radcliffe tombstones for their own burials! It was bought back by the Collegiate Church in 1815.

The remaining space between this area and the Jesus Chapel, in the South East corner of the Nave, was occupied by the **Chapel of St Nicholas**, the chantry of the De Trafford family, and probably endowed around 1486. The south wall here contains a **memorial to the emergency services** expressing thanks for their bravery on 15th June, 1996, and the fact that no-one was killed by the IRA bomb. The adjacent **tablet commemorating the Booth Charity** also relates to this incident. Humphrey Booth died in 1633, leaving the income from property for the relief of the poor. The succeeding centuries, with a rapid escalation of property values since industrialisation, have turned Humphrey's income into something more substantial. His charity paid for the restoration of the cathedral after the bomb, together with the fitting out of a care centre for the homeless. However, the principal attraction in this area of the Nave is the **display of charters**. They were issued by Henry V (1421), establishing the College with a Warden, eight fellows, four clerks, and six choristers; Elizabeth I (1578), re-founding the College as a Protestant institution; and Charles I (1635). There is also a modern **memorial to John Bradford (**p.20)

Our circuit of the Nave has brought us back to the 'pulpitum', or screen. It is time to pass through its three sets of doors into the **Choir or Chancel**. The mediaeval church claimed to be the body of Christ on earth, a mediator between God and man, dispensing God's grace through the sacraments. The sacrifice by which sin was redeemed was repeated in the mass, so that all who heard this service would benefit spiritually. Consequently, the sacred mystery must take place here, in a part of the church restricted to the clergy. The church was then, above all, concerned with ceremony. Ordinary folk tended to see it as a repository of useful supernatural power, akin to magic. The priest must have been seen very much as a local shaman, dispensing magical gifts. Indeed, this probably sat quite easily in the common mind with a persisting belief in the old fertility cults, as evidenced elsewhere in the cathedral.

The chancel is the oldest part of the church, and was begun in 1422 by John Huntington, the first Warden and Rector of Ashton-under-Lyne. He is vested for celebrating mass in his **brass** of 1458, located on the floor of the Choir in front of the High Altar. His remains lie somewhere near here, buried with his ring, chalice, and patten, so that he might render an account of his stewardship on the great day of judgement. The magnificent **carved choir stalls** are obviously the creation of master craftsmen. James Stanley, the second Warden, and later Bishop of Ely, paid for this work, completed in 1508. (In addition to wealthy merchants, the Collegiate Church had some powerful patrons at this time.) There are twelve stalls on either side, and each contains a **'misericord'**. In the course of long services, the clergy leant against a ledge when the seat was in the upright position. The carvings below the ledges include the following:

- ❖ A hare cooking the hunter and his dog.
- ❖ A pilgrim robbed by monkeys.
- ❖ A man who has broken his wife's cooking pot.
- ❖ Two men playing backgammon.
- ❖ A pig playing the harp.
- ❖ A fox (with a birch rod!) teaching cubs.

There are also the grotesque faces of the 'green man', thought to be a reference to the old fertility cult. The **canopies** over the stalls are a riot of carving. The **Bishop's Throne**, on the right-hand side towards the altar, was built for Bishop Moorhouse. He had also been Bishop of Melbourne, so look for the two carved kangaroos! The modern **East Window** is best seen from this point. The local worthies are John

Detail from wood carvings in the cathedral choir

Byrom (p.10), Thomas Langley (Warden), Hugh Oldham (p.23), and Humphrey Chetham (p.24). St Aidan and St Chad, the 'apostles to the north' in Saxon times, are also included.

Exit into the south aisle of the Chancel, noticing the **organ** (1952) replacing the one destroyed in the war. Across the aisle may be found the **Jesus Chapel**. A (badly worn) **brass of Sir John Byrom and his wife Margaret** may be found to the right of the entrance to the chapel. It probably dates from around 1460, and was originally on the floor of the Lady Chapel prior to its destruction by bombing. The **old screen** dates from 1506, the year that Richard Bexwicke (or Beswick), a "merchant prince" of the town, defrayed the costs of its construction. The "Master, Wardens, and Yeomen of the Guild of St Saviour and the Name of Jesus" went on to furnish the chapel as a chantry. (Richard made sure that he had his own private chantry here, as well!) The Guild, like the lesser 'Guild of St George', was a kind of religious society enabling ordinary men to make provision for the afterlife, a facility that goes far beyond the scope of a modern insurance policy! The chapel contains the 17th-century **brasses of the Mosley family** (p.97), who were Lords of the Manor at the time. It was ultimately used as the private chapel and burial place of the Byrom family (p.10). A descendent surrendered the chapel to the cathedral in 1904, on condition that the screens be retained – a fact recorded in a small **plaque** in the south-west corner.

Return to the south aisle and walk towards the east end of the cathedral, pausing at the entrance to the **Chapter House**. Although the bishop uses a cathedral as his headquarters in the diocese, it is actually run by a Dean, assisted by a council or Chapter of clergymen. They meet in the Chapter House, just as the Warden and Fellows of the college did, starting their meetings with a 'chapter' of scripture. There are **two interesting brass plaques** to the right of the Chapter House door. One bears a Latin inscription in honour of **Warden Heyrick**. He managed to retain his Wardenship of the Collegiate Church at the restoration of Charles II, despite being a founder member of the presbyterian 'Classis' (local church organisation) during the Commonwealth period, when the state church was all but abolished. Was he, as the inscription suggests, a genuine moderate and conciliator, or was he a self-serving creep? The other records the death and burial of **Lady Barbara Fitzroy** in 1734. She was the daughter of the Duke of Cleveland, an illegitimate son of Charles II and one of his more notorious mistresses. Nobody knows what this granddaughter of a king was doing in Manchester, though she appears to have been estranged from her family. The **paintings over the door** (by Carel Weight, 1963) illustrate the beatitudes. They include a man 'hungering and thirsting after righteousness' (outside a bank!), ignored by businessmen and office workers. The Chapter House itself (entered through a pair of doors) was erected by James Stanley in the time of Henry VIII, though the roof is modern. A **Victorian effigy of Hugh Birley**, in the then popular mediaeval style, may be found near the Fraser Chapel. He was former MP for the city, and a champion of the established church. The south aisle terminates by the **Fraser Chapel** (1890), which contains an **effigy** in the Mediaeval style of the 'people's bishop' (p.44). The Fraser Chapel's latest addition is a **modern altarpiece by Mark Cazalet**. The Holy Family are seen to be enjoying a meal of chips (washed down with Boddington's beer!) in Castlefield. To the left, St. George releases the dragon that we all, to some extent, are chained to, against a background of urban dereliction. To the right, St Denys carries his head from his place of execution, the Mount of Martyrs (Montmartre), to his place of burial (St Denis, north of Paris) by way of Market Street! It is reserved for private prayer. The recent **sculpture of 'The Holy Night'** (by Josefin de Vasconcellos), popular with many visitors, is usually placed in the area behind the High Altar.

The **Lady Chapel** is situated to the right of this area, at the extreme east end of the church. The Mediaeval church encouraged the patronage of a variety of saints – as a way of approaching God through an intermediary. Chief amongst these was the Virgin Mary, the centre of a considerable cult. The chapel was built by Huntington, who was also probably responsible for the **screen** (1440) with the mutilated figure of St George. His **'rebus'** (or pun), in the form of a hunting scene and a 'tun' or barrel of ale, can be seen either side of the screen arch! Warden West endowed a chantry here in 1518. The chapel was rebuilt after complete destruction in the war, and is now set aside for prayer and meditation. Continue along the east end, noticing the **display of the cathedral silver**, before turning left into the north aisle.

The **Regimental Chapel** occupies the whole of the north side of the chancel area. It was formerly the Chapel of St John the Baptist, or Stanley Chapel. The Stanley family came into favour in the reign of Henry VII, becoming the Earls of Derby. (A malicious story has one of them awaiting the outcome of Bosworth Field in a wood, before joining the winning side!) They were very influential in the north-west, and great patrons of the collegiate church in Manchester. The chapel was built in 1513, and is said to be the thank offering for a safe return from Flodden Field. While Henry VIII was otherwise engaged in France, the Scots invaded. A scratch army, which included archers and foot soldiers from Cheshire and Lancashire, was assembled. The Scottish King, and the majority of his nobility, were killed in what proved to be a famous victory. Many Manchester men distinguished themselves in this battle.

Charge, Chester, charge! On, Stanley, on!
These were the last words of Marmion.

The family endowed a chantry for themselves in 1515. It became the Manchester Regiment Chapel in 1936. The fragments of brasses, to the left of the entrance to the Chapel, are of **Sir Alexander Radcliffe and his wife**, dating from around 1540. They were once on the floor of the Choir. The English custom is to hang the **battle flags** of local regiments in church when they are replaced or the unit is disbanded, and most of these date to the First World War. The **books of the rolls of honour**, in the wooden cases, record those members of the Manchester Regiment who died in that conflict. Many enlisted together in 'pals' battalions of workmates (p.122). The slaughter was terrible, particularly on the Somme. "Out of the north parts, a great army and a mighty host." The books carry on through the last war and continue (as the King's Regiment) to the present. The blood red **'fire window'** remembers Sir Hubert Worthington, the architect responsible for the post-war restoration. The last remnants of the historic stained glass were destroyed in the war, for Manchester was the most damaged cathedral after Coventry – as the photographs in the chapel show. A **brass of James Stanley, Bishop of Ely**, may be found to the left of the altar steps. He is in his Episcopal robes and carries a mitre. The brass was originally placed on a tomb in the Ely Chapel, which stood to the north of the Regimental Chapel. It too was destroyed in the war, but was never rebuilt. Other salvaged **remains of brasses** may be found to the side of the chapel entrance from the North Aisle.

Exit by the South Porch, but please be sure to make a donation towards the upkeep of this ancient church before leaving.

Returning to Cathedral Yard, turn left and notice the modern timber balcony and patterned stucco at the rear of the Old Shambles. Another left turn leads into Cathedral Street, originally a narrow lane alongside the churchyard called Half Street. Here, two hundred years ago, was the shop of old Jane Clowes. She sold sweets and engaged in extensive sugar boiling, and, like many Lancashire folk, she disliked pretension. On a visit to a Liverpool sugar broker, she turned up in her old-fashioned clothes and black bonnet, and was promptly shown the door. A second visit (dressed in her landlady's gown) resulted in a different attitude, so she promptly placed an order too large for the company to fulfil! One wonders if her wraith annoys the staff of the new upmarket clothes shops in the Corn Exchange.

Her best customer was Joshua (Jotty) Brooks, a parson and member of the Collegiate Church. Eccentric but kindly, his behaviour (which included slipping over the churchyard wall to the shop in the middle of services) was the talk of the town. He was in his element during the mass marriages and baptisms (the Church was then the only place available for such rites). Amid hundreds of people, he would marshal couples or godparents with acid comments and heckling. He is well described in 'The Manchester Man', a greatly loved novel about the old town.

There are a number of **blue plaques** *(9)* along the low stone wall on the left. One commemorates John Bradford, a native of the town and an early Protestant. He, and others, thought that all that mattered was the cultivation of a close personal relationship with God. The church as an institution was secondary to this, for grace could come through this relationship instead of ceremony. Thus, God transformed the human personality. "There, but for the grace of God," he remarked as a condemned man passed him, "goes John Bradford". These views undermined the powers and pretensions of the old mediaeval church. As a result, he was burned alive in London in the reign of Mary. "What am I Lord, that thou should thus magnify me?" A large number of Mancunians, rightly or wrongly, and whether believers or not, carry this concept one stage further – thinking that anyone who leads a good life and helps his or her fellow has just as good a chance of entering the pearly gates as any regular churchgoer. Edward Barlow was a post-Reformation Roman Catholic martyr. There is a plaque to William Temple, the 'people's Archbishop' famous for his left-wing sympathies, but (strangely) not one to Bishop Fraser (p.44). However, Peter Green (p.234) is included. The reconstructed east end of the cathedral, behind the wall, has a simple and moving **'Madonna and Child'** by Sir Charles Wheeler.

The City Park

Cathedral Street leads to the new **City Park**, also known as 'Cathedral Gardens'. The park springs on several axes from **'Cathedral Gateway'**, a rectangular paved area *(10)*. Make a short detour along the left-hand axis, past the 'Cathedral Green' on the north side of the cathedral towards the river. Part of the paving runs over the lane where the Apple Market was once held. There is a brief glimpse of Chetham's College (p.3) to the right, though most of the view is masked by trees. Until some years ago, a curious lean-to wooden shop once inhabited the angle *(11)* between Chetham's gateway and the corner building (with the blocked entrance). The windows were full of old railway and bus enthusiast publications, together with 'glamour' magazines and ancient sex 'manuals' that ought to have graced a museum of social history, all bleached by the sun. Sadly, the old gentleman in the dustcoat behind the counter was murdered, and within a short time it was as if he and his shop had never existed.

Retracing our footsteps to Cathedral Gateway, note the **stepped stone podium** on the right-hand corner, from which water issues to supply a **water feature** along Long Millgate. We now explore the right-hand axis, comprising Fennel Street (probably derived from the Anglo-Saxon 'vennel', meaning a narrow lane). For a long time it was just known as 'Th' Back o' th' Church'. Thomas Deacon (p.40) was a notable resident. He belonged to the 'True British Catholic Church', which appointed its own bishops, including himself, for he held 'services' over a shop in this street. This curious sect seems to have been a front organisation for the Jacobites in Manchester, and his three sons joined the Pretender's army in 1745. One was hanged. His head was placed on a spike on top of the Old Exchange building in the Market Place (p.72), and old Mr Deacon went to view it, removing his hat in respect. On the north side of the street is a large landscaped area – including a collection of trees (called the **'Orchard'**, by the way!), lawns, and a wedged-shaped section terminating in a paved area directly in front of Urbis that can be used as a performance area, and can be accessed from both Fennel Street and Long Millgate. So, make your way to the new Plaza.

Urbis – pictured in 2002

The 'Welcome Arm' of the £30m

Urbis (Ian Simpson Architects) embraces the Plaza. The 2,200 glazed units clad a structure that rises like the prow of a ship, thrusting into the City Park. A restaurant and bar occupy the fifth floor, with fine views over the city centre (reached by a separate ground-floor entrance). 'Urbis' means 'of the city' in Latin, and the contents are intended to explore the many sides of the modern metropolis around the world, in the present and the future, through visual, audio, and interactive features.

Urbis (open daily 10.00 – 6.00, free admission) had a rather chequered existence after it opened. The actual purpose of the building seemed lost on most people, the interactive displays did not seem to have been well thought out, and the entrance fee was considered rather high. The result was a major rethink. The internal arrangement was altered, and free admission was introduced (except for special exhibitions).

The ground floor is a public foyer with a very minimalist feel. Visitors should proceed to the **information point** to obtain a free ticket for the next funicular ride. Tickets for the current exhibition may be purchased (if desired, the exhibition can be directly entered by the stairs to the first floor gallery). There is a **shop**, an adjacent **café** and other facilities including cloakroom and very useful toilets. Visitors then ride an unusual **funicular lift** for a two-minute ascent to the **fourth level**.

We arrive at a sound and light show (beware strobe lighting effect) introducing **'Arrive'** – a range of exhibits that recreate the impressions of entering a vast, busy, metropolis for the first time. As we try to make sense of it all, the questions are asked. Why do we come to cities, and what do we expect of them? In the first display area are 'astounding facts' (the GDP of New York exceeds that of Brazil, that sort of thing) and the contents of **new arrivals' bags** from the 'runaway' to the 'shopper'. That of the 'funster'(?) includes condoms, facepaint, and handcuffs! Drum like cases (related to videos) depict the most precious **belongings of a number of Mancunians** (look out for the tin in which Heidi keeps her dreams).

We descend to the **third level** (lift available) and enter **'Change'**, a sequence of interactive installations that show how different people and communities influence the city, and are influenced by it. It is better to proceed in a clockwise direction, coming first to the **viewing balcony**. After looking down, attention is drawn to two audio visual shows. The first offers a number of options relating to **changing Manchester and its communities** – an overview of two hundred years of change; the story of Jewish Manchester; the German legacy; and the post-war years. (After making the choice, slide your foot along the 'time line' in the floor to alter the show!) The second display illustrates **change in the districts of Manchester**. The choice includes Chinatown (p.123), the Gay Village (p.143), Ancoats (p.152), Hulme (p.260), Moss Side, the University (p.222), and Rusholme (selection by rollerball). A curious collection of vaguely human-shaped structures follows, each being transformed into one of a number of **city people** as you pass, talking about themselves. It is also possible to stand in front of (and be incorporated into) a screen showing a series of **city tours** of Paris, Tokyo, and St. Petersburg. Lastly, **city voices** introduce a number of city characters, including 'Rambo' the tattooist.

On the **second level**, enter a white area, where the theme of **'Order'** is examined. We are confronted by a wall of **visitors' pictures**, representing people as names and possibly numbers. Bear in mind that, if you wish, you can make your own **identity badge** as a souvenir. The first stage in this process is to stand in front of the mirror to have your image recorded by CCTV. (You can record your opinions on sheets of paper in the room beyond.) **Items of street furniture**, such as bus shelters or lamp posts are interactive devices, dealing with the following topics – urban disorder;

crime and punishment (interesting to see what is illegal, and where!); noise (experience it within the yellow cone); the use of public space; utilities (particularly transport); and maps. **Urbis Court** deals with the issues of privacy within an urban setting (place your ear against the glasses on the walls), street trading, and busking. You can see what is happening in the rest of Urbis on the screens in the **CCTV Control Room**. Be sure to get your identity badge printed out. **Level one** comprises the **Exhibition Gallery**, which can only be entered by ticket.

Returning to the rectangular paved area of Cathedral Gateway *(10)*, the way now lies along Long Millgate, the remaining axis of City Park, in the direction of Victoria Station. The winding nature of this street indicates its origin as a country lane leading to the water mills and bridges on the Irk. The mediaeval inhabitants were compelled to use the original water mill and an associated bakehouse here, a useful source of income to the manorial lords. Fulling mills and tanneries were later established on the Irk. A **border of water** runs along the right-hand side of the paving, fronting **'Pillow Lawns'** with its trees and benches, and terminating in a **second water feature** near the Todd Street corner. The whole of this area, including the Urbis centre, is on the site of a 19th-century shopping arcade, a glass and iron structure said to have originated as a women's prison! It sadly disappeared in the 1970s.

The main points of interest are, however, on the opposite side of the street. The large battlemented brick structure, with Gothic windows and a tower, is the old **Grammar School** building, erected 1867-1880. (The original schoolhouse was taken down in 1776.) Hugh Oldham, Bishop of Exeter, founded the Grammar School in 1515. As a local man, who had risen to power on the coat tails of the Stanley family, Hugh wanted to found a school in his native Lancashire. He considered that "children in the same county, having pregnant wit, have been most part brought up rudely and idly and not in virtue, cunning, erudition, literature, and in good manners". Some things never change! The school moved to a new site in Fallowfield in 1931, and the building is now part of the Chetham's complex. Thomas De Quincy was a grammar school pupil, and his schooldays here are recounted in his 'Confessions of an English Opium Eater'.

Chetham's College

Between the school building and a modern (though tasteful) student residence, may be found the **gatehouse entrance** *(12)* to **Chetham's College –** now 'Chetham's School of Music'. The College started life as the manor house, carefully positioned in an ideal defensive site on a sandstone bluff in the angle of the Irk and Irwell. The Hanging Ditch and its extension defended the remaining side. Archaeological evidence points to an inner ditch as well. It was the seat of the Lord of the Barony of Manchester, a manor at the head of a loose federation of subordinate manors across a large part of southern Lancashire. A manor did not merely consist of a landed estate, but was also a collection of rights and privileges that could be demanded of the inhabitants, legal rights that would increase the lord's power, status, and income. All this had originally been granted, after the Norman Conquest, to the De Grelle or Grelley family by Roger the Poiteven, in return for military service. In the baronial hall, the Barons would entertain guests, receive rents, and hold their own private court of law. However, they mainly appear to have resided elsewhere, and used the manor house as a hunting lodge. A mediaeval survey records the kennels for their dogs (p.27).

The present appearance and layout of the building probably dates from 1422, when Thomas de la Warre donated the site to his College of Priests, and thus forms one of the best examples of a non-monastic mediaeval religious building in Britain. This institution was dissolved by Edward VI, and refounded in a Protestant guise by Elizabeth I in 1578. However, the former building was purchased by the Earls of Derby. Lord Strange, one of their number, came here in 1642 with the purpose of seizing the powder and match (fuses) that were kept as part of the county militia magazine. This was seen by the townspeople as a hostile act, for he was rumoured to be collecting an army for the king. The young Lord was invited to dinner in the hope that things would pass off smoothly. Meanwhile, his supporters began parading the streets with a drum, shouting "the town's ours!". Bloodshed ensued and Richard Percival, a linen weaver, became the first recorded casualty in the English Civil War. Lord Strange later besieged the town (p.12).

Humphrey Chetham (1580-1653) was a wealthy local merchant. Although a moderate puritan, he supplemented his income by money lending, and was not averse to holding royal offices in the county. Either from a natural charitable impulse, or from guilt, he purchased the buildings for £400 and left the interest from a sum of £7000 to educate forty poor boys in a school. He also left £1000 to create a library, the first free library in Britain. The school and the library opened in these premises in 1656, and a Royal Charter was obtained in 1665. It was known as a 'bluecoat school', after the manner of the boys' dress (p.16), and continued as such until 1969. The institution was incorporated with Nicholl's Hospital (founded 1881) in that year to form 'Chetham's School of Music', catering for musically gifted children. Entry is by competition. One mediaeval tradition is still followed – the school provides the cathedral choir.

The public may visit the **Library** on weekdays (9.00-12.30, 1.30-4.30), and the Baronial Hall is often used for free lunchtime concerts (enquire at reception). Please be sure to check with security before entering the school precinct.

The **gateway** *(12)* front was rebuilt in 1816, but the rear (with the steps) is origi-

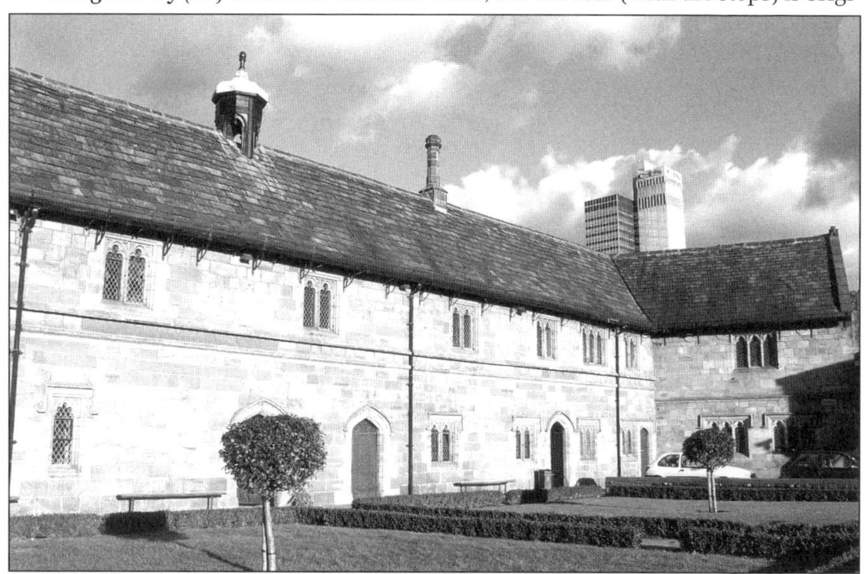

College House, Chetham's School of Music

nal work. The College building is 'L' shaped with the main block across the yard, directly ahead, and a wing running between it and the gateway, on the right. The latter contained the 'hospitium' (for receiving visitors), brewery, bakery, and kitchens. The main block consists of the Baronial Hall, with the Warden's accommodation to the left. Walk towards the left-hand side of this building, and enter the door round the corner *(13)*. The entrance corridor has a view of the lovely **cloister garth**, surrounded by the cells of the former Fellows. Visitors ring the bell at the door on the left for entrance to the library, before ascending a flight of stairs. An old printing press is in the corner of two wings. The main wing, straight ahead, was the dormitory of the clerks (lesser priests) and choristers. Here are the original **17th-century bookcases** (the precious books were chained until 1745) and the curious 18th-century gates between them.

The right-hand wing was formerly the College chapel (dedicated to the Virgin), leading to the **reading room**. This was the Warden's upper room. There is some fine **plasterwork** over the fireplace, containing the arms of Humphrey Chetham flanked by figures of a cockerel and a pelican feeding her chicks with her own blood (a symbol of Christian charity). The **portrait of Chetham** is said to have been painted from life. It is clear that there was once a curved plaster roof, and the eagle's claw and portcullis of the Earls of Derby may be seen along the top of the **wooden panelling**. The **oval table** is Cromwellian in date, and the painting of **'The Reconciliation of Steele and Addison'** is by Kneller. A fine **clock** is the earliest known (1695) gift of a former 'Bluecoat Boy'. Perhaps the most precious object is the chest with the inscription "The gift of Humphrey Chetham esquire, 1655". (The staff will usually open it if politely requested.) It contains a small **17th-century chained library** of religious books. Chetham donated five of these to local churches, but only this (from Gorton) survives. The lovely little **bay window** was a favourite place of Karl Marx, who used the library when he came to Manchester to visit Engels.

Fox Court, the cloister garth, tucked away behind the library

The Library now contains over 100,000 volumes (60,000 published before 1851) and many rare manuscripts. Nowadays, it acquires books on the history and topography of Manchester. Anyone may become a reader upon application to the librarian.

We return to the College Yard. The **Baronial Hall** is entered (for concerts) by means of a **screen passage**, which ran between it and the kitchens – a typical mediaeval arrangement. The Warden and other important people sat upon the raised **dais**. The original fire would have been in the centre of the room, for the fine **fireplace** was installed in the 17th century. It opens through to the delightful Victorian **'inglenook'**, with views of the cloister. A **'ladies bay'** is on the same level as the dais. It is sometimes possible to view the **'Audit Room'**, which was part of the Warden's residence. Dr. John Dee, 'Queen Elizabeth's Merlin', is cited as a famous occupant, though he probably resided at the Deanery (p.68). His occult interests and activities (which included raising the dead in a churchyard near Preston) caused a public scandal, but he had a powerful patron in the Queen. An old table is preserved here. This bears the **'devil's footprint'**, pointed out as Dee's handiwork by generations of Chetham's lads. On the other hand, the room has been used by accountants ...

Victoria Station

Back in Long Millgate, the walk continues to the left, along Victoria Station Approach (a private road created by the railway company). The curious structure on the corner marks the entrance (round the back) to the station undercroft, now a club for railway employees. The building itself contains *Snippers* hairdressers. The fine **station canopy** *(14)* belongs to the Edwardian extension, and contains the names of popular destinations at that time. There is Blackpool (the workers' playground), Ireland (by boat from Fleetwood), London (courtesy of the Midland Railway), and Belgium (by boat from Hull to Zeebrugge). A flight of steps on the left leads to **Walkers Croft**. A 'croft' was a piece of land on which cloth was put 'on tenterhooks' for bleaching. (Many textile processes were introduced to Manchester by Flemings, who were locally known as 'walkers'.) This curious cobbled lane is built over the Irk, which still flows beneath. As we walk along, there is a fine view of Chetham's College, and it is easy to imagine this great stone mass perched on top of the sandstone rise, with the river flowing at the foot. There is a carved beast on the tower at the end of the range of buildings. Around the corner (in Victoria Street) is

The frontage of Victoria Station, with popular destinations on the station canopy

Palatine Buildings, a hotel speculation of 1842. It is now used as the College's music practice rooms.

However, the way lies along Hunt's Bank, on the right. The name is a reminder of the hunting proclivities of the manorial lords, and it is thought that the hunting dogs were kept near here. The 'House of Correction' was in this street until the opening of the New Bailey Prison in 1790. The wretched prisoners dangled cups from the barred windows to beg alms from passers-by. The enormous flight of steps on the left is used as an exit from performances at the 'Manchester Evening News Arena' (p.28). Hunt's Bank was transformed by the arrival of the railway. The **original Victoria Station of 1844**, then the largest in the world and named "by permission of her Majesty", still survives *(15)*. The main block, at the corner of Hunt's Bank and the station approach, still has the mounting for the clock, which ought to be replaced. The single-storey wing to the left was the part used by the Liverpool and Manchester Railway (it was then a joint station). The station became the headquarters of the Lancashire and Yorkshire Railway, expanding many times – the frontage along the station approach was completed in 1909. The functional 'new' part of the canopy *(14)* fills the gap where an overall roof spanned the roadway between the station and the now vanished railway offices. 'T'owd Lanky' may not have been the largest railway company, but the 'business line' was certainly one of the busiest. It retains the affections of local enthusiasts to this day.

Enter **Victoria Station** by the left-hand archway of the two entrances *(16)*. This houses a fine tile **map of the system** (though the rival LNWR route to Yorkshire, between Stalybridge and Huddersfield, is somehow omitted) above the impressive First World War memorial – with its tableau of St George and the Dragon. A left turn (past a smaller memorial to the dead of the goods department) reveals a block formerly devoted to passenger services, with mosaic signs typical of the period before 1914. The **buffet** interior (complete with dome) has been restored, and should be briefly visited – even if the prospect of railway food is not appetising. ***Northern Belle***, a company specialising in themed railway excursions (including the 'Orient Express') now occupies the site of the old bookstall. Broad flights of steps (which some people mistake for the footbridge!) lead to the **'City Room'**, which acts as a vestibule to the Arena. Except before and after a perfor-

The Edwardian exterior of Victoria Station

Former bookstall, Victoria Station

mance, it is an empty and soulless place, mainly used for the ATM's, though there are a few shops and a *McDonald's*.

The **Manchester Evening News Arena** (DLA Ellerbie Beckett), Europe's largest multi-purpose indoor sports and events arena (maximum capacity of 20,500), is built over part of the station and the old Manchester Workhouse. Developers and architects ought to have a sense of history. When they accidentally stumbled on the old pauper graveyard, it was obvious that, in this case, they had not. The Arena is used for everything from rock concerts to sporting events, and is also the home of 'Manchester Storm', a local ice hockey team. The complex includes a multi-screen cinema and a multi-storey car park.

Back in **Victoria Station**, the path continues past the **stylish booking offices** and other passenger facilities, replete with glazed tiling and curved doorframes. (The Metrolink station is opposite, on the left.) ***The Good Life***, in an archway to the right, is recommended for a quick snack. The archway on the left, formerly the entrance to the old fish dock, is one of the saddest places in Manchester, and is truly **'the gates of hell'**. The leave trains in the First World War departed from here, and a little bronze plaque (easily missed) records this fact: "To the memory of the many thousands of men who passed through this door to the Great War 1914-1918 and of those who did not return." Exit from the station is into Long Millgate by **'cigar alley'**, which once catered (complete with bank) for the needs of busy city 'gents'.

The Co-operative Movement

The way across to Corporation Street follows the tramlines, and passes the spot where the 'Manchester Arms' stood. The pub had once been the starting point for a coach to Bury, but was really a converted 18th-century house. In the 1970s, it was one of the first Manchester pubs to introduce strippers, who performed to an audience of goggle eyed railway porters. And all this was lost to make way for a road that was never built. We must all have been mad! The opposite side of Corporation Street is the **stronghold of the Co-operative movement** (p.268). From left to right is a 'streamlined' classical building of 1928, followed by a fine Edwardian centrepiece (faced with red and grey granite) in the 'Baroque revival' style of 1905, and ending with a nondescript brick rectangle, built to house the bankers in 1980. Follow the tram lines to the corner of Balloon Street. Notice the **plaque** to James Sadler ("pioneer aeronaut"), who made the first manned ascent at Manchester in a hydrogen balloon from a garden that was once here.

There is a modern **statue of Robert Owen** (p.35) on the opposite corner *(17)*. Owen came to Manchester from Newtown in Wales. He later became an important mill owner, but a benevolent one. An interest in the effect of the working environment upon his employees led him to formulate theories, which he published in 'A New View of Society.' This earned him the title of 'father of British socialism'. He was also the first to suggest the idea of co-operation, and is seen as the founder of the co-operative movement (p.268). The excursion to Bury can be commenced at this point (p.251).

Robert Owen, founder of the Co-operative movement

Walk down Corporation Street in the direction of Exchange Square. The street is an 'improvement' of 1845-1848, and was intended to clear a way out of the town by avoiding the congestion of Long Millgate. City Buildings, on the corner of Todd Street on the right, is a fine example of a late **Victorian office block**, complete with clock tower and wrought iron work. Todd Street, formerly 'Toad' or 'T'Owd (old) Lane', was once described as "one of the filthiest suburbs of the town, so confined that the winds of heaven could scarcely penetrate it". It ran along the extension of the Hanging Ditch towards the Irk. Ann Lee was born in the lane in 1736. A "woman clothed with the sun", she was the founder and prophetess of the Shakers. After disrupting a service in the old Collegiate Church, she was imprisoned. Christ then appeared to her, and inspired her and her followers to emigrate and settle in the American colonies. The Shakers believed that it was necessary to release the spiritual nature from its imprisonment in the world of matter. Consequently, any artefact must be as simple in design as possible.

'Tis a gift to be simple, 'tis a gift to be free,
'Tis a gift to come round where we ought to be.
And when we come round it will be all right,
We will dwell in the valley of love and delight.
Where pure simplicity is gained,
To bow and to bend we will not be ashamed.
We'll turn, turn, turn with all our might,
And, in turning, we will come round right!

The Shakers have all but died out (they preached celibacy and expanded mainly

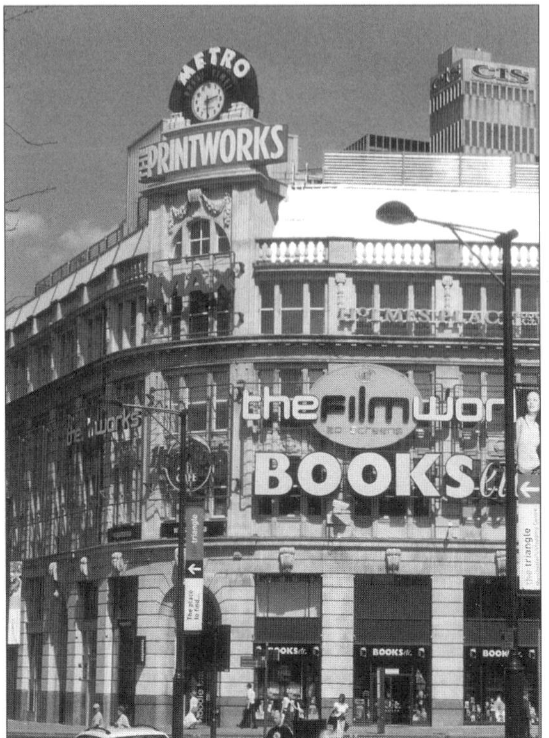

The Printworks complex

through recruitment), but Shaker furniture and artefacts are greatly prized and widely collected.

Walking along Corporation Street, notice how the Corn Exchange has included a previous bank building and associated offices at the Fennel Street corner. Ahead, there is a fine view of Exchange Square, *Marks and Spencer,* and the bridge to the *Arndale Centre.*

Printworks

The ***Printworks*** is on the corner of Corporation Street and Withy Grove (p.167), distinguished by the **large digital video screen** over the main entrance and numerous neon lights. Formerly known as Kemsley House (at one point 'Maxwell House'!), it developed piecemeal after 1929 as the largest newspaper office and printworks in Britain, printing such long-forgotten papers as the *Sunday Graphic,* as well as the northern edition of the *Daily Telegraph.* The £110m conversion (only the frontage survives) has produced a major leisure complex.

The 'themed' cobbled streets (complete with 'weather effects'!) run from Corporation Street and the main Withy Grove entrance to ... well, a side street, but a passage will no doubt later appear to the intended transport interchange. The central attraction is, without doubt, a 20-screen cinema, incorporating a giant **IMAX '3D' screen** (26 by 23 metres) and a 'luxury' viewing facility (complete with refreshments served at one's seat!). One hopes that there will be enough films to show in these city centre cinema complexes! The rest of the Printworks appears little more than an extended cinema foyer, dominated by a variety of **'big name' eateries** (including *Hard Rock Café, Henry J. Bean's*). There is also a ***Virgin*** family entertainment centre, ***Tiger Tiger*** (a four-floor bar and club complex), a branch of ***Books Etc***, and a health club. The interior decoration, meant to invoke a variety of 'moods' (with 'hidden' printing presses roaring away through the grills), falls far short of the mark and cannot be remotely compared with the 'Trafford Centre' (p.266).

After quitting this leisure complex, Exchange Square, where the walk began, is just a short distance further along Corporation Street.

Rear entrance to the Town Hall Extension on Lloyd Street, St Peter's Square

2 Exchange Square to Albert Square

Start: Exchange Square

Estimated time of walk: 1 hour

Interiors: Royal Exchange – 15 min; St Ann's – 30 min; The 'Hidden Gem' – 30 min; Town Hall – 30 min; Cross Street Chapel – 15 min

Highlights: The home of cotton, a mini-Crystal Palace, two beautiful churches, hidden alleyways, Abraham Lincoln, the civic heart of the city, an unusual place of worship, and the pillar box that defied the terrorists.

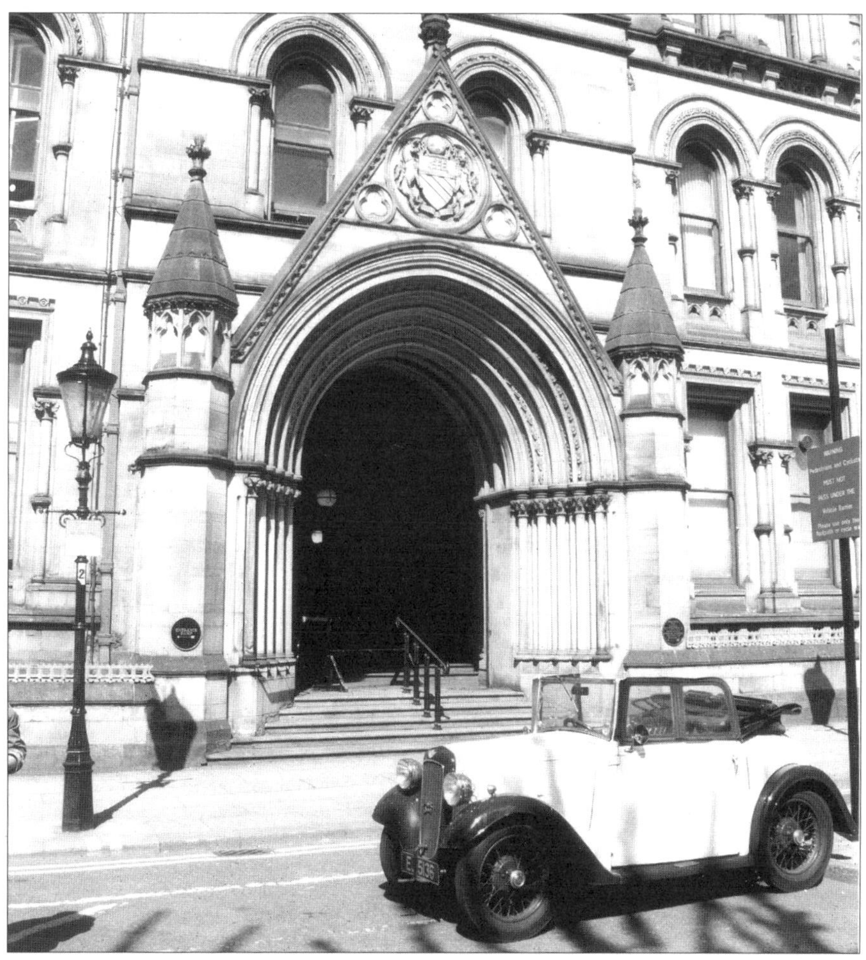

Once again, we are standing on New Cathedral Street steps (p.6). The previously noted axis, or line of sight, between St Ann's Church and the Old Shambles now draws us in the opposite direction to the previous walk, along New Cathedral Street. You are standing on the third level here, for there are two lower levels below the street, used for deliveries to *Marks and Spencer* (p.6) and pedestrian access to and from the large underground car park (which is entered from Deansgate, behind the West Shambles development).

The street partly follows the course of Old Millgate, which probably first appeared in the 12th century. Over a hundred years ago, in the course of demolition, workmen found a strange underground room near here. It may have been a folly – perhaps a banqueting chamber for 18th-century jollifications. On the other hand, it was not far from John Byrom's house, and it may have been a meeting place for Jacobites or perhaps for an occult secret society! (p.10). The **West Shambles** development, on the right, contains offices, housing, and shops fronting New Cathedral Street and Exchange Square, including a branch of ***Harvey Nichols*** (seen as the cachet for Manchester's claim as an international shopping centre.) The narrow lane called Smithy Door, which ran between the Market Place (p.72) and Deansgate, lay somewhere underneath this development. Once upon a time, a blacksmith lived there, a man who could only claim a debt in court by producing the door upon which he chalked his business accounts!

The shop window of Kays, Exchange Square

The street terminates at the junction with Market Street, St Mary's Gate, and Exchange Street *(1)*, one of the busiest in the city (if speaking of pedestrians). Steps in front of *Marks and Spencer* (p.6), to the left, indicate the fall of the roadway towards the Irwell. The jeweller's frontage of ***Arthur Kay and Brothers***, on the opposite corner, contains the original 1901 advertisements. Proceed directly ahead into Exchange Street. This marks the first attempt at town planning in Manchester, replacing a narrow passage called 'Dark Entry' after 1777. 'The Gardens' (David Backhouse, 1987), with the ***Disney Store*** at street level, is a revamp of a boring post-war building in a striking but jolly mixture of classical and what seem to be 'art nouveau' elements.

The Royal Exchange

However, the massive frontage of the **Royal Exchange** takes up the street (and the subsequent Square) on the left-hand side. A row of classical pillars alternates with pilasters at the corners and entrances, and an impressive 180ft (55m) **circular**

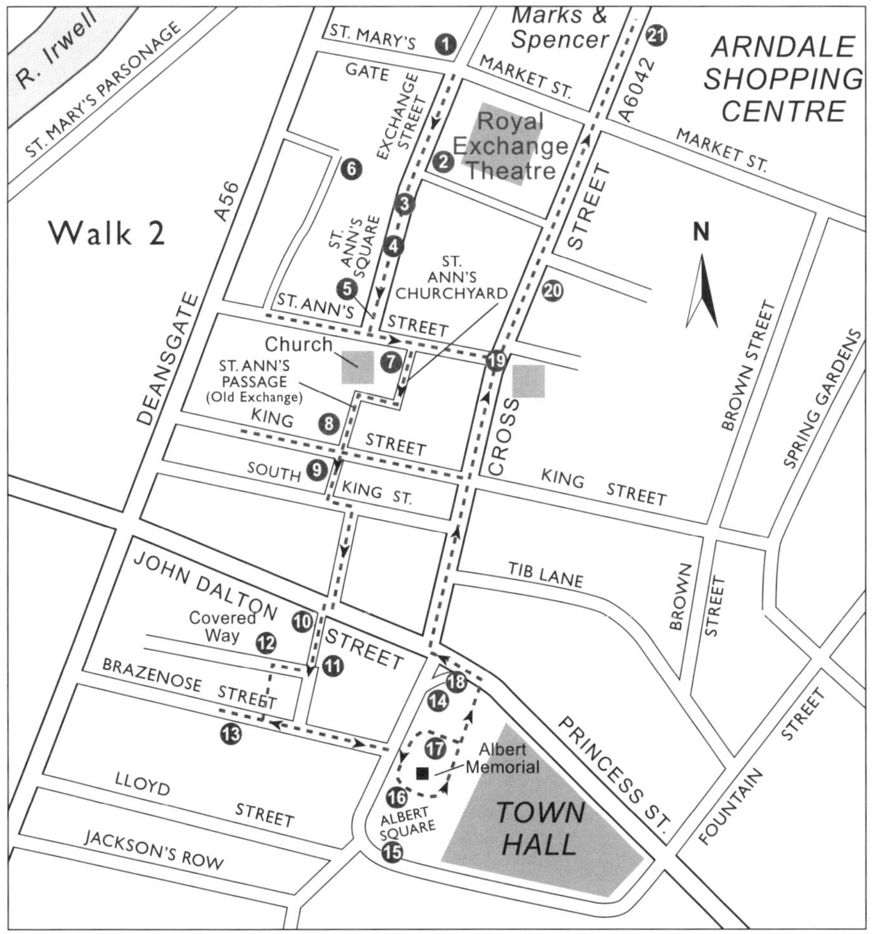

tower graces the Exchange Street corner. Cotton from all over the world was bought and sold here. The first Exchange, a meeting place for businessmen, opened in the old Market Place in 1729 (p.72). As the cotton trade took off, a larger hall was needed, and a second Exchange, on the present site, opened in 1809. The Master of this institution was attracted by a disturbance in 1834, for John Bright (p.44) had decided to make a public stand against the Corn Laws, and addressed the members by standing on a chair. Receiving a mixed reception, he desisted after being threatened with ejection by the police. The event could be said to be start of the Anti Corn Law League (p.113). Additions to the structure began in 1836, and a greatly enlarged building opened with a grand ball in 1849.

Even this soon proved inadequate. A third Exchange, extending over the site of Newall's Buildings (once the headquarters of the Anti Corn Law League), was begun in 1867, and opened in 1874. It had a fine classical portico on Cross Street (p.48), that is sadly no longer with us, but the tower is still a prominent landmark. The last phase of construction started just before the First World War in 1914, and was only completed in 1921. The Exchange had 11,000 members in its heyday, but only half that number after 1945. Membership continued to decline with the cotton trade, and trading ceased by 1961. "England's bread hangs by Lancashire's thread." The entrance to the ***Royal Exchange Shopping Centre*** is on the left. (Notice the **plaque** recording the rebuilding of the city centre after the IRA bomb.) There are three floors, though the antique market in the basement is, sadly, no longer with us.

ICE plaque on the outside of the Royal Exchange

The entrance to the **Exchange** itself is a rather grand flight of steps. A lift, inserted into the staircase, communicates with a projecting approach from the main floor. On either side are inscriptions relating to the construction and opening of the present building. The interior is a massive rectangular space, surrounded by classical pillars and pilasters, and surmounted by a **dome**, 62ft (19m) in diameter. A long aisle runs directly ahead to the Cross Street entrance (p.48), divided from the main hall by a line of double pillars and square columns. The Exchange was held twice a week, when mill owners, brokers and merchants involved with the cloth trade flooded into Manchester from all over the county. The main business was conducted quietly (members were expected to behave like gentlemen) in the Great Hall. Each member was allocated fifteen square feet of floorspace, determined by the intersection of invisible lines extrapolated from numbered and lettered placards affixed to the walls! Those who serviced the trade, including shippers and engineering companies, might be found in the aisles. The **indicators**, high on the

Main entrance to the Royal Exchange, on St Ann's Square

wall at the Exchange Street end, show the closing prices on the last ever day of trading here. A ***café*** may be found below them, with the ***theatre bar*** to the left. The Royal Exchange was badly bombed in the last war. Look for the **plaque** unveiled by Princess Margaret in 1953, to mark the rebuilding.

Like a giant lunar module, the steel-framed **Royal Exchange Theatre** seems as if it has just landed in the centre of the Great Hall. The heavy load of the theatre is greater than the hall floor could bear, and is thus directed by the framework to the inner structure of the Great Hall. It is a 740-seat theatre in the round – no one is more than a few yards away from the performers and the action on stage. The theatre attracts international stars of the stage and its repertoire is a mixture of classics and new (sometimes, experimental) plays. The **box office**, together with a ***craft shop***, **bookshop**, and ***bar*** (with bar snacks) are located in the aisle. Notice that the **names of patrons** and sponsors are recorded in little metal plates in the floor!

Back outside, take a brief detour into the ***Exchange Arcade*** *(2)*, marking the site of Bank Street (built over in the last Exchange extension around 1914). It contains a good ***Oxfam*** 'fair trade' shop, with a variety of gifts and products from most parts of the 'third world'. Do not miss the **plaque** in memory of Robert Owen (p.29) near the

The massive dome of the Royal Exchange

entrance. He first obtained employment in Satterfield's Drapery that once stood in the vicinity.

St Ann's Square

The frontage of the Royal Exchange continues into **St Ann's Square**, which we now enter. Henry III granted Robert Grelley, Lord of the Manor, the right to hold an annual fair here in 1227, a useful source of income to the Grelleys and their successors. The site was then called Acresfield, and the fair was held on and around St Matthew's day (20th-22nd September), mainly as a mart for livestock and horses. Some historians have suggested that a cross stood at some point so that bargains could be solemnised, and that this is the origin of Cross Street (p.48). The fair continued, much to the inconvenience of residents and shopkeepers alike, until it was removed to Knott Mill (p.182) in 1823. After the construction of St Ann's Church, the area was developed as a fashionable square, rivalling the best that London could offer. (There were trees between 1718 and 1822.) The Square's finest moment came after the Reform Act of 1832, when the 'hustings' for Manchester's first MPs were held here. The candidates processed into the Square behind a band. St Ann's Square is still associated with 'society' in Manchester, with upmarket shopping and prestigious weddings on Saturdays at the Church, with everyone in big hats or suits from Moss Bros.

The Square was pedestrianised and remodelled a few years ago, though many dislike the **'balls'**! The **Boer War Memorial** (by Thorneycroft, 1908) depicts a wounded soldier passing ammunition to a defiant comrade *(3)*. And that is how the country saw it at the time, a war for the defence of an Empire defiant in the face of adversity. This view encouraged large numbers of part-time volunteer soldiers to opt for service overseas. More died of dysentery and typhoid than were killed in action, and the mismanagement of the campaign in its early stages, together with the physical condition of many of the recruits and volunteers, brought about much needed military and social reforms. The sculptor embraced this new realism, and the statue depicts an actual incident during the fighting at Ladysmith (the figures were modelled on two privates of the Manchester Regiment).

The recent **fountain** *(4)* represents a cotton bud, though hardly anyone knows that. The distinguished person who inaugurated it was unimpressed by the original 'artistic' effect, mumbling "is that it?". The water now flows a little faster. The former chairman of the Anti Corn Law League (p.113) unveiled the **statue of Richard Cobden** *(5)* in 1867, just as the old headquarters down the road was consigned to dust. Cobden came to Manchester in the 1830s, and created a successful calico printing business. He was perhaps the most outstanding figure in the League, and also inaugurated the movement to incorporate the town (p.78). In later life, he championed the cause of international peace.

Beyond the Exchange, on the left-hand side of the Square, are **Old Bank Chambers** (1920s), once the home of Manchester Liners, trading to Canada by the Ship Canal. Look out for the ship's prow of Jason and the Argonauts, carved on the corner. The 'bank' in question was the 'Manchester Bank' of 1771 (the first in the town) that also gave its name to the street nearby. It was founded by a partnership that included Edward Byrom (p.60) and William Allen (p.61). The latter became sole proprietor, and went bankrupt in 1788. However the bank was rescued by the Heywood family of Liverpool, who later moved to new premises in St Ann Street (p.39). The strikingly painted wedding-cake Victorian Classicism of **Mansfield Chambers** is next door.

The opposite side of the Square is far more interesting, for the opening out from Exchange Street to the original width of Acresfield has been preserved. At this point is the entrance passage to the **Barton Arcade** *(6)*, with ***Sportspages*** (devoted to sports books and publications). Enter the Arcade and find a mini Crystal Palace in glass and iron, assembled from prefabricated parts manufactured in Glasgow in 1871. Above the shops, which include the fascinating ***House of Lamps***, are wrought iron verandas giving access to offices. The Arcade leads through to Deansgate (p.52). Upon regaining the Square, notice that the **range of buildings** on this side, though much altered and rebuilt, preserve the original scale of the 18th-century houses. **St Ann's Arcade** (which many people miss) has some interesting shops, including a dealer in classic cameras.

St Ann's Church

However, one is always drawn to the major attraction at the end of the Square – **St Ann's Church**. In the early 18th century, two facts were clear. The town was growing beyond the capacity of the old Collegiate Church (p.14), and that ancient institution was a stronghold of High Toryism, if not a coterie of closet Jacobites. For these reasons, a second church was clearly needed, and Lady Ann Bland, Lady of the Manor and leader of fashionable society in Manchester (p.40), was determined to do something about it. She laid the first stone of the new church in 1709 and the Bishop of Chester consecrated it in 1712. The dedication was a complement to both the founder and the Queen. The Church naturally attracted a Whig low-church congregation, but the majority of Mancunians followed the example of John Byrom (p.10) in attending St Ann's in the morning and the Collegiate Church in the evening, or vice versa, just to be on the safe side! As the city later developed, more and more of the population moved out of the centre, and St Ann's lost its congregation. Nowadays, it is a 'city church', ministering to all who work in the city centre with lunchtime services, events, and recitals. It is also the official church of numerous Manchester organisations, including the police force. Finally, St Ann's is famous as a stronghold of adherents to the 1662 Book of Common Prayer. This, together with a fine choir, attracts growing numbers to Sunday services.

The church was built in the new style popularised by Sir Christopher Wren, who is supposed to have had a hand in the design. However, the actual architect was probably John Barker, responsible for St Alkmund, Whitchurch. It exemplified an age of reason. Newton had mapped out the universe with mathematics, and it seemed that even God might be ultimately knowable in the same way. It comes as no surprise that the architecture was based on harmonies produced by mathematical proportion. The original design included a cupola on top of the **tower**. After 1777, this was replaced by a spire, but removed shortly afterwards when the tower was reconstructed. Note the **position of the original clock**. St Ann's has been restored in 1837 and 1887-1889, when a great deal of the stonework was replaced. The ornamentation was originally in a different coloured stone, but the restorations have produced a piebald effect. A **brass plaque** (near the vestry door on the left) details the history of the Square, and there is a commemorative **inscription to John Shaw** (p.11) at the base of the tower. The church is open daily, and everyone is welcome to attend the services and events. So enter, and enjoy.

"Our churches must be made for auditories," wrote Wren (auditories are buildings where the congregation could hear and see the preacher distinctly). St Ann's is really a box, which was once centred on a massive 'three-decker' pulpit at the east end, towering above desks for the parson and the clerk. Preaching was the most important activity that the church could undertake, to seek to turn men towards God, to aspire to the personal relationship that Protestants consider so important. The altar table was almost hidden behind in the circular apse. However, the Anglican Church was influenced by the 'ritualism', fashionable in the last quarter of the 19th century. Consequently, a 'sanctuary' or **Chancel** was created at the east end in the last major restoration by Alfred Waterhouse. The **screens and beautiful ironwork** are notable. The original **pulpit** was removed to the left of the Chancel and (to reduce the height) placed in a 'moat' surrounded by the **old communion rails**. The **stained glass in the apse** is by Frederick Shields, and the centre window is a memorial to Bishop Fraser (p.44).

The **Lady Chapel**, to the right of the Chancel, contains the **original altar table** (the gift of Lady Ann Bland), a fine piece of Queen Ann workmanship. The **'Descent from the Cross'** was painted by Annibale Carracci (1561-1609), and purchased in the 18th century by a Mancunian in the course of an Italian tour. It was originally presented to St Peter's Church (p.108). The modern **perspex window** is the gift of the Northern School of Music.

The richer inhabitants rented the **church pews**, while ordinary folk crowded into the **galleries**. The fine **organ** of 1730 was originally located at the west end, and the **font** is inscribed "The gift of Francis Latham of London, Gent. 1711". The

Interior of St Ann's Church

stained glass by the choir vestry entrance, to the left of the chancel, is 18th-century work by William Peckit of York, and was formerly the east window of St John's (p.60). There are many **memorial tablets** in the church, but the most interesting is to Sergeant Charles Brett in the area under the tower. (The tablet was originally in St Barnabas's Church.) A number of Fenians (Irish nationalists) had been arrested in 1867. While being transported to Belle Vue Prison, the van was ambushed on Hyde Road in an attempt to free the prisoners. Sergeant Brett refused to hand over the keys, an act for which he paid with his life, and his assailants were later tried and executed. The 'Manchester Martyrs' have their own memorial elsewhere, but one ought to remember the courage of poor Sergeant Brett as well, for he was only trying to do his duty. Please leave a donation for the upkeep of St Ann's before you leave.

Exit, and inspect St Ann's Street in front of the building. The section to the left, between the church and Deansgate, was called Toll Lane. Here, the Lord of the Manor levied a toll on beasts bound for the fair. A curious custom involved the inhabitants assembling here on the first morning of the fair, and pelting the unfortunate first animal to pass by with acorns, while others goaded it with whips! The rather plain top floor of the building above ***Habitat***, in contrast to the rest, is evidence of wartime destruction. But it is the other section of this street, between the church and Cross Street, that has the most interesting buildings. Starting at the corner of the Square, ***The Royal Bank of Scotland*** was erected in a loose interpretation of the Palladian style in 1848. The actual bank was to the left of the entrance arch, and the manager's house of brick faced with stone to the right. The original occupant was a bank founded by the Heywood family (p.44), who were great benefactors to the city. The elaborate decoration of **Alliance House** (1900) on the Cross

Street corner does not chime in with the utilitarian frontage of the building society on the ground floor.

The Conservative Club, which opened in 1875, was located in National House on the opposite corner. It is an elaborate work, intent on making a statement that the party had 'arrived'. Indeed, the modern Conservative Party only made a significant impact in Manchester after its philosophy had been redefined by Benjamin Disraeli, and after Gladstone alienated many liberals by adopting 'home rule' for Ireland. Nowadays, the party has all but disappeared from the electoral life of the city. The building is a marvellous concoction of pediments, classical columns, and armorial devices. Notice the oriel windows at the Cross Street corner. **Winter's Buildings** (1901), on the churchyard corner, is a mixture of brick, terracotta, and stone, typical of the period.

The paved area at the east end of the Church is all that is left of **St Ann's Churchyard** *(7)*. The **'chest tomb' nearest the railings** is that of Thomas Deacon (p.21), "the greatest of sinners and the most unworthy of primitive bishops". The **upright stone** against the curving apse wall, with its Latin inscription, marks the grave of the Rev. Joseph Hoole. As Rector of St Ann's, he preached against the Jacobite rebellion. Death spared him the experience of it on his own doorstep, but fate had a curious surprise in store. As his hurried funeral took place, some of the Highland officers entered the Square and, in complete ignorance of the political opinions of the deceased, doffed their bonnets and joined the funeral procession! No doubt they wanted to create a good impression, but it is interesting to speculate how many of the dead on Culloden Moor attended a funeral in Manchester and followed the body of a man whose name they probably did not know. Another **'chest tomb' to the left** has a terrible list of child mortality, set out like a football pools coupon. Immediately behind it is the **stone of John Howard**, "a respectable grocer and an honest man". He just made the 19th century by a few days at the age of eighty-four. Born in a small country town, and dying in a place starting to resound with the thump of steam engines and the clattering of machinery, what changes he must have seen in that time!

Walk round the back of the church and turn left under the archway of St Ann's Passage, or **Old Exchange Passage** *(8)*. This curious little spot started life as a footpath from Acresfield. Lady Ann Bland established an assembly room over the passage for soirees and dancing. Her deadly rival was Madam Drake (who presided over a rival Tory salon). This lady was not so refined – gossip suggested that while Lady Bland exemplified the height of fashion, Madam received guests with a pipe in one hand and a mug of beer in the other. However, Madam Drake had gone so far as to decorate her coach and horses with the Royal Stewart Tartan, and something had to be done. So, one fine evening, Lady Bland and her company came out of the room attired with orange blossom (the colour of the 1688 revolution) and danced in King Street by the light of the moon! Businessmen met in this room between 1792 and 1805, the period between the first and second Exchanges – hence the name. The present structure is a conceit of 1896, replacing an original 18th-century building. Until a few years ago, there was a French food shop in the passage, distinguished by a young lady in fishnet stockings and a beret who sold a remarkable amount of French bread!

The popular King Street shopping area

King Street

Follow the passage through to emerge in King Street. This 18th-century street was intended for fashionable residences, but after Cross Street (p.48) cut across it, the two halves went their separate ways, this particular portion retaining the original scale. Seek out **Dr Peter Waring's fine brick mansion** of 1736, complete with railings and steps. It is the only house to survive in anything like the original condition, probably because it was turned into a bank around 1788. However, only the frontage remains, tastefully incorporated into the façade of a *Virgin* store. Interestingly enough, the easily missed nondescript stucco-exterior opposite the preserved frontage, with the 'dolls' house' windows and the two lots of ghastly post-war balcony railings, hides what is thought to be a **town house dating to circa 1700** (above a branch of *Reed*).

A short detour to the Deansgate end of the street reveals a magnificent **pastiche of mediaeval timber framing** on the corner of Police Street. The street name commemorates the site of the Police Office. It stood in this place at a time when much of the day-to-day administration of Manchester was still the responsibility of a manorial official known as the Boroughreeve. The infamous Joseph Nadin occupied this office with a responsibility for maintaining law and order, but he seemed to spend more time persecuting political radicals than chasing criminals. After Peterloo (p.131), his outrageous behaviour was a spur to obtaining proper local government.

After noticing the Victorian iron colonnade above ***Ted Baker Woman***, the way continues through **Boardman's Entry** *(9)* situated beside *Blu*. This, and subsequent passages, have design features associated with John Dalton (p.46). He was never without his umbrella, so look upwards! Walk through to St James's Square (possibly named by Jacobite sympathisers), showing how small some of these 18th-century developments could be.

We are now in John Dalton Street. The buildings are mainly modern construction, though **Trinity Court** (1865) has a fine frontage of polychromatic brickwork with Venetian features. It once sold 'Mediaeval furniture', very popular in the age of the Pre-Raphaelites. Although rather new, the ***Ape and Apple*** is a tastefully designed pub, popular for its quality beer and good food at quite reasonable prices. The ***John Dalton Café*** can also be recommended. **New Church House** (established in 1782) is the home of the Swedenborgian Church. This Protestant sect established itself in Manchester in the 18th century and caused quite a stir. Its most famous creation was a circular church near Ancoats, now sadly demolished. Continue through **Dalton Entry** *(10)* by the side of New Church House, looking for the chemical apparatus in the decorative roundels. This leads through to **Mulberry Passage** *(11)*, where the design motif continues.

St Mary's RC Church

On exiting, a right turn leads to St Mary's Roman Catholic Church, better known as **The Hidden Gem** *(12)*. The church originally ministered to a slum area packed with Irish immigrants, and was established in 1794, though the present building (inspired by a Spanish church and incorporating Byzantine features) dates from 1848. The design aroused Pugin, the great panjandrum of the Gothic revival, to a state of apoplexy, complaining that it "shows to what depths of error even good men fall when they abandon the true thing and go whoring after strange styles". The name refers both to the location and the fact that the simple exterior conceals an amazing surprise.

Enter (but be careful not to disturb anyone at their devotions) and admire the great **reredos** of Caen marble behind the altar, a giant cluster of life sized sculptured figures that seem to have strayed from a great Baroque church in Rome. From left to right are Our Lady, St Stephen, St Patrick, St Peter, Our Lord (above the tabernacle), St John, St Hilda of Whitby, St Augustine, and St Joseph. The left-hand chapel has a fine **pieta**, and the right-hand one a **statue of 'Our Lady of Manchester'**, with scenes of the nativity and the presentation in the temple. Little is known about "Mr Lane of Preston" who executed the whole work in the 1870s. Do not miss the wooden **oratory** (part of the priest's house) to the rear of the right-hand side aisle, as it contains a **painting of 'Our Lady of Manchester' by Harold Riley**, which is sometimes visible. The church also has a powerful modern interpretation of the **'Stations of the Cross'** by Norman Adams R.A., and the **font** is worth a glance. Illustrated guide books are available from the priest's residence next door at all reasonable times. Again, please leave a donation before you go.

After leaving, proceed through the covered way to Brazenose Street, a thoroughfare that has been completely rebuilt in the last few decades. The unusual name is derived from the fact that the land here belonged to William Hulme's Charity (p.166), as the income derived from it financed a number of scholarships to Brazenose College. Brazenose Street might have been much grander – a tree-lined processional way from Albert Square to the River Irwell was proposed in the 1945 city redevelopment plan. The concept has been revived in the form of a series of linked pedestrianised streets, and the original intention may be realised in the Spinningfield development (p.57). In recent years, the quiet tree-lined **Lincoln Square** has been created (by demolition) to one side of the street. Mainly used by office workers for taking a break, the Square will repay a brief inspection. It affords a good view of the ***Rising Sun*** in Queen Street, which gives an indication of how the area probably appeared in the early 19th century. The truly awful **Centurian House** looms over all, blocking the view towards Deansgate. The architect obviously had a bad day at the office.

A dramatic **statue of Abraham Lincoln** *(13)* dominates the Square. In 1917, Mr and Mrs Taft offered a copy of the statue of Lincoln in their home city of Cincinnati (by George Barnard) to London, as symbolic of Anglo-American unity. But the capital did not want "the tramp with colic" and Manchester immediately offered a 'temporary' site in Platt Fields, where the statue was unveiled in 1919. It was moved to the new square in 1986. It depicts Lincoln as an ordinary man, just starting his career in the law and politics. The large plinth contains a variety of inscriptions (very badly worn), including the text of a resolution to Lincoln passed by Manchester working men at a public meeting in 1862. Manchester was then experiencing terrible hardship because of the 'cotton famine' caused by the Union naval blockade, and it might be thought that public opinion would have inclined to the Confederacy. In fact, despite their suffering, the Liberal establishment of the city and its organised working class supported the Union cause. Lincoln was so touched that he sent a reply in which he described the resolution as "the sublimest example of Christian heroism". This text is also on the plinth, but someone changed "working men" to read "working people", which is not what the great man said. Political correctness may have its good points, but this is idiocy and was greatly criticised at the time. In front of Lincoln is a **brick rectangle**, usually planted with bulbs. The plaque indicates that this was a fountain (which obviously did not work) in honour of Prince Charles's wedding in 1981. Beside it is a more recent plaque commemorating Lady Diana.

Albert Square

Brazenose Street exits into **Albert Square**, the civic heart of Manchester, where the walk resumes. After attaining the status of a city in 1853, the first Town Hall (p.80) began to seem inadequate. The appearance of the city centre was attracting some criticism at the same time, and an Act of Parliament was obtained in 1866 to demolish an area of slum property and create space for an impressive new Town Hall and a civic square worthy of the city. The centrepiece of the new civic centre, then as now, would be the **Albert Memorial**. Prince Albert of Saxe-Coburg-Gotha appeared as a figure of fun, a "penniless German sausage monger" on the make, when he married Queen Victoria. However, he soon won the hearts of the public as a model family man and a patron of the arts and sciences. His greatest achievement in this field was the Great Exhibition of 1851, which gave birth to many important national institutions and museums. He introduced the Christmas Tree to Britain and also averted a potential war with America. His premature death caused an outpouring of national grief.

The memorial, designed by Thomas Worthington, was inaugurated in 1867 and cost £6,250. It comprises an open arched four-sided **Gothic canopy** with a spire 75ft (23m) high containing a **marble statue of the prince** by Noble. Each gable above the arches contains an elaborate pierced panel surrounded by **sculpted heads**. They are representatives of the arts and sciences, and include Raphael, Wren, and Shakespeare.

The four pinnacles on top of the pillars contain the **allegorical groups of figures** that Victorians loved, again representing the arts and sciences (art supported by music, sculpture, painting, and architecture, that sort of thing). The fact that hardly any of this ornamentation can be seen from the ground did not seem to matter at the time. Perhaps they peered at it through opera glasses. The five-stepped base is decorated with armorial devices.

The contrasting **Jubilee Fountain** *(14)* marks two important events – the Queen's Jubilee in 1897, and the opening of the scheme to bring drinking water to Manchester from a reservoir at Thirlmere in the Lake District. The jolly fish and the water spouting gargoyles are great favourites with children.

The Square contains a number of statues. **Gladstone** (by Raggi, 1901) is at the Mount Street end *(15)* and shows the 'people's William'. He was the political exemplification of the 'Manchester School' – the advocacy of the greatest degree of personal liberty in the political, religious, social, and economic spheres, commensurate with decency and civilised behaviour. The logic of this propelled him into a battle to obtain political autonomy for Ireland, and he is depicted making a point in the 'home rule debate' of 1893. "My mission is to pacify Ireland". He split the Liberal Party because of this issue, resulting in many of the Manchester industrial elite gravitating towards the (now acceptable) Conservatives. A deeply religious man, he was in the habit of searching out prostitutes to bring back to Downing Street, for soup and sympathy from his wife. Sadly, many people thought him rather pompous – Queen Victoria claimed that he addressed her as if she was a public meeting.

Oliver Heywood (Bruce-Joy, 1894) is next to him *(16)*, a member of the distinguished banking family. His wealth enabled him to devote his time to good works, particularly the progress of education in Manchester. The statue of **John Bright** *(17)* may be found on the other side of the Albert Memorial (Bruce-Joy, 1891). With Cobden, this Rochdale mill owner led the Anti Corn Law League (p.113). The repeal of the duties on imported corn in 1846 was the symbolic victory of free trade or 'Manchester School' principles and seemed to usher in an age of peace and progress. He was also a Manchester MP.

Bishop Fraser (Woolner, 1888) is shown in his everyday clothes, including gaiters *(18)*. This is appropriate, for he was the 'people's bishop', the 'bishop of all denominations'. He was very tolerant of other religious groups, and had a profound sympathy for the working people of the city. His death was such a shock that business was suspended on the Royal Exchange. The plinth is illustrated with scenes from his ministry, including him addressing workmen.

There is an interesting **range of buildings at the Mount Street end** of the Square, in several variations of the Gothic style. On the corner of Mount Street is St Andrew's Chambers (1872, by a pupil of Waterhouse in the style of the Town Hall), with a statue of the saint holding his cross on the Mount Street side. It was built for the Scottish Widows Friendly Society, a savings organisation started after the Napoleonic Wars. Fronting the Square is a frieze in which money is being handed over to what is presumably a Scottish widow. To the right is Carlton House (1872), once the home of the Manchester Arts Club and the Bridgewater Canal offices, in 13th-century Gothic. It is followed by Albert Chambers (1873), with a bust of the Prince, built for the Corporation Gas Works in a debased Venetian Gothic. Finally, on the corner of Southmill Street, is a superb example of the genuine article (by

Thomas Worthington, 1866). It was built to commemorate the 2000 ministers who left the Anglican Church in 1662, as a result of the Act of Uniformity, and was a home to religious groups and learned societies. The three floors of brick are pierced with 14th-century Venetian windows – the whole was inspired by a palazzo on the Grand Canal. It now contains *The Square Albert* pub.

Carnival time in Albert Square

The **buildings facing the Town Hall** are more mundane rectangular modern brick, though the ground floor colonnades are a useful feature, being used by the outdoor tables of fashionable cafés. Note the classical Abbey National building (1900), on the Corner of John Dalton Street. The lavish Northern Assurance building (1902), at the **Princess Street end**, is also worth a look. *Wippels* will sell you anything from a university gown and mortarboard to ecclesiastical vestments.

The Town Hall

The Square is, above all, a setting for the **Town Hall**. The foundation stone was laid in 1868, but it was not until 1877 that the opening ceremony could take place. In the meantime, Alfred Waterhouse had created one of the finest public buildings in Britain. Two styles were available for town halls at the time. The neo-classical, with its emphasis upon the public virtues of Greece and Rome, was still popular, but fading. The Victorian obsession with the Middle Ages also translated into civic terms. Was not Manchester the equivalent of mediaeval Venice, Bruges, or Antwerp? Consequently, the new town Hall would recreate the glories of the 'cloth halls' of Flanders. John Ruskin had made fun of such pretensions. As an 'architectural man milliner', he advised aldermen with delusions of grandeur to ornament their civic palaces with bulging moneybags.

The site is almost triangular, and the three principal wings (containing continuous corridors around the building, servicing 314 rooms) are constructed around a central space. This, in turn, is divided into a series of small courtyards by a great rectangular ceremonial hall. The main Albert Square frontage has a **clock tower** 286ft (87m) high, with a peal of 21 bells – the grand entrance is at the base. All the windows and arches are in the best Gothic, with great attention to detail. The principal **first-floor rooms** are, from left to right, the Banqueting Chamber, Reception Room, and (on the other side of the tower), the Mayor's Parlour and the Old Council Chamber (still in use for committee and public meetings).

Study the **grand entrance**. St George is placed on the gable above it, with Henry III and Elizabeth I in niches below. Agricola (founder of the Roman Fort) is situated above the entrance itself. The main **range of statues on the Princess Street corner** depict (from the left) Thomas De Grelle, who gave a charter to Manchester in 1301; Thomas De La Warre; John Bradford; General Charles Worsley, the first MP for the town in Cromwell's parliament; Humphrey Chetham; and the first Duke of Lancaster. There are **other sculptures** – Edward III, in whose reign Flemish weavers arrived in Manchester, is on Princess Street, and Edward the Elder, who conquered the Danelaw, and sent men to Manchester to 'repair and man it', graces the Cooper Street entrance.

Tours of the Town Hall can be arranged, and are sometimes included in the city walks programme, but the public are usually able to see the Great Hall (ask at the reception desk). The left side of the **Entrance Hall** contains a **statue of John Dalton** by Chantry. The statue is a likeness made in 1839 for the Royal Institution (p.100), and was placed here in 1884. Dalton was a Quaker schoolmaster from Cumbria who settled in the town. One day, his maid served him a cup of tea with too much milk in it. He suddenly realised that the nature of substances related to the proportions of the ingredients. The Ancient Greeks had developed the concept of the atom. He took this one stage further, and posited the theory that all elements were composed of atoms, but mixtures of different atoms (two of hydrogen, one of oxygen, for example) create substances such as water. Like Kant, he was a creature of habit, whose routine hardly ever varied (taking a holiday in the Lake District the same weeks every year). At times, his eccentricity could be alarming. An acquaintance asked why he had not visited. Dalton replied that he was too busy, but "if you agree, I will come and stay with you". And so it proved – he remained as a guest for the rest of his life. **James Joule** (by Gilbert, 1893) is opposite (p.237). Notice the (damaged) metal instrument in his hand.

A wide corridor prefaces the staircase, but the **Sculpture Hall**, a sort of pantheon of Victorian worthies, should be visited first (it is also used for temporary exhibitions). There are few modern memorials, but there is a fine **plaque honouring the Manchester Contingent of the International Brigade**, a **wood sculpture in tribute to Nelson Mandela**, and a striking **sculpture of Sir John Barbirolli** conducting (p.135). The **Grand Staircase** is next ascended, but do not miss the **painted statue of Henry of Grosmont**, the first Duke of Lancaster. His elevation was accompanied by the creation of the County Palatine of Lancaster, in effect, the creation of the county of Lancashire. A lovely **spiral stair** rises next to the left-hand side staircase, and a **statue of John Bright** (p.44), executed by Theed in 1878, ornaments the right-hand flight. Bees, symbolic of industry, are a design motif throughout the building, and can be found in the **mosaic floor** of the landing. Enter the **Great Hall**, a grand room of 100ft (30m) by 50ft (15m), with a magnificent **organ** at one end. One of the statue niches is empty because there was an argument about whoever was worthy enough to fill it! A **ceiling** decorated with the arms of places with which Manchester traded, supports a **hammer beam roof**. The hall is lit by six elaborate **'gasoliers'** (now converted to electricity).

However, the **frescoes executed by Ford Maddox Brown**, the great Pre-Raphaelite master, constitute the glory of this room. The Council specially selected the subjects, indicating how Mancunians saw their history at that time. The description starts with the left wall near the entrance and proceeds in a clockwise direction.

The Romans are building a fort at Manchester. Woad-painted Ancient Britons are assisting!

The baptism of Edwin takes place in a wooden Church at York, a significant event in the conversion of the North of England.

The expulsion of the Danes from Manchester is depicted. A piece of Victorian whimsy – even some of the warriors are smirking!

Manchester sees the establishment of Flemish weavers in 1363. The city's textile heritage is thus a long one, and Queen Phillipa of Hainult is shown visiting. A weaver is distracted and his apprentice takes the opportunity to make eyes at the daughter!

A dramatic incident in the trial of John Wycliffe is shown. A religious reformer who prefigured Protestantism, his trial is interrupted by his protector, John of Gaunt, Duke of Lancaster. The figure at the end of the table, in a green head-dress and taking notes, is Geoffrey Chaucer.

A bellman proclaims weights and measures in old Manchester. The city's reputation for honest trading is established at an early date. Notice the Chetham's boy in his 'bluecoat' uniform.

Crabtree observes the transit of Venus in the upstairs of his shop, 1639. The humble puritan draper becomes an important astronomer and mathematician. Anyone can 'pull themselves up by their own bootstraps'.

Chetham imagines his life's dream, 1640. A child plays cricket with the original style of bat, and the dream still includes a master with a birch rod.

An image of Bradshaw's stout defence of Manchester in 1642. The gallant captain and his 'forty musketeers' are firing at the royalists (in the foreground) on the Salford side, across the old bridge.

John Kay's house is attacked by a mob, 1753. The inventor of the 'flying shuttle' is smuggled out. It is useless to fight against the idea of progress, one must find an accommodation with it. 'What Manchester does today, the world does tomorrow'.

The ceremonies at the opening of the Bridgewater Canal, 1761. This conduit for cheap coal lays the foundations for future industrialisation.

Dalton, the schoolmaster scientist, is collecting marsh fire gas – an indication that great inventions and progress often come through the efforts of ordinary men.

Exit the Town Hall by the corridor through to Lloyd Street, noticing the **stair** on the left (the corner staircases are modelled on the Chateau of Blois).

Cross Street

Continue the walk by leaving Albert Square at Cross Street. This street started life as a country lane, became built up in the 18th century, and the first of several 'improvements' started in 1831. (Piecemeal alterations and widening of Manchester streets were often financed out of the profits of the town gas works!) Consequently, 'Pool Fold', 'Cross Street', and 'Red Cross Street', were united under one name.

We reach the spot where King Street cuts across. At the corner of the left-hand portion, the **Eagle Insurance Building** (now the *Leeds Building Society*) advertises itself by an eagle perched on top of a semi-circular pediment. This feature draws the eye into a structure of chimneys, pedimented dormer roofs, and an iron balustrade, a good example the Edwardian Baroque constructed in 1911. The architect was the popular Charles Heathcote, also responsible for (in the right-hand portion of King Street) the Flemish Renaissance **Northern Rock building** of 1895 (now the *Diesel* fashion shop), and ***Lloyd's Bank***. The bank (completed 1915) might have been his masterpiece, but it is much too fussy, if not a little pretentious. Take a peep at the **glazed coffered vault** over the banking hall (entrance in King Street).

Most bankers dwell in marble halls,
To encourage deposits, and not withdrawals....

The bank stands on the site (in King Street) of Manchester's first Town Hall (p.80). In contrast, the brick structure with corkscrew chimneys (on the other side of Cross Street, opposite *Lloyd's*) was the **Ottoman Bank** of 1889, when the Levant was a source of cotton. ***Mr Thomas's Chop House*** is next door, in charming Baroque terracotta dating from 1901. The decor is little changed from then, when it was one of many establishments catering for hurried businessmen who always dined at one. (Dinner is a mid-day meal in Lancashire, and don't you forget it!) The former Conservative Club is on the corner of St Ann Street.

Cross Street Chapel *(19)* is directly opposite, next to *Lloyd's Bank*. Henry Newcombe, a Fellow of the Collegiate Church, was unable to comply with the Act of Uniformity in 1662 and headed a small group of Presbyterians who established a Chapel on this site in 1694. It was destroyed in 1715 by a Jacobite mob led by Tom Sydall, a local blacksmith (who was later executed), but rebuilt with government compensation. The Chapel became Unitarian in the course of the 18th century. (Unitarians, a widespread group in Lancashire, deny the doctrine of the Trinity and proclaim the oneness of God.) In the 19th century, William Gaskell ministered here.

His wife was the novelist Elizabeth Gaskell, author of 'North and South', 'Cranford', and 'Mary Barton'. The old Chapel was destroyed in an air raid in 1940, and after a period in a second building, a third Chapel was constructed within the Observatory property development, opening in 1998. (The Unitarians still own the freehold.) It is open on weekdays at all reasonable times (ring the bell), and you may get a guided tour.

The new Chapel is surrounded by a circular ambulatory, containing **historical relics**. There are pictures of the first two Chapels, a memorial tablet to Mrs Gaskell (note the war damage), a 'settle' made from timber from St Mary's Church (p.68), and a sculpture symbolising 'rebirth' carved from a burnt timber from the bombing of 1940. The upstairs is usually shown upon request. The corridor has a **portrait of William Gaskell**, and the **'Gaskell Room'** contains historical relics of the family. Again, please leave a donation or purchase one of the booklets.

A little further down Cross Street, on the right, is a little half-hidden passage called **Back Pool Fold** *(20)*. The 'Pool' boasted the town 'ducking stool', described in 1586 as an instrument "... for the punyshment of Lewed women and Scoldes". It was a chair attached to a long pole, levered into the water by means of wooden blocks at the edge of the pool. A new stool was erected at the Daub Holes (p.90) in 1619. Of course, the name could equally describe the moated Pool Fold Hall (sometimes known as Radcliffe Hall), which probably stood on the present site of *Boots*. This was the home of the Radcliffes, a modest, if substantial, Manchester family, who may have been distantly related to the Radcliffes of Ordsall. William Radcliffe was one half of the partnership that masterminded the defence of the town against the royalist Lord Strange in 1642. The house (and its associated property) was sold to the Brown family towards the end of the 17th century, and ended its days as a tavern before demolition in 1810.

The Arndale Centre from Exchange Square

An eccentric bookseller had his shop in the passage in the early 19th century. He was fond of leaving little rhymes.

I, John Hopp,
Can't come to my shop.
Because I, John Hopp, am ill;
But I, John Hopp,
Will come to my shop,
When I, John Hopp, get well.

The passage itself has a nice 18th-century (?) frontage, set back from Cross Street.

The branch of ***Boots Chemist*** also stands on the old site of *The*

Manchester Guardian Offices (p.57). It is a part of the *Arndale Centre*, revamped since the IRA bomb, and is an improvement over the previous lavatorial tiles. The new high-tech 'minimalist' interior decor of *Boots* is perhaps a little too brutal for most tastes – one almost expects the staff to be equipped with whips. The Royal Exchange and its Arcade *(2)* are on the other side of the street. Proceed into Corporation Street, noticing that the ***Arndale*** **frontage** on the right has been reconstructed in brick, with eye-catching circular towers at the corners. There is a good view of the **futuristic bridge** *(21)* linking the *Arndale* and *Marks and Spencer* (p.30). Here the IRA bomb was placed in a van, and the **pillar box** (inscription) took the full force of the blast but escaped comparatively unscathed. This was the photograph that went round the world – the image of survival. Exchange Square is a little further, just round the corner.

The view from Spinningfield across Deansgate to the Town Hall

3 Deansgate and the Deanery

Start: Exchange Square

Estimated time of walk: 1½ hours

Interiors: John Rylands Library – 20 min; Pump House Museum – 1 hour

Highlights: The first 'department store', a world-famous library, the majesty of the law, the only museum of working-class history in Britain, and the lost world of Manchester's Deanery.

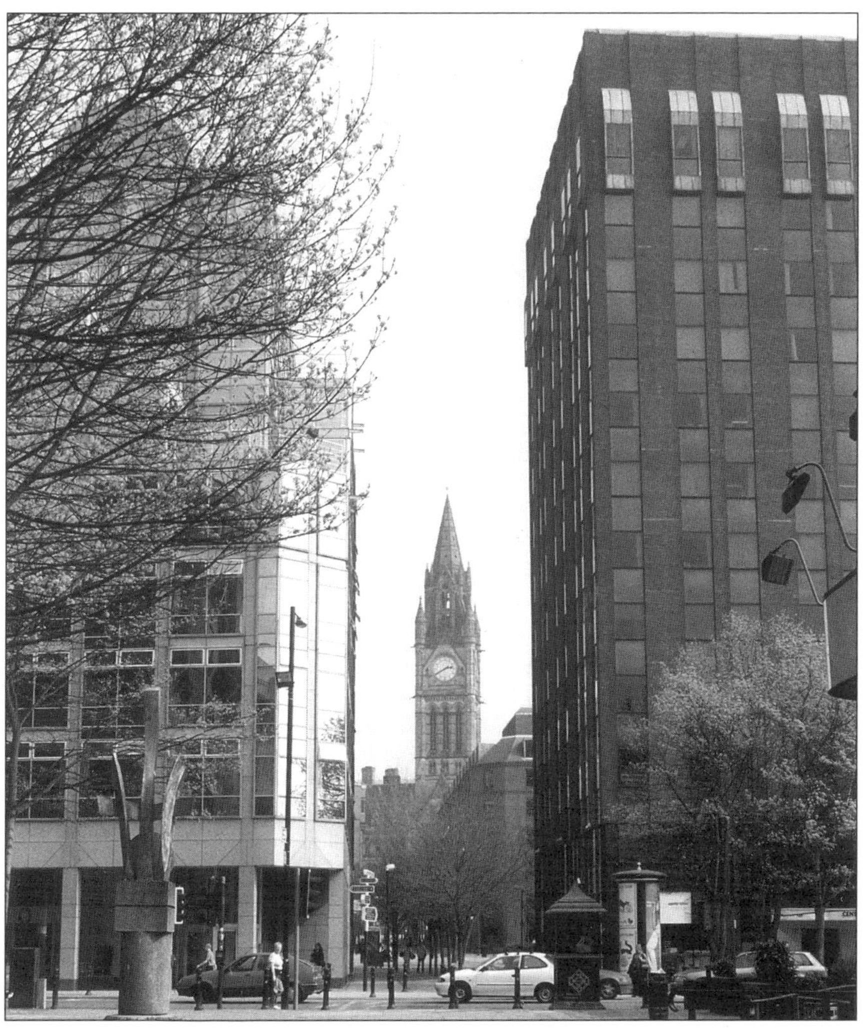

Deansgate is the street of the Danes. After all, the North West was part of the Danelaw in Anglo-Saxon times, and many present-day residents still have Norse blood in their veins. The suffix 'gate', common to many Manchester thoroughfares, is similar to 'gatten', the word for a street in several Scandinavian languages. Deansgate may be far older, for some scholars think that it may have followed part of the Roman road between the important legionary bases of Chester and York. Nevertheless, until the 17th century, it was a country road leading to the residence of the Steward of the Court Leet (p.77). By the mid-19th century, it had become a cluttered street barely 30ft (9m) wide, and widening and straightening it began in 1869. This continued in a piecemeal fashion over the next decade, when the first horse tramway route in the city was laid down it.

Deansgate

Again, the walk starts at Exchange Square, which we leave by way of Cateaton Street. Deansgate proper begins at the end of this street, and we turn left to navigate the first leg of it to the junction with St Mary's Gate. This short section once had the most impressive buildings (including two hotels and a shopping arcade), but all was destroyed in the last war. The West Shambles is on the left, with its twelve-storey residential accommodation on the corner with St Mary's Gate. It is rumoured that the penthouse on top of **'Number One, Deansgate'** *(1)* was offered at £2m. The number of residents in the city centre is rapidly increasing, transforming the character of the area, and assisting in the development of a '24-hour city'. In contrast, one of the ugliest buildings in Manchester is on the right, a former sixties office development which now partly houses the ***Ramada Renaissance Manchester Hotel***. The hotel entrance is round the corner in Blackfriars Street. Hopefully, a planned refurbishment will have opened the hotel reception area to daylight.

St Mary's Gate, to the left of the crossroads, is an ancient thoroughfare. Local historians have suggested that the name may have been derived from the possible original site of the mediaeval parish church at the Deanery (p.68). **Speakers House** (1963), on the corner of St Mary's Gate, indicates that it is built on a bomb site that was used after the war as a 'speakers corner', a facility still very much missed. It contains the *American Express* offices. Next door, on the Deansgate side, is the long Italianate frontage of the **Barton Arcade** (p.37), distinguished by an iron veranda *(2)*.

Continuing down Deansgate, we notice a charming building on the right, opposite the Barton Arcade. Fine street-level arches decorated with carving belong to the former china shop at **Regency Court** (1875), and the motif is continued above. This frontage has been described "as if a frock-coated mourner at a funeral displayed every now and then a lace handkerchief". It prefaces a row of continental-style cafés and bars, with tables and chairs often spilling out onto the pavement. The first is the *Moon under the Water*, a conversion of the former 'Deansgate Picture House' (1916). The original cavernous interior has been put to good use, as the new hostelry's chief claim to fame is an entry in 'The Guinness Book of Records' as **the largest pub in Britain**. The name is taken from the ideal pub described in an essay by George Orwell – which did not, of course, exist! Next is *La Tasca*, a popular Spanish bar and restaurant, with a basement Latin club. *Bar Med* is followed by *The Living Room*, with live music in the evening and people who want to 'see and be seen'. Finally, *Café Rouge* typifies the places that have sprung up in Manchester in recent years.

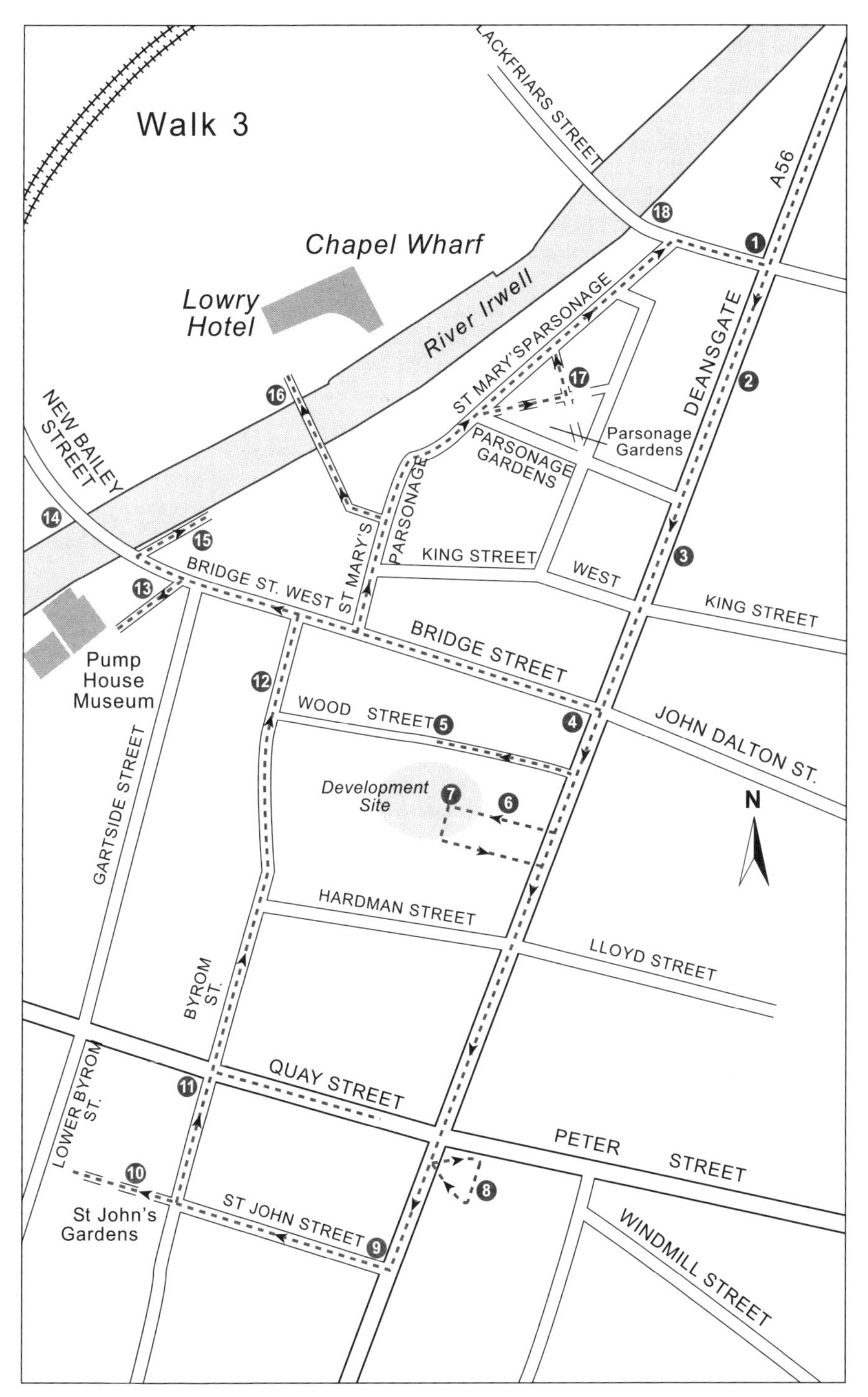

Walk 3
LACKFRIARS STREET
A56
Chapel Wharf
Lowry Hotel
River Irwell
ST MARY'S PARSONAGE
DEANSGATE
NEW BAILEY STREET
PARSONAGE GARDENS
Parsonage Gardens
PARSONAGE
ST MARY'S
KING STREET
WEST
BRIDGE ST. WEST
KING STREET
BRIDGE STREET
Pump House Museum
WOOD STREET
JOHN DALTON ST.
N
Development Site
GARTSIDE STREET
HARDMAN STREET
LLOYD STREET
BYROM ST.
QUAY STREET
LOWER BYROM ST.
PETER STREET
St John's Gardens
ST JOHN STREET
WINDMILL STREET
1
2
3
4
5
6
7
8
9
10
11
12
13
14
15
16
17
18

Kendal Milne

Over the road, on the corner of St Anne Street, is the original part of *Kendal Milne*. The S. and J. Watts concern (p.120) opened a shop here as early as 1796, and as their business expanded, it became an outlet for a growing variety of goods from their warehouse. It is thus claimed by some as the **world's first 'department store'** *(3)*. The partnership of Kendal, Milne and Faulkner (the latter died in 1862) acquired the enterprise in 1835, and soon the business outgrew the premises. The present structure, built in the popular Italianate style in 1873, had amazing innovations, such as a lift, a 'Moorish' tea room, and furnishings displayed in a tableaux of rooms, all very unusual for that time. The store cultivated an upmarket clientele, and furnished the décor for the facilities used during royal visits to the city. It also sold William Morris wallpaper. Until the 1970s, the basement still contained a tiled food hall similar to the one in London's *Harrods*.

The business eventually expanded across the street, and the striking concrete design (by J. Beaumont) of the present ***Kendal Milne*** store dates from 1938, a modernist statement in which the vertical function of parts of the structure are emphasised by windows running the whole height. The new building did not open until after the war, and was connected by a pedestrian subway with the original store across the street. *Kendals* was the place to observe the ladies of the 'Cheshire Set' in their natural habitat, but, for some reason, a decline set in and the original building closed. The store has since re-established itself after a rethink. The old premises are largely tenanted by *Waterstones*. This is agreed to be the best of all their bookstores – three floors of books, helpful staff, sofas, a coffee shop, a reading room, and late night opening. The shop is often the venue for talks by famous authors about their work.

Kendals – previously Kendal Milne

Another former **outpost of the S. and J. Watts** commercial empire, dating from the 1860s, is located just beyond the old building, at the corner of King Street. Their monogram is still entwined over the door, together with allegorical figures of art and craft. Beyond the new store, on the corner of King Street West, is a building in the Queen Ann revival style (late-1870s), containing the children's paradise of ***Daisy and Tom***, with five floors of everything you can possibly think of for the baby and toddler.

The ***Halifax Building Society*** (Turner Lansdowne Holt, 1983), an interesting modern use of brick, is situated next door, on the corner of Bridge Street. Look across Deansgate. **Queen's Chambers**, on the corner of John Dalton Street, is in the Gothic style with battlemented balconies and gargoyles. It was constructed in 1876 as government offices, which accounts for the royal arms over the corner entrance and a statue of Queen Victoria high on the John Dalton Street side.

The **Sawyer's Arms** is unmissable *(4)*, retaining one of the best Victorian pub frontages (of 1898) in the city. The interior was once gutted to create an 'open plan' monstrosity, but has now been sympathetically restored. Further along Deansgate, the curious building above the *Basha Café* on the right, with its Jacobean gable with a worn coat of arms and other carving, is easily missed. It dates from the 1880s and was the **Corporation Gas offices**. It is a delicious thought to imagine the Lord Mayor announcing the latest charges from the balcony, accompanied by a peal of trumpets. Or perhaps the architect got carried away. A short detour to the right reveals the **Wood Street Mission** *(5)*, founded in 1869, rebuilt in 1905, and still used for charitable purposes.

The John Rylands Library

Back on Deansgate, you are now stopped dead in your tracks. The effect of **The John Rylands Library** *(closed for renovations until 2006)* can be overpowering. It was built in memory of John Rylands, a rich Manchester cotton merchant. After inheriting the family concern in 1847, he built up a business empire based on textiles, cabinet making, and printing equipment. At the height of his powers, he controlled seventeen mills and factories, and employed 15,000 workers. Not surprisingly, he became Manchester's first multi-millionaire, and left a fortune of £2,750,000 when he died in 1888. A labourer at that time would consider himself lucky to earn more than a pound a week! His wife commissioned Basil Champneys, architect of Mansfield College, Oxford (a foundation supported by northern Nonconformists), to house what was intended as the finest library in Britain. The library took ten years to build, and probably cost £230,000, an immense sum at the time.

The John Rylands Library

It is said that the design was

inspired by Ruskin's 'Seven Lamps of Architecture', though the Gothic style was then going out of fashion. However, the church-like appearance is deliberate, for Champneys wanted to emphasise the connection between monasticism and scholarship. The Penrith stone frontage is built to create a theatrical effect, though notice that it is set at an angle from the street, an indication of Deansgate's unplanned development. The **filigree of window tracery** is perpendicular in style, and the **twin towers** are similar to the lantern tower of Ely Cathedral. Mrs Rylands supervised every detail of the design and construction, ensuring the provision of modern fireproof floors. Prior to the opening to the public on New Years Day, 1900, she embarked on a buying spree that purchased as many collections of rare books as she could lay her hands on to add to her late husband's collection. Although merged with Manchester University Library in 1972, it still operates as a completely separate entity. The library offers guided tours (charge) on Wednesdays at noon, but members of the public can view the reading room from the issue desk and visit exhibitions on weekdays (10.00-5.30) and Saturday (10.00-1.00). So, enter the cool dark interior. (The building is currently undergoing restoration, so access may be restricted.)

The progression to the reading room is intended to be an unfolding sequence of vistas. Enter through the **art nouveau bronze gates** into the **entrance hall**. A group representing **'Theology Directing the Labours of Science and Art'** (by John Cassidy) is situated at the foot of the **stairs**. These are lit by tall Gothic windows, and give access from a landing to an arched and panelled **room used for temporary exhibitions** of the library's treasures. Look for the **old printing press** before continuing up the stairs to the **reading room**, which can be inspected from the area with display cases in front of the desk. The long vaulted nave of the room is like the library of an Oxford College, with reading bays and a gallery on either side, decorated with **figures** representing eminent men in the history of the arts and sciences. They were selected by Mrs Rylands, and emphasise religion and literature, though John Dalton is paired with Sir Isaac Newton. All the fixtures and fittings (using a great deal of Polish oak) are original and designed to be all of a piece with the structure. Some of the **electric light fittings** remain, utilising a turning knob instead of a switch! At either end of the room are **statues** (also by Cassidy) **of Mr and Mrs Rylands**.

The library collection contains some five million items, both western and oriental, including Ryland's own collection of theological works. The library numbers the following precious items amongst its collections – the **earliest known fragment of the New Testament** (from St John's Gospel dating from the 2nd century), the **oldest dated piece of Western printing** (a print of St Christopher of 1423), and a rare example of the **'wicked' bible** (in which the printer has omitted 'not' from the seventh commandment). In addition to rare books and manuscripts, the collection also extends to more mundane but valuable books, tracts, pamphlets, sheet music, and magazines. It is available to genuine researchers upon application to the librarians.

Before leaving, be sure to pay a visit to the public lavatories, resplendent in the original mahogany, marbling, and polished copper piping.

Across Deansgate is a contrast (or antidote) to the Library in the shape of **Lincoln House** (by Halford Associates, 1986). When it opened, it was Manchester's first all glass building. However, it almost never got beyond the drawing board – the deputy of the planning officer is reputed to have said to his chief "look at this before we turn it down".

Spinningfield and the Education Offices

Spinningfield *(6)* is next door to John Rylands, and is being refashioned as part of an ambitious development project (called after the name of the old street). Allied London Properties intend to create four million square feet of offices, shops, civic buildings, and public squares – one of the largest business centre developments in Europe. It will include a paved square at this point, hopefully restoring the sculpture that stood here. When unveiled in 1971, it marked a turning point. Not only was it the first abstract public sculpture in the city (by Keith Godwin of Manchester Polytechnic), it was also the first new Manchester sculpture in several decades. The Scott Trust marked the anniversary of the Manchester Evening News by donating it to the city, and choosing the title **'Vigilence'**. Once, like most of the little streets off Deansgate, Spinningfield was a haunt of vice and depravity, obviously the perfect location for modern newspaper offices. *The Guardian*, *Observer*, and *Manchester Evening News* are to be found in the building that juts out into the half-completed square.

The Manchester Guardian (as it was) was no ordinary newspaper. Founded by John Edward Taylor in 1821, it rapidly established itself as Britain's foremost radical and progressive national newspaper, a description that is still true today. It remains left of centre in a national press dominated by right wing proprietors. It probably experienced its greatest days under the guiding hand of C. P. Scott, who edited the paper from 1872 to 1929. He was one of the sights of the city, cycling between the old offices in Cross Street (p.50) and his home in Fallowfield. Once, he came off his bicycle, and the policeman was puzzled as to why someone of his age was out so late. Scott explained that he had been working at *The Guardian* office. "Well," the policeman observed, "all I can say, sir, is that if the newspaper keeps an old gentleman like yourself working until this time of night, they ought to be bloody well ashamed of themselves!" Some years ago, they were clearing out the old Cross Street offices before removal to this site. There, in the back of a forgotten cupboard, was Scott's puncture kit! The Scott Trust guarantees editorial independence for both *The Guardian* and *The Observer* (an associated Sunday paper) alike. Alas, it has lost its 'Manchester' prefix and the paper is now based in London, but a special 'northern edition' is produced. It can be maddening at times, and a little idiosyncratic (an article on the Middle East was once headlined 'No Great Sheiks'), but *Guardian* readers are an amazingly loyal bunch.

Proceed to the right hand side of the newspaper offices, noticing the wall plaque commemorating the **site of the Old Manchester Poor House** (1764-92) on the left. This was built by authority of Gilbert's Act, which permitted parishes and townships to construct establishments where the able bodied poor could be set to work, thus discouraging idleness. Directly ahead is the fine new **City Magistrates and Coroners Court** (TPS Consult)*(7)*. The former is a minor court (sitting without a jury) usually dealing with petty cases and assorted vandals, drunks, and low life. The coroner (sometimes with the help of a jury) enquires into suspicious and sudden deaths. The sandstone frontage frames a noble glass atrium with eighteen courts on one side and the administrative offices on the other. There is a car park underneath. You can walk round the back of the newspaper building (which will eventually be replaced), past a future passageway to Crown Square (p.63) on the right, before returning to Deansgate.

We next pass **No 1 Spinningfield Square**, a new glass office block at the corner of Hardman Street. The frontage in this street is a sweeping curved façade that overhangs the ground floor, impressively supported by cantilevered struts. It stands on the site of Northcliffe House, a rather nice art deco structure. A sad loss. Hardman Street itself will soon be transformed into a paved tree lined avenue, communicating with the proposed Spinningfield Bridge. Further along Deansgate, the sober Palladian Classicism of **number 184 and 186** (1896), once used by the Inland Revenue, follows. It is now used by the County Court, which largely deals with civil cases, including debt.

Elliot House lies across the road at this point. Built in 1888, and extended in 1904 and 1914, it is perhaps the best example of the then popular Queen Ann style in the city. Inspired by Flemish and English renaissance features, everything is here – tall sash windows, shaped gables, dormer windows, and fine brickwork. The **carved cherubs** at the corners and the oval windows are particularly noteworthy. It was built to house the Manchester School Board, set up under the auspices of the 1870 Education Act, and entirely concerned with local education. The electoral arrangements permitted women to serve on the Boards and protected the interests of political and religious minorities. Consequently, the Manchester Board was a progressive undertaking. From the panelled Board Room, they established a system of state education second to none, going beyond the provision of 'elementary schools' to create 'higher grade schools' which taught scientific and commercial subjects. This interfered with too many vested interests (particularly the independent grammar schools) and resulted in the abolition of the Boards in the 1902 Education Act. The Act transferred responsibility for state education to the (politically) safer local authorities, and the doleful effects of this retrograde step were not remedied until 1944.

Next door, **201 Piccadilly** (by Holford Associates, 1997) epitomises what has been called the 'Manchester Style', utilising the traditional materials of stone and brick with glass in a modern way, and winning a civic trust award in 1998. It partly stands on the site of the old Quaker Burial Ground (p.116). (The bodies were exhumed and reburied a long time ago.) The adjacent **Onward Buildings** (1903-05) was the headquarters of the Band of Hope, a missionary organisation that emphasised abstinence from alcohol. It now contains the ***Model Shop*** (the model aeroplane and model railway variety!) and the ***Topkapi Palace***, which can be recommended for superb kebabs. The Baroque revival **Royal London House** (1904) is situated opposite, on the corner of Quay Street.

Great Northern

The junction of Deansgate with Peter Street is marked by a modern pylon construction, which indicates the commencement of the **Great Northern Warehouse Complex** by a newly created open space *(8)*. The circular sunken **events arena**, part pavement and part grass, with a water feature in front, is perhaps a little clinical – obviously meant to set off the high-tech and angular ***Bar 38***. (Not to be confused with a related bar of the same name in the Gay Village!) The bar has two wedged-shaped floors of steel and glass above a large basement area opening out onto the 'piazza'. The whole area prefaces the main entrance to the new leisure complex.

The Great Northern Railway serviced the eastern side of the country, but had no lines in the North-West of England. It solved the problem by participating in the

Cheshire Lines project, a jointly owned railway company responsible for Central Station (p.132), and by obtaining 'running powers' over other railways, particularly the Great Central. Growing traffic resulted in the construction of a large goods station and warehouse on acres of slum land in the period 1896-8, occupying most of the left-hand side of Deansgate from this point. The great **rectangular brick warehouse** looks as if it would stand until the crack of doom (with walls eight brick courses thick), proclaiming its ownership in glazed brick. Rail traffic entered at viaduct level, road traffic at both ground and first-floor level (accessed by ramps), and a canal ran underneath (p.186). The upper floors were used for storage, and hoists communicated between all the levels. The company took care to build a row of shops along Deansgate (with railway offices above), and this is thought to be the **longest Victorian street frontage** in existence. It became part of the London and North Eastern Railway in 1923, and the sign indicating the destinations served (over the **cart entrance on Deansgate**) dates from this time.

The complex has been recently redeveloped in a £145m project. After noting ***Persia***, Manchester's first Iranian restaurant, proceed from the 'piazza' through the main entrance. The ground floor of the warehouse building is given over to a variety of **food outlets**, including restaurants and cafés. There is also a small **historical interpretation centre** at this level. The **first floor** is filled with **shops** (the subsequent floors are used as a multi-storey car park). An **'atrium'**, also accessed by a flight of steps from Deansgate, connects the old part of the complex with a new structure. A mezzanine level accommodates a large health club facility, and the first and second floors of the new building house a **24-screen cinema** with associated retail and leisure area.

You can exit by the atrium steps but the walk is resumed at the Peter Street corner. We then continue past **Deansgate Court** (1900), once Congregational

Great Northern Railway warehouse complex and performance area

Church House, to the corner of St John Street. The **plaque** *(9)* repays attention. Deansgate once led to Aldport Lodge, a Saxon name meaning an old town or fortress (we are not far from the site of the Roman Fort). A large house stood somewhere near the corner of Liverpool Road, in the midst of a park of about 100 acres that extended from Knott Mill (p.131) to Quay Street, and from Deansgate to the Irwell. A survey in 1322 stated that the oak trees alone were worth £300. The archery butts were placed here in the 16th century, when the law compelled every able bodied man to practice on Sundays after church. The house and park became part of the Stanley patrimony, and Edward, Third Earl of Derby, resided here for a period between 1556 and 1568. Quite why the old man who, in his youth, had attended Henry VIII upon the 'Field of the Cloth of Gold' would be content to act as Steward of the Court Leet of the Manor of Manchester is something of a mystery. Perhaps he had a good reason for a discreet retirement. He died in 1572, and the property passed to the Mosley family, Lords of the Manor (p.97).

As the plaque indicates, Lord Strange occupied the house for a few days during the siege of Manchester in 1642 (p.12) and placed his cannon at this point. His artillery fire along Deansgate destroyed a few houses and barns, but the defenders (who possessed a brass cannon piece of their own) hit back. A lucky shot is said to have started a blaze that consumed the whole house. It was never rebuilt. *(This walk can here be combined with the Castlefield Walk by walking to Pioneer Quay near the end of Deansgate, see page 171.)*

St John Street

St John Street

Turn right into St John Street. This thoroughfare is said to be the 'Harley Street' of Manchester, although the consultant doctors are in danger of being dispossessed by the lawyers. It has a perfect **terrace of Georgian houses** on the right-hand side. The street terminates at the pretty **St John's Gardens**, which should be entered. Edward Byrom, the son of the more famous John (p.10), lived on Quay Street, near the corner of the street named after him. He dabbled, like other rich men of the town, with a number of projects. He helped create Manchester's first bank, and also pursued a career as a property developer. He paid for a church dedicated to St John, which stood on this spot, no doubt intended as the centrepiece of a prestigious new residential district. The Bishop of Chester consecrated the church in 1769, but, like other city centre churches, it lost its congregation in the flight to suburbia. The redundant structure was demolished in 1931, but a clause in a family will ensured that the land could never be built upon. Hence, the pleasant garden with the **stone cross** *(10)*. It casually records that you are in the midst of the remains of nearly 22,000 people who were buried in the churchyard and vaults. Somewhere here lie the remains of John Owens (p.61). The gardens have a good view of Granada Studios, which incorporates the old accumulator tower of the former railway goods yard on the left.

We retrace our steps and turn left into Byrom Street. The Jacobean style frontage of the **Rechabite Friendly Society** (1896) brings to mind a verse by William McGonnagle about a party of Scottish Rechabites "who had resolved themselves to see some sights". To continue the Scottish theme, the **plaque** on the building opposite states that "Bonnie Prince Charlie" used the area as an artillery park on his way through Manchester in November, 1745 (his gunners managed to fire for all of 20 minutes at the opening of the battle of Culloden).

St John's Gardens

Quay Street

We have now reached Quay Street. Look for the **roll of honour** (at left-hand corner of Byrom Street) recording the dead of St John's Ward in the First World War *(11)*. There were several of these, particularly in working class districts, across Manchester. They sadly disappeared in the demolition and redevelopment of the sixties and seventies. It is affixed to the side of a **large Georgian house**, so turn left into Quay Street to view the main frontage. It was built around 1750 by William Allen, a partner in, and later sole proprietor of, the Manchester Bank. He was charitable by nature and fond of ostentatious living, so the failure of the bank must have been a cruel blow. The house passed to William Hardman, who made a fortune from property speculation. He showed great taste in amassing an art collection valued at £30,000, an immense sum in the early 19th century. Indeed, the house, with its gallery, concert room, and gardens, was described as a "Chatsworth in miniature". His memory is perpetuated in a nearby street name. After a period of occupation by Richard Cobden (p.37), the tenancy passed to George Faulkner.

Faulkner was the friend (perhaps the only real one) of John Owens, a successful Manchester merchant. Despite his wealth and position, Owens took little or no part in the social life of the town, and seemed to have had few interests. One evening, after dinner in this house, he confided to Faulkner that he would leave all his

The Opera House

money to him. George was touched, but replied that he had more than enough of his own. Why not use it for some public purpose, such as promoting education? Owens pondered this, and, in 1846, left the sum of £96,642 to establish a College for the education of young men – open to all, irrespective of political or religious views. Faulkner's house seemed the natural home for the new venture.

Owens College opened its doors for the first time in 1851, offering the external BA of the University of London. It was soon struggling – by 1856, it was down to only 33 students. One evening, Henry Roscoe (the professor of chemistry, and later a famous scientist) was taking an airing on the steps when a poor man paused on his way past.

"Maister, is this th' neet (night) asylum?"
"Not yet, my man, but if you come in six months time I fear it will be!"

Nevertheless, the project did not wither on the vine. It began to expand, and moved to a new building on Oxford Road in 1873. There, Owens College became the nucleus for the present University of Manchester (p.222).

Quay Street recalls the fact that the Irwell was once an important waterway and that the road led to the principal wharf. The old Skin Hospital stood on the opposite corner to the Georgian house, the first outside London to install x-ray apparatus. But if we venture down the street in the Deansgate direction, we find the 3,000-seat **Opera House** on the left. It opened in 1912 (with a performance of 'Kismet') as the New Theatre, and is (vaguely) in the French Empire style. There is an heroic frieze of what appears to be Apollo in his chariot within the Pediment. The architects bemoaned the fact that theatre promoters never paid their bills on time, and cannot have been too concerned when sewer rats appeared amongst the audience on the opening night. The name was changed in 1920, and after a sad period of sporadic films and bingo, the theatre was refurbished in 1984 – reopening with a presentation of 'Barnum'. The theatre's repertoire generally comprises touring shows and musicals (Phantom of the Opera, etc.). "The play mirrors life" – at the moment, Andrew Lloyd Webber's.

A little past the theatre is **Sunlight House**, Manchester's first really 'modern movement' building, and the first speculation by Joseph Sunlight, an expatriate Russian (he needed an English name and chose that of a popular brand of soap!). It was the tallest in the city, the first to eclipse the Town Hall tower, when it opened in 1932. (Joe had show business contacts, so Douglas Fairbanks inaugurated the basement swimming pool.) Notice the polygonal lift tower. (Sunlight, who had some eccentric ways, would work the lift himself in the lunch hour, rather than pay for a relief man!) In contrast, the rest of the street is rather boring, though (after retracing your steps) look out for the offices (1992) in the form of a **pastiche of a Georgian terrace**, visible from the Byrom Street corner.

Crown Square

Turn right, and continue down Byrom Street to **Crown Square**. The Square is a post-war creation, intended as the climax of a processional way from Albert Square – civic grandeur (as it were) leading to the majesty of the law. The steps to the right do indeed lead to Spinningfield and Deansgate, but something went horribly wrong with the grand concept, and a lot of mediocre buildings were allowed to get in the way. The Square was closed to traffic in 1971, and trees were planted in regimented rows. When you read these lines, the scene may be very different. The Square and the surrounding area constitute a 20 acre development (with shops and a hotel) by Allied London, which will include the replacement of the Magistrates Courts, together with the elimination of the newspaper, education, and legal offices between the Square and Spinningfield. The Crown Courts will remain, and Hardman Street will become a tree-lined boulevard stretching from Deansgate to the Irwell, which will be crossed by a new bridge.

The largest structure in the Square is the **Crown Courts** (by the then city architect, L. C. Howitt, 1962), a modern reworking of a classical theme, with a long façade of 'columns'. It is clad in Portland stone and sports a triple arched aluminium canopy at the entrance. This is only used on ceremonial occasions, and the public entrance *(12)* is in the 'extension building' to the right of the façade (visitors pass through a metal detector). Stairs lead from it to the public concourse on the main floor, running the length of the building and giving access to six courtrooms. When the courts are in session, it is usually filled with witnesses, police officers, and barristers in their traditional wigs. (In the English legal system, crown courts tend to deal with serious offences, and barristers alone can plead in them. Ordinary members of the public can only deal with barristers through an intermediary, usually a general lawyer known as a 'solicitor'.)

The present building replaced the old Assize Courts (destroyed in the war) that stood on Great Ducie Street, in front of Strangeways Prison. That building was decorated with a large number of **statues executed by Thomas Woolner**, the Pre-Raphaelite, around 1861, and several of these were saved for posterity – some are displayed along the concourse. They comprise figures of 'Mercy'; Judge Gascoigne, who taught roistering Prince Hal (later Henry V) that even a royal is not above the law; Sir Thomas More; and Sir Matthew Hale. Others are placed in what must be Manchester's least known museum (permission to view required), situated under the main staircase. The relics of the old building here include figures of Alfred the Great and Edward I (the 'English Justinian'). It is usually possible (if you are inclined that way) to watch a trial. Ask at reception.

The **Magistrates' Courts** (Yorke, Rosenberg, and Mardall, 1971) are to the left of the main façade of the Crown Courts, situated on a podium that contains a car park, reception yards, service areas, and a cafeteria. The building itself is a dark glass box, suspended in a white frame (a tile clad structure beyond the main walls on posts). The exterior indicates the internal arrangements, as the central main floors are twice as tall as the administrative mezzanine floors on either side. The blank wall at the top conceals a top lit cell block and service plant. The public concourse (reached by the steps) prefaces the courts that form the core of the structure. It seems a pity that one of the few interesting buildings from this period will shorlty disappear.

Exit Crown Square by way of Dolefield (land once rented to finance 'doles' of bread and other necessaries to the poor), with the **Crown Court Extension** (Property Services Agency, 1986, and now comprising the public entrance) on the left *(12)* and the high office block of **Scottish Life House**, now Manchester House, (1965) opposite. The only significant thing about this building was its peculiar mode of construction. The concrete floors were cast on the ground and hoisted up into position around a central column. It was apparently the best show in town for a while.

A left turn brings us to **Albert Bridge**. The 'New Bailey Bridge', its ancestor, was opened by a company in 1785 – using the tolls to finance property speculation in Bridge Street. They were bought out in 1803 (when the tolls were abolished), and a new public bridge was constructed in 1844 by Jesse Hartley (the celebrated engineer of Albert Dock in Liverpool) and named in honour of the Prince Consort. A sculpture entitled **'Doves of Peace'** (the work of Michael Lyons of Manchester Polytechnic) was placed in front of the bridge in 1986 *(13)*. This work was the runner up in a competition for the peace monument (p.107), and was said to be originally inspired by the artist's study of a pine cone.

There is a good view of the ***Mark Addy***, across the river *(14)*. A quay has been situated here since the 18th century, and was used as the point of departure for swift 'packet boats' to Warrington and Runcorn. These carried passengers and 'packets' of mail, and were hurried along by relays of horses stationed along the towpath. When the roadway on the Salford side of the river was widened in 1857, some of the supporting arches were used to accommodate the packet station, which (despite rail competition) was still in business. They now contain the pub, and the old quay is used as a riverside beer garden. (Mark Addy was a well-known publican and resident of Salford in late Victorian times. He was famous for his record number of British Humane Society medals, awarded for rescuing drowning people from the Irwell.)

The New Bailey Prison was located near the *Mark Addy*. Founded in 1790 to replace the old House of Correction (p.27), this institution was visited by Elizabeth Fry, the prison reformer, in 1818. A treadmill was introduced in 1824, and subsequent extensions produced all the amenities and horrors of a Victorian prison. Abel Heywood, a prominent citizen, was imprisoned here in 1832 for selling untaxed newspapers. (He courted martyrdom to make a political point, but the authorities were too stupid to realise it.) The last public execution in Britain is thought to have taken place outside the prison on 4th April, 1868. (Further information can be obtained from a Tourist Information Point, situated across the bridge.)

Pump House Museum

The **Pump House Museum** may be found immediately to the left. It is located in a building constructed for the Manchester Hydraulic Power Company in 1909. Three or four steam engines pumped water up to tanks in the roof, where it was stored at a high pressure. The water was then distributed by a system of mains throughout the city centre, where it powered hoists in warehouses, machines, lifts, and even a public clock! The last vestiges of the system lasted until the nineteen fifties. The building now contains a selection from the collections of the **People's History Museum**, formerly at Limehouse in London. (When evicted from their home in the

The Pump House Museum

capital, Manchester offered a home to an important part of our national heritage.) The museum uses the Mechanic's Institute (p.142) as a store and restoration workshop. The Pump House is open (admission charge but free on Fridays) Tuesday to Sunday, 11.00 – 4.30.

An **audio-visual introduction** (by Glenda Jackson) precedes the first gallery. A small display details the importance of the cotton industry in Lancashire, and relates it to the issue of the slave trade. (However, it is a myth to suggest that this trade financed the industrial revolution. The evidence points to the contrary.) The modern history of the labour movement starts with the 'thinkers' of the 18th and early 19th centuries (notice **Tom Paine's death mask**), and continues through parliamentary reform and the **Chartists**. The latter formed the first truly national working-class movement in this country. The 'People's Charter' had six demands – a vote for every adult male, equally sized constituencies, vote by ballot, annual parliaments, payment of MPs and the abolition of members' property qualifications. With the exception of (impractical) yearly elections, all these are now the cornerstones of our democratic system, but were then considered revolutionary. Notice the **medal commemorating Fergus O'Connor**, the Chartist leader.

The display on the **Peterloo Massacre** (p.131) is sobering, with a cannon used to 'maintain order' at the time, and yeomanry sabres. A horsehair **yeomanry cavalry plume**, captured as a trophy by Middleton weavers, and a **truncheon** wrested from a special constable, show that there were many in the crowd prepared to fight back. In contrast, the contemporary **cartoon of a meeting demanding women's rights** puts into the speakers' mouths a farrago of double entendres! There is a viewing point for the fine collection of **trade union banners** along a wall of the basement gallery. Notice the use of biblical texts in the older ones, indicating the close link between the cause of labour and nonconformity. A flight of stairs leads to the **basement gallery**.

A new recruit is inducted into **the mysteries of the Tinplate Worker's Trade Society**. Early unions based their ritual on the masons – notice the figure of the skeleton. 'Remember thine end.' Other sections deal with **radical prints**, **agricultural workers**, and the **rise of the skilled craft unions** which also offered protection against hardship (death benefit is paid to a widow in a **Gorton parlour of 1886**). There is a colourful display of **friendly society regalia** (these were working class insurance societies) and a reminder that some people were just too downtrodden, as in the tableau of **'sweated labour'** making boxes at home. The next area deals with agitation and campaigns, including the **founding of the Labour Party** (look for the **art work of William Morris and Walter Crane**) and the story of the campaign for female suffrage, including the **kitchen of a Manchester suffragette**! A display focuses upon **'The Ragged Trousered Philanthropists'**, a famous socialist novel about building workers in Edwardian Hastings by Robert Tressel. They are philanthropists because they beggar themselves using their skills to make a small minority rich.

A colourful selection of posters leads to an area with sections on the **co-operative movement** (with a store counter); the struggles of the dock workers (giving rise to modern mass trade unions), and the **general strike of 1926**. A photograph of mounted special constables in pith helmets (!) sums up all you have ever hated about the English class system. The post-war victory of the Labour Party and the creation of the welfare state centres on a **1945 parlour**. Realities nearer our own time, are brought home in displays about the miners and other recent disputes. Note the **shelter used in the 1989 ambulance workers' strike**. The final area deals with working class leisure in the form of sport, music, and seaside holidays. Two **upstairs galleries** are used for temporary exhibitions, and there is a good view up the river.

Returning to the bridge, cross the street and look for the easily missed steps. These lead to a river terrace, part of a river walkway that has, as yet, not really got off the ground. Peeping through the foliage is a **statue of Joseph Brotherton** (by Noble, 1858), and it is perhaps worth asking who he was and what he is doing in such an out of the way spot *(15)*. Brotherton was one of those Victorian businessmen who made enough money to retire young and devote himself to good works, particularly town improvements and the cause of education. All in his native Salford! Consequently, the statue was erected over the river in Peel Park (p.236), but it was removed to make way for an extension to what is now Salford University in 1954. And so, he was put in store and forgotten about. When rediscovered, no new plinth awaited him, for he was sold to Gawsworth Hall near Macclesfield. Poor old Joseph was finally purchased by Manchester Council (because he was elected MP for the town in 1832) in 1986, and placed in this position where he can gaze across the river at his ungrateful posterity. He is portrayed with the fresh buttonhole that he wore every day.

Bridge Street

Walk down Bridge Street in the Deansgate direction. The large building on the left is **Albert Bridge House** (Ministry of Works, 1958-9), the current seat of the Inland Revenue, and inhabited by over 800 tax officials. It is a well-proportioned, straightforward design for a modern building, and that is really all that can be said. Directly ahead is an **anonymous little square** at the junction of Bridge Street and King Street West, with trees and concrete balls probably left over from the St Ann's Square job. Here, in the 'swinging sixties', George Best (the first of a new breed of footballer) opened a boutique.

Bridge Street was the scene of events associated with the case of the 'Manchester Ophelia'. Lavinia Robinson was engaged to be married to a surgeon who lived at number 66, and on the evening of 16th December, 1813, was to have stayed the night with relatives a few doors down. She disappeared instead. The surgeon, a man called Holroyd, said that they had parted after a lover's tiff, and he knew nothing of her whereabouts. The winter of 1813-14 was a particularly harsh one, and the Irwell froze. However, the spring thaw cracked the ice at Barton, and her body (which had been trapped on a sandbank) rose to the surface, perfectly preserved. The events caused a great sensation and the young victim was buried in St John's churchyard. Although nothing could be proved, Holroyd left town pretty fast, and later appears to have committed suicide.

The section of the street between the square and Deansgate is worth a detour. The rather plain exterior of the **Masonic Temple** (1929), on the right, hides a magnificent neo-classical interior, with a coffered vault over the main hall, supported on Ionic columns. It may even be possible to see it without rolling up a trouser leg. On the same side can be found the façade of the **Manchester and Salford Children's**

Mission (late-1880s), with children's faces; the terracotta panels of **Rational Chambers** (1879); and the elaborate floriated terracotta pediments of **Bridge Street Chambers** (1898). On the left are the Italianate **Kenworthy's Buildings** (1902). (For *Sawyer's Arms*, see p.55.)

Back at the square, the way lies right, along St Mary Parsonage. However, another short detour should be made to the left of this street, down the footpath between the railings to **Trinity Bridge** *(16)*. This was designed by Santiago Calatrava (his only British commission), and opened by the Lord Mayors of Manchester and Salford in 1995. The footbridge consists of a triangular boxed section, supported by stays attached to a 41ft (12m) pylon. But why is there a bridge here? The intention was to open up to pedestrians an area of derelict railway land across the river, and it seems to have worked. **Chapel Wharf**, on the Salford side, is now occupied by a number of developments. **Trinity Bridge House** (Leach, Rhodes, Walker, 1998-9), is set back on the left, yet another Inland Revenue office. (They must be breeding like rabbits!) The same architects were responsible for **Aldine House** (1967) adjacent to this development. However, the most recent structure to appear is to the right – the five-star ***Lowry Hotel***. There is a fine view upstream towards the bridges and the cathedral. Back at St Mary parsonage, notice the **plaque** on the left on Alberton House, marking the site of the first municipal gasworks in Britain to sell gas to the public, established on this spot in 1817.

St Mary's Gardens

We now arrive at **St Mary's Gardens**, the site of the ancient Deanery of Manchester. A survey dated 1320 records "two acres of land and a place of pasture without the gate ... joined to the rectory of Manchester," and goes on to state that it comprised three large fields of four oxgangs (as much as could be worked by an ox-plough in one day) given to the church in Manchester by Albert de Grelle, the third Baron. Scholars have suggested that the tenure is far older than that. Indeed, the area was probably the original site of the Saxon Church, placed here to perhaps service the Royal Hall across the river. (Salford was a royal manor before the Norman Conquest, and probably used for hunting, see p.130.) It was certainly the location of the 'Parsonage House', later called the 'Deanery' and 'Deansgate House', and used by the clergy since time immemorial. This would be the place designated as a residence for the Warden of the College in the charter of Elizabeth I (1578).

Warden Murray, an early occupant, preached before James I on the text "I am not ashamed of the gospel of Christ". The king was not amused. "Thou art not ashamed of the gospel of Christ, but by ***** the gospel of Christ may be ashamed of thee!" Manchester College was thus marked out for re-organisation, but had to wait until the reign of Charles I. Later, a quite different Warden resided at the Deanery, of a type still familiar in corporate bodies today. "Silver tongued Wroe" knew exactly what to say on any occasion. He rebuilt the parsonage or Deanery House, and lived here in some style (with wine cellars cut into the rock, it would appear). 'Deansgate House' later passed into secular hands, and was probably situated (with its gardens, summerhouse, and orchards) at the west end of the gardens. Traces of it survived as late as the 1900s.

The pleasant **gardens** *(17)* are the site of St Mary's Church, consecrated in 1756, and thus the third place of worship to be built in the town. It was closed as early as

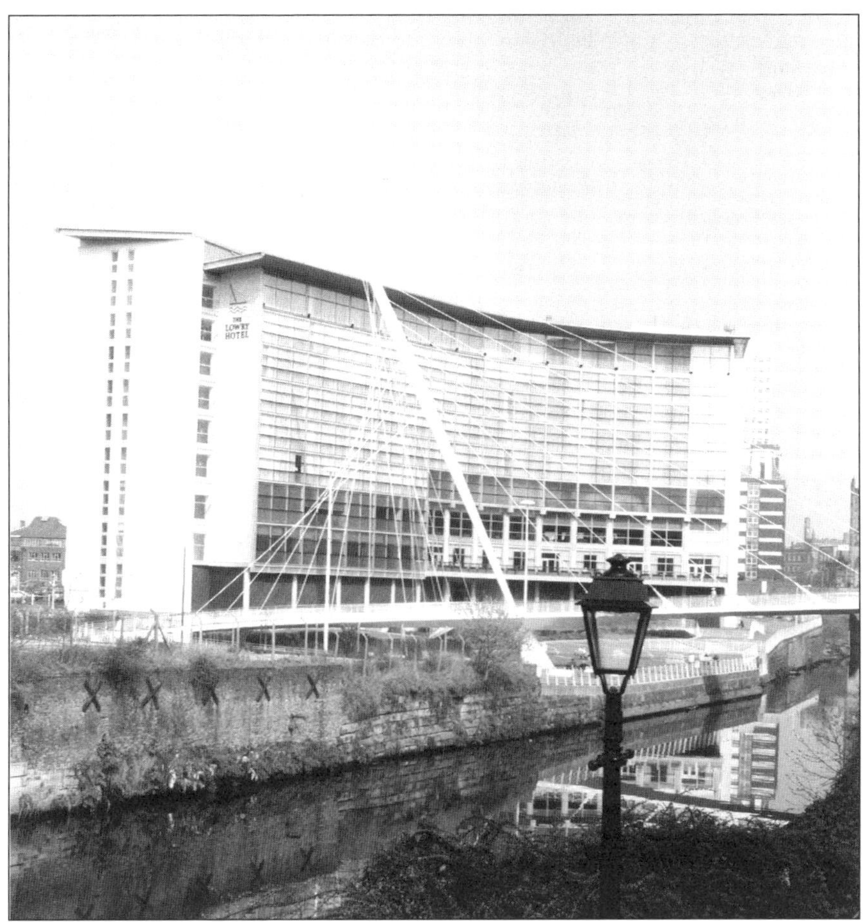

Looking across the River Irwell to the Lowry Hotel

1890, God crowded out by mammon, as it were, but lingered on until demolition in 1928. The gardens, particularly on a fine day, are a haven of peace not far from busy Deansgate and a resort of office workers in their lunch hour.

Two large office buildings dominate the gardens. **Arkwright House**, built in 1927 for the English Sewing Cotton Company, fronts the street that leads to Deansgate. It has giant Corinthian pilasters, rising to support an entablature and cornice in the usual neo-classical style (there are two fine Corinthian columns round the corner, in the direction of Deansgate), all in the best Portland stone. **National Buildings** stands in front of the river. It was the head office of the National Boiler and Generator Insurance Company, and was built in brick and terracotta in the popular Baroque revival style, between 1905 and 1909. Notice the lions' heads on the fifth storey. The extension building dates from 1968 but was given a brick cladding in 1994, when two storeys were added. It is said to contain the **most expensive apartment in Manchester**.

We leave the gardens by way of the continuation of St Mary's parsonage, noting the name of Back College Land, a reference to the link with the Collegiate Church. **Blackfriars House**, on the corner of Blackfriars Street, the former offices of the Bleacher's Association, dates from 1923. Interestingly enough, all the modern buildings mentioned in connection with the parsonage were, over a period of nearly a hundred years, designed by the same architectural practice.

A left turn brings us to **Blackfriars Bridge** *(18)*. This owes its origin to a group of actors who erected a wooden footbridge (approached by 39 steps down the rocky Manchester side) in the 18th century, to enable the public to reach their theatre in Salford. Indeed, it is named after the Blackfriars Theatre in London. The present stone bridge, built by a private company, opened in 1820. It was purchased by public subscription to eliminate the tolls in 1847. The bridge witnessed high old times for a brief period in 1901. The horse tram company had spanned both Manchester and Salford with its system, but both municipal corporations decided to establish their own electric tramway systems to replace it. Of course, the municipalities would have to co-operate. (Salford had no city centre and intended to use Deansgate as a terminal loop line.) Unfortunately, the two councils fell out prior to opening, and Manchester instituted 'a tramway blockade'. Thus, rival trams terminated on the bridge on a stretch of shared track that constituted a sort of 'no man's land', watched by an audience of aldermen, council members, lawyers, police, and bemused ratepayers. Meanwhile, Dr. Tait, the noted Professor of Mediaeval History at the University, suggested that it was all the fault of the original manorial lords who had allowed the separation of Manchester from Salford in the first place! *(The Salford walk starts at this point on p.227.)*

You can now return to Exchange Square by walking down St Mary's Gate and New Cathedral Street.

The revamped Arndale Centre at Market Street corner

4 Market Street and District

Start: junction of Market Street with Exchange Street

Estimated time of walk: 1 hour

Highlights: The 'largest public lavatory in the world', the financial heart of the city, the lost theatres of Manchester, a haunted pub, and Mr Lewis's enterprise.

Market Street starts at a point adjacent to the old Market Place, and this seems a convenient point to begin this walk. So follow the now familiar path from Exchange Square along New Cathedral Street to its junction *(1)* with St Mary's Gate, Market Street, and Exchange Street.

Market Place

Sadly, the Market Place no longer exists. The site lies somewhere under the present *Marks and Spencer* store (p.6). It was the heart of the old town, a spot to hear the latest news and gossip. This aspect of life centred on the mediaeval cross, which survived until 1752. Here the 'bellman' read proclamations and made announcements, here public oaths were sworn, and here (sometimes) sermons were preached. Before the Reformation, the latter was the province of wandering friars. By the 17th century, it was the business of puritan 'lecturers', supplementing the shortcomings of some of the local clergy by advocating a more personal religious experience and 'amending manners'. In such a public place, the instruments of punishment might be found – the stocks and the pillory.

A conduit was constructed in 1550, to conduct a much needed water supply to the Market Place from nearby springs. (It sometimes ran red with wine, for such events as the restoration of Charles II in 1660.) The greater part of the space was taken up every Saturday with the 'Market Stead' or 'Stid', which attracted country people from far and near. A two-storey building with booths (stalls) on the ground floor, housed the 'Sessions House' where the Court Leet met from time to time (p.52).

There were many regulations to enforce in connection with market activity, including measures against 'engrossing' (buying up too much to create a monopoly) and 'forestalling' (trying to intercept incoming country traders before they arrived at Manchester, or before the market opened). 'Lookers for Fish and Flesh' and 'Lookers for Bread and Ale' checked quality and prices. (Standard commodity prices were fixed by the county magistrates at an 'Assize of Bread and Ale'.) The 'Ale Conner' would test the quality of this vital product (which everyone drank in preference to unhealthy water) by pouring a quantity on a stool and sitting on it in his leather breeches. If the brew was too weak, the stool would stick to the seat of his pants! Last but not least, duly appointed 'Scavengers' would make sure that the market refuse would not block the gutters or the ditch that drained into the Hanging Ditch (p.8). Particular areas of the Market Place were used for various produce – the butchers in the nearby 'Shambles' (p.9) and the fishmongers in the adjacent Smithy Door (p.32).

The Market Place was the natural choice for the site of the first Exchange in 1729 (p.33). Elizabeth Raffald moved to a shop next to the 'Bull's Head' there in 1766. She had been a housekeeper to Arley Hall in Cheshire and published (in 1769) 'The Experienced English Housekeeper', probably the first important work on cookery and domestic science in Britain, and the start of a tradition extending through Mrs Beeton to Delia Smith. The versatile lady also ran a servants' employment agency, and produced the first directory of the inhabitants of the town in 1772. A large part of the Market Place disappeared as a consequence of Victorian road 'improvements', and what was left was destroyed in the 1940 blitz. The 'Old Shambles' alone

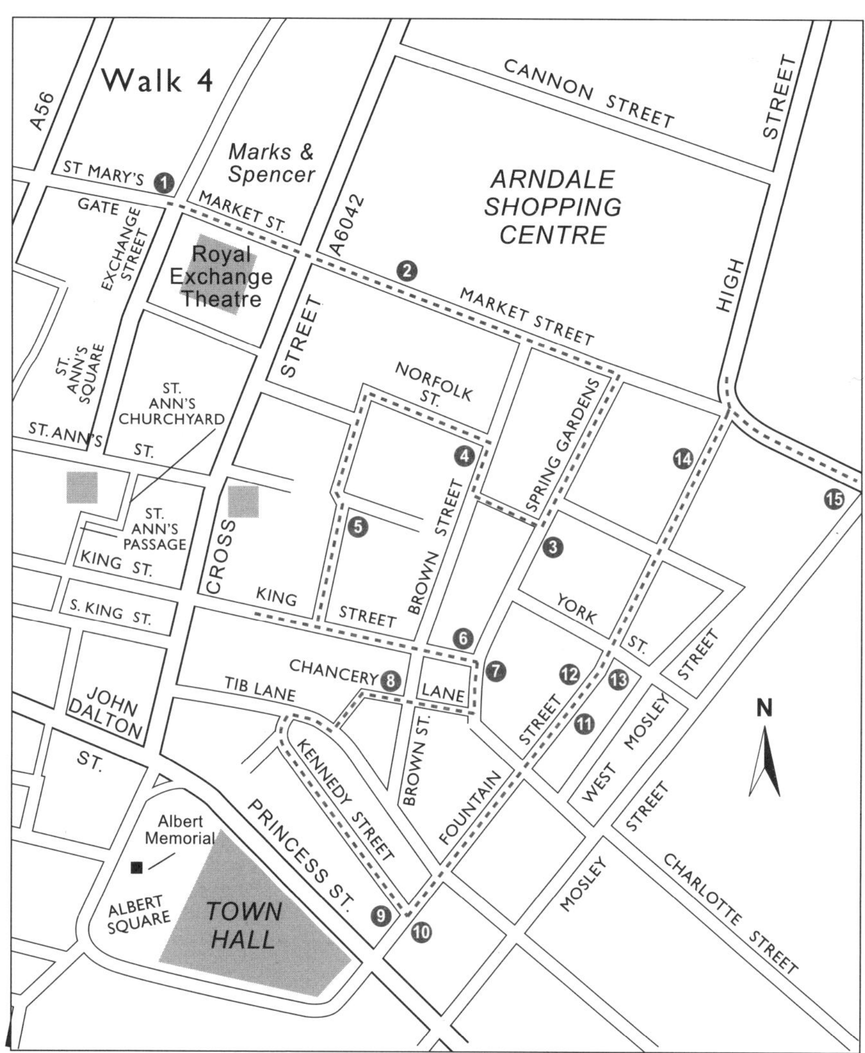

survived, but it has been since been moved on two successive occasions, its new position currently fronting Exchange Square.

The 'Market Stead Lane' ran from the Market Place in a southerly direction, climbing the steep incline up from the river. At places it was incredibly narrow, being five yards wide at the Market Place corner, and fourteen yards in the vicinity of Brown Street.

Once Market Street was so narrow,
There was hardly room to wheel a barrow.

It was not straight either, but wound at various angles so that it was impossible to see from end to end. The condition of the thoroughfare was usually deplorable. The Court Leet forbade the inhabitants to use the earth surface as building material in 1554, and continued to complain for a century afterwards about encroachments by private 'dunghills' (manure was a valuable commodity in a pre-industrial agrarian age) and pigsties. As late as the 18th century, travellers still had to negotiate a pond at one point. An open sewer, running down one side of the street, completed the picture. An Act of Parliament was obtained to widen and improve the street in 1821 (including easing out the slope) and work started the following year. Like all such undertakings in Manchester, the task was undertaken in fits and starts as funding became available. The sum of £232,925 was spent between 1822 and 1834, and a great many historic half-timbered buildings were demolished in the process. One William Yates purchased many fragments for re-use in Knowle House, a magnificent Tudor folly that he erected for himself on Bury New Road in Broughton. This was demolished a few years ago, in a gross act of architectural vandalism.

Market Street

The new Market Street rapidly established itself as the principal thoroughfare in the city, and a major shopping street, replete with most of the principal department stores. It was pedestrianised in 1983, but something remains not quite right, and the layout is forever being altered. The latest format has removed some of the clutter of the street furniture, but the treatment of the street traders remains a thorny issue.

And so we pass between *Marks and Spencer* (p.6) and the Royal Exchange (p.33) towards the great crossroads with Cross Street and Corporation Street. This was once the busiest corner in Manchester and witnessed perhaps one of the first traffic light installations in Britain. The vehicular traffic has been tamed in recent years, and large parts of the city centre are a little more civilised as a result.

Arndale Centre

The ***Arndale Centre*** dominates the view ahead. The Arndale Property Trust had been buying up land in the area since 1952, prior to being taken over by Town and City Properties of Bradford (pioneers of the closed shopping mall in Britain) in 1963. The latter submitted a plan for redeveloping a 25-acre site in 1965, the second major post-war development after Piccadilly Plaza. Money proved to be the main problem, but the council was so keen on the project that they advanced loans of over £160m in 1973. As part of the deal, they purchased the freehold of the site for leaseback to the developers. (The lease later passed to P and O Properties, and is now owned by Prudential.) Wilson and Walmersley, who had just masterminded the Educational Precinct, were chosen as architects and the whole project was completed in 1980.

This massive complex comprised a main two-level shopping block astride Cannon Street (originally incorporating a bus station), an extension alongside Cross Street (p.48), a multi-storey car park, a tall office block, and a market area. It is often remarked that 'a camel is a horse designed by a committee'. In this case, the infighting between the council, the developers, and the architects (together with the interventions of council engineers who were planning roads that would never be built) produced a veritable dog's dinner. Exterior shop fronts were initially forbidden on Corporation Street and High Street as express roads were intended. The architects wanted internal streets covered with glazed roofs. The developers wanted enclosed malls on the American model, but without any redeeming design features.

Consequently, Mancunians have had a love-hate relationship with the *Arndale* from the first. On the one hand, many people like the idea of a multitude of main-stream shops, well known multiples, department stores, and cafeterias, all under one roof. In this, the *Arndale* has a similar appeal to Meadowhall in Sheffield, or the Metrocentre in Gateshead. However, the place can be confusing, the malls are undifferentiated, and people get lost. (Because of the Market street slope, enter by the High Street entrance and find yourself eventually on the first floor!) The original managers had some equally quirky ideas, including dressing the first security staff in pith helmets! But it is the tiled exterior to which most people object. It is truly hideous, resulting in the local joke about 'the largest public lavatory in the world'. "Manchester's Arndale Centre is so castle-like ... that any passing mediaeval army would automatically besiege it rather than shop in it."

As in other things, the IRA bomb has wrought a transformation. The Corporation Street and Cross Street frontages have been rebuilt, and the long Market Street façade has been transformed. The entire section beyond Canon Street (with the exception of the multi-storey car park) is being reconstructed, enclosing Canon Street (the disliked bus station vanished some years ago) as an indoor glass enclosed 'high street mall' (p.6). Prudential are undertaking an ongoing refurbishment of the interior malls – Hallé Square is now illuminated by a new glass superstructure. Hopefully, something will be done with the tower block too. You should at least enter the new ***Foodchain*** catering court (which spans Market Street) by means of the elephant's trunk of an escalator to the rear *(2)*, if only for the fine views up and down Market Street (and some convenient public lavatories).

Market Street itself is full of vanished landmarks, ancient and modern. To the right of the 'elephant's trunk' is Pall Mall, named after the 18th-century game of 'pell-mell', in which a ball was hit by a mallet through an iron hoop suspended several feet above the ground. It was originally a cul-de-sac, entered by two alleyways underneath premises tenanted by a carver and guilder, but was turned into a street by the improvement commissioners. The *Arndale* entrance, opposite, leads to a mall called Cromford Court, adjacent to the site of the original of the same name, where Richard Arkwright (p.191) established his warehouse. It was probably called after the Derbyshire location of his first large mill. Mr Hyde's Grocers Shop, a magnificent Tudor half-timbered building, stood in the way of the 19th-century street improvements. Look at its former location at ***Virgin***, on the right, and imagine what we have lost. The Bank of Manchester, the first joint-stock bank in the town, stood on the corner of Brown Street. It opened in 1828, with "a profusion of mahogany and brass," something that no-one in the town had seen in a bank before. It obviously started a trend.

The left-hand side of Market Street has been reconstructed – the tiles are no more! About half way along this range was the 'Cinephone', opened in 1914 as the 'Market Street Picture House'. It reinvented itself after 1950 as 'Manchester's Continental Cinema'. And in the 1950s and 1960s, we all knew what that meant, didn't we? The association of foreign films with salaciousness led to some eclectic programming, to say the least. Fellini's 'Juliet of the Spirits' played in 1966. But 'Last Year in Marienbad' might be followed next week by 'Days of Desire', and Bergman's latest offering might be supported by 'Naked as Nature Intended'. ("Oh look, darling, we've just passed a nudist camp ... let's stop and find out what goes on there

...") The management eventually made provision for the different markets. The matronly lady in the box office would put aside her knitting and spot the suit, the duffel coat, or the university scarf that signalled 'film buff'. "Oh, you'll want the circle, love (it was about sixpence extra) ... a much nicer view." Meanwhile, a group of men in raincoats lived up to their stereotype in the stalls.

A number of fine brick mansions were erected on Market Street in the early 18th century, reflecting the rising prosperity of the town and new fashions in architecture. Where ***Foot Locker*** is now situated, on the left, the Dickenson family of Birch built a grand town house. It was two storeys high, topped by an ornamental balustrade, and fronted by a garden surrounded by railings. The fact that the 'Horse Pool' stretched from the front door to the corner of High Street did not seem to bother anyone at that time. John Dickenson entertained the Young Pretender, otherwise known as 'Bonny Prince Charlie', here in 1745, and the house was forever after known as 'The Palace'. After becoming an inn, it was demolished in Victorian times.

The Dickensons were landed gentry, but James Marsden was a nouveau-riche textile merchant, who seems to have spent a great deal of his time in property development (particularly on the site of ***British Home Stores***), and naming streets after himself. Quite clearly, he had 'arrived', and aped the manners of local society, including the Jacobite sympathies in vogue at the time. If John Dickenson could not host the Prince in 1745, he made do with the Duke of Athole. He built an even grander house opposite 'The Palace', with a doorway approached by a flight of nine steps, three floors, fluted pillars, a cornice supporting four life sized figures, and a cupola with a flagpole. One comes across cases of 'keeping up with the Jones's', but this is ridiculous!

Building development in this part of the town had hitherto just followed the line of Market Street with open fields beyond on either side. But Manchester began to expand to the south and west in the course of the 18th century. The Brown family was foremost in this development. Joshua Brown, a rich dyer, acquired Pool Fold Hall (p.49) in the previous century, and enlarged the estate by the purchase of other property in the locality. By 1723, there was only one heir left to this estate. Unfortunately, Thomas Brown was a sea captain whose whereabouts were not exactly known. Responding to an advertisement in a London newspaper, the good captain certainly 'learned something to his advantage'. He rapidly claimed his inheritance, took one look at the new St Ann's Square, and obtained a private Act of Parliament enabling him to grant building leases on the land in his possession. All the property bounded by Market Street, Cross Street, King Street, and Mosley Street, was thus parcelled into building plots by a deed of 1747.

Spring Gardens

We will now explore this area by turning right into Spring Gardens. The street is called after the spring of water, which was directed by pipes of elm trunks along it, continuing via Market Street to the Market Place. This 'conduit' was first installed in 1550-58 as a result of the generosity of Isabella Beck, a widow and heiress of the Bexwicke or Beswick family (p.18).

There were only a few houses built in the street by the time of the mid-18th century, with open fields to the south. Then it became engulfed in a mass of speculative building. Nowadays, modern financial buildings intrude, so continue past the cellular concrete tower block containing the ***National Westminster Bank*** to arrive at the ***Atheneum Bar***, at the corner of York Street *(3)*. This was Parr's Bank, an essay in sandstone by the ubiquitous Charles Heathcote in 1902. The large arched windows of the former banking hall are flanked by ostentatious paired Doric columns, whose shield and scroll brackets appear to support nothing in particular. The impressive corner doorway has columns rising the height of the building and culminating in a pediment and finial. A drum and cupola rounds the whole arrangement off. The internal Pyrenean marble columns were shipped whole to Manchester via the Ship Canal. The building was saved from demolition in 1972 by a petition of over 11,000 names, organised by the Victorian Society.

Imagine the garden that used to be here, with a well from which the spring itself bubbled forth. Taking advantage of a new Act of Parliament that permitted provincial theatres, the first Theatre Royal (p.85) opened on the site in 1775. (This caused the spring to dry up, but not the actors.) The famous Mrs Siddons appeared in productions, and it was a lucky time for the theatrical Farren family – Miss Farren married the theatre loving Earl of Derby and her youngest daughter went on to captivate, and marry, the Earl of Wilton. The theatre was rebuilt after a disastrous fire in 1789 and hosted such attractions as 'the Young Roscius', a boy prodigy who played Richard III, Hamlet, and other Shakespearean characters in the course of an evening's entertainment. The Theatre Royal moved to grander premises in 1807 but the redundant building was soon occupied by 'The Amphitheatre', with circus, equestrian events, trained animals, and equally trained variety performers. It ended its days as the Queen's Theatre, with a repertoire of Victorian melodrama. The remains of the well were revealed upon demolition in 1869.

Retrace your footsteps a short distance, then turn left down Marriott's Court. Joshua Marriott, a merchant and dealer in thread, had obtained one of Thomas Brown's leases and erected a house fronting onto Brown Street at this point. It was a fine brick three-storey mansion, with a coat of arms over the door. His grandson was involved in the tortuous affairs of Roger Aytoun (p.140), and was one of the initiators of the first Theatre Royal. The unmemorable 1960s **Post Office** is the third to be located on Brown Street, a replacement for the far better 19th-century Post Office building that stood on this site. Since many postmen were (and are) ex-soldiers and military reservists, the Victorian structure included a rifle range! Turning right into Brown Street, well, you have to rub your eyes: someone has plonked down a **Norman castle**, complete with turret, battlements, and arches, in the middle of the town centre *(4)*. The main entrance is in Norfolk Street, round the corner, and the building is an Edwardian folly of an office block (1909) in Portland stone – ideal for someone hiding from their creditors, no doubt.

The first Post Office site on Brown Street was a little further up in the direction of Market Street than the site of the second and third, though on the same side. Oswald Mosley, the Lord of the Manor, erected a room for the Court Leet (p.52) at this location in 1824, with space for a number of butcher's stalls beneath. He then used the court to enforce an arcane mediaeval privilege, whereby he could regulate butchers. Any who wished to operate a shop in the town had to take a stall in his new 'shambles'. As the Court still exercised a local government function in the town, this boosted the cause of incorporation no end. The ubiquitous Richard

Cobden (p.37), serving as a juryman, was moved to fury. "Is it in this great town of Manchester we are still living under the feudal system? Does Sir Oswald Mosley, living up in Derbyshire, send his mandate down here for us to come into this dingy hole to elect a government for Manchester? Why, now I will put an end to this thing." When Manchester became a corporation, the vacant space was used for a much-needed large Post Office. It moved to the present site in 1884.

Turn left into Norfolk Street, and enjoy the **'castle'** a little further. Next door to it are the Baroque revival (1907) offices of the **former Northern Stock Exchange**. Until the 1980s, the London Stock Exchange had a monopoly in the buying and selling of stocks and shares, controlled by a cosy oligarchy of 'jobbers', who ran the Exchange and restricted entry to its hallowed halls. They vetted and admitted 'brokers', who acted as an intermediary between them and the customer. Of course, not everyone could base themselves in London, and the importance of the industrial north required a branch in Manchester, though run under the same regulations (the latest prices were 'wired' to it). This was the Exchange's final home in the city, before the financial 'big bang' of the 1980s abolished the monopoly. Norfolk Street contained another spring in 'Marriott's Field', which also fed the conduit.

Pall Mall and Court

Another left turn leads into Pall Mall, with a new building on the right incorporating the features of the original **'Princes Chambers'**, including the doorway. Marsden Street commences to the left, at the end of Pall Mall. The Marsden Street Theatre was the first in Manchester, established in 1753, long before the Act which permitted 'subversive' theatrical performances to be given outside of 'sophisticated' London. However, it was possible to give a concert and charge admission, as a playbill of 30th April, 1760, indicates. The recital (in six parts, front seats two shillings, back seats one shilling) was "to begin at six o' clock in the evening to whatever company may happen to be in the house. (!) Between the parts of the concert, for the further amusement of the ladies and gentlemen, will be presented, gratis, a tragedy called 'Theodosius, or the Force of Love', all the characters exhibited by persons without hire, gain, or reward; to which will be added a farce 'The Old Man Taught Wisdom, or the Virgin Unmask'd'." In the same year, an argument at rehearsal led to a duel, in which a man was killed! The theatre closed in 1775, though the premises were sometimes used for the exhibition of giant painted 'panoramas'. B.R. Hayden, a panorama painter and showman, visited in 1831, and perceived the need for a School of Design in the town. Unfortunately, the ensuing attempt to found one proved abortive.

To the right is Chapel Walks, leading to the entrance to Back Pool Fold (p.49), guarded by a fine **'mock Tudor' pastiche**. However, our way lies straight ahead through Pall Mall Court *(5)*. The raised surface, including an odd **little square** with a few trees, masks an underground car park. Look left, where the cellular bronzed glass walls of the **Sun Alliance building** (Lionel, Brett, and Pollen, 1969) overcomes limited space by wrapping itself like a reverse figure two around the boring sixties **Norwich Union building** on King Street. Opposite, also fronting on to King Street, is the **former northern headquarters of the National Westminster Bank** (Casson Conder, and Partners 1968). The genius of Sir Hugh Casson (of 'Festival of Britain' fame) presided over a great simple, if rather stark, concrete free-standing shell, as if anticipating future re-use. The strange colour of the Swedish granite exterior was intended to match the soot stained surroundings. However, since most of the stonework in Manchester has been cleaned, it is now the building that stands out like a sore thumb. The bank controlled over 700 branches from here, but it was sold to Orbit Developments in 1999, and refurbished as offices and shops (amongst which is a large branch of ***Calvin Klein***). A plaque commemorating Harrison Ainsworth, the Victorian novelist, should be noticed on the wall. (He was born in a house on this site.) His romantic historical novels include 'Rookwood', which created the legend of Dick Turpin's ride from London to York.

King Street

Pass through into King Street. ***Lloyds Bank*** stands on the corner of Cross Street. By the end of the 18th century, the Court Leet (p.52) could not handle the problems of the growing town, and a number of ad-hoc bodies came into existence. The Manchester and Salford Police Act of 1792 created the Police Commissioners. The Court Leet, through the auspices of the Boroughreeve and the infamous Joseph Nadin (p.41), provided only a limited police function during daylight hours. The new body created an organised system of night policing. But it also assumed responsibility for cleansing, street lighting, water supply, and highway improvement. It was,

The Lloyds TSB building in King Street

however, elected on a restricted franchise by those who occupied property worth £30 a year. After some initial friction with the old Court, it settled down under the leadership of Thomas Fleming (p.16).

It based itself in a house on the site of the bank. (The premises were previously the home of Dr. Charles White, a pioneer in medical teaching, and a leading promoter of the Infirmary. He is commemorated by a **plaque**.) However, as the work grew, something grander was needed. The house was demolished, and construction began in 1825 on what was to become Manchester's first Town Hall. It eventually took eighteen years, several extensions, and the expenditure of £40,000, before the Commissioners were satisfied. The Old Town Hall was a large and elegant building with a façade of classical columns. But this state of affairs could not last. In the political aftermath of the Great Reform Act of 1832, the momentum for incorporation became unstoppable. A Charter of Incorporation was granted to Manchester in 1837, and the first elections for the new town council were held the following year. The Commissioners, in particular, refused to accept defeat. Not only did they not contest the elections (allowing the liberals and reformers to win all the seats) but they also denied them the use of their building.

Thus, the first council meetings were held in the York Hotel, a large inn with a 'commercial room' suitable for the purpose. The hotel was also the venue of several meetings to promote some of the early railway schemes which linked Manchester to other parts of the country, and the scene of inauguration of the Anti Corn Law League in 1838 (p.113). The site of this establishment is marked by a **plaque** on the National Westminster Bank building. The Queen's Bench confirmed the charter of incorporation in 1841, and the Council eventually occupied what would become their Town Hall. The Court Leet lingered until 1848, when the old manorial rights were purchased. And everyone lived happily ever after... The Old Town Hall became the public library when the present Town Hall opened in 1877, and was demolished in 1912. The columned façade may still be seen as the backdrop to Heaton Park boating lake (p.254).

This portion of King Street developed very differently from its other half across Cross Street. The roadway became wider to accommodate the grand buildings, for this developed into the financial heart of the town. The ***DKNY* fashion shop**, opposite *Lloyd's*, was built for Prudential Insurance, and later housed the Manchester Stock Exchange. Alfred Waterhouse designed it (in a vaguely mediaeval style) in 1881, using columns, round headed windows, and dogtooth moulding. (It has sadly lost its tower and gabled roof.) But he used glazed red Accrington brick and terracotta, earning the epithet 'slaughterhouse Gothic'. Its restoration as a shop won a Civic Society award in 1999.

King Street's finest building is next door, opposite the former National Westminster Bank. As the industrial districts began to expand, the Bank of England decided to open a Manchester branch in 1826. C.R. Cockerill was responsible for the **Bank of England** building, which dates to 1845. (He had previously conducted archaeological excavations in Italy and Greece.) There are tall windows for the inevitable banking hall (the King Street entrance is a later addition), six giant Tuscan columns of the Doric order supporting a frieze, and a second storey of pilasters underneath a central pediment. Enter, and find the hall stripped of furniture and fittings, for it has become the entrance foyer to a new office development.

Notice the round **cast iron columns** and the barrel vaulted ceiling. Cockerill freely interpreted classical conventions, so there is rather a Baroque feel to it. Tasteful water features flank the entrance to a stair well in the **modern building** (Holford Associates, 1996). Outside, observe the marriage of the old structure and the new, rather controversial lofty tower block, fifteen storeys high. But it is not brutal in conception, and the whole thing eventually grows on you.

Cross Pall Mall (which intersects King Street at this point) to find the temple of high fashion called ***Emporio Armani***. The original façade of the Manchester and Salford Savings Bank here appears to have been incorporated, some time in the 1850s, into what was the Sun Life and Fire Offices. Certainly, the rusticated ground floor arcade must have once lit a banking hall. There are Doric pilasters and a decorated frieze above. Two large structures dominate the rest of the street on this side. The first is **Ship Canal House** (H.S. Fairhurst, 1924-26), erected of reinforced concrete around a steel frame in the heyday of the great waterway. Nevertheless, the façade is very traditional, with a rusticated stone ground floor, ashlar first floor, a prominent string-course (projecting line of masonry), and several more storeys terminating in a colonnade of paired Corinthian columns. The whole ensemble is rounded off by a cornice and parapet, and surmounted by sculptured figures. The group is difficult to see, so cross the road for a glimpse of **Neptune brandishing his trident**. Construction required a special Act of Parliament because of the building's great height. It was anticipated that any future neighbours would also be tall, but the 'Mary Ann' tiling (that Fairhurst did not intend to be on view) can be clearly seen on the walk up from Cross Street.

The rather odd **Atlas Assurance** building (1929), next door, is tall and narrow to take advantage of a small site. The man himself, holding the world on his shoulders, is placed over a very elaborate **bronze doorframe**. Interestingly enough, the building was designed by the grandson of Alfred Waterhouse, and was erected on the site of the last Georgian house to survive in this part of King Street. It now contains a branch of *Georgio Armani*.

The range of buildings on this side of King Street ends in the imposing **Midland Bank** of Edwin Lutyens, designed in 1929, but not built until 1933-35. Lutyens wished to create an imposing building by combining mass and solidity with simplicity. A tall steel frame is clad with Portland stone, but the corners and the upper storeys are proportionally cut back, with the windows and architectural features designed to emphasise distortions of height and perspective to create a structure that seems to soar. Unfortunately, Reginald McKenna (Bank Chairman and frustrated liberal politician) interfered and foisted the fussy top storey on the architect. But his other advice was eminently practical. A marble border to the banking hall floor should be omitted "in view of the fact that a considerable number of people in Manchester wear nails in their boots ... the risk of slipping is even greater than it is in London". (He was talking about boot wearing businessmen and manufacturers, not just bank employees. At that time, older 'city gents' in these parts still considered shoes and wrist watches a sign of decadence!) Lutyens, it is said, never ventured north for a commission again.

The **Reform Club** *(6)* stands on the opposite corner of this end of King Street. The Liberal Party had dominated Manchester politics since the Reform Act of 1832 (as it had dominated most of the north west of England). The club, founded in 1867, reflected the dawn of a new age of mass politics and party organisation and was a combined headquarters and gentleman's club for Liberals in the city. In effect, it constituted a home for a large part of the local political establishment of merchants, manufacturers and professional men. They engaged the renowned Edward Salomans to design a building in the popular 'Venetian palazzo' style, the last great Manchester manifestation of what had been an affectation in the town. 'Venetian Gothic' reflected the trading republic (democracy?) par excellence, and (along with the mediaeval Flanders cloth towns) was, perhaps, a role model that many Manchester citizens aspired to. Salomans, assisted by John Philip Jones, created an exceptionally fine building in York sandstone. The large first-floor 'piano nobile' (containing a meeting room) is lit by a series of **two-lighted windows**, each framed by a polychrome (multi-coloured) **Venetian window arch**. A large balcony, supported by columns, is situated over the main entrance. Notice the lovely **oriel windows** at the corners, which commence **turrets terminating in minaret-like towers** with domed roofs (originally gazebos). There are **friezes** above these windows representing the arts and sciences. The building once also had a pitched roof and a fleche spire in the Flemish style ('fleche' meaning 'feathered arrow' – a smaller and more decorative style than usual).

The club opened on 19th October, 1871, amidst much speechmaking and political demonstration. Many prominent British political figures, including the young Winston Churchill, have addressed the Manchester electorate from the first-floor balcony. But the nature of politics and the political system have changed. Party politics are no longer the preserve of local elites in quite the same way, and party organisation seems to have been eclipsed by the mass media. The building has been recently refurbished after lying empty for a number of years. You can glimpse the **grand staircase** through the main entrance, though it now only leads to solicitor's offices. A purchase in the shop on the left of the main entrance, or perhaps a polite request, may reveal the original **mahogany and green marble-lined lavatories** of the 1890s improvements.

The grand first-floor room contains the ***Reform Restaurant***, said to be Manchester's finest. It is entered round the corner in Spring Gardens, by a fine staircase (with a **statue of Gladstone** at the top) to the very plush bar and restaurant (designed by Bernard Carroll). This is located in the principal room with the large Venetian windows. A smaller room, often used as an overflow or for private functions, was a **card room**, decorated with painted panels. The restaurant has been patronised by Manchester United players (Sir Alex Ferguson had his testimonial party here), soap stars, and a variety of celebrities (including Monica Lewinsky). As far as is known, David Beckham and 'Posh Spice' have not yet greeted the world from the balcony.

Turn towards the fine row of buildings at the top end of the street *(7)* and examine them from left to right. The **former National Provincial Bank** (1888-90, Alfred Waterhouse) is on the corner of York Street. The large windows are flanked by giant Doric pilasters, and the upper two storeys are linked by Ionic pilasters. Notice the attic rooms, lit by small gabled windows. The two rather elaborate doorways are crowned with curved pediments, with triangular pediments above, topped with balconies. The first headquarters of the Manchester Ship Canal Company was located here for a brief period. The **Lancashire and Yorkshire Bank** (1890), next door, directly faces King Street. It sports massive mullioned and transomed win-

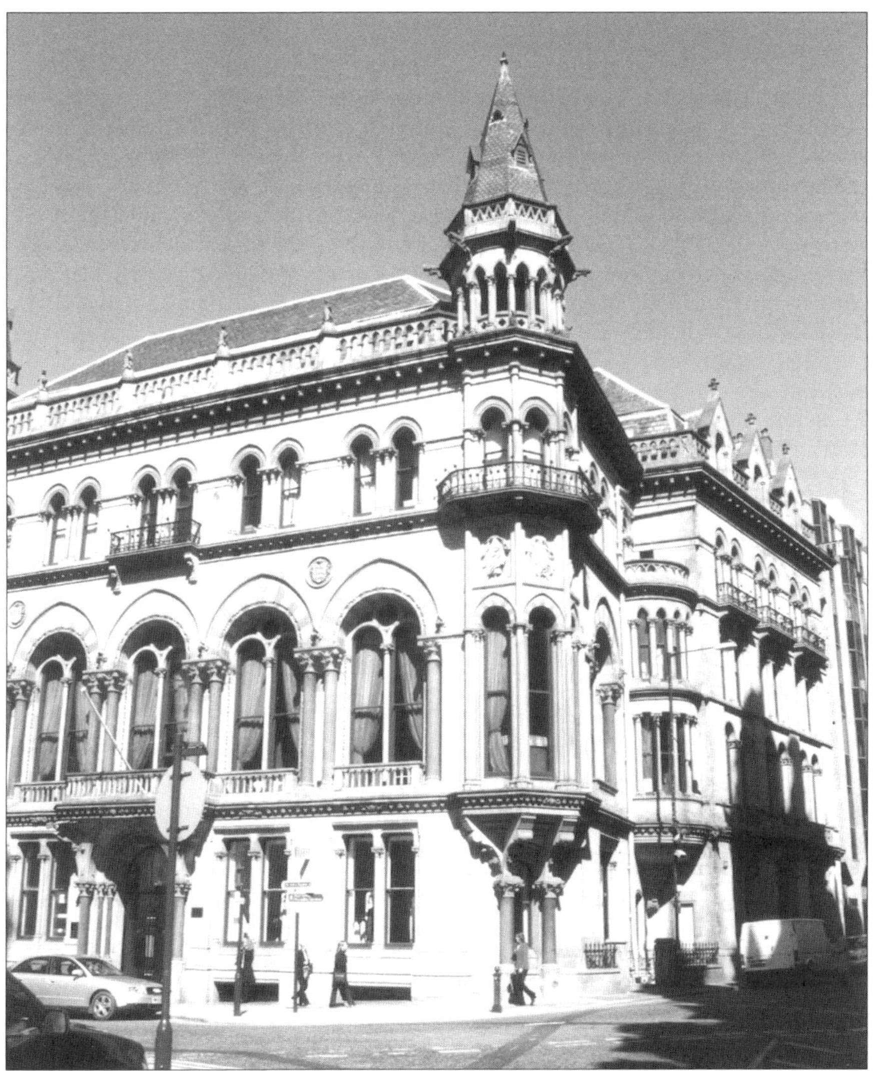

The Reform Club – on the corner of King Street and Spring Gardens

dows, rusticated stone, and the usual piers of square Doric columns terminating in an entablature. But this former bank also has a huge and imposing asymmetrical doorway with a tower above (complete with drum and cupola), and the massive gable is reminiscent of a Baroque church. It is now home to *Rothwells*. To the right is the **Commercial Union Assurance building** (another Heathcote confection of 1881), later occupied by Martin's Bank. The ground floor windows are again surrounded by Doric pilasters, but their decoration is more 17th-century Jacobean than classical. Note the three roof turrets, and the apsidal or curving corner on to Concert Lane.

Chancery Lane

We turn right and right again, in a peregrination of the Midland Bank, to find ourselves in Chancery Lane. Chancery Buildings may be found on the corner of Brown Street. The façade of the original warehouse has been preserved on Brown Street side, with a new apartment development constructed behind it. This is a common redevelopment technique in the city centre area. **Lombard Chambers**, all that remains of Cunliffe's Bank, stands on the opposite corner, to the rear of the Atlas Assurance building *(8)*. Sir William Cunliffe Brooks, MP for East Cheshire, was a very wealthy banker indeed. He resided most of the time at Barlow Hall (near Manchester) but had other houses in London, the Highlands of Scotland, and the Mediterranean. He rather fancied himself as a second Medici, lending money in what he regarded as the modern equivalent of renaissance Florence. Consequently, he engaged George Truefitt (a passionate mediaevalist, who had introduced the 'Cheshire Magpie' style of mock half-timbered building to Manchester and the North West) in 1868 to design a bank worthy enough to house his financial operations.

The original building stretched through to front King Street, where Ship Canal House stands, and the great hall was lined with Sienna marble, and divided by gilt columns and brass screens. The surviving portion is a mixture of Gothic and Italian styles, with the usual tall round-headed windows on the ground floor, a corbelled string-course above, and dormer windows. The most notable features are the **wrought iron work** – the balconies, and the corner tower with its spiky metal cage on top. The elaborate floriated carving is a delight, and contains the monogram of the bank – Brooks's initials.

Leftwards, down Chancery Place, brings us to Booth Street. **Greg's Building** (1845), on the right-hand corner, was built for the son of Samuel Greg, the owner of Styal Mill. The left side of Booth Street (in the direction of Chancery Place) repays some attention, as it has preserved something like its original Victorian appearance. From left to right are the **Manchester and Salford Savings Bank** (1872), Italianate in Darley Dale stone, with carved heads above the windows; **Massey Chambers** (1879, replacing the Buck Hotel), with veiled heads and 'putti' supporting a high gable; and **Clarence Buildings** (1880s), sandstone, with Jacobean style pilasters. The ***Town Hall Tavern*** is directly ahead, down Tib Lane.

But our walk turns left into Clarence Street, and left again, down Kennedy Street. The leather-bound collections of the **Manchester Law Library** (1885) can be seen through the perpendicular windows on the right. Notice the stained glass panels of bewigged judges below the carved inscription. Kennedy Street has a number of 'Gothic revival' warehouses, but the real gems are **two 18th-century houses** near the corner of Cooper Street. They were altered in the 19th century (notice the loom shop window lights) and are now home to two pubs, *The City Arms* (with green tiles in the corridor) and *The Vine (9)*. We have now reached Cooper Street. The **former Freemason's Hall** (erected in 1863) is facing us, with classical pilasters, columns, and a pediment with a group of sculptured figures *(10)*. The virtues of the Masonic 'craft' are represented on the frontage by **statues** of 'Prudence', 'Fortitude', 'Temperance', and 'Justice'. The masons moved to their new premises in 1924, and it is now an everyday office block called Waldorf House.

Proceed to the left, up Cooper Street, to the start of Fountain Street. The name is a reference to another tributary of the Market Place conduit. Like other streets in the neighbourhood, this was a fashionable address in the 18th century, particularly as it was the location of a Concert Hall and a Theatre. But banks, offices, and warehouses soon displaced the original residents. A rather fine **Venetian polychromatic brick warehouse** (1868), possibly by Salomans, stands at the left-hand corner of Booth Street. To the right is **'81st on Fountain Street'** (Holford Associates, 1990), the ground floor in polished marble, and upper storeys in deep rectangles of white stone. (It is noticeable how much of the modern architecture is inspired by the Victorian context.) **Gan House**, on the left, is a Waterhouse creation of 1882 in the 'restrained palazzo style', with dormer windows and corner turrets. A new office structure was created behind the façade in the 1980s. The street that now cuts across was not an original part of Spring Gardens. It contains (in the right-hand section, **numbers 54-72**) the warehouse (1851) of William Romaine Callender, a major Conservative figure in the political life of the late-Victorian city.

The Second Theatre Royal

Beyond this intersection, between Spring Gardens and the present York House, was the site of the second Theatre Royal. The foundation stone for the second Theatre Royal was laid with some ceremony here *(11)* in 1806. The theatre opened the following year with a performance of 'Folly as it Flies'. It was of an enormous size, with a lobby wide enough to admit a coach. The famous Grimaldi appeared in 1811 and 1813, Paganini played the violin, and the cultural sensibilities of the audience were not above enjoying Astley's Circus. A great music festival was held in 1828 (culminating in a fancy dress ball). This was repeated in 1836, when the theatre was joined to the Assembly Rooms and the Portico Library (p.99) by covered passages in the streets. The event produced a sensation. The great Madame Malibran could not disappoint her public, sang against medical advice, and promptly collapsed. She died soon after, and the mortified authorities gave her a lavish public funeral, which the whole town marked or attended, at the Collegiate Church. The Anti Corn Law League (p.113) held a fund raising Bazaar in 1842, and a performance of 'A Christmas Carol', was given on 6 May, 1844. The theatre burned down early the next morning.

Notice, on the left of the street, how the modern Barclays Bank Offices (1980) extend into a fine example of a 19th-century warehouse on the corner of Spring Gardens. Next door, distinguished by the fine coat of arms, were the **offices of the Overseers and Churchwardens of Manchester** *(12)*. Every Anglican (state church) parish has a body of elected churchwardens and sidesmen. The former assist the clergyman in the management and the maintenance of the church, and the latter formerly kept order in the services and made sure that the local ale houses were shut (nowadays they take the collection!) The wardens and sidesmen did not, in the past, have a good reputation. Sidesmen were advised to:

See all, hear all, and say nowt (nothing).
Eat all, drink all, and take aught (anything).
And when your wardens drunken roam,
Your duty is to see them home.

The Victorian wardens of the old Collegiate Church (and later the cathedral) were a power in the land, managing property and investments that were rapidly increasing in value, and overseeing some very wealthy local charities. Thomas Worthington was responsible for the first two floors, in modest brick and York stone, in 1851-3, and the top floors were added in 1858. A large boardroom extended the entire width of the building.

The 'Gentleman's Concert Hall' stood at the corner of York Street, extending to Concert Lane. It opened in 1777 with a music festival, said to be the first one to be held in provincial England. The original 1,200 patrons of the Hall paid an annual subscription of four guineas (£4.20). The nobility of the building, with its "elegant glass chandeliers" does not seem to have been reflected in the behaviour of the audience. They held loud conversations during performances, shouted out demands for certain pieces of music to be played, and took "the liberty to express dissatisfaction by hisses". Much of this sounds like the activity of the 'claque', by which a group of the performer's friends (though a 'claque' might also be hired) went along to either support him, or denigrate a rival. The Hall could also be used, like the Theatre Royal, for balls and assemblies. The Concerts removed to a new venue in Peter Street, and the Hall closed for performances in 1829. York Street itself first appeared in 1793, built up as far as Mosley Street. Two interesting modern buildings face each other at the corners of Fountain Street. **York House** (Leach, Rhodes, Walker, 1975) is set back from York Street, piers of dark brown brick alternating with cream tiles for ten storeys above the podium *(13)*. **Clock House** (Cassidy and Ashton, 1996), opposite, might be described as a post-modernist interpretation of the classical idiom. Worth a second glance, anyway.

As we approach Market Street, it is impossible to miss the ***Shakespeare*** public house *(14)*. An inn has been here since 1771, but the present building is probably Victorian, and its 'mock Tudor' façade is modern. However, it includes **ancient timbers and carvings** taken in 1928 from 'The Shambles' inn in Chester, and re-erected here. The pub has spirits in more ways than one. The ghost of a Victorian maidservant reputedly haunts it. One version states that the poor girl set fire to herself while lighting candles, but the other has a wicked chef raping and then murdering her. The chef is said to have then hanged himself from a beam (the marks are supposed to be still visible) and he also haunts the place. You really can't get the staff! This end of the street was the location of the oatmeal market (under the former Lewis's department store). Oatmeal, along with potatoes, constituted the diet of the working population during the industrial revolution.

At that time, everyone, high or low, dined at home. Consequently, James Hudswell took a bold step in opening 'The Fountain Street Refectory' in 1824. It was, in effect, Manchester's first restaurant, and was an overnight sensation.

> Since Hudswell first in Manchester began,
> A guttling (eating) mania hath assail'd the town,
> At one o'clock, to gulp his good things down.

But, by 1838, there were still only eighteen eating establishments in a town where it was still possible to reach anywhere (including home) on foot.

Lewis's and Pauldens

We have now reached the final stretch of Market Street, dominated by two large department stores, with the Metrolink station in between. The former **Lewis's**

The impressive frontage of the Debenhams store

(*Primark*) became something of a Manchester institution. David Lewis, a Londoner, was enamoured by the concept of a 'department store' (said to have originated in 19th-century America or France, but see page 54), and is credited with pioneering the institution in Britain. He came north and opened his first store in Liverpool in 1856. The firm was always associated with entrepreneurial flair, even showmanship. (Brunel's 'Great Eastern' was chartered, before being broken up, and anchored as a floating advertisement in the Mersey.) The original Manchester store, opening in 1877 in the French renaissance style, with a showy corner tower, followed in this tradition. Intended initially as a men's and boys' drapers, women's clothing, and even food, were soon added. The store's famous 'two shillings and ninepence' (about 14p) pocket watch was one of its many attractions – along with distorting mirrors, a 'magic lantern' show in the shop windows, and a basement full of slot machines. At one point, the basement was flooded with 2ft (60cm) of water in a recreation of Venice, complete with gondolas!

The company negotiated with the Council for room to expand, and exchanged some pavement space for the right to enclose two inconvenient back streets as an arcade. Lewis's Arcade, until the late-1950s, was one of the sights of the town, being the haunt of a battalion of jolly tarts *(15)*. It also contained the entrance to the children's paradise of Wyles, with two floors of toys and renderings of both the Blackpool and Eiffel Towers in Meccano. (The Market Street entrance was where ***FT5k*** is situated, and the remains of the other entrance is round the corner in Mosley Street.) The new extension, which subsumed the old building, was completed in 1915. It included a great dome, 100ft (30m) high by 36ft (11m) in diameter. This was the centrepiece of the Christmas decorations, and every Manchester child was taken at some time to see it. The extension also boasted the first escalators outside of London, and the 'largest soda fountain in the Empire'. Upstairs might also be found a ballroom sprung on ball bearings, the venue of tea dances. This room was also used for a variety of exhibitions, promotions, and a Christmas toy fair until the 1960s. The final extension, on the Mosley Street side, was completed in 1929. The interior of the store was extensively remodelled in the 1960s, and the dome disappeared.

Many people date the start of a long and slow decline from this period. It was painful to witness, for it seemed that the management had a death wish. When the last tills rang on a sad Saturday in February, 2001, people sensed it was the end of an era. In the midst of the bear garden of the closing down sale, both the shopping public and the staff took photographs for posterity. Lewis's, after some refurbishment, has been reopened by *Primark*, a discount retailer.

Debenham's, across Market Street, was built in 1929-32 for the Ryland's store company. Although built to the design of P. Garland Fairhurst, Ted Adams (as project architect) should take a lot of the credit for solving the problems on the ground. It is built on an irregular site, and no angle is true. The substantial **corner towers** are intended to mask this fact, and the vertical mass offsets the horizontal of six storeys. It is a steel-framed building, clad with Portland stone, and intended for adaptation to a multitude of uses. The ground and first floor were originally leased to a number of shops and a bank, while the rest was used as a warehouse. A beacon and revolving searchlight (visible for up to sixty miles) was placed on the roof as a marker for Ringway (now Manchester) Airport. Paulden's store moved here in 1953, shortly before their premises on Stretford Road were destroyed in one of Manchester's most spectacular post-war blazes. This was the making of the site, for Paulden's was just as much an institution as *Lewis's*. "That one ... if she fell off Paulden's, she'd land in a posh coat." It is now home to *Debenham's*. We have now, at long last, arrived at Piccadilly and Piccadilly Gardens.

A Metrolink tram leaving Piccadilly

5 Piccadilly to St Peter's Square

Start: Piccadilly Gardens

Estimated time of walk: 1 hour

Interiors: City Art Gallery – 1 hour; Portico Library – 15 min; Central Library – 20 min

Highlights: The 'centre' of Manchester, a private library, the City Art Gallery, Central Library, where Mr Rolls met Mr Royce, and the home of Free Trade.

After exhausting the possibilities of Exchange Square, we will now make Piccadilly our base and starting point for the next couple of walks. But what is Piccadilly? The majority of Mancunians, if asked for the centre of Manchester, will inevitably direct the visitor to Piccadilly. For them, it is the heart of their native city, a place that inevitably comes into the mind of an exile or expatriate. In short, the words Manchester and Piccadilly go together.

But it was not always thus. Up to the end of the 18th century, the area was on the outskirts of the town. The foot traveller came to the limit of the Market Stead Lane, and crossed a trickle of water known as the Tib by a large flat stone, the other traffic splashing straight through. Lever Hall stood to the left, and to the right ... well, there were the 'Daub Holes'. At that time, most of the buildings in Manchester were timber-framed with 'wattle' (woven twigs or reeds) filling the spaces between. Since time immemorial, the citizens had dug the clayey earth at this spot to make the 'daub' to be smeared over the 'wattle' filling. The rain had filled the expanding pits to create some rather unwholesome stagnant ponds. It was just the place to erect the new 'Ducking Stool' in the early 17th century (p.49).

Ahead lay open fields stretching as far as the Derbyshire hills on the horizon. Indeed, witnesses could recall, many years later, a day in 1778 when Squire Trafford and the 'Harriers' killed a hare in the vicinity of the present Portland Street. It was the Lancashire custom to follow the hounds on foot, and spectators sometimes joined in the chase! Curiously enough, the daughter of the master of the hunt drowned herself in the largest of the ponds.

The construction of the Infirmary proved to be the catalyst to transform this place into an erstwhile city centre. Dr. Charles White was the inspiration for the provision of a much needed charity hospital. The subscription list was opened in 1752, and land was purchased (facing the London road across the 'Daub Holes') from Sir Oswald Mosley in 1754. A forty-bed 'Manchester Infirmary' opened on the site the following year, but soon proved inadequate for the needs of the town. More land was obtained and an extension, including a dispensary, was added in 1792. Some of the cost was defrayed by the proceeds of a balloon ascent from the Infirmary grounds. The infirmary soon acquired a clock in a turret with a weathervane.

The scope of the institution's activities was extended to the whole Greater Manchester area at this time. Prominent men became trustees for life by a payment of twenty guineas (£21). The trustees could nominate medical men for vacant positions and vote in the ensuing election, but most of the subscribers saw their donation as a way of providing the certainty of medical attendance for their employees in the event of industrial accidents. By 1825, the building was encased in stone (which included four fluted classical columns) and lit by gas – including the clock. William IV became a patron, and the epithet 'Royal' was added to the title. The 'Manchester Royal Infirmary' was completely reconstructed between 1847 and 1853, when north and south wings were added and the central portion received a dome and a new clock. Part of the cost of the north wing was defrayed by the sum of £3,000, raised by a concert given by Jenny Lind, the 'Swedish Nightingale'.

A small lunatic asylum was erected on the Portland Street side in 1765, and was extended three times between 1772 and 1788. Either the pressures of the expanding town were increasing or behaviour previously ignored was being reclassified. Perhaps both. Nevertheless, the inmates were removed to a new asylum at Cheadle in

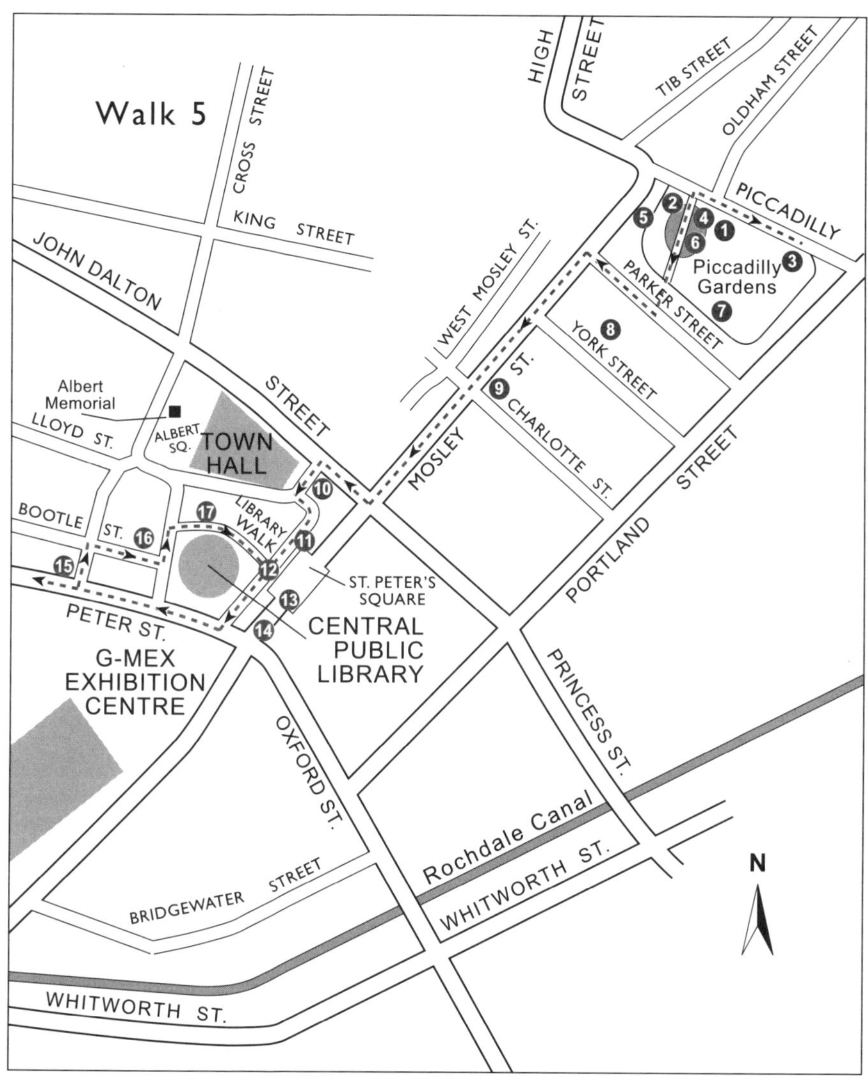

1847. Even more ephemeral was the existence of baths located on the Mosley Street side, established in 1781. The proceeds of hot, tepid, cold, and vapour baths went to Infirmary funds, but visitors could also 'purge their humours' by bloodletting, with a choice of cupping (opening a vein with a knife) or the application of leaches!

The development of the Infirmary was but one factor in the creation of a fashionable area. The other was the fate of the Lever estate. Lever Hall appeared as a quaint half-timbered old house, standing in the midst of gardens and orchards, the town residence of the Levers of Alkrington (near Middleton). The last tenant was Ashton Lever, a gentleman who (like many of his time) had a 'cabinet of curiosities'. However, in this case, the collecting mania got the better of him, and probably devoured a large part of his inheritance. A visitor in 1773 described a collection requiring 1,300 glass cases in three rooms. It attracted large numbers of local visitors (3,320 on one 'opening day'), so its owner decided to recoup his losses by taking it to London. Unfortunately, it proved to be one attraction among many, and Mr Lever was reduced to disposing of it by lottery. Even this failed, and the insolvent gentleman committed suicide at the Bull's Head, Market Place, in 1788.

His landed estate had been sold to a property speculator, who lost no time in dividing it up into building plots. The Hall later became the 'White Bear' coaching inn, which stood on the site of the former Kardomah building (see below). The roadway, an extension of Market Stead Lane past the Infirmary, became known as Lever's Row. In 1812, the former became Market Street, and the latter Piccadilly. Some have suggested an aping of the fashionable London name, but it should be remembered that the name itself is probably derived from the peccadil, a flower that was much used as a vegetable dye in the infant textile industry.

Of course, there remained the 'Daub Holes'. Sir Oswald Mosley was happy to donate the land in front of the Infirmary for the construction of an ornamental pond, provided that it remained in public use in perpetuity. Mosley cannot be considered a pure altruist, for the pond was also to be used as a reservoir forming part of a private water supply system he was installing. The area around the pond became a fashionable promenade. It was a popular place for drilling the volunteer regiments after church on Sunday – the Manchester and Salford Volunteer Infantry received their colours here in 1798. When Mosley's money-spinner was superseded by the advent of the Manchester and Salford Waterworks, the pond became stagnant and noisome. Fountains were proposed, and three were actually erected for Queen Victoria's visit in 1851. But the public had had enough of aquatic features, and the area was filled in to form an **Esplanade** (now known as the Boulevard) in 1853. This was soon populated with public statues.

The Statues of Piccadilly

An exploration of the area should start here, in the centre of Piccadilly Gardens. Although **Queen Victoria** *(1)* is the centrepiece, this monument is the newest. She had come to the throne in 1837, the year that Manchester had been incorporated, and saw the century out by dying in January 1901. Her reign had been one of peace and increasing prosperity. In that time, industrialisation had made Britain a world power with the greatest empire ever known. It was an age of startling progress in virtually every field. The Victorians came to believe that such progress was continuous, and that poverty and ignorance would eventually completely disappear. However, rapid social change had posed immense challenges, but it seemed as if the Queen had presided over a successful transition to a constitutional monarchy and a modern mass democracy. In all this, she had appeared a symbol of stability and assurance – even, at times, a mother figure.

Part of the 1897 Jubilee Fund had been earmarked for a statue, and Onslow Ford was selected as the sculptor. The Queen herself had sat for him and pronounced herself delighted with the results. Alas, she died before the monument was completed. Victoria is depicted seated in the imperial robes of state with orb and sceptre (some critics thought she had been made too stiff and formal). To the rear is a figure representing 'Maternity', with a baby in each arm and a faded inscription from Shakespeare. "Let me but bear your love, I'll bear your cares." There is also a small

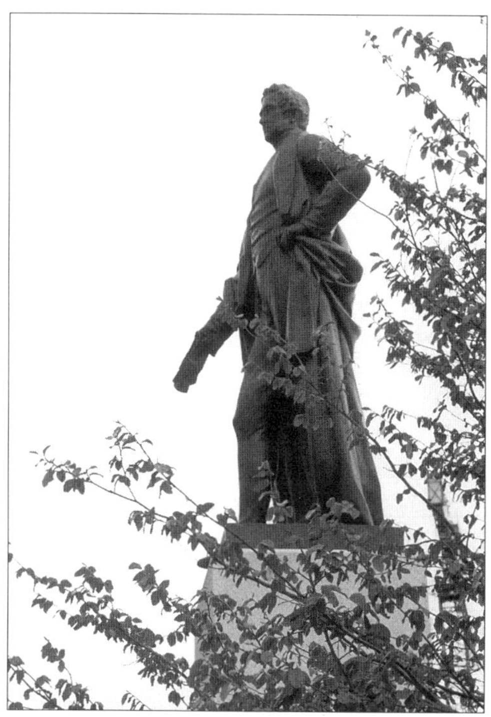
The statue of Sir Robert Peel in Piccadilly Gardens

group of 'St George and the Dragon' on top of the monument. The statue was unveiled in 1901 by Lord Roberts (Kipling's 'Bobs'), the Boer War hero. The behaviour of the crowd, who created a crush by straining to get a better view, was such that the VIP's were trapped in their temporary grandstand. The Vice Chancellor of Manchester University was observed removing his academic dress before climbing down the scaffolding!

Victoria is flanked by (for Manchester at the time) two unusual heroes. **Sir Robert Peel** *(2)* is located at the Market Street end. His father was a local mill owner (Robert was born in Bury) who became a Tory MP – a very rare bird in these parts. The family transformed themselves into landed gentry, living on an estate in the Midlands, and Robert succeeded his father as a member of a group of 'Tory reformers'. Upon becoming party leader, he inherited a political faction of landed aristocrats and gentry, seemingly intent on a collision course with the new industrial and commercial elite. Peel's great achievement was to reconcile the old establishment with the new by obtaining the repeal of the Corn Laws in 1846. He is thus regarded as the father of the modern Conservative party. His role in the repeal of a hated piece of legislation (p.113) added him to the ranks of free trade heroes in Manchester, as elsewhere. Sadly, he died prematurely in 1850 (in a riding accident), at the height of his fame and personal popularity. The dramatic circumstances resulted in a rash of statues throughout the industrial districts. Nowadays, Peel is mainly remembered for the creation of the Metropolitan Police in 1829, and British policemen are still called 'bobbies' to this day.

William Calder Marshall was selected (after a competition) as sculptor, and rejected the fashion of depicting public men in antique Roman togas. There are, however, two allegorical figures of 'Manchester' (resting her arm on a cotton bale) and 'Arts and Sciences'. Notice that the Manchester coat of arms rests on a sheaf of corn, a coded reference to the town's role in the repeal of the Corn Laws. The statue was unveiled in 1853. It has since been repositioned in connection with the Piccadilly redevelopment.

The **Duke of Wellington** *(3)* has stood in the vicinity of Portland Street since 1856, though he used to be nearer the corner. The hero of the Battle of Waterloo in 1815 went on to become a very reactionary Tory prime minister. His participation in the ill-fated opening ceremony of the Liverpool and Manchester Railway (p.183) was sufficient to provoke a near riot (iron shutters were fitted to his London home because people kept breaking his windows). However, the Duke lived to an immense age, and gradually became a respected elder statesman, who was clearly devoted to the young Queen. It was also pointed out that his victory had ushered in an unprecedented age of peace and stability in British foreign policy, and that this had underpinned economic expansion and prosperity. His death provoked an outburst of national mourning. "Bury the Great Duke with an Empire's lamentations."

The statue stirred immense controversy. Some people wanted Wellington depicted as a martial warrior astride a horse, while others alleged that James Prince Lee (the Bishop of Manchester) had fixed the competition in favour of Matthew Noble, then a comparatively unknown sculptor. Noble produced a Wellington as an 'elder statesman', with four symbolic figures suited to Manchester opinion – 'Minerva' (Wisdom); 'Mars' with a sword (Valour); 'Victory' with a wreath; and 'Peace' bearing a cornucopia of plenty. The panels depict the Battle of Assaye (in India); the victory of Waterloo; Wellington receiving the thanks of the House of Commons (in 1814); and the great statesman at the Congress of Vienna (1815), helping to settle the peace of Europe.

Two subsidiary statues once flanked the Infirmary entrance. **James Watt** (1857) is a copy of the Chantrey statue in Westminster Abbey, and is intended to commemorate the importance of the steam engine in the history of the city. He has been moved to a new site on the fringe of the water feature *(4)*, upstaging Victoria a little. Her Majesty would definitely not have been amused! The other statue of John Dalton (1855) was removed in the 1960s to make way for an electricity sub station (p.211). The old boy would probably have approved!

Piccadilly Gardens

Now take in the view over **Piccadilly Gardens**. The Infirmary had quite clearly outgrown the limitations of its location by the end of the 19th century. It was removed to a green field site on Oxford Road and the old building was demolished in 1909. Unfortunately, no-one knew quite what to do with the vacant area that remained. There were proposals for a library, an art gallery, even a new town hall, but they all came to nothing. Finally, it was turned into Piccadilly Gardens in the 1930s, a municipal park in miniature, with flower beds, a fountain, and a bandstand. Clearance of the Parker Street area (for a bus station) added to the sense of space. The whole area thus became one of the largest city squares in Britain, to which the name 'Piccadilly' was popularly applied. Sadly, the Gardens were allowed to decline after the 1960s, and the site was often used for fairground rides and the associated fast food stands. Piccadilly Gardens have recently been extensively remodelled, along with the entire context, though aspects of the design may not be everybody's cup of tea.

The Gardens area is framed by paved areas, with a **geometric pattern of squares** centred upon the Queen Victoria statue. The patterned paving is extended to every approach or 'gateway'. (The purpose is to bring together previously disassociated elements.) Traffic has been virtually eliminated in this new dispensation. Only Portland Street retains a normal flow of vehicles, shielded by a new building development. Piccadilly itself, from Oldham Street to Newton Street, is now a tree-lined Boulevard for the use of buses and taxis. Parker Street remains a bus station, while only the Metrolink trams disturb the Mosley Street side.

The principal new feature is the **Grove** *(5)*, a group of trees intended to be a focus of interest from both sides. They draw the eye towards the Market Street exit from the Gardens, whilst also providing an interesting feature on the other side by gradually becoming visible from Market Street itself. These trees are rooted in a wide paved area, pierced by the tramlines, which is an extension of the Market Street and Oldham Street pavements. The paving gives access to a pedestrian route across the Gardens by means of a **'catwalk'**. We cross a **water feature** *(6)*by this means, consisting of a phalanx of miniature fountains, illuminated at night, a feature intended to draw the eye to the **Gardens** themselves. Unfortunately, the effort is repaid by a minimalist interpretation, for all that most people will see is a clinical area of grass. One can't help thinking that some flowers would be nice. The pedestrian axis continues to the curved wall that indicates the Parker Street edge of the Gardens. The wall is the basis for a **Pavilion** *(7)*, on either side of the exit to the bus and tram station. One contains a convenient **café**. The pedestrian axis continues across the tramlines and the bus station to connect with the new Mall in Piccadilly Plaza, which is, in turn, the new gateway to Chinatown (p.123).

Take some time out to inspect the buildings on the opposite side of the **Boulevard** (Piccadilly), moving from left to right. The corner of Tib Street is graced by a **delightful conceit** of 1879, all brightly painted panelled bays and bands. The rather **new façade** stands on the site of the old Kardomah Coffee Company building (constructed in the Moorish style) that some idiot in planning allowed to be demolished. All is still not perfect in these enlightened times. Lever Hall and (latterly) the White Bear (see above) stood somewhere in this vicinity. The former **Piccadilly Picture Theatre**, to the right, opened in 1922, with a café, restaurant, and a dance hall in the basement, all in the 'beaux art' classical style. Despite a first rate location, the venture closed in 1937. The building stands on the site of the old Mosley hotel. An **'Italianate' office block** in York stone (1881) marks the Oldham Street corner.

The opposite corner used to be a branch of Woolworths, opened in 1928 where the Albion Hotel used to be. It was the scene of a spectacular and tragic fire in the 1970s, and the refurbished structure now contains ***Nobles' Amusements and Piccadilly Disco***. The windows can usually be relied upon to elevate kitsch into an art form. Next door is the **Manchester and County Bank**, also dating from 1928, with Ionic pilasters and a row of rather cute lions. The National Westminster Bank has now colonised the entire building, but the upper floors once constituted the Imperial Hotel, meant to be one of the finest in the city. However, the BBC took over in the 1930s, making it one of their regional headquarters (complete with studios) until the more recent move to Oxford Road.

Across Lever Street, **Weatherspoons** has opened a branch in 'palazzo' style offices of 1892. Notice the **small brick building** to the left, the sole survivor from the late eighteenth or early nineteenth century of what was the original building scale. Two buildings, that appear to be like bookends, box in the ***Gardens Hotel***. They were designed by the same architect, and obviously intended to flank a third that somehow never materialised. That to the left (1904) is 'Flemish revival' with tall gables. That to the right (1907) is Clayton House. One floor contains the **library of the Manchester and Lancashire Family History Society**, the ideal port of call if you are cultivating (or pruning?) your family tree. Visitors are welcome by appointment. The **main hotel building** between these two is the structure that stubbornly persisted. It is another 'palazzo' in sandstone from the 1880s, later the headquarters of Manchester Corporation Tramways. The city had the third largest tram system in Britain, but the last 'car' ran in 1949. Fortunately, this mode of transport has been reincarnated in the excellent Metrolink system as Manchester leads the field again. **St Margaret's Chambers** (1890s) is on the corner of Newton Street. This has a superb 'Elizabethan revival' frontage with huge gables and beautiful panels over the first-floor windows.

The view toward Portland Street is blocked by a rather 'naff' sixties retro brick box, an indication that planners and councillors can still be out of touch. The Portland Street side of Piccadilly, behind the new monstrosity, has **a fine range of warehouses**, reflecting Victorian vision and pride. (These buildings are described on p.119.) They can be reached by an arcade in the new structure.

Apart from the office block at the Market Street corner, the frontage of the former ***Lewis's*** largely occupies the **Mosley Street side** of Piccadilly. It is, in fact, an extension to the store, dating from 1929. The entrance to the former Lewis's arcade is still clearly visible (p.87).

Piccadilly Plaza

The remaining side of Piccadilly is the domain of ***Piccadilly Plaza***. The tall warehouses that stood behind Parker Street were destroyed in the 'Christmas Blitz' of 1940, creating the largest bombsite in Manchester. This was the scene of the first major post-war development in the city. Covell, Matthews, and Partners produced a 'spectacular' design that was to be the first phase in a project that would extend all the way to Oxford Road. Work commenced in 1959, but the entire *Plaza* was not completed until 1965. A nine-storey hotel is carried upon a concrete cradle, supported by columns and 'piloti'. Sunley Tower (24 storeys high, together with three floors of plant at the top) is curiously placed so that it is sideways on to the main viewpoint. And Bernard House was given an 'experimental roof' that reminded many Mancunians of a Chinese pagoda – 'honky tonk Han', perhaps. Finally, at street level, a shopping complex acted as a base for all these structures. The inhabitants of Manchester do not greatly love *Piccadilly Plaza*, nor can it be described as a successful building. It constitutes a barrier, blocking off Princess Street and Oxford Street in a way that few other buildings could do. It is surely haunted – blood curdling screams echo at night along the deserted malls, as the shade of Sir John Betjeman throttles the architect.

The Hotel did not get off to a good start, for a ceiling collapsed shortly after opening. However, the main problem was its design. The architects assumed that everyone would arrive by car, so the main entrance (approached from York Street, round the back!) was placed adjacent to the car park ramp on the top of the shopping areas. They no doubt expected that taxi drivers would welcome an unscheduled tour of part of the complex. Anyone seeking entry on foot had to find a way to the upper mall, and then look for a private escalator. It was thus possible to encounter, in Piccadilly Gardens, an exasperated individual (complete with dinner jacket and en route to a function) plaintively asking all and sundry how you "bloody well get into this place?" Hey presto! There is now a proper entrance at ground level in Portland

Street, and the ***Hotel Piccadilly*** could be recommended as one of the best places to stay in Manchester.

The Upper Mall 'Piazza' was a failure from the first, as the public stayed away in droves. By 1967, only eleven of the forty available shops had been let. Of course, the almost gale force winds that blew through the place (resulting from the down draft created by Sunley Tower) did not help matters. The provision of a fibreglass and Perspex overall roof did not solve the problem. Until a few years ago, an exploration of the almost deserted upper Piazza was like an excursion to the former East Berlin.

Although many would like to see the place blown up, another fate lay in store. The complex was purchased, for £22m, by Portfolio Holdings of London. A major refurbishment project began, though it is not expected to be complete before 2005. The old Piazza is no more, and new **arcades** have gone a long way to opening up the shopping area – two now lead to York Street *(8)*, acting as a 'gateway' to Chinatown. (p.123) (These are sometimes closed at weekends.) A very useful *Marks and Spencer* food supermarket has appeared at the Mosley Street corner. Bernard House has been replaced by a more conventional structure, but **Sunley Tower** (mainly occupied by government departments) awaits refurbishment, when it will be re-clad in a more acceptable style. Last, but not least, the old ghosts may be exorcised by a change of name to *Piccadilly Exchange*.

Mosley Street

Leave Piccadilly by Mosley Street, named in honour of the Mosley Family, once Lords of the Manor of Manchester. This conjures up some vision of a feudal knight, feasting his household and guests in the old hall crowning the bank of the Irwell. The truth is rather more prosaic. The Mosleys were minor gentry, who made their money in the 16th-century woollen trade. Nicholas Mosley represented the family business in London (he was Lord Mayor in 1599), but returned home to retire. He purchased the manorial rights of Manchester for £30,000, and the family ended up owning property and residences in and around the town. Nicholas was buried in the church at Didsbury, other family members at the old Collegiate Church. Despite supporting the King in the Civil War, their confiscated estates were later restored. Another generation supported the Pretender in the 1745 Jacobite rebellion, but this did not affect the family fortunes.

A large part of their income in the 18th century was derived from the market at Manchester, and a move to set up a rival market at Pool Fold (p.49) was ruthlessly crushed. The subsequent attempts by the family to use the archaic institutions of the town as their personal milch cow became so exasperating that they hastened the cause of municipal incorporation (p.78). After a great deal of haggling, the Corporation of Manchester purchased the manorial rights from the Mosleys in 1845. A later descendent of the family, Sir Oswald Mosley, achieved some political notoriety in the 1930s. A gifted and intelligent man, he was influenced by the radical economic ideas of the time. However, his participation as a minor minister in the second labour government resulted in a complete disillusionment with the British political system. He consequently flirted with fascism, and founded the British Union of Fascists, a decision that exiled him to the political fringe as a figure of ridicule. When visiting Hough Hall, the last ancestral Manchester home of the family, he spoke a profound truth. "I wandered through the deserted stables and outhouses ... perhaps we should never have left."

The new street was laid out in the last quarter of the 18th century. By 1791, it was a most fashionable address, a street of prestigious schools, places of worship, and public buildings. Nowadays, the banks and offices have taken over, but more than enough survives to interest the visitor. Moreover, it contains Manchester City Art Gallery, recently reopened after an extensive refurbishment, and incorporating a new extension.

Notable buildings

That part of the street facing Piccadilly has already been dealt with, so we start at the Metrolink Tram Station (which is only used by outward trams) alongside the continuing façade of Piccadilly Plaza. In contrast, the opposite side of the street is a riot of architectural invention. The ***Bradford and Bingley Building Society*** inhabits a Greek temple, complete with Corinthian fluted columns and a pediment, built for the Manchester and Salford Bank in 1836. ***Lloyds Bank*** occupies a brick building, with rusticated stone surrounds, and has colonised next door. Number 16, known as **Harvest House**, is an early version of the 'palazzo' style (1839). **Colwyn Chambers** (1898) graces the corner of York Street, once the Mercantile Bank. It is embellished with handsome Ionic columns and fluted pilasters. Crouching figures hold up an arched pediment on the corner door, enabling patrons to enter the hair salon of *Toni and Guy*.

None of these can compare with the gorgeous neo-classicism of the place where the ***Royal Bank of Scotland*** currently dwells. It was constructed for the Manchester and Salford Bank, who moved here from down the road in 1862. Oddly enough, if this bank's first building was the start of a new trend, its new home marked the end, for this is Edward Walter's swansong. The architect of the Free Trade Hall designed the last flowering of the 'palazzo' style in the city. Two impressive floors of Italianate pedimented windows surmount the tall banking hall, and the whole façade is rounded off at the top by an elegant balustrade. You don't have to be in need of funds to take time out and enter it, to enjoy the sumptuous banking hall. As most bankers know a good asset when they see one, the lights are often left on at night, so that the ceiling might be seen from the street. Pity about the modern light fittings, though. It is interesting to compare this building with the bank's modern branch across the street – **the only office building in Manchester with trees on the roof!**

Part of the old bank stands on the site of a house (at the York Street corner) in which Nathan Meyer Rothschild briefly resided. He was sent by his father from Frankfurt to buy Manchester goods, but departed to London in 1812. He later received news of Napoleon's escape from Elba a full 25 hours before the British government, a coup that led to the establishment of the family fortune in this country.

The later extension to the old bank covers the ground once occupied by the Assembly Rooms. Such a new and fashionable street obviously required a select place of assembly, for balls and refined social gatherings. The establishment opened in 1792, admission being restricted to those one hundred gentlemen (and their guests) who had each paid £70 towards the cost of erection. What did they get for their money? A first-floor ballroom, fifteen glass chandeliers, upholstered seats, Chinese wallpaper, card rooms, a tearoom and, presumably, the very best in female

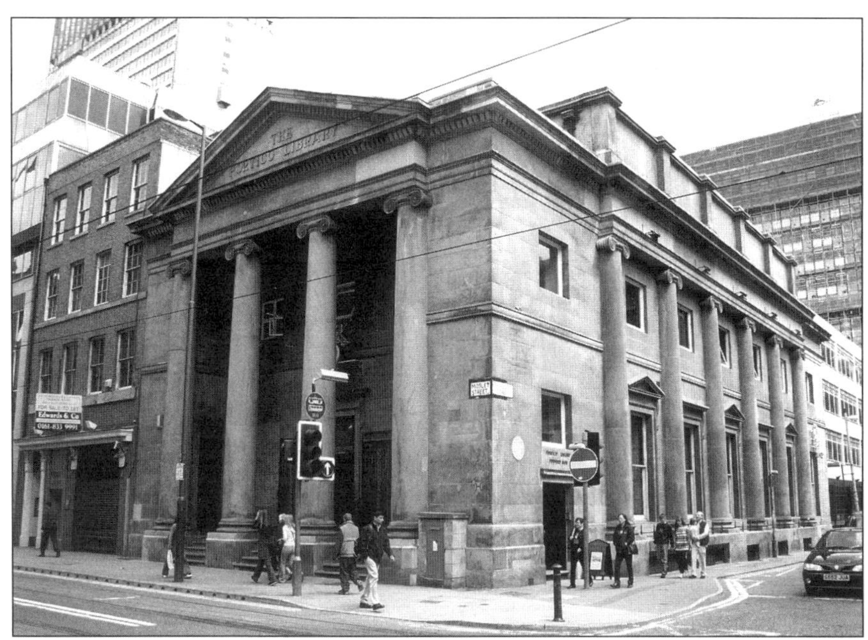

The Portico Library building, also housing the *Forgery and Firkin*

company, as the rules stated that gentlemen had to change partners after every second dance. Fashions change, the select people moved out of the street, and the Assembly Room contents ended up being sold at auction. The building itself was demolished in 1850.

Another gem lies at the corner of Charlotte Street. This is the **Portico Library**, so named for its fine neo-classical façade. One Robert Robinson, in the course of a visit to Liverpool, saw an impressive library and newsroom. He was told that it was a private facility, organised by some gentlemen of that town upon the basis of an annual subscription. What was good enough for Liverpool was surely good enough for Manchester. After some initial difficulty, a meeting of prominent townsmen took up the idea, and the library opened in 1806. Thomas Harrison, the celebrated Chester architect, designed the building, producing perhaps one of the finest examples of Classicism in the country. The roll call of members and users of the library down the years is illustrious, and includes John Dalton (p.46), Thomas De Quincy (p.23), and Paul Roget (of 'Thesaurus' fame).The place is still run as the founders intended, as it is owned by shareholding members who elect a management committee (new members are proposed and seconded by existing members). The members have access to newspapers and magazines, private reading rooms, and a service of refreshments. They can also request the purchase of books to add to the collection.

Do not be misled. The old bank premises, which fronted on to Mosley Street, are now transformed into the *Forgery and Firkin* (if you happen to like that sort of thing). Otherwise, go round the corner into Charlotte Street *(9)* and ring the bell for admission. (The library is open to visitors Monday-Friday, 9.30-4.30.) Walk up the stairs to the **'Portico Gallery'**, a large public room, often used for art exhibitions. Look up at Harrison's **great dome**, before fixing your gaze on the **portrait of Richard**

Cobden (p.37). Above it is a **wind gauge**, a dial connected to the rooftop weathervane, showing the direction of the wind. The walls are lined with books, the majority in antique leather bindings. The library's collection reveals much about the literary and academic tastes of past Mancunians. Several rare first editions of novels by Mrs Gaskell and the Brontë sisters were discovered in a stock check some years ago. Genuine researchers can, of course, use the library on application to the librarian.

On the opposite side of the road is perhaps the **most hideous building in the city centre**, built for the Royal London Assurance Company in 1973. After a tenancy by Eagle Star Insurance, it remained empty for a number of years.

The Manchester City Art Gallery

A little further on we come to the most important building on Mosley Street – **Manchester Art Gallery** (open Tuesday-Sunday and Bank Holidays, 10.00–5.00, free admission). The current Gallery is a complex of three buildings. Each is described, starting with the main (and earliest) structure facing Mosley Street. The 'Royal Institution of Manchester' owed its origin to a public meeting, held in 1823, to further the interests of literature, science, and the arts in the town. The organisation it created led to a venue in which lectures, scientific demonstrations, and exhibitions took place, in addition to functioning as a school of art and design. Sir Charles Barry (later known as the architect of the Houses of Parliament) was the winner of a competition for the design of the building, proposing an edifice in the best Grecian manner. He had studied classical architecture and absorbed the concept that beauty resulted from mathematical proportion. His 'non-de-plume' for the contest was "beauty is nothing without utility". It was erected between 1825 and 1834, and whatever was left of the original funds was spent on works of art.

By the last quarter of the 19th century, the Institution was in difficulties. Fortunately, the Corporation had been stung by criticism that such a progressive city could not provide itself with an art gallery. Manchester had become a laughing stock and the building and contents were thus purchased from the Royal Institution in 1882, on the understanding that a fixed sum of ratepayers' money would be spent annually for the next twenty years, on the purchase of works of art for the collection! One can imagine the response if this were to happen today.

(A note of caution. Despite a seemingly large area of new space for temporary exhibitions, the Manchester City Art Gallery has introduced a policy of changing the pictures in some of the smaller galleries from time to time. If your favourite picture is missing, be sure to complain!)

We enter the Gallery under the six-columned portico, pretty much as Barry intended. The **grand entrance hall** is lighted from the roof, and a wide staircase leads to a (now blocked) doorway. This formerly gave access to a large auditorium, which served as a lecture theatre. Stairs ascend from either side of the landing to a balcony around three sides of the hall. Look up, and note the **decorative casts of the Elgin Marbles**, the gift of George IV. (The originals are in the British Museum, and portray the annual procession to the Parthenon, in honour of the goddess Athena.) **Visitor information** (including the hire of audio guides) may be obtained from the small room to the left, and a cloakroom is located to the right. The entrance hall also accesses a large and well-equipped shop, a restaurant, and a café.

Manchester City Art Gallery and Atheneum annexe

The **CIS Manchester Gallery**, illustrating the history and topography of the city in works of art, is entered to the left of the hall. Ten themed displays highlight how art and design is woven into the fabric of Manchester.The display includes works by **L.S. Lowry** (p.245) and **Adolph Valette** (see below). **The MEN Exhibition Gallery** is adjacent. The ground floor of the new wing is devoted to the concept of 'life-long learning', and includes an **education centre** and a **lecture theatre**.

We climb the stairs to a series of galleries at first-floor level. Galleries one to three contain works from the 17th and 18th centuries, illustrating the development of painting in Britain and Europe. There was a gradual move away from religious subjects, although this area remained important. Increasingly, the classical world provided a vehicle for comment upon the human condition, usually in the form of an allegory. Landscape developed from an adjunct to composition into a subject in its own right. The wealthy required portraiture and the ideal of beauty was translated into the female nude. Techniques also changed – 'Mannerism', for example, distorted both proportion and perspective to produce an effect.

Two paintings depict different aspects of 18th-century British art in **Gallery One**. The large canvas of the **Cheetah and Stag with Two Indians** is by George Stubbs, one of the foremost animal painters in the history of European art. The painting commemorates a gift to George III from the Governor of Madras. Stubbs is able to capture the vitality of these exotic creatures, in the company of equally exotic attendants. There is also a fine Gainsborough, **A Peasant Girl Gathering Faggots**. This artist's work is an antidote to the stuffiness of much of the 18th-century classicism, introducing a freshness and naturalism to the subject matter.

Gallery Two depicts art in the era of the 'Grand Tour'. This was an extended educational holiday, in which aristocratic young men were expected to acquire experience of the world, and complete their education. They also acquired whatever artistic taste they had, often bringing back antiquities and works of art. The **Portrait of Sir Gregory Page Turner**, by Pompeo Batoni, is typical of a formal 18th-century portrait. Batoni resided in Rome, and specialised in painting rich and aristocratic gentlemen. Compare this with the portrait of **Miss Cornelia Knight**. It was painted by Angelica Kauffman, one of the few female artists in Western painting before the modern era. Although a founder member of the Royal Academy, she was not allowed to attend the 'life classes' held there! The subject was a personal friend, and the picture was painted out of love, as a gift. It shows.

English taste in this period also inclined towards the landscape, a genre that began to develop in the 17th century. The **Adoration of the Golden Calf**, by Claude Lorraine, illustrates a critical point in the evolution of the landscape. Although intended as a classical rendition of the biblical story (in the absence of Moses, the children of Israel revert to idolatry), the composition is set in a large landscape. The artist has manufactured the appearance of nature in an ideal way, but it has more or less taken over the picture.

Compare this with **Thomson's Aeolian Harp.** The harp in question is an ancient Greek invention, rediscovered in the 18th century. It is set up in a garden or rural setting, and produces music as the wind blows through the strings. However, despite the disporting nymphs, the picture is a great landscape of the Thames in the vicinity of Richmond. It is painted by the young J.W. Turner in his best academy manner, but is fresh and sparkling. His approach evolved into the style exemplified in 'Now For the Painter' in Gallery Four.

There are several large and monumental figure compositions, often exaggerating the physique to create a monumental effect. But ignore these classical allegories, and search out G.F. Watts' rendition of **The Good Samaritan** in **Gallery Three.** It portrays the rescue of the Jewish victim by the despised Samaritan in terms of almost Herculean figures. (Watts gave the painting to the city as a tribute to Thomas Wright, the 'prisoner's friend', see p.212.) The Gallery contains works representing 19th-century painting.

Gallery Four is devoted (more or less) to the 19th-century Romantic movement. Nowadays, we associate the word with Mills and Boon, but it originated with a whole philosophy based upon the primacy of the emotions. Storms were thus popular subjects, and the angry sea is the subject of **'Now For the Painter', (Calais Beach)** by J.M. Turner. A little joke of his, for the 'painter' referred to is a nautical rope! But the picture goes far beyond jokes and romantic metaphors. It is easy to see how his preoccupation with the light and shade in nature inspired the later Impressionists, as he raved on his deathbed, "the sun is God!".

The endeavours of the **Pre-Raphaelite Brotherhood** are displayed in galleries five and eight. This group of painters, as the name suggests, was convinced that art had lost its way after Raphael, seen by the Victorians as the peak of perfection in the Italian 'High Renaissance'. Thereafter, art had become entrapped in technique and conceited 'effects'. The answer was to go back to the simple beginnings of the Renaissance, in the late Middle Ages. Painters should paint a meaningful interpretation of what they see. Millais, Hunt, Brown, and Rossetti were part and parcel of a general fascination with the Gothic and the Mediaeval, which provided the context for religious, social, and political developments at the time. The rich industrialists and businessmen of Manchester eagerly purchased their paintings.

The paintings in **Gallery Five** are typical of their work. The **Hireling Shepherd**, by Holman Hunt (one of two versions), illustrates the saying in the gospels – only the true shepherd knoweth his sheep and will ultimately lay down his life for them. (Contemporaries also applied the metaphor to certain Victorian clergymen!) The work goes beyond biblical allegory, even beyond the depiction of the scene of dalliance. For we then concentrate our minds upon the incredible detail, as Hunt meticulously assembles his version of reality. (For the preliminary studies, an assistant in the studio held the sheep in particular positions.) The man was a perfectionist. Examples of his other work include **'The Shadow of Death'** (in which the young carpenter pauses in work, stretches, and the shadow cast predicts the later crucifixion) and **'The Light of the World'** ("behold, I stand at the door and knock"). The latter featured on a banner carried by one of the churches in the local Whit Walks (p.197).

'Work', by Ford Maddox Brown is an allegory of a different sort. We have here a message to the great 'Victorian Middle Class' concerning the importance and dignity of labour. Notice the bourgeois gentleman, whose way is impeded by the progress of the road works, the same way that his understanding is impeded by prejudice and ignorance. This little tableau is sardonically observed by the figures on the right. They are Thomas Carlyle and Frederick Maurice, Victorian thinkers who (like the artist) sympathised with the plight of the working man.

Many Pre-Raphaelite paintings may strike the casual visitor as odd. **The Scapegoat** (another version is at The Lady Lever Gallery, Port Sunlight) depicts the goat upon which the villagers have projected their sins and feelings of guilt, real or imagined. The poor animal is then released into the wilderness, in the belief that its imminent death will liberate the community. The allegory refers, on another level, to the redemptive sacrifice of Christ. The artist actually went to the shores of the Dead Sea to ensure realism – and presumably obtained a local goat! The neighbourhood bandits gave him a wide berth as he pretended to be mad by waltzing with his rifle – but they decided he was mad from the first. The picture has strange and haunting qualities, though whether it was worth the effort is another question.

Some of Dante Gabriel Rossetti's work, as in **The Bower Meadow**, has a curiously dreamy quality, and much of it portrays a mediaeval fantasy world. This approach may be contrasted with the work of John Millais, perhaps the most conventional painter of the brotherhood. **Autumn Leaves** exemplifies a more 'mainstream' version of the Pre-Raphaelite Brotherhood ethos.

We pass into the world of 'Victorian Life and Landscapes' in **Gallery Six**. Many visitors (like their Victorian ancestors) are drawn to the vast panorama and detail of William Frith's **Derby Day**, a painting teeming with dramatic incident. Frith's paintings were spectacles themselves when they went on view – policemen and barriers were employed to control the crowds. Nevertheless, 'domestic' dramas, the situations of everyday life, were also in vogue. James Tissot made a career out of this comedy of manners, as **'Hush'** clearly illustrates. Yet, it is worth noticing the 'social realism' approach to the dramas of everyday life. In some pieces, the darker side of life, the hideous gulf between the rich and the poor, is allowed to intrude.

In fact, the Victorians elevated the dramas of life into something approaching the intensity of a Greek tragedy, particularly in an historical garb. For they thought art had an educative, even a redemptive function. It must tell a story, and that story must have a moral. This began with scripture. Then, the moralising was extended into a school of 'history painting'. There are several examples of this genre in **Gallery Seven**. And so the knight of storybook legend enters the evil forest, armed only with a simple faith in God. You can capture the moment of decision in **In Manus Tuas Domine**, by Briton Riviere. The moralising often had an historical setting. **Prince Arthur and Hubert** illustrates the point when the little prince's gaoler must decide whether to carry out the orders of the King, and blind or kill the boy.

At the other end of the market, history became fun. Here is the **Chariot Race**, reconstructed for your delectation. And there is a **Viking Funeral**. In fact, historical reconstruction became something of an obsession. This 'auto didactic' approach became a straitjacket, almost dooming British art to a fate similar to that imposed by 'social realism' in Soviet Russia. But all was not lost, as we shall soon see.

We meet the Pre-Raphaelites again in **Gallery Eight**, along with other examples of late Victorian art. Rossetti's **Astarte Syriaca**, is an unusual departure for this artist. It depicts an earlier, cruel man-hating edition of the goddess transformed by the Greeks into Aphrodite. It is a portrait of Janey Morris, at the end of the affair. (The pomegranates are symbols of desire.) Rosseti was also a poet, and the painting accompanies a sonnet of his, part of which is quoted on the frame. You may pick out his portrait **Jolie Coeur**, which typifies the 'Pre-Raphaelite woman'. Notice a fine example of a refined form of 'history painting': Frederick, Lord Leighton, depicts the moment after the Greeks vanquish Troy. **Captive Andromache**, reduced to a mere servant, waits to draw water. She is thinking of her slain husband and children. Andromache, the isolated figure in the middle of the painting, may reflect the angst of the artist. Frederick Leighton had arrived – he was rich, had a fine house, and was the first British artist to be elevated to the peerage. But he always felt an outsider – he never married, never felt that he belonged anywhere in particular. It can also be seen in the work of Sir Lawrence Alma-Tadema. **Silver Favourites** is typical of this style of painting, and it is easy to see how the work of such artists influenced the 'Hollywood epic'.

Gallery Eight, is the final gallery of the old building. The displays in this gallery are subject to change.

The Art Gallery Extension

Returning to Gallery Five, we cross, by way of the **'glass bridge'**, to the new **Extension Building**. Directly ahead is the **Clore Interactive Gallery**, with a variety of exhibits (including those of a 'hands on' nature) designed to appeal to children. However, the greater part of the first floor level is given over to **Twentieth Century Art**. It is fairly predictable with all the usual suspects. Fortunately, the gallery has not greatly succumbed to the minimalist trend in abstract art, nor the diversions of abstract expressionism. The Tate Northern it ain't.

Gallery Fourteen, to the left, details the impact of the Post-Impressionists upon Britain. The portrait **Mama Mia Poveretta** is the work of **Walter Sickert,** the doyen of the British impressionists, and nominal head of the so-called 'Camden Town school'. (The work of Adolphe Valette is in another part of the complex.)

Go through to **Gallery Fifteen**. A rather idiosyncratic individual, Francis Bacon, is responsible for **Portrait of Henrietta Moraes on a Blue Couch**. His expressionist take upon the everyday perception of reality is particularly disturbing. The remaining gallery has a small selection of recent work.

Retracing our path, we now enter the old **Atheneum** building, fronting Princes Street. A word of explanation is required. The idea of an institution to promote the improvement of young men (in an entertaining and not too solemn way) originated with John Walker, a surgeon. The great-hearted doctor died of a fever, caught through his work in the local slums, but his idea lived on. It was launched at a public meeting in 1835 (the occasion of Richard Cobden's first public speech), resulting in £10,000 being raised in three weeks. The building opened with a banquet in 1839. It also was designed by Barry, proving to be the first manifestation of the popular 'Italian Renaissance' style in the town. Inside were coffee rooms, lecture halls, a fine library, and a gymnasium. Unlike the Mechanic's Institute (p. 142), the Atheneum tended to the wants of young managers and businessmen. So there was more of an emphasis on the social event than formal classes. Charles Dickens presided at a 'soirée' in 1843, and gave some of his 'dramatic readings' (murder of Nancy, death of Little Nell) here in later years, a practice that may have hastened his death. Ralph Waldo Emerson also put in an appearance. The Atheneum, like many things, outlived its usefulness, and the building was taken over by the Art Gallery as an annexe. It is now completely integrated into the Gallery complex.

Gallery Ten houses paintings by Adolphe Valette. Valette settled in Manchester, where he taught at the Art School (p. 214) and numbered Lowry amongst his pupils. His work is in the Post-Impressionist idiom, and he found the Manchester weather very much to his taste in depicting the vagaries of light and shade. Many notable Manchester landmarks are discernible in the paintings.

The room accesses two smaller galleries. That to the right is an interactive display relating to drawing, but that to the left (dedicated to religious pictures) includes some of the **oldest works in the collection**. They depict two contrasting artistic approaches, both rooted in the patronage of the late mediaeval church and its devotees. Many of these works were altar pieces, and it is well to remember that they were enclosed by hinged side panels, opened with ceremony on feast days, or at solemn moments in the liturgy, to the awe of the congregation. The side panels often depicted the donors, being presented as candidates for salvation by their patron saints. Other works were smaller, perhaps intended for private devotion.

The **Duccio Crucifixion** is a fine example of early Italian painting. Although we now value the skill and imagination of the individual artist, such works were often created on what amounted to a production line – the more talented apprentices painting the fabric, for example, and the master contenting himself with the finishing touches. These pictures were painted in tempera, a medium in which the pigment was mixed with the yoke of an egg. It dried extremely quickly, so the work was executed in short, thin brush strokes. Shading required the parallel strokes of different gradations of colour. From such beginnings, Italian artists systematised the art of drawing and painting. This can be placed within the context of a rediscovery of the old learning, involving Platonic debates about the nature of beauty and mathematical proportion, leading to a discovery of the principles of perspective, composition, and colour. The nature of this process is illustrated by a number of works, which also denote the introduction of oil painting to Italy as a technique.

In contrast, the work of the northern school (concentrated on Flanders) developed from the craft of manuscript illustration. The Flemish artists invented oil painting in which the pigment was mixed with linseed oil. The medium was malleable and slow drying – amazing effects could be obtained by mixing (or overlaying) one stroke with another. The Flemish masters painted what they saw. They were not interested in abstract ideas of the nature of reality, for they merely wished to record it for posterity. Look at the panel of the **Virgin and Child**, and see that they have gone a long way to creating the first portraiture. The tradition of religious painting continues, as may be seen in the strange **A Village in Heaven (Cookham)**, painted by that interesting individualist, Stanley Spencer.

Gallery Eleven contains changing displays drawn from the print and drawing collection. Proceed into **Gallery Twelve**, titled 'Life and Death in the Seventeenth Century'. The majority of the works displayed are **Dutch Genre**, part of the valuable Assheton Bennet collection. Dutch painting of this period is perhaps an acquired taste. Although clever in execution, one can only view so many tavern scenes, churches, domestic interiors, ships, the contents of kitchen tables, and frozen water with equanimity. It tends to shade off into a mere assemblage of objects and possessions, which some historians have ascribed to a developing 'bourgeois mentality'.

However, **Sir Thomas Aston at the Deathbed of his Wife** is undoubtedly English in origin. This odd painting is the work of John Souch, the 17th-century Chester heraldic painter. He started his life painting ceremonial coats of arms, but evidently received some artistic training (probably in the Netherlands) before turning to portraiture. Thomas's wife is shown both alive and dead, and it has been suggested that the family heads were taken from life in preparation for a portrait celebrating the impending birth. Alas, both mother and child perished. The picture is full of rich symbolism. The son, for example, holds a cross-staff, an instrument of navigation. This is not only emblematic of the Christian cross, but also indicates that the stars in their courses might be measurable, but poor Thomas's grief is not.

The top floor (a vast high-ceiling room, once the Atheneum's theatre) has been turned into a **Gallery of Craft and Design**, containing an introduction to decorative art, craft, and design, over 1,300 pieces in all, displayed in a thematic way. The original fine moulded ceiling is particularly noteworthy. The **fine silver** from the Assheton-Bennet bequest is located near the entrance, with the Thomas Greg collection of **British ceramics** to one side. Turn left, and proceed around the large room in a clockwise direction. Small children will be immediately drawn to the **historic doll's house** of 1850 and the other dolls and toys collected by Mary Greg.

Items associated with **'personal rituals'** include a **cosmetic jug** (illustrated with a cartoon of 'old women ground young'!). A superb **christening robe** exemplifies the theme of **'life events'**, while a number of items such as **tea pots and caddies** introduce **'social rituals'**. The displays are now themed according to the material or technique of manufacture – **artefacts made of glass and wood** (particularly furniture). A variety of objects constitute a **'touch experience'** along one of the walls, before we explore the world of synthetic materials, including plastics. The display themes now move on to **shape and colour**, before returning to the social context of **applied art and craft**. Objects utilised in **religious ritual and devotion** represent the 'spiritual' life. Amongst them may be found the exquisite **Madonna With a Goldfinch**, an early Italian work, painted in tempera on a (gilded) wooden panel. (Legend has it that a goldfinch once impaled itself upon Christ's crown of thorns, thus accounting for the hue of its breast. Thus, in the picture, is the cosmic event foretold.) The **'telling tales'** section is full of souvenir items, but the **'industrial'** section is perhaps more significant. Here, the exhibits derive from the former Horsefall Museum in Ancoats, intended to educate and inform the late Victorian working class about the development of industrial design and artistic taste. The rest of this floor, overlooking Nicholas Street, contains a **Temporary Exhibitions Gallery**.

Princess Street

After regaining Mosley Street, turn right into Princess Street. Look out for the superb patterned brick of the **office chambers** (1870s) on the corner of Cooper Street, and **the row of 18th-century houses** (now fronting a *Weatherspoons* pub) beyond. Cross over to the **Messenger of Peace** (Barbara Pearson, 1986), a popular and much-photographed statue *(10)*. It is placed in a small paved area with seats, an ideal spot to while away the time on a fine day. On one side is the shortest side of the Town Hall, and an entrance surmounted by a statue of Edward the Elder, the Saxon King who re-occupied Manchester after the Danes had been expelled. On the other lies the greenery of the **Peace Gardens**. Both the statue and the gardens symbolise a time in the seventies and eighties when Manchester City Council, rightly or wrongly, espoused the cause of peace with grand political gestures; the most controversial of these was the declaration that the city had become a 'nuclear free zone'. The gardens contain a **foundry pattern** of a cogged wheel, meant to symbolise Manchester's industrial past.

The **Tourist Information Centre** is directly opposite the Peace monument. In addition to dispensing information, the Centre can book accommodation (visitors can book ahead to other town and cities on their itinerary, in addition to Manchester), sell bus and train tickets, and handle bookings for theatre and other entertainment venues. It also has a well-stocked shop for the purchase of books and souvenirs. A programme of walking tours, most of which start at the Centre, can be recommended.

The TIC is housed in the **Town Hall Extension** (1934-1938). The sandstone exterior of this building is plain, but rather striking. Colonnades on both the Mount Street and St Peter's Square sides gave access to gas and electricity showrooms (these municipal departments were very commercially minded). The passage side, adjacent to Central Library boasted a magnificent **curving counter area**, where people came to pay their bills. Parts of it are still visible through the windows. The first floor still contains the **Council Chamber**. (The seating, for 145 councillors, is of English oak with hogskin upholstery.) There is an associated library, ante-room, and panelled committee rooms. You can, if you wish, see the spectacle of council business transacted from the public gallery – but only do so if you have a real interest in 'parish pump' matters.

The way lies along the colonnade, but notice (to the left) what has been described as **'the most expensive playground in the world'** *(11)*. Certainly, a great deal of stone and tasteful wrought iron was used in its construction, but the toddlers from the Town Hall crèche greatly enjoy it, as might be demonstrated on a fine day. Another sculpture now appears. Popularly known as the **Burghers of Manchester** *(12)*, the actual title is 'Struggle for Peace and Freedom' (Philip Jackson, 1988). The group of figures forms a solid wall as they advance forward, indicating that unity of purpose is strength.

St Peter's Square

St Peter's Square has now been reached. It is named after St Peter's Church, which once stood in the midst of it. The Reverend Samuel Hall, formerly the curate of St Ann's, founded the church – and thereby hangs a tale. He was also honorary chaplain to the Volunteers, and omitted the Athanasian Creed at church parades in deference to the nonconformists in the ranks. For this heinous offence, he was refused election as a Fellow of the Collegiate Church when a vacancy occurred. His disgusted supporters rallied round, raised the necessary funds, and built him St Peter's church. Consecrated in 1794, it was a rather grand affair, with a steeple (added in 1822) and an equally grand and very fashionable congregation. This state of affairs soon changed, and the congregation had all but disappeared by the turn of the century. The building was demolished in 1907. The fine organ, at one time said to be the largest in England, was removed to another church, now also demolished. It was last sighted in a warehouse in Lincolnshire, but its present whereabouts are unknown. The painting from over the altar is now in St Ann's, (p.38). But what to do with the large underground vault, crammed full of decaying coffins? It was deemed best to seal it, and then turn the site into gardens. A commemorative **stone cross** *(13)*, with suitable inscriptions, was placed in the gardens in 1908.

After the Great War of 1914-1918, a war memorial was erected. Like many British towns and cities, Manchester opted for a **cenotaph**. (The original, in London, was designed by Lutyens, and was intended to symbolise an empty tomb.) Note the recumbent effigy of a soldier on the top, like a fallen mediaeval knight, a paladin of chivalry. The memorial now also honours the dead of the Second World War and other conflicts *(14)*. There are **individual memorials** to the Manchester Italians, who fought as brothers in arms, 1915-1918; to the dead of the Korean War,

St Peter's Square and the Central Library

1950-1953; and a special memorial, the gift of the Royal British Legion. On Armistice Sunday, the trams stop, a short service is held, and wreaths are laid. A two-minutes silence at 11.00am (the time the guns stopped in 1918) ends with the sounding of the 'last post' and 'reveille' on the bugles. Afterwards, members of the public place their poppies or crosses of remembrance on the lawn area.

> When you go home,
> Tell them of us, and say:
> "For your tomorrow,
> We gave our today."

Central Library

The Square might have been expanded to make a fine civic space, but the plot of land on the corner of Dickinson Street (occupied by **Century House**, dating from 1934) was allowed to go to a developer by default of one council vote! **Elizabeth House** (1959-1960), dominating one side of the Square, is a nondescript box. (It should have been stone clad, but the money ran out.) However, **Central Library** redeems the appearance of the Square. The saga of the municipal library in Manchester is told elsewhere (p.188). Suffice it to say that the City Fathers decided to make a grand gesture, and build the largest municipal library in Britain. Designed by Vincent Harris, and modelled on the Pantheon, the great steel framed circular structure dates to 1934 (the **foundation stone inscriptions** repay inspection). The lower levels are clad in rusticated stone, the upper storeys are hidden behind Doric columns, and a **grand portico** fronts the main entrance. The Library has suffered from financial stringency in recent years, and is, in many ways, a shadow of its former self. As a major regional asset, it should not rely on the City council for its

Central Library

upkeep. There really ought to be a levy, to which the other local authorities and the local universities and colleges (whose students seem to take over the place at term time) ought to contribute. And then there might be balm in Gillead once more.

We pass under the classical portico, and continue through the doorway to arrive in the grand **entrance hall**. Turn round, for a moment, to inspect the **stained glass windows** depicting characters from Shakespeare. The **roof** is decorated with the arms of Manchester and the other heraldic devices associated with the region.

The **Commercial Library** is to the left. In addition to company information and similar reference material, it also contains a European Union Briefing Unit. A rather lacklustre **Lending Library** is to the right. (Most of the serious lending stock is now upstairs. Goodness knows why.) A lift may be found opposite the main entrance, but it is far better to use the staircases on either side.

There is a ***coffee bar*** in the basement, together with the **Library Theatre**. In this small and intimate theatre, a repertory company present a mixed programme of old favourites (particularly whatever Shakespeare is on the exam syllabus) and new work. A children's production always features at Christmas. Look out for the **portrait of Miss Horniman** (p.113).

Ascend one of the grand staircases, and enter the Social Science Reading Room, under the **Great Dome**. This is the largest reading room outside the (old) British Museum library, with accommodation for over 300 readers. It is surrounded by an apt **quotation from Ecclesiastes**, and has a superb echo – you can sometimes hear a page being turned! The original conception has largely survived. Books and other reading matter are ordered from the central desk, above which towers the **clock and its Baroque mounting**. The great desks, some sporting the carved mementoes of previous generations of readers, fill the rest of the space. (Sadly, uniformed attendants no longer deliver the requested items to your seat.) The large metal light stands, and the bookcases lining the circular walls, are also original. The latter once contained a variety of reference works, but now are full of lending stock.

An outer circular passage accesses a series of specialist libraries, including the **Technical Library** (with a Patent Library within), the inevitable internet facility, a **microfilm study area** (usually populated by those in search of their family tree), and a **Local Studies (History) Library**. The large Jewish community in the city created the **Jewish Library**, one of the most important in the country. Unfortunately, financial cuts have resulted in it being dispersed in the general Social Science stock.

Take the lift to the next floor for the **Art Library** and the **Henry Watson Music Library**. Henry Watson, an ordinary Mancunian, amassed a collection second to none, including many rare musical scores. The **Language and Literature Library** is located on the top floor.

The Midland Hotel

We leave the Library, and make our way towards the ***Midland Hotel*** (now the Crowne Plaza Manchester – The Midland Hotel) at the top end of the Square. The Midland Railway, inspired by William Towle (their very capable hotel chief), decided to build one of the greatest hotels in Europe in the city of Manchester. The hotel opened, to great applause, in 1903, and rapidly became a Manchester institution. It had everything – 400 luxurious bedrooms, a French restaurant, a Turkish bath, winter gardens, a ballroom with a sprung floor, and its own theatre. An

The view across Windmill Street towards the impressive rear elevation of the Crowne Plaza Manchester – The Midland Hotel

orchestra (with vocal renditions) played at dinner, a string quartet at lunch and tea, and there was even music on the famous roof garden (the bass player wore a cloth cap on breezy days), a favourite place to take tea on a fine day. The hotel went through a sticky patch after the last war, and did not really move with the times. (David Hockney, it is said, was refused admission for wearing odd socks.) However, after a thorough restoration programme, the hotel is back where it belongs, and is awash with celebrities once more – see if there are any teens waiting at the entrance to catch sight of their current idol.

Charles Trubshaw, the company's architect, produced a rather florid design, combining a variety of styles, but had the good sense to choose glazed terracotta for the exterior surfaces (granite is employed in the lower section). Thus, the building effectively cleans itself. The **two large arches** were cab entrances and exits. Look for the **Wyvern**, a mythological beast representing the Saxon kingdom of Mercia, which featured in the railway's coat of arms. There is a **memorial tablet,** within the entrance on the right, to the historic meeting of Charles Rolls and Henry Royce, an event that took place in 1904. The two were like chalk and cheese. Rolls was a rich playboy, with a passion for fast cars and flying. Royce was a gruff, no-nonsense engineer, struggling to build motor cars in a back street in Hulme. But they genuinely hit it off, and Royce was deeply upset when his partner was killed in a flying accident.

Enter without fear, for even 'posh' places are friendly enough in this part of the world. Taking tea at the Midland is fun (served between 2.30 and 5.30pm). The **grand entrance hall** once led to a now vanished Winter Garden at the heart of the building. The **Octagon Court**, to the left, is beneath a light well that was once taller, and capped with a glass dome. On New Year's Eve, a lavish ball would be held. When the wealthy businessmen and their guests were celebrating at the bar in the Court area, it was the custom for the youngest resident of the hotel (in the days when the staff lived in) to be lowered down to the floor in a basket. These rich men would then pin banknotes to the baby or toddler's blanket as a good luck gesture for the coming year. There are resident ghosts. The 'grey lady' scared the life out of a group of airline cabin crew some years ago. (It made such an impression on them that they always asked to be shown the room in question on subsequent visits.) She is said to have been an elderly guest who made the hotel her home (a common practice before the war). Apparently, the spirit resents her room being let to anyone else – though she is now at peace as the room is now used as a store. A charming small girl also sometimes appears to guests.

Peter Street

Upon leaving the hotel, turn left and proceed down Peter Street. This thoroughfare was created in 1790, linking Deansgate with the new road to the south. Within a few decades, it had become the entertainment centre of the city, crowded with theatres, music halls, and 'gin palaces'. After a relatively fallow period, entertainment is once more to the fore, in the form of new bars and discos.

St George's House, adjacent to the Midland, was formerly the home of the Young Men's Christian Association, who moved to this site in 1875. In 1911, the present structure was built, a beautiful concoction of terracotta, with art nouveau panels, all set off by a **reproduction of Donatello's statue of St George**. It was the first building with a reinforced concrete frame in the city, indeed, one of the first in the country. This supported a large hall, a cinema, smoking lounge, a dining room, a swimming pool on the fourth floor, and a gymnasium (with a 'galleried' running track) on the sixth! The YMCA decided to sell the building and use the proceeds to finance the new 'Y' Hotel in Castlefield, and it is now converted into offices.

St George's house occupies the location of the Natural History Museum (as the street round the corner testifies). The Manchester Society for the Promotion of Natural History started in 1821, and opened the Museum in 1835. At first, it was purely for the use of the members, but the collection was expanded and the public soon admitted. The contents were offered to Owen's College (p.61) in 1867, and some of the exhibits can still be seen at the Manchester Museum. One former exhibit definitely not on display is the 'Mummy of Birchin Bower'. Hannah Beswick, who lived at this isolated country spot, had a dread of being buried alive. She consequently arranged with her doctor, Charles White, for her body to be kept above ground. She died in 1758, and Dr White embalmed her with tar, leaving the face exposed. Eventually, he removed her to his house, where she was kept in the case of a grandfather clock! Her face appeared where the dial should be, covered in a velvet cloth. Once a year, as the will instructed, two "witnesses of credit" were procured, the cloth drawn back, and an inspection was made for signs of life. At length, the 'mummy' became an exhibit at the Museum in Peter Street, alongside the stuffed remains of

Billy, a celebrity carthorse that had lived 61 years. The old girl was finally laid to rest (presumably quite dead) at Harpurhey Cemetery in 1868. However, something must still trouble her, for she haunts the electronics factory in Failsworth that now stands on the site of Birchin Bower.

Television House (1959-1960), the first home of Granada Television in Manchester, is situated on the right-hand corner of Mount Street.

A **blue plaque** on the building marks the site of the vanished Gaiety Theatre. This place had its heyday just before the First World War, under the redoubtable cigar-smoking Annie Horniman. Miss Horniman liked to encourage new talent, even if considered a little 'avant guard'. Her audience was satirised as comprising "intellectuals from the university, vegetarians, nature lovers, weekend hikers in the Derbyshire hills, and general marchers in the advanced guard of public opinion". (This fantasy description still haunts readers of the Daily Mail.) In this context, Stanley Houghton and Harold Brighouse created the 'Manchester school' of playwriting, a new form of social realism all the more potent because it was shot through with humanity and humour and featured strong female characters. 'Hindle Wakes' and 'Hobson's Choice' are still widely performed by amateur groups in the region, and are sometimes revived in repertory. Like many theatres, it was haunted. Now that the Gaiety is no more, does the ghostly flute music still echo on the site?

The **Theatre Royal (*Infinity*)**, the last remaining theatre building on the street, is next door to St George's House. After the second theatre of that name burned down, the present one opened in 1845 with a performance of 'Time Works Wonders'. (The owners were taking no chances this time, for a 20,000-gallon water tank was placed in the roof space.) Notice the classical portico and the **statue of a rather smug Shakespeare**. The roll call of the great who have trod the boards here is long, and includes Henry Irving, Macready, and Jenny Lind. The first performance of *La Bohème* in English was given here in 1897, with Puccini in the audience. The theatre also pioneered that grand institution, the Christmas pantomime, in Manchester. It now contains a rather large disco.

The Free Trade Hall

We have now arrived at one of the major sights of the city. The façade of the imposing **Free Trade Hall** dominates the left side of Peter Street. In 1815, a British government dominated by a landed aristocracy passed the notorious Corn Laws, which restricted the importation of grain until the home price had reached eighty shillings a quarter. It was a measure designed to safeguard agricultural rents, then the principal source of income for the political establishment. But, for the poor, it meant high bread prices. And much else besides. The law was seen as a direct challenge to the free trade principles of the new industrial and commercial elite. The new urban middle class would assert itself and involve itself in the political process by targeting the Corn Laws. In the aftermath of Peterloo (p.131), it would enlist the support of the new working class. And Manchester would lead the way.

The Anti Corn Law League is perhaps the first example of a successful pressure group in modern politics. In 1840, Richard Cobden (p.37), a founder member, gave a plot of land on Peter Street for the use of the society. A temporary wooden pavilion was erected in eleven days, and opened by a banquet at which Daniel ('The Liberator') O'Connel was a guest. John Bright (p.44) made his debut as the delegate for

Rochdale. A second, larger, building was erected in 1843, with a roof supported by iron pillars. Both structures were venues for a variety of political meetings and fund raising activities. Fortunately, Sir Robert Peel (p.93) was able to persuade the old Tory aristocracy to agree to repeal of the measure, thus reconciling the existing political establishment to the new industrial elite, and creating the modern Conservative party. The law was repealed in 1846, but did not finally come into operation until 1849. A great banquet was held in the hall, and at midnight the chairman called out "the Corn Law is dead!" This was followed by three cheers, then everyone burst into a rendition of a popular song of the time – 'There's a Good Time Coming'.

The Free Trade Hall – by kind permission of the Hallé Concerts Society

Meanwhile, the hall had been used for a variety of events, ranging from amateur theatricals starring Charles Dickens and Wilkie Collins to Chartist (p.66) meetings. Consequently, a private company was formed to build a third hall, and the present building, designed by Edward Walters (and probably inspired by the Gran Guardia Vecchia at Verona), was inaugurated in 1856. The frontage is in the Lombardo Venetian style, with carvings by John Thomas. The **arms of the towns** associated with the movement appear in the spandrels of the arcade arches. **Allegorical figures** appear between double columns with Ionic capitals. The **figures over the windows** represent 'Arts', 'Manufactures', 'Commerce', and 'Agriculture'. 'Free Trade' is depicted as a female figure in a central position, her arms extended to receive the products of all nations. The building was badly bombed and the interior was reconstructed after the last war.

In addition to becoming the home of the Hallé Orchestra (p.135), the Free Trade Hall has witnessed many notable speeches and events. Charles Dickens, Winston Churchill, and the Sex Pistols have all appeared here. On a night in 1966, the audience booed Bob Dylan and chanted 'Judas' when he eschewed folk for rock music

The Albert Hall

and famously took up an electric guitar in his second half. With the opening of the Bridgewater Hall, the future was unsure. A plan to graft on to it an appalling tower development was fortunately defeated. However, the Free Trade Hall is now the *Radisson Edwardian Manchester*, with 263 rooms, two 'presidential suites', and 18 'de-luxe' winter garden rooms, together with a conference centre. The contrast between the old and the new building is not as shocking as might be supposed.

Continue down Peter Street as far as the new square (p.58). The Methodist church opened the **Albert Hall**, opposite, as a meeting centre in 1910. It has been reincarnated as *Brannigans*, a nightspot with a reputation for raucous (but friendly) entertainment – "eating, dancing, and cavorting," as the notice says. This probably explains the angry behaviour of the ghost, a malevolent entity said to reside in the tower.

Retrace your footsteps and turn left under the arch across Marron Place *(15)*. Watch out for police vehicles, for the archway is in line with the courtyard entrance of the **Manchester City Police Headquarters**, on Bootle Street. This building (a structure in ferro-concrete around a central parade ground, with a large underground area) opened in 1936. The whole is faced in Portland stone. (The Manchester force is now part of Greater Manchester Police. For the Police Museum, see p.162). The ***Sir Ralph Abercrombie***, a pub dating to the early 19th century, lies down Bootle Street in the Deansgate direction. (Lunchtime food available.) Though now forgotten, Abercrombie was a hero of the Napoleonic Wars. Along with Sir John Moore, he reorganised and reformed the British army, making it an instrument of victory in the hands of the Duke of Wellington. Abercrombie met a tragic end in battle. As he lay dying, he asked what he was lying on, and was displeased when he found out. "Only a soldier's blanket! Be sure to return it to him immediately!" It is said that a victim of 'Peterloo' (p.131) expired on the bar, though this may be a reference to a jury viewing a body at an inquest, often held in pubs at the time.

Friends Meeting House

Turn round, and retrace your steps. The entrance to ***The Little Bookshop***, on the left, is easily missed *(16)*. This second-hand bookshop can be recommended, and the friendly proprietor is very knowledgeable. It is in the basement of the **Friends Meeting House**, which we reach by turning left into Mount Street. The Society of Friends, which most people know as the Quakers, was founded by George Fox (who had visited Manchester as a young man) in the aftermath of the English Civil War. The earliest stronghold was in Cumbria and Lancashire, and the tradition continues. Quakers believe that the spirit of God enters the soul of the individual during periods of quietness and contemplation. There is no structure to their religious meetings. Anyone can say (or sing!) what is in their hearts. Quakers are pacifists – but they have served as medical personnel (often under fire or in places of danger) in both World Wars. Because of their tolerant outlook, and sympathy for social reform, the Meeting Houses are sometimes used by a variety of groups advocating many causes – as is the case here.

The original Meeting House was located on Deansgate, but the congregation grew too large. It moved to the present site in 1795, and it is said that this first building offered sanctuary to those fleeing from St Peter's Fields in 1819 (p.131). The present Meeting House, with a fine classical frontage, dates from 1830. It was the place of worship of John Dalton (p.46) and, rather curiously, Thomas Edmondson (inventor of the railway ticket), and George Bradshaw (editor of the first railway timetable). The interior is much altered, and not of any particular interest, though some of the **early gravestones** still survive at the side of the building.

The adjacent ***Citrus Restaurant*** inhabits the ground floor of a building formerly used by the Inland Revenue (1874), hence the **royal beasts** either side of the main entrance. (Victoria herself is on the Mount Street side.) Note, also, the fine carved supports for the projecting oriel windows. The opposite side of the street is taken up by the Town Hall extension, complete with an **interesting foundation stone**, and Central Library. Walk down the **impressive curved passageway** *(17)* between the two, and find yourself back at St Peter's Square.

The Elizabethan, Italianate and French Renaissance architecture of the S. and J. Watts warehouse – now the Britannia Hotel

6 Piccadilly to Knott Mill

Start: Piccadilly Gardens

Estimated time of walk: 1½-2 hours

Highlights: The greatest warehouse in Manchester, Chinatown and the Chinese Arch, an upside-down building, the site of the Hacienda, Sir Lancelot's encounter, G-Mex, 'Peterloo', and the Bridgewater Hall.

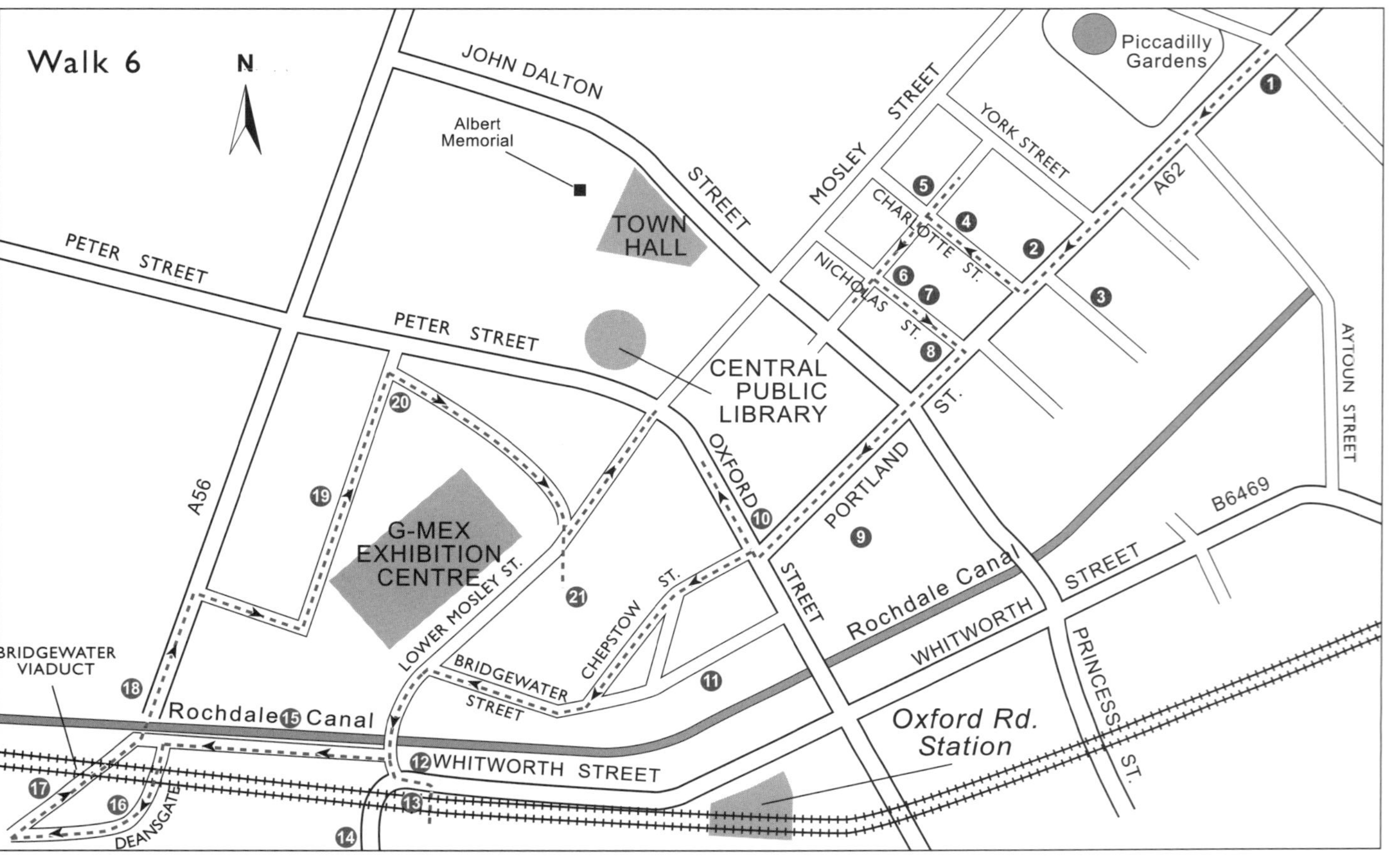
Walk 6
N
JOHN DALTON STREET
Albert Memorial
TOWN HALL
Piccadilly Gardens
MOSLEY STREET
YORK STREET
A62
CHARLOTTE ST.
NICHOLAS ST.
PETER STREET
PETER STREET
CENTRAL PUBLIC LIBRARY
PORTLAND ST.
AYTOUN STREET
OXFORD STREET
B6469
A56
G-MEX EXHIBITION CENTRE
LOWER MOSLEY ST.
CHEPSTOW ST.
BRIDGEWATER STREET
Rochdale Canal
WHITWORTH STREET
PRINCESS ST.
BRIDGEWATER VIADUCT
Rochdale Canal
WHITWORTH STREET
Oxford Rd. Station
DEANSGATE

Once more, sally forth from Piccadilly. This time, we leave the area by way of Portland Street, paralleling the routing of the previous walk for a large part of the way before exploring an area that epitomises the regeneration of the city from industrial dereliction. It also touches upon a spot where an event took place that changed the course of British history.

Portland Street

Portland Street itself is a mid-Victorian creation. Imagine a narrow country road, winding from here to the banks of the Medlock, passing Garret Hall (p.147). Then think of part of this ancient thoroughfare being transformed into a wide street so that it would communicate with Oxford Street, well placed on the fringe of a fashionable district extending across from Mosley Street, a district complete with a new church. Finally, consider a great change in the textile industry, with the introduction of modern means of mass marketing and distribution. The latter came to pass in the second half of the 19th century, when Manchester became the principal distribution centre for the trade in cotton cloth, and Portland Street (and the district around it) became the warehouse quarter.

A new generation of ever larger and greater warehouses were designed for a new generation of merchants, often in the renaissance 'palazzo' style or more northern Gothic. Both styles recalled the 'merchant princes' of Flanders and Italy in the Middle Ages. The new structures soon evolved a standard plan. The ground floor and basement were devoted to packing, usually using hydraulic or steam powered presses. Goods came and went by a cart entrance to one side or round the back. A far grander entrance (complete with staircase) led to the showrooms and offices on the first or second floors. The remaining floors were used for storage, accessed by a number of hoists.

As indicated in the previous walk, the Portland Street side of Piccadilly is masked by an office block. This is a pity, as it has **a fine range of warehouses** *(1)* reflecting Victorian vision and pride. (Unfortunately, the Queen's Hotel of 1845, which stood on the Piccadilly corner, has been replaced by a conventional steel frame box of bronzed glass, but the rest of the frontage more than makes up for this loss.) The tallest structure in the middle of this warehouse group, six storeys high, was constructed with a York stone and ashlar façade in 1852 for the firm of Kershaw, Leese, and Sidebottom. At street level, it is distinguished by a fine arcade (ornamented with wreaths) supporting a principal floor or 'piano nobile' marked by window pediments. The top storey is a more modern addition, way above the cornice. The E. and J. Jackson warehouse of 1858, on the left, is a more modest and plainer affair (though still rather grand, with a suite of fine rooms on the second floor indicated by arched window pediments). However, the façade to the right of the central building continues with large rusticated arches enclosing a semi-basement (the second storey is again the main floor). It was built all of a piece with the central warehouse in 1851-2 for Brown and Son. All three structures are the work of Edward Walters, the architect of the Free Trade Hall. He seems to have cornered the market in warehouse design for a time.

Both the Jackson and the Kershaw warehouses now form the ***Portland Thistle Hotel***, with little but the façades remaining. The Brown warehouse, at the corner of Aytoun Street, is the **headquarters of the Greater Manchester Passenger Trans-**

port Authority and its associated Executive. This body is responsible for planning a public transport strategy for the area, and is attempting to co-ordinate and improve local train, bus, and tram services, a task not made easier by misguided deregulation and privatisation policies.

The other corner of Aytoun Street was the **former headquarters of Greater Manchester Council**. The Greater Manchester County was formed in 1974, with the object of providing a strategic authority for an area of 2.7m people (the third largest Metropolitan County in Britain). It was responsible, amongst other things, for strategic planning; fire, police, and ambulance services; major transport infrastructure; and tourism development. In the latter field, it created Country Parks based on the river valleys and initiated the Castlefield development. The municipalities retained responsibility for purely local matters. Unfortunately, relations with some of the more boneheaded local councils were often strained. The authority was abolished in an act of gross political spite by the Thatcher government. In some ways, the Greater Manchester area is still recovering from the consequences of that act. The GMC was housed in a bleak six-storey box, built in 1971. A concrete lid tops the alternating bands of brick, concrete, and glass. The street-level podium has since been opened out with the provision of glass windows and retail facilities.

From S. and J. Watts to the Britannia Hotel

Stand in front of the **former Bank of England Northern Headquarters** (Fitzroy, Robinson, and Partners, 1971). This Lego-like structure consists of twelve storeys of bronze glazing and black-and-white cladding, placed on a concrete podium fronted with polished black granite *(2)*. Now look across the road. The **S. and J. Watt's Warehouse (*Britannia Hotel*)** is the finest and most spectacular warehouse in the city, with a street frontage of 300ft (91m) and a façade 100ft (30m) high. The brothers Samuel and James came to Manchester to seek their fortunes, and built up a fabulous commercial empire, traces of which may be seen all over the city. James, in particular, was typical of the 'Manchester man' of his day – self-made, entrepreneurial, a free trade advocate, liberal in politics and nonconformist in religion. Indeed, he probably thought he had fulfilled a biblical saying when he entertained the Prince Consort at Abney Hall, his Cheshire home. "Seest thou a man diligent in his business? He shall stand before kings." Moreover, genealogists had 'discovered' a line of descent for the family that led back to King Alfred!

The warehouse, constructed by Travis and Magnall between 1855 and 1858, reflected this new confidence and pride. It also reflected common sense and an eye for the main chance, for the impressive stone façade was tacked on to an iron framed brick box, as is apparent from a visit to the goods entrances round the back. No matter, all eyes were on the front, a veritable architectural encyclopaedia, with each storey representing a different style. It started with an 'Italianate' ground floor, followed by 'Elizabethan', 'Italianate' again, 'French Renaissance', and 'Italianate' for a final time. The great box-like towers are very noticeable, sporting traceried rose windows, reminiscent of a French cathedral.

Over 600 staff worked inside. The warehouse had a department (each with its own showroom) on each floor, and perhaps had more in common with a great store. The range of finished goods was amazing, from carpets to print dresses, from umbrellas to corsets. One room was reputed to contain a stock of ribbons worth

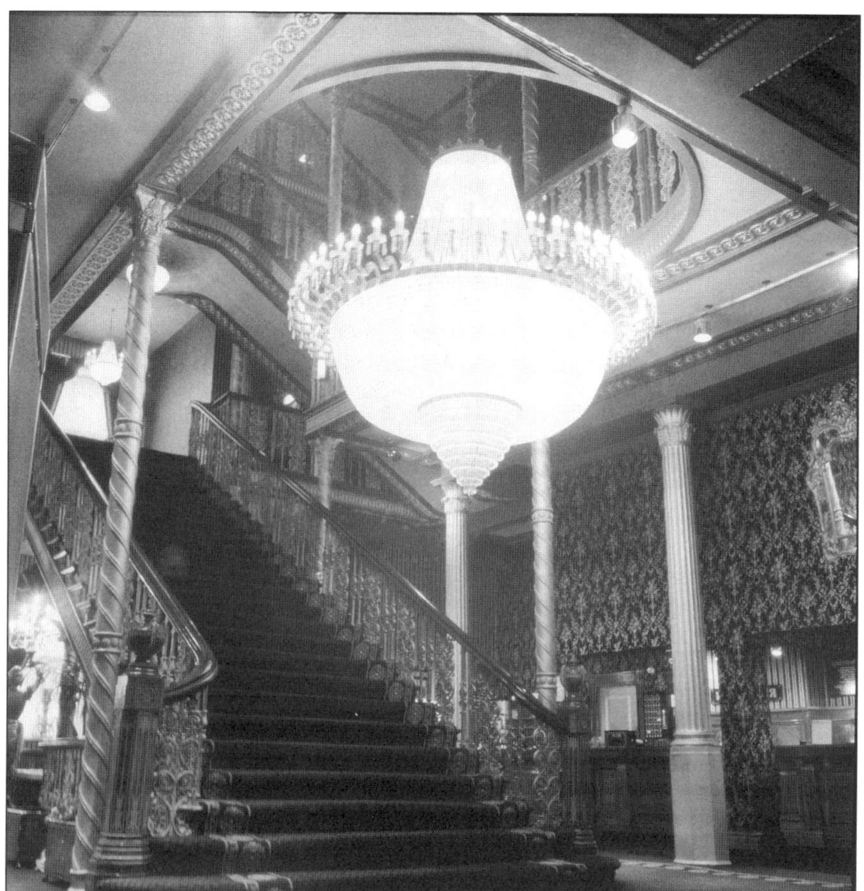

The grand staircase in the Britannia Hotel *(by kind permission of the Britannia Hotel)*

£40,000, almost a king's ransom at the time. Consequently, the firm became one of the 'lions' of Victorian Manchester, a kind of tourist attraction. Distinguished visitors to the city were eager to obtain a card of admission, guaranteeing a conducted tour.

Members of the Watt family were philanthropic employers (or paternalists, depending on your point of view). At one time or another, they encouraged savings banks, sports teams, social events, a choir, and a band. In return, a job at the warehouse often meant a good job for life, and the employees were a remarkably loyal bunch with a great 'esprit de corps'. In December, 1940, with much of the district set alight by incendiary bombs, the chief of the company fire brigade (what else!) was ordered to abandon the building. He refused. When the water supply was cut off, he and a team of his firemen (all employees) improvised fire beaters from whatever was to hand and saved the day. Changed economic conditions in the post war period accomplished what the Luftwaffe had failed to do. The company became part of the Courtauld Group in 1969, and the surplus warehouse was sold off. The grand façade is now incorporated into a rather grand hotel (where reunions are sometimes held by the old S. and J. Watt's staff). One wonders what the upright James might have thought, "for the night cometh, when no man may work".

Go inside the Hotel lobby. The sumptuous entrance hall still contains the **magnificent iron grand staircase** (once exclusively for the use of customers and distinguished visitors) which communicated with the show rooms on every floor. Do not neglect the moving **war memorial** at the entrance. When war broke out in 1914, some influential citizens suggested that the principle of allowing friends and workmates to enlist and serve together might encourage recruitment. A 'Clerks and Warehouseman's Battalion' was advertised, aimed at the elite of working Manchester. The response was overwhelming – several so-called 'Pals' Battalions' were recruited. The initial expenses were borne by local businesses, with the big warehouse companies leading the way. These were amongst the best units in the British army, but were squandered in bloody battles in the Flanders mud. "The paths of glory lead but to the grave."

Don't forget to glance down Chorlton Street, to the right of the *Britannia Hotel*, for a view of the enormous **'matchstick men'** abseiling down the side of Arthur House *(3)*. **St Andrews House** (Portland Tower), adjacent to the Hotel, stands in front of Chorlton Street Coach Station (p.142) that was part of the same development. All 21 storeys (Leach, Rhodes, Walker, 1962) were built for the Scottish Widow's Fund, but were recently extensively refurbished. **Telephone House**, to the right (1959-61) was one of the earliest 'curtain walled' modern buildings in the city.

Charlotte Street

A right turn into Charlotte Street reveals an impressive **frontage of Victorian warehouses**, indicating what the entire district must once have looked like. The range of buildings from the Portland Street corner starts with Fraser House (1856), with a Siamese restaurant at street level. Then follow Manchester Associated Mills (1855), in functional brick; Hanover House (1983), a curious modern reproduction in the 'palazzo' style; and a Victorian warehouse with prominent chimneys on the office front (insurers forbade open fires in the storage areas). Charlotte House (1857), beyond George Street, is a fine mixture of brick and sandstone, with strangely corbelled windows on the second floor. All of these structures (except the modern building) were the work of Edward Walters, architect of the Free Trade Hall. Notice the Portico Library at the Mosley Street end (p.99).

Pause at St James's House, across the road (4). This recently refurbished office block stands on the site of St James's Church, consecrated in 1786 as a 'chapel of ease' to cater for a fashionable suburb. (The early 'chapel' status was to ensure that the profitable monopoly of baptisms and marriages, then held by the Collegiate Church, was not challenged.) Consequently, there was not much love lost between the two institutions, particularly where the Rev. Cornelius Bayley was concerned. The founding minister was a charismatic preacher with a keen sense of humour. When the bishop saw his dark skin, he became convinced that Bayley was a Jew, and refused to ordain him. Bayley immediately requested a dish of pork, providing the onions were well done! His preaching attracted a large congregation, and his low-church sympathies appealed to nonconformists, who attended his church in addition to their chapels. Upon being told (by a lapsed member of the Collegiate Church congregation) that St James's was now more convenient, the Rev. Joshua

Brooks (p.20) was moved to scorn. "Oh, he's a rank Methody, and you may as well go to John Wesley's preaching shop in Owdham Street at once!"

If Bayley could not baptise or marry, his church could at least offer a first rate place of burial in capacious vaults under the structure. Many prominent citizens were interred here, including the notorious Joseph Nadin (p.41). When it happened that Bayley's coffin found its way here, his devoted widow began to spend a period each day sitting on a chair beside it in the vault. In time, her coffin was eventually placed beside her husband's, on the spot where she was wont to sit. The fashionable congregation was ephemeral, soon replaced by the poor of the district, until even they were displaced by commerce. The church closed in 1928, and the burials were exhumed and removed by 1970.

A Medical School, founded by the surgeon Thomas Turner in 1825, was situated behind the church. It was the first of its kind outside London, and William IV granted the title ' Manchester Royal School of Medicine and Surgery' in 1836. This prestigious institution became part of Owens's College (p.61) in 1873, and formed the basis of the future University Medical School. (The University also absorbed the Medical Society Library in Faulkner Street.)

George Street and Chinatown

Turn right into George Street, and notice the **wall plaque** *(5)*. Here stood the home of the Literary and Philosophical Society, one of the oldest learned societies in Britain, dating to 1781. It developed out of a 'salon' or discussion group, meeting at the home of Thomas Percival (another surgeon). The meetings became so well attended that, after a period in which they met in a tavern, land was purchased for a permanent venue on George Street. The Society opened its doors here in 1804. Many famous men have been members, including James Joule (p.237), Henry Roscoe (p.62), and Ernest Rutherford (p.222). The Society is forever associated with John Dalton (p.46). Dalton became President in 1817, and had his laboratory here. The Society continues its work, and an annual programme of lectures is open to the public.

A glance down the street will reveal **Rutherford House** (1967) at the left-hand corner of York Street. A secret telephone exchange, and an associated nuclear bunker, was constructed underneath it (by specially vetted construction workers) at the height of the cold war.

Proceed down George Street in the opposite direction, and enter **Chinatown**. Manchester has the largest Chinese community outside London – there are over 30,000 people of Chinese descent in and around the city, mainly Cantonese in origin. The Chinese quarter is an eclectic mixture of supermarkets, banks, herbalists, travel agents, and a variety of other businesses, all catering for the needs of this community. And, of course, it is full of an incredible variety of Chinese and other Asian restaurants. At one end of the market stands the ***Yang Sing***, re-housed in almost palatial surroundings on Princess Street, and considered by aficionados as one of the best in the country. It pioneered the 'banquet' concept, in which the party negotiates a 'tailor made' menu with the waiter. It is not as expensive as you might think – on average it works out at about £15 a head (in 2002). The ***Wong Chu***, on Faulkner Street, typifies the cheaper end of the market, and is patronised for every-

The Chinese Arch – Chinatown

day meals by the local Chinese themselves. With its hanging ducks in the window, it could almost be on a back street in Hong Kong.

The Chinese Quarter really comes alive on a Sunday morning, when Chinese restaurant and chip shop owners arrive from all over the North West to buy in provisions for the week ahead. Everyone brings his or her family and friends, as it is an excuse to meet and have a good gossip. One of the highlights of the Manchester tourist calendar is a spectacular Dragon Dance during celebrations of the Chinese New Year.

At the Nicholas Street intersection, notice the new Art Gallery Extension on the right, before turning left. The car park to the left is fronted by a row of oriental plants, set off by **two delightful pavilions** that are used by the community as meeting places. A junk in full sale is rendered in coloured brick on the wall behind *(6)*. The **warehouse** on the opposite side of the street is in the 'Elizabethan revival' style

(1870) and contains a microcosm of Chinatown, with a craft shop, a herbalist, and a practitioner in acupuncture. A much-photographed Manchester feature marks the junction with Faulkner Street. The **Chinese Arch** *(7)* was assembled by a group of twelve craftsmen from the People's Republic of China from parts shipped from thence, and unveiled to the public in 1987. It is decorated with red and gold dragons and phoenixes, colours and symbols of luck and prosperity. Through it may be glimpsed, rather incongruously, a **Doric columned warehouse** dating from 1846. Nowadays Faulkner Street is famous for ***Ho's Bakery***, the source of delicious honey buns. Continue along Nicholas Street to return to Portland Street, where the right-hand corner is marked by yet another **'palazzo' warehouse** of 1873.

Portland Street

The next stretch of Portland Street, on the right, has preserved a range of what are probably **early 19th-century buildings**, some with a row of top lights illuminating the former 'loom shops' *(8)*. Handloom weaving was the last of the textile processes to be mechanised, and required a good light. These buildings represent a time when all the vacant land in the area was used for the erection of cheap and shoddy workers' housing, often grouped around insanitary courtyards. Dr. Kay could describe, in 1832, "courts in the neighbourhood of Portland Street, some of which are not more than a yard and a quarter wide, and contain houses frequently three storeys high, the lowest of which storeys is occasionally used as a receptacle of excrementitious *(sic)* matter". Of course, the good doctor did not realise that manure, human or animal, was a saleable commodity. A manure heap on their doorstep was, to the poor inhabitants of the courts, a price worth paying for the promise of additional income. However, as cholera visited the town in that year, perhaps not.

Notice the two pubs, both with original cellar entrances and railings, unspoilt interiors, no 'muzak', and lots of lovely 'real ale'! The ***Grey Horse*** inn consists of two rooms partly made into one, with a generally mature clientele. The ***Circus Tavern*** claims to be the smallest pub in Manchester – the two rooms will only hold about forty people. It is a friendly place (well, it would have to be!), and the only noise is the hum of conversation. (At busy times, the door is shut, so it is worth knocking.) The ***Colin Jellico Gallery*** may be found in between them, something of a Manchester institution. It totally lacks pretension, as local artists exhibit and the prices are comparatively cheap. The ***Princess Hotel*** is situated in Pickles Building, on the left-hand corner of Princess Street, an Italianate (but perhaps rather debased Gothic) construction of 1870.

Cross Princess Street (p. 107), and continue in the direction of Oxford Street. The **'Piazza' development**, to the right, comprises the *Hotel Ibis*, a restaurant, and a variety of retail outlets. Anyone remotely interested in architecture and design should, at this point, make a beeline across the road to the ***Royal Institute of British Architects Bookshop*** and associated ***Cube Gallery*** (an acronym formed from 'Centre for the Understanding of the Built Environment'). A number of galleries are used in a programme of fascinating exhibitions, and the converted space of a former warehouse is worth a look in itself. (Usually open Tuesday-Friday, 12.00-5.30; weekends, 12.00-4.00.)

Have a quick look up Dickinson Street, to the left, for a view of **Linley House** *(9)*.

It stands on the site of Manchester's first Electric Power Station, opened in 1893. By 1923, it had been reduced to the status of a substation, but a moment of fame was at hand. The BBC had started broadcasting from Manchester with a station called 2ZY, transmitting from the top of the Metropolitan Vickers water tower in Trafford Park. A studio was opened in an attic of the Dickenson Street power station offices. (The aerial was strung between the chimney and the chimney of the adjacent Bloom Street electricity station!) The announcer got uproariously drunk one night, and the sub station staff 'detained' him in a lift halted between two floors. In the meantime, one of the engineers stepped into the breach, and none of the listeners noticed the difference! The BBC migrated to Piccadilly once the pioneering days were over. Notice **Beaver House**, a packing warehouse of the 1920s, on the corner of Dickenson Street.

The remainder of this side of Portland Street, extending as far as Oxford Street and thence round the corner, is taken up with **Behren's Warehouse** (Portland Buildings). In contrast to the S. and J. Watt's phenomenon, this equally impressive building is plain and functional. A series of brick piers terminate in round-headed arches, and a stone-clad ground floor includes cart entrances and grander office and show room entrances. Indeed, the offices are to be found on the Oxford Road frontage, framed in iron. Here was the Koh-i-Nor, Manchester's first Indian restaurant, and the sensation of 1938. The opposite corner of the Oxford Street junction comprises the ***Circus*** development (extending into Oxford Street), the latest in the fashion of using historic façades, in this case, including a Portland Street frontage of 1866. It contains the *Travel Inn* (a 240 bed 'budget' hotel), leisure facilities, a restaurant at street level, and a large basement health club. A new **plaque** *(10)* records that the complex stands on the site of property that was part of Humphrey Booth's charitable endowment (p.17).

Oxford Street

Make a brief detour to the right, into the part of Oxford Road going towards St Peter's Square. The ***Odeon Cinemas*** conceal the last surviving pre-war city centre 'picture house'. The 'Paramount' opened in 1930 with a performance of 'The Love Parade' (starring Maurice Chevalier and Jeanette MacDonald) and a 'parade of beauty' (starlets direct from the studios). It was a state of the art 3000-seat fantasy palace of pleasure, complete with its own Wurlitzer organ and troupe of 'Tiller' (dancing) girls to entertain in the intervals. The 'Odeon', as it became, was transformed in the 1970s. The organ was removed (fortunately, preserved by an enthusiast) and the 'art deco' interior was converted into a multi-screen establishment. Take a good look at **Prince's Building**, opposite. This 1903 structure of brick and buff terracotta betrays some 'art nouveau' influence. The prominent **chimneys**, connected by curved parapets, are particularly noticeable. Of course, local people will tell you that the Irish foreman got the plans upside down! The façade is incorporated into a modern development, fronting Oxford Court. (The rest of Oxford Street is described on p.205.)

A branch of McDonald's has been opened in the former cinema on the corner of Chepstow Street. **'The Picture House'** (the sculptured sign remains) opened in 1911 as the first purpose-built cinema in the city. The first films were shown as part of music hall programmes or by touring showmen at fairgrounds. As the popularity of the medium increased, more sophisticated examples of the product began to be shown in rented halls and converted premises. The owners of this establishment were evidently in pursuit of a better audience – they provided a café, and accompanied the films with a string orchestra. The opening performance was inaugurated by the Lord Mayor, no less, and included film of Captain Scott's polar exploration (Mrs Scott was in the audience). The last film was shown in 1980.

Chepstow Street

Proceed down Chepstow Street. Oxford Court, to the right, is an attempt to disguise a modern office development as a collection of **Georgian houses**. **Canada House** is just across the road, a five-storey (plus attic) structure of 1909 by William G. Higginbottom. It was erected round an iron frame (visible from the rear) and clad in buff terracotta with an 'art nouveau' gate. Alongside, a vacant area opens towards Great Bridgewater Street and a view of **Lee House** *(11)*. H.S. Fairhurst, the architect, had visited America in 1926. A commission by Tootal Broadhurst to add an extension to their Oxford Street building was an absolute godsend, as he had been particularly taken by the 'skyscrapers' and wanted to design one. Fairhurst therefore planned a seventeen-storey tower, which would have then been the tallest building in Europe. However, only the first phase was built, between 1928 and 1931, a thoroughly modern steel frame structure, with concrete floors, brick walls, bronze framed windows, and a stone clad ground floor. In contrast, the modern sheet glass of **100 Barbirolli Square** prefaces a **view across the restored canal basin** towards the G-Mex Centre.

The great brick bulk of **Chepstow House** lies directly ahead. This was Sam Mendel's warehouse, and has a strange story to tell. Sam was born in Liverpool, and was brought to Manchester by his father, who had set himself up in the business of rope manufacturer. The young lad entered the service of a local merchant, and travelled extensively on his behalf in Germany and South America. After setting up his own textile business, Mendel developed a great business empire, and erected this large warehouse in 1874, when he was at the height of his powers. He was a phenomenon. His dealings in 'grey' goods, for export to India and China, took the form of orders so huge that his dealings sometimes seriously affected the market. Yet he was a "gentleman from top to toe", always ready to receive courteously the humblest salesman. As Manchester's greatest 'merchant prince' at that time, he lived in great splendour at Manley Park on the south side of the city.

The Suez Canal opened the year after this warehouse, transforming the cotton market. In the vastly changed commercial conditions, Sam lost everything. The contents of his mansion were auctioned, and the pictures (including works by Turner and Constable), silver plate, furniture, and Sèvres and Chelsea porcelain, featured in a catalogue of 209 pages. (It took six days to sell his wine collection!) Poor old Sam died in poverty at Balham, London, in 1884. One hopes that the thrice-married gentleman had consoled himself with some happy memories. The old warehouse has been converted into seventy-six flats, though the **boiler room chimney** remains. And over the door is a **symbolic carving** relating to the eternal quest for the elusive 'golden fleece'.

Notice the ***Peveril of the Peak***, a pub dating from 1820, and built by a retired coachman. The name refers to a stage coach that performed the journey from

Market street to London (via Derbyshire) in 23 hours! (The historical Derbyshire character, after which the coach was named, inspired a Walter Scott novel.) The attractive tile exterior dates from the 1920s.

Great Bridgewater Street

Cross the paved area and enter Great Bridgewater Street. Expensive canalside housing now populates the area between this thoroughfare and the Rochdale Canal on the left. Note the ***Rain Bar***, a very popular mixture of bar and café (with canalside terrace), housed in a former umbrella factory. A canal arm, leading to the Barbirolli Square basin is spanned by a reconstructed bridge. The **wrought ironwork** between the battlements, with a motif of musical notes, refers to the Bridgewater Hall on the right. After passing the new ***Jury's Inn*** hotel, we come to Lower Mosley Street.

Notice the great **bowstring bridge** – used by the Metrolink trams after climbing the ramp at the side of the G-Mex Centre. The ***Britons' Protection Hotel*** is situated on the left-hand corner. This old pub dates from 1806, and the name indicates an association with the local volunteers, determined to resist an invasion by Bonaparte. It is worth a visit for its panelled interior, military murals, beer garden, and a collection of over 150 malt whiskies. The upstairs room is the venue for several local societies. Turn left into Lower Mosley Street. The iron-framed Gothic windows at ***Matthew's Office Furniture*** are worth a glance, before pausing on the Rochdale Canal Bridge. In the distance may be discerned the Refuge tower (p.210), but don't miss the broken classical columns belonging to the ***Acqua Coffee Bar***, in the foreground. The intersection with Whitworth Street West is now reached.

The elaborate tiled and panelled corridor leading to the ladies' toilet in The Britons' Protection

The left-hand corner is the site of the legendary **Hacienda Club** *(12)*. It opened in 1982, in a former warehouse-cum-yacht showroom, one of the creations of Anthony H. Wilson, the guru of Manchester's music scene. At one time, it was the most famous club in the world, featuring on the cover of 'Newsweek'. (Rod Stewart claimed, in the 1980s, that Los Angeles, London, and Manchester were the best music venues in the world.) However, the club became more commercial, and problems arose with unwelcome drug pushers and bad management. (It was rumoured that so many people were on the take that it was impossible to make a profit!) The club closed in 1997.

Cross over to the open railway arches at the corner of Albion Street

(13). Here are exhibited **relics of Gaythorn Gas Works** (established in 1817). In the area beyond the viaduct, there is a fine view of the futuristic glass structure of **'Number 1 City Road'** *(14)*. The way now lies along Whitworth Street West, past the ***City Road Inn***, with an exterior typical of the late-19th century. From this point on, the street runs alongside the Rochdale Canal (p.154), visible over the wall to the right. It is the scene of ***Deansgate Locks*** *(15)*, an interesting development in which retail units in a series of railway arches (forming the old approach to Central Station, now G-Mex) are accessed by a continuous balcony, connected with the street by a series of bridges across the canal. The tenants include the ***Comedy Store***. The latter is evidence of the proposition that stand up 'alternative' comedy is the rock music of the present time. The locks in question are numbers 90 and 91, part of the infamous 'Rochdale Nine', familiar to boaters on the 'Cheshire Ring'. A **lock keeper's house** is visible at the end of the street, before the canal enters the Gaythorn Tunnel. A fine **plaque** on the bridge parapet gives the date of construction (1902) decorated with the city coat of arms.

Deansgate and Knott Mill

A rival form of transport is marked by **Deansgate Station**, across the road. The railways in Manchester were built in a somewhat haphazard fashion, the original lines terminating in what was then the suburbs, with little thought given to connecting the different undertakings. When this soon became necessary, a problem arose – the expense and difficulty of constructing a line across a crowded built up area. The 'Manchester South Junction and Altrincham Railway' had this end in view, as it intended to connect London Road (now Piccadilly) Station with the Liverpool and Manchester line at Ordsall (the Altrincham branch was an afterthought). The land conveyancing was so complex that two solicitors were employed full time for over a year (the pressure of work gave one a breakdown). The line runs on a continuous brick viaduct of 224 arches containing 50 million bricks.

The station opened (as Knott Mill), along with the rest of the line, in 1849. It was rebuilt in its present form in the last quarter of the 19th century, incorporating mock battlements and a **fake portcullis** in tribute to the nearby Roman Fort, along with the **company arms**. (The station yard entrance has a **'pun'** in the form of a carving of a reef knot!) Interestingly enough, the Altrincham branch came into its own as Manchester's first suburban railway, servicing the growing residential suburbs to the south west of the city, which accounts for the size of the reconstructed station. The line was electrified in 1931. The station is joined to the Metrolink Station and the G-Mex Centre by a futuristic **footbridge**. (There is also a **flight of steps** up to the trams at the corner of Deansgate.)

A sculpture in the form of a **gigantic bicycle** marks the start of the lower section of Deansgate, to the left, now little more than a backwater since the construction of the Bridgewater Viaduct (see below). The ***Atlas* bar**, situated to the right, under an arch of the viaduct, is particularly popular, and serves food. There is a fine range of food and drink on sale in the ***Atlas Deli***, to the left, owned by the same company. Continue under the bridge, past the ***Pack Horse Inn*** (noting the slope to the river). The ***Castlefield Gallery*** (open Wed to Sun 1.00 – 6.00pm, late opening Thurs, free) may be found nearby in Hewitt Street. It sells a variety of (mostly affordable) art, often featuring local artists. Only the left-hand parapet of the bridge survives, distinguished by an **old boundary stone** indicating the border between Manchester and Hulme township. There may have been a ford over the Medlock here in Roman times, but the bridge is certainly mediaeval in origin, on the main route into the town from the west. The 'mill' ground corn in the vicinity from an uncertain date.

In olden times, none other than Sir Lancelot, upon a knightly quest, came by this place. Here lived the giant Sir Tarquin, who hung a basin on the bough of a tree. None might pass unless they struck the basin with their lance, thereby challenging the wicked knight to a fight. Sir Lancelot vanquished the giant and freed the local people from his tyranny. A large part of the Arthurian Legend (Sir Gawain's exploits with the Green Knight, for example) is set in the North West of England. Since they largely derive from Celtic oral tradition, this is not surprising, as this border area lay on the edge of the Anglo-Saxon kingdoms and was the last to retain its original culture. Some scholars think that the 'giant of Knott Mill' is a faint echo of some bardic propaganda for a Pennine dark-age chieftain. However, some amateur local historians will tell you that Camelot lay in Salford!

We are on firmer ground with the Saxon era, for 'Knott' refers to King Canute. Everyone remembers him as the foolish king who placed his throne on a beach, tried to command the tide not to come in, and thus got his feet wet. The whole point of the story is misunderstood. He was actually trying to demonstrate to his sycophantic Witan (Council) that there were strict limits to the power of a king. Knut (to give him his proper name) was a Dane who had seized the English throne. However, he maintained order, made wise laws, and was a great friend to the church. In short, not a bad chap.

> Merry sungen the monkes of Ely,
> When Knut Kyng rowed thereby.
> "Row Knichts, nearer to the land,
> That we may hear these monkes sing!"

He may even have visited Manchester, for the town then lay within the Royal Manor of Salford, much used as a kingly hunting lodge. An old tradition also states that the Saxon kings thus owned the mill, hence the name.

James Brindley used the Medlock as the source of his canal in 1764. It opened out into the Bridgewater Basin (p.175) on the right, but he had to guard against the problem of periodic floods. Consequently, the excess water flowed through a sluice (in the form of an ingenious hollow gate, which tipped over when full) which diverted the water into an underground tunnel, leading to the Irwell. The sewage of Hulme went this way after 1848! The 'old Warehouse' stood at the head of the basin, athwart the river, but its place is now taken by **Deansgate Quay**, a new brick apartment development. Take a detour through the arch for a **view over the basin** as far as the Bridgewater Viaduct.

Double back on to the **Bridgewater Viaduct** *(17)*, opened in 1841 as a measure to improve traffic access to the town from the west. There is a fine view over the Bridgewater Basin and a large part of Castlefield. We now pass the old chapel, walk under the railway bridge, and find ourselves at Pioneer Quay. **The Castlefield Walk** (p.171) starts at this point *(18)*.

However, our walk continues under the second railway bridge. Opposite the old **Free Library Building** (p.188), turn right into Great Bridgewater Street (passing a possible sight for a future Hilton Hotel on the right). Just before the Central Station viaduct, go left into Watson Street *(19)* – a curious thoroughfare that runs between the Great Northern Leisure Complex on the left and G-Mex on the right. We emerge alongside Great Northern Square (p.58) before a right turn into Windmill Street. On the right-hand corner, adjacent to the G-Mex Centre, is the new sandstone-walled **International Convention Centre** *(20)*, leased by Manchester Council to the G-Mex Centre (with which it is linked). In addition to the 2000 m^2-hall and an 800-seat auditorium, the complex includes banqueting and seminar rooms, translation facilities, and a range of media and catering services. It is expected to attract 50,000 extra visitors per year to the city.

The **rear of the Free Trade Hall** (p.113), with the new hotel extension, is opposite the Centre. The adjacent ***Betty's Bar***, an unusual brick building with an intriguing balcony, is worth a look. Stop at this point, and try to imagine this area a little after the beginning of the 19th century. Everything from the *Midland Hotel* to the Free Trade Hall, including a large part of the G-Mex Centre site was open ground, called (after the church, see p.108) **St Peter's Fields**.

Peterloo

The period after the Napoleonic Wars was a hard time, with a combination of economic depression and high food prices. The poor lived off potatoes and a kind of stew made from nettles and dock leaves called 'Waterloo porridge'. But something was very different. The first period of industrialisation had created an industrial working class, a group that was starting to flex its muscles and organise. The cause of political reform had fallen into their hands, for groups of workers had become convinced that the times would only mend when a reformed parliament was achieved.

Henry 'Orator' Hunt was to address a great reform demonstration at St Peter's Fields on 16th August, 1819. The immense crowd was augmented by contingents marching in from the surrounding towns. This was no mob. It was more frightening than that, as far as the establishment was concerned, for the crowd was orderly and disciplined – even dressed in their Sunday clothes. (Reports of secret drilling on the moors around the town, were probably connected with organising the marching contingents.) Unfortunately, as Manchester had no proper local government at the time, legal jurisdiction lay in the hands of unelected magistrates. This panic stricken reactionary group, watching the proceedings from a nearby cottage, ordered the military force at their disposal to arrest Hunt.

This force was the Manchester Yeomanry, a volunteer cavalry regiment left over from the wars, and officered by the sons of local landowners and merchants. They had to force their way through the crowd to reach the stand with Hunt and his fellow speakers upon it. They lost control, and started lashing out in all directions with their sabres. Some reports state that many of the Yeomanry were drunk. In other cases, individual officers sought out local radicals for retribution in an early form of class warfare. The officers of a detachment of Hussars (regular army) were appalled, and spent as much time trying to control their fellow military as dispersing the crowd. "Fie gentlemen! For shame!" a Hussar officer cried, as he knocked up some Yeomanry swords. "What are you at? The people cannot get away!" Some of the crowd fought back, and gave as good as they got.

Altogether, sixteen people died, and over six hundred were injured. But this is a conservative estimate, for many were no doubt spirited away by their family and friends. Interestingly enough, the authorities had not crushed the political movement. The out-of-town contingents marched back in good order, and a mood of defiance emerged. Manchester did not explode into anarchy, for not only the town, but the greater part of the country, were united in an expression of universal disgust and loathing at what had happened. The event was christened 'Peterloo' for "Waterloo (in which one of the dead had fought) had been a battle, but St Peter's Fields was bloody murder". Peterloo was a turning point, and an alliance was forged between the middle and working classes to achieve parliamentary reform. Unfortunately, the urban working classes were cheated in the Reform Act of 1832, and had to wait until 1867 to obtain the vote.

These soldiers mow'd folks down like flies,
Thi' sabres drip'd wi' blood.
Thi' heeded man nor woman's cries,
But slew them where thi' stood.

Salute we now these men o' yore,
Who were t'concience true.
An' gave thi' blood for t'common good,
On't fields o' Peterloo!

We have been passing through a vast acreage of former railway property. From the late sixties, this was largely derelict, the preserve of temporary car parking, the part of Manchester that was best hidden. It has now given birth to three classic examples of urban regeneration. The International Convention Centre has already been mentioned, and the Great Northern development is dealt with in a previous walk (p.58). So we must deal with the third (and pioneer) project.

G-Mex

So, stop at the forecourt of the **G-Mex Centre**. The Midland, Manchester, Sheffield and Lincolnshire (later Great Central), and Great Northern railways decided to break the monopoly of the London and North Western between Manchester and Liverpool. They formed a joint company, that (since it would also comprise a line to Chester) would be called 'The Cheshire Lines Railway'. (It was the only railway in Britain with carriages and wagons, but no locomotives – the constituent companies provided the latter.) The new route was an instant success, especially the punctual expresses that ran every hour to Liverpool in forty minutes. Such an undertaking needed grand terminus, and Central Station opened in 1880. The impressive arched girder frame is the **second widest unsupported train shed span after St Pancras**, upon which it is modelled. However, unlike St Pancras, horizontal beams do not secure the thrust of the arch. Instead, the great girders run straight through the undercroft to anchor themselves in the underlying rock. The undercroft, intended as a goods station, used over 34 million bricks in its construction. In addition to Cheshire Lines trains, the constituent railways transferred the great majority of their express services here from London Road (now Piccadilly) Station, together with some of their local trains. It was intended to build a grand station entrance block, but the companies could never agree on the allocation of the costs. Consequently, the (temporary) wooden buildings, with few alterations, lasted until the station closed!

Central station closed in 1969. For many years it lay derelict, until the old Greater Manchester Council decided that the city needed a good exhibition hall.

The G-Mex Exhibition Centre

The **Greater Manchester Exhibition and Event Centre (G-Mex)**, to give it its proper title, was the consequence of a unique public and private sector partnership, and is definitely an asset to the city. The **large hall** is 10,000 metres in extent, although it can be subdivided into smaller exhibition halls by moveable screens. Look up at the **clock**. In the course of its restoration, a time capsule left by the original workmen was discovered. You can usually enter the foyer, and take a peep through the hall doors. The Centre hosts a mixture of trade and public exhibitions, an indoor funfair around Christmas and New Year, and has staged concerts and sporting events, though the latter now faces stiff competition from the Manchester Evening News Arena (p.28).

At this point, we must really consider the street name. Windmill Street is named after a windmill that lay in the vicinity, grinding materials for dyestuff. As the name of Mount Street testifies, this was the highest piece of land to the West of the city. On one side, it sloped towards the Irwell, and on the other, southwards towards the Medlock stream. Not much of a hill, though, and some said that the choice of name was a little 'tongue in cheek'. The mill was sold in 1811 and disappeared shortly after. The remains of the grand entrance to the ***Midland Hotel*** (p.110), opposite G-Mex, may still be made out. When most guests arrived and departed by rail, this was the principal hotel entrance, and a covered way extended from it across the street and up the forecourt to the station! The hotel stands on the site of a cottage and extensive gardens owned by a Mr Cooper. He is said to have walked there and back to Doncaster, every year for forty years, to see the St Leger horse race!

Barbirolli Square and the Bridgewater Hall

You should now cross Lower Mosley Street to reach **Barbirolli Square** *(21)*, a fine viewpoint over the restored canal basin. The square is paved in York stone, with

Modern architecture in Barbirolli Square

bands of granite, and a few plane trees. The most conspicuous object is the **pebble**, an 18-ton piece of polished marble (said to have cost £20,000!) by the Japanese sculptor, Kan Yasuda. Steps lead down to the basin, which is graced with the inevitable water feature. (It would be nice if some narrow boats actually tied up here. Perhaps some concert-goers might arrive by barge!) Some lime trees dot the quayside, and the ***Pitcher and Piano*** bar and restaurant fronts the water's edge. The bar is actually in the basement of **100 Barbirolli Square**, clad in Sardinian grey granite.

It should be recorded that this building stands on the site of ***Tommy Duck's***, one of the great pubs of Manchester. It was located in a late 18th-century house, and got its name in a most singular way. A signwriter was inscribing the name of the landlord, one Thomas Duckworth, on the fascia boarding – but ran out of space. Thus ***Duckworth's*** became ***Duck's***! In its final incarnation, the interior was unique, owing nothing whatsoever to a 'designer' but deriving from the interests and eccentricities of the landlord and his cronies. There was a priceless collection of Victorian theatre and music hall posters, a skeleton within a glass-lidded coffin, and the 'pièce de résistance', a ceiling covered with a fine collection of ladies knickers. These ranged from the skimpiest pieces of lace to capacious 'bloomers'. (Female regulars were asked to donate a pair, which was duly autographed, dated, and pinned up with due ceremony.) A raid by a group of women who were determined to reclaim them soon passed into the city's folklore. Sadly, the pub was demolished in a rather dubious episode. It is said that the perpetrators were fined for knocking down a listed structure without consent. 'Hanging, drawing, and quartering' would have been more appropriate. To the rear of the basin is a good view of Sam Mendel's Warehouse (p.127).

The chief function of the Square is to act as an introduction to the **Bridgewater Hall** (Nicholas Thompson, 1996). Manchester, from the 18th century onwards, has always been a centre for the performing arts, particularly music. In the nineteenth century, the cosmopolitan nature of the city encouraged this trend. Charles Hallé, a brilliant German musician, settled in a place with a thriving and cultured German community, and created the world famous orchestra that bears his name (popularly known by older residents as the 'Hallé band'). The orchestra made the Free Trade Hall (p.113) its home, and is usually associated with Sir John Barbirolli, the legendary conductor after whom the square is named. A large bronze bust of him is placed near the entrance, and it is interesting to compare this with the sculpture in the Town Hall. Changing circumstances necessitated a move to a new venue. The result is the Bridgewater Hall, the first purpose built musical auditorium in Britain since the Royal Festival Hall of 1951. The BBC Philharmonic and the Manchester Camerata orchestras joined them here. However, it must not be thought that the new place is purely a temple to orchestral classical music. A wide programme is offered, from popular music to stand up comedy.

The entire building is mounted on 270 giant bearings, which act as shock absorbers. No vibration is transmitted to the auditorium. The **exterior** is placed on a plinth of sandstone blocks, supporting angular walls of glass and metal cladding. A suspended glass curtain of four levels of foyers and bars focus on the Square, with views of the canal basin on one side, and the box office, shops, and offices against Mosley Street. It is best seen illuminated at night, for some have compared it to the prow of a great liner, with people at various levels gazing at the reflections in the water. The exterior of the auditorium

Dappled sun reflects onto the entrance to the Bridgewater Hall

is encased in Jura limestone, terminating in a stainless steel roof. Enter and explore the outer area, noticing the **carpet**, inspired by Monet's Water Lilies, and the inclined auditorium wall. Tours of the Complex are available (charge), but you can usually inspect the **auditorium** if no rehearsals or performances are taking place. It is finished in natural materials – the veneer colours were inspired by some autumn leaves collected by the architect. Notice the fine **organ**, and the fact that the tipped up empty seats reflect the sound back to the performance area. The Bridgewater Hall is open Monday-Saturday from 10am.

The walk continues by following the tramlines along Lower Mosley Street, alongside the *Midland Hotel*. This part of the building stands on the spot once occupied by the Gentlemen's Concert Hall, which moved here in 1830. Liszt, Paganini, and Chopin performed in its heyday, a factor that induced Charles Hallé to settle in Manchester. (The People's Concert Hall was round the corner, and, in this case, the audience certainly weren't gentlemen – a wire net was sometimes hung over the stage to protect the performers!) The Hall became a theatre after 1893, witnessing the first performance of Ibsen in the city. The old place was sold to the railway in 1897, on the understanding that their proposed hotel would include a theatre. The ***Premier Lodge Hotel*** is on the opposite side of the street.

The walk terminates in St Peter's Square. You can now return to Piccadilly by Mosley Street (described in reverse order from p.107).

The Rochdale canal at Canal Street

7 Alternative Manchester (1): The Gay Village

Start: Piccadilly (Newton Street corner)

Estimated time of walk: 1 hour

Highlights: The tale of 'Spanking Roger', Britain's only Gay Village, the inventor of the computer, and the legend of Garret Hall.

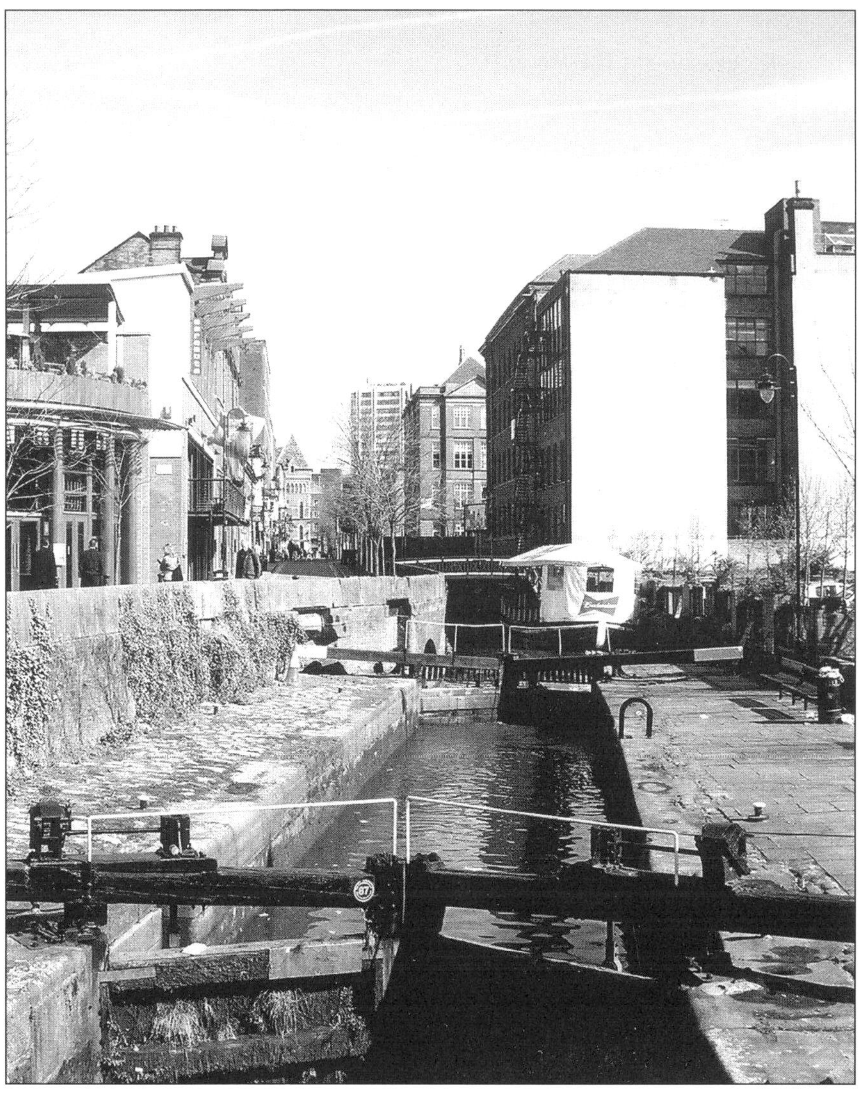

This is the first of three short walks. They can be taken in any combination, or independently, but all have a unifying theme – the 'alternative' Manchester that most visitors can easily miss. Two of the walks start from Piccadilly, and the third can be linked to either or both.

So let us start again at that part of Piccadilly proper (the street, rather than the amorphous area to which the name has been loosely applied) which runs in a southerly direction beyond the great open space. To most people, it is nothing more than a wide road to and from Piccadilly Station, usually taken in a hurry. But there is more to it than that. The street has recently been 'improved' and a line of trees has been planted. Pause a while to admire the fine row of buildings along the left-hand side.

Piccadilly to Auburn Street

Start at the corner of Newton Street *(1)*. **Prince of Wales Chambers** is in the Italianate style, a brick and stone structure of the 1850s rendered in stucco. *The Piccadilly Tavern* graces the street level of the adjacent **Hall's Buildings** (1870s). However, cross the road for a good view of the fun building next door. Someone who had a sense of humour designed **Number 77-83** in 1877. Notice the frieze and the **little seated men either side of the corner tower**, propping up the ends of the balustrades! There is a good (and cheap!) café, together with the *Bier Keller* (with a resident 'oompah band'), on the ground floor.

The new red brick of **Murray House** replaces a building destroyed in a fire some years ago. A number of middle-aged housewives, working for Christmas money, were trapped by the fire in an upstairs room. They managed to summon help by telephone, but it arrived too late – they were suffocated by the smoke. Spare them a thought as you pass by. The ***Brunswick Hotel*** is thought to date from the eighteenth century. **Number 107** was designed by C.H. Heathcote for Messrs. Sparrow Hardwick in 1898. It is 'Baroque revival' in style, with corner turrets and gables. The words "Founded 1848" can still be seen. It has metamorphosed into the 61-bedroom (with five penthouse suites) *Rossetti* hotel. The eclectic interior (including pre-war German mannequins) also include the *Café Paradiso*.

The battlemented **gateway of the Rochdale Canal basin** (p.154) can be glimpsed at the bottom of Lena Street *(2)*. Indeed, the adjacent tower block is constructed over one of the canal locks (still accessible from the towpath). The eighteen-storey Rodwell Tower (Douglas, Stapleton, and Partners, 1965-66) experienced major problems with crumbling concrete in the 1980s. Some citizens hoped it would be demolished, but the structure was stabilised by means of a protective coating and re-launched as **'111 Piccadilly'**.

The opposite side of the road has far less to show for itself. The rather bland frontage between Hope Street and Chatham Street conceals the site of Circus Street behind. This was named after a circus arena leased by the appropriately named Mr Handy in 1794. Hailing from London, he brought his own circus troupe to perform here a number of times. Shortly after an appearance in 1797, it proceeded to Liverpool to embark on the 'Viceroy' for a tour of Ireland. Mr Handy was to follow a few days later, but news came that the ship was lost with all hands in a storm. The proprietor was never the same again, and the arena remained largely silent until demolition in 1808.

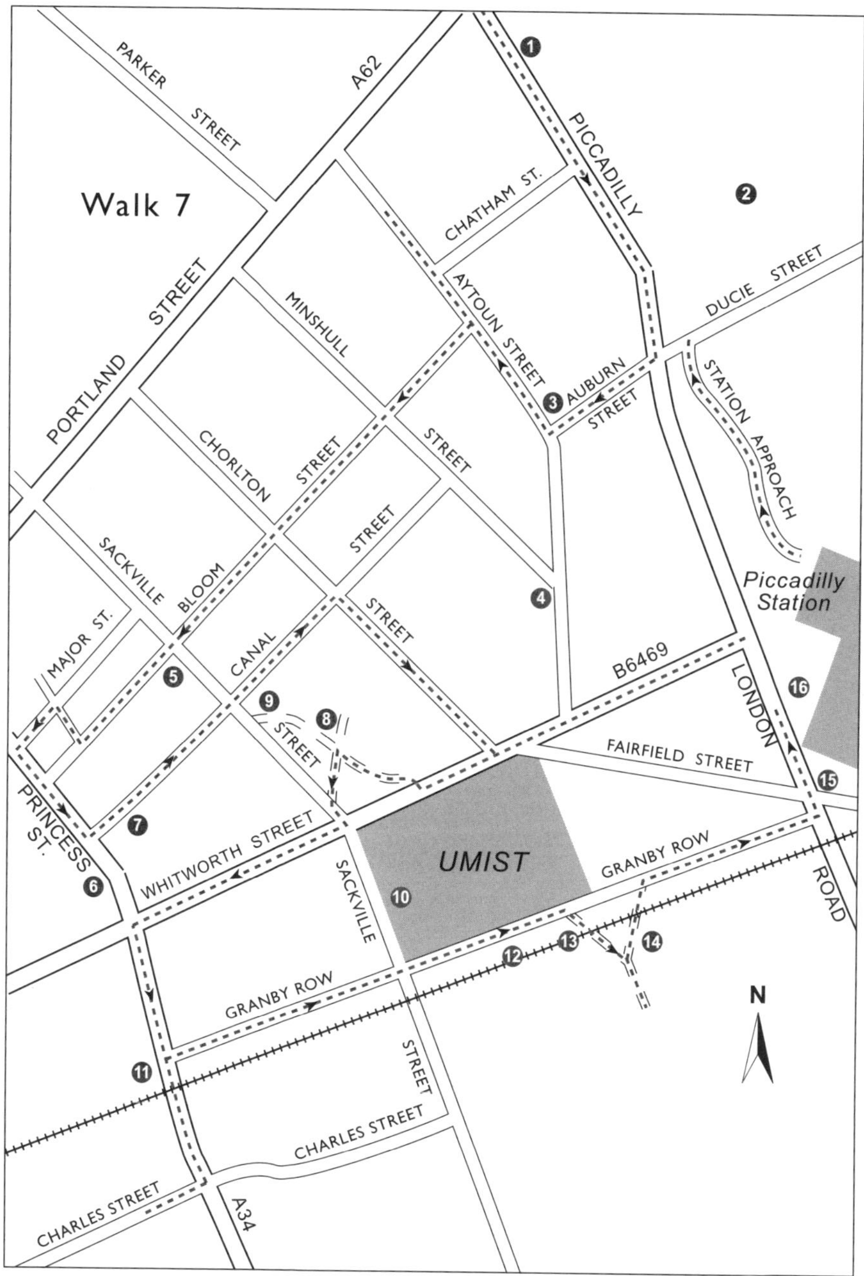

The Portland stone of ***Barclays Bank*** dates from 1911, the name of "Union Bank of Manchester" still proudly carved upon it. Further along may be found the warehouse of Joshua Hoyle and Son, erected in the period 1904-06. It was the distribution point of a textile empire located in the Rossendale Valley. Hoyle's virtually

Main entrance of the Malmaison Hotel from the bottom of the Piccadilly Station Approach

cornered the market at one time in the supply of dark blue uniform cloth – there were contracts with British Railways, the Post Office, and about half the police forces and corporation transport departments in the country. Since 1998, it has been occupied by the four-star, 120-bedroom ***Malmaison Hotel***, including a 'traditional brasserie'. The new right-hand wing stands on the site of the Imperial Hotel, the birthplace of the Football Association. One might have thought that the pub façade would have been preserved and incorporated into the new structure, but no-one seemed interested.

Piccadilly, at this point, becomes London Road. The extreme width of the thoroughfare reflects its past use as a market for the millworkers and factory operatives. We turn right into Auburn Street, alongside the canal, to reach Aytoun Street.

Aytoun Street

In the course of the 17th and 18th centuries, the greater part of the property in this area of Manchester was acquired by the Mynshull family. Barbara Nabb, the widow of Thomas Samuel Mynshull, became the sole heiress of this estate in 1755. One fateful day in 1769, she attended the fashionable Kersal races and met Roger Aytoun. 'Spanking Roger' (after his pugnacious manners, and not a reference to some personal habit!), 6ft 4in (1.9m) of handsome physique in military uniform, swept the lady off her feet. Less than one month after this meeting, the young Scotsman and the 65-year-old widow were married in the Collegiate Church. Aytoun nourished a military career. With some financial assistance from his wife, he raised his own regiment, the 72nd Regiment of Foot (Manchester Volunteers) to serve in the latter stages of the American War of Independence. He paraded the Manchester streets with a watch pinned to a banner, promising it to the day's first recruit. Other

The UMIST campus (now amalgamated with Manchester University)

times he would challenge likely candidates to a fight – on the understanding that they would enlist if he won! The local archive still preserves a poster advertising a football match as a recruiting ploy. The Manchester Volunteers never went to America. Instead, they formed part of the garrison of Gibraltar, which was then besieged by the Spanish. The long siege produced conditions of great privation, and members of the regiment were driven to desertion and suicide. Nevertheless, Gibraltar was held.

Aytoun returned to Manchester as a hero, but then revealed a dark side to his nature. Barbara died in 1783. Roger had squandered the entire family fortune by 1792, and had mortgaged the landed property. His debts were reduced (!) to over £11,000 by 1797, and finally cleared by the sale of Chorlton Hall. But Aytoun had already left Manchester for pastures new. He married another heiress in his native Scotland in 1794, and died a rich man in 1810! His tangled affairs resulted in land sales that led to a rash of speculative building on the south side of the town.

Standing at the Aytoun Street corner *(3)*, the Business School (see below) campus of the Manchester Metropolitan University is down to the left, though only the grim **College of Commerce building** (1962) is visible *(4)*. The great pile of the UMIST Building broods in the background. Turn right into Aytoun Street itself, a wide thoroughfare with tram tracks, and proceed as far as the ***'Grand'*** on the right. It is on the site of the 'House of Recovery', founded in 1796, and later absorbed by the Manchester Royal Infirmary. This 100-bed fever hospital is credited with saving the town from a number of potentially disastrous typhus epidemics in the early stages of the industrial revolution. A warehouse for A. Collie and Co. was built here in 1867, handling over five million 'pieces' of cloth per annum. This warehouse was converted into the Grand Hotel in 1880 and the façade is now incorporated into a development of luxury apartments. In 1998, when they went on sale at prices from £50,000 to £300,000, potential customers queued all night! Notice the **red granite doorway** set into the original frontage of Darley Dale stone.

The plain box of the old GMC Headquarters (p.120) is opposite. However, the best view is back down the street across to the **Old Crown Court**. It was soon apparent that the interior of the new Town Hall would have no room for the Police Courts. In these, members of the Council, acting as magistrates, remanded prisoners to higher courts or dealt with petty offences such as drunkenness. The omission was remedied by holding a competition for the design of a new set of courts, which was won by Thomas Worthington. The winning design had to accommodate the problems associated with a cramped site, the courts being placed in the centre and surrounded by a network of corridors and offices. It is perhaps one of the finest buildings of the period in the popular Venetian style, although financial stringency dictated the use of brick. Nevertheless, the **stonework decoration** is handsomely carved, and includes mythical creatures at the side of the doorways. Inevitably, the eye is drawn to the **great clock and bell tower**. The structure was completed in 1873, at a cost of £81,000.

The destruction of the Assize Courts in World War II resulted in the transfer of the Crown Courts to this building. And here they have stayed, despite the opening of the new Crown Court in Crown Square. Indeed, the interior was refurbished in the 1990s to create four new courts. This works programme also included a **new wing** that incorporates an entrance on Aytoun Street, in a style very much in sympathy with the original.

Bloom Street

After examining the exterior (though you may be able to pop in and see a trial), walk down Bloom Street, by the side of the Crown Court. Note the interesting **warehouse** at the intersection with Mynshull Street. Bloom Street continues beyond the Chorlton Street intersection, past the large **Coach Station**. This, together with the multi-storey car park on top, was part of the St Andrew's House development (Leach, Rhodes, and Walker, 1963). The coach station became notorious for the first impression of the city that it created – a general air of decay and all round seediness. After a great deal of municipal and public pressure, a major refurbishment programme began in 2001, and was completed in time for the Commonwealth Games. ***Paddy's Goose***, on the left, is a traditional pub building. It is sometimes patronised by not so traditional cross dressers, as we are now entering the Gay Village.

Napoleon's, at the corner of Sackville Street, introduces a range of original buildings, indicating how the area must once have appeared *(5)*. Continue beyond them and turn right down Abingdon Street, before turning left into Major Street. Here, the **Mechanics' Institute** stands at the corner of Princess Street. This institution resulted from a conversation, held in 1824, between William Fairbairn, the noted engineer, and two friends. Fairbairn suggested that Manchester needed a forum in which the application of science to manufacturing and engineering might be taught. The inevitable public meeting launched the project, funds were raised, and the institute opened its doors the following year. By 1841, 1,300 members paid a £1 subscription to enrol in a series of adult classes (advanced tuition often took the form of 'mutual improvement' with the class members assisting each other). There was also a social dimension, together with a series of guest lectures. Ralph Waldo Emerson appeared, and Fanny Kemble, the greatest actress of the time, gave readings from Shakespeare.

"The Mechanics' Institute for the Diffusion of Useful Knowledge and the Encouragement of the Educable Working Class" moved to this site in 1854, and the building is in the popular 'palazzo style'. The Institute metamorphosed into a Technical school in 1882, and, as such, proved to be the nucleus of the future University of Manchester Institute of Science and Technology. The building now houses the archive, store, and restoration and conservation workshops of the National Museum of Labour History. It is not open to the public, though genuine researchers may access the archive collection upon application. (The museum galleries are to be found at the Pumphouse, and are described on p.65.) Note the **plaque** upon the Major Street side, recording the fact that the Trades Union Congress held their first meeting here in 1868.

Turn left into Princess Street, and walk as far as the **bridge** over the Rochdale Canal (p.154). On the way, we pass (on the left) Princess House (1860s) and No. 109, a pair of **yellow brick warehouses**. But look directly ahead, over the canal bridge, on the right. **Capital House** *(6)*, stretching from the canal to Whitworth Street, is an amazing creation in the 'Scottish baronial style', complete with corner turrets. It is now divided into serviced apartments.

Canal Street

We turn left into Canal Street, where narrow boats can sometimes be observed negotiating **Princess Street Lock** *(7)*. The canal towpath finished at this point, and the horses crossed the **narrow iron bridge** (by the side of the road bridge) to reach Canal Street. They continued their work along the (restored) strip of **cobbles**, which some people mistake for the pavement. Pause awhile here.

Canal Street is the heart of the **Gay Village**. The *Rembrandt* and the *Union* pubs hosted a gay clientele from the 1940s onwards. Indeed, the landlord of the latter was imprisoned as late as 1965 for "outraging public decency". On release he recommenced operations at his old hostelry, re-christened the ***New Union***. It stands at the corner of Princess Street and is still one of the most popular haunts in the Village. *Napoleon's* nightclub became the unofficial headquarters of the scene in the 1970s, when things began to change. The Central Manchester Development Corporation started to improve the area, a number of 'gay' entrepreneurs were alive to the possibilities, and the notion of a 'Gay Village' really took off. In one area, it was argued, gay men and women could be themselves. They could frequent their own cafés, bars, pubs and clubs (some devoted to their particular interests), shop for fashion and life style items, and, above all, feel safe. *Mash and Air,* the first of a new breed of café bar, opened on Chorlton Street in 1996, and *Manto* has inspired several imitators.

The Gay Village is now one of Manchester's major tourist attractions, with 20,000 visitors crowding into the village on a summer weekend. (It should be noted that at least 2,000 people are resident in the village area.) The gay 'Mardi Gras' festival attracts over 100,000 visitors from all over the world. Consequently, the 'pink pound' is now entrenched in the city's economy. However, the village is perhaps a victim of its own success – large numbers of 'straight' tourist visitors often overrun the area at weekends. Consequently, some of the establishments now impose (with varying degrees of tact) a strict entry code.

Canal Street

Canal Street itself has been transformed into a vibrant continental setting, with the clientele of the various cafés and bars spilling out into the street in fine weather. Notice that the street sign is placed at some height on the wall of ***Spirit*** **bar**. This is because the sort of people who put detergent in fountains consider it funny to block out the first letters of each word on the sign. ***Manto*** (Benedict Smith and Associates, 1989) was the first bar on the street, in brick and steel, with large street-level windows that allow its customers to be seen! (There is a breakfast club here, 02.00-06.00 on Friday/Saturday.) ***Sarasota***, above, is a very fashionable rooftop restaurant. One almost expects Hercule Poirot to emerge from the ***Abbaye Belgian Brasserie*** (specialising in mussels) next door. A **wooden bridge** leads over the canal to ***Metz***, a 'mid-European' café and bar, complete with a **floating drinking area**. Continue down the street. The ***Rembrandt Hotel*** (with a conspicuous enclosed balcony) is on the corner of Sackville Street. It is currently popular with 'macho' dressers. Continue alongside the canal as far as Chorlton Street, noting the 'Beacon of Hope' (see below) on the fringe of Sackville Park on the right. There is a view of *Churchill's* pub and other **18th-century survivors** at the end of the street.

Turn right into Chorlton Street, with an **early stone warehouse** on the left, marking the crossing of the canal. **Mynshull House** is part of Manchester Metropolitan University, as are the rest of the subsequent buildings on this side of the street. The brick building, set back from the car park, is the home of the **North West Film Archive**. The North West area featured prominently in the early history of British cinema, and some of the first films (several from the 1890s) have been preserved. The collection includes a variety of both professional and amateur footage of past events, customs, and ways of life that have disappeared. The range terminates in the **Business School of the University** (Mills, Beaumont, and Leavy, 1994) embracing the Old College Building and containing the library, with a very visible **grand staircase** that is usually hung with works of art. The screen of metal strips at the first-floor level is intended to shade the computer suite.

UMIST

We have now reached the junction of Whitworth and Fairfield Streets, and the view across the road is dominated by the great front of the main UMIST building. In reality, this is the **Municipal Technical School Extension**, commenced in 1927, but not completed until 1957! Much influenced by the work of Norman Shaw, it continues the terracotta frontage of the original building and incorporates a rather solid looking tower. Turn right into Whitworth Street, and then pause in front of the **Sheena Simon College**, a school of the performing arts. It was formerly the Central Higher Grade Board School, opened on this site in 1900 and intended by the Manchester School Board to undertake a higher level of technical instruction. The premises became a military hospital in the First World War, and there may still be some Mancunians who remember a pale figure in 'hospital blues', propped up at a window, and attempting to recover from the effects of a gas attack. The College students sometimes give public performances.

The adjacent **Sackville Park**, on the corner, originated as land purchased by the City Council in the 1880s. They were so proud of the new Technical School across the way that they wanted a good place from which to view it. The gardens contain a **monument to Alan Turing** (Glyn Hughes, 2001), the 'father of the computer' *(8)*. Turing conceived the idea of a 'universal machine' in the 1930s, a theoretical concept from which modern computing is derived. He put his ideas into practice by constructing 'The Bomb', a code breaking machine based at Bletchley Park during the last war. It enabled the allies to read the German 'enigma' codes, and was a key factor in the resulting victory.

Turing and his team developed 'The Baby', the first modern computer, at Manchester University in the post-war years. Unfortunately, he began to encounter problems with the authorities relating to his homosexuality. After an ill-advised course of hormone treatment, a life of great potential was terminated by suicide. Such was the reward from a grateful country. The statue is made of silicon bronze (what else!) and depicts Turing seated on a park bench holding an apple in his

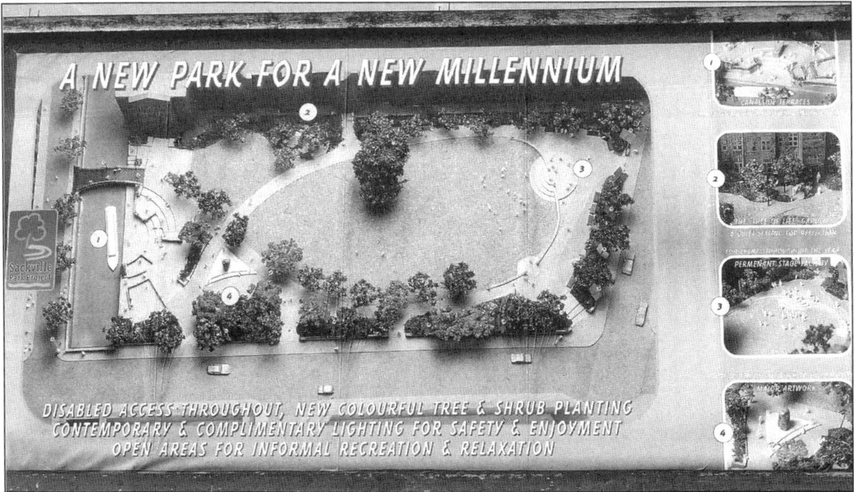

Plan for the development of Sackville Park

The Alan Turing monument

hand. The reference has a sting in the tail – on the face of it, the symbol recalls Newton, the father of modern mathematical and physical theory. But the apple is also a symbol of forbidden love. And Turing's choice of method of release from his personal agony was an apple laced with cyanide. The memorial was unveiled on the anniversary of his birth, and it should be noted that the major computer companies did not exactly fall over themselves to contribute to the memorial.

Appropriately enough, there are two memorials to Aids victims in the park. The **Tree of Life** was planted on World Aids Day in 1993. The **Beacon of Hope** may be found nearby *(9)*, overlooking the canal. This commemorates the victims of the Aids epidemic – their names are recorded in the capsule, and the list is updated each World Aids Day. A time line around the Beacon represents the spread of the virus and records the progress of the battle against it.

Exit the park and make a short detour by crossing Whitworth Street and walking for a short distance down Sackville Street. This brings us to the entrance to the original **Municipal Technical School** *(10)*. Sir Joseph Whitworth (p.224) was largely responsible for creating a new home for the recently formed Technical School, refashioned from the old Mechanic's Institute. As the inscriptions record, the trustees of his legacy disbursed the sum of £66,000 for the purchase of the site and the building fund. Over £13,000 came from the receipts of the Royal Jubilee Exhibition, held at Manchester in 1887. The six-storey structure was mainly erected (from designs by Spalding and Cross) in the 'French Renaissance' style between 1895 and 1912, using Accrington brick and terracotta. The **grand entrance hall** (once populated with casts of 'antique' sculptures) comprises an area of 40,000sq ft (3673 sq m), clad in marble tiling. Sir Arthur Whitten Brown (the Brown of Alcock and Brown, who made the first flight across the Atlantic in a Vickers Vimy in 1919), was one of the students at this time – commemorated by an **internal plaque**. The Technical School later became the University of Manchester Institute of Science and Technology (UMIST). UMIST has now amalgamated with Manchester University.

The building contains the comparatively unknown **Godlee Observatory**, built in 1902, and in the care of the Manchester Astronomical Society. It is located on G Floor, and accessed by a spiral wrought iron staircase. The original telescope is there to be used, but there is also a fine view out over the city centre. (The observatory is open to the public on Thursdays, 7pm to 10pm, admission free.)

Garret Hall

Retrace your footsteps to continue along Whitworth Street, and then turn left into Princess Street. **Lancaster House** is on the right-hand corner, but that side of the street is dominated by **Asia House** and **Manchester House**. The former (1900-10) has three upper floors of large Ionic pilasters, and the latter is very similar. If the **gate** *(11)* is open, walk down the passage between these two buildings and take a peep at the winding Medlock, surrounded by the **tiled backs of the great buildings** fronting onto Oxford Road and Whitworth Street. Continue along Princess Street under the railway viaduct to ***Joshua Brooks***, named after the famous Manchester character (p. 20). Turn right at this point into Charles Street, where the famous ***Lass o' Gowrie*** is situated beyond the Medlock bridge. It mainly attracts university people during the day – and sometimes a 'celebrity' from the nearby B.B.C. The pub has an attractive **tiled interior** and **brews its own beer**! Look for the **plaque** on the Medlock side of the pub, indicating the site of Manchester's oldest 'pissotiere' – last used in 1896!

Return along Charles and Princess Streets to the ***Old Garret***. This modern pub is situated near the former Garrett Hall, to which a curious legend is attached. An 18th-century owner journeyed to London on business, and was never heard from again. This caused problems when his son came of age, for the deeds of the property could not be found. His mother, who persisted in the view that her long vanished husband was still alive, placed an advertisement in a London paper. Surprisingly enough, this elicited a reply. The son was instructed to go to an address in the capital, where he was blindfolded and taken to a mysterious destination. The blindfold was removed to reveal his father! The gentleman eventually explained that, in the course of his original visit, he had fallen in love with a London girl. Consequently, he concealed his past life in Manchester and committed bigamy. He made his son swear never to reveal this information, expressed himself well satisfied with the young man's education and upbringing, and handed over the necessary documents. Finally, he promised that word would be sent of his death, which occurred some years later.

UMIST Campus

The way now lies to the right, along Granby Row. **Orient House** (1914), with its white glazed neo-classical façade, and **Granby House** (1911) are at the heart of the conversion of warehousing into flats. The latter blazed the trail with an £11m, sixty-two apartment conversion. Notice what is currently on offer in the estate agents window! The street now passes alongside the UMIST building, with a pleasant grassed area to the right. Here are a number of modern sculptures. The **Vimto sculpture** (Kerry Morrison, 1992), a large wooden bottle surrounded by fruit, is a favourite with children *(12)*. 'Vimto' began life as a 'temperance drink', an alternative to beer. John Nichols mixed the first batch of this popular drink on Granby Row in 1908. Further on may be found the **Technology Arch** (Axel Wolkenhauer, 1989), made of industrial strength steel rope *(13)*. A detour along the path to the railway arch reveals **Archimedes** *(14)*. The old boy is portrayed rising from his bath and uttering 'Eureka!' at the very moment of his discovery that the area of an irregularly shaped object can be measured through the amount of displaced water. There is a fine view over the **UMIST Campus** from this point.

Return to Granby Row, and proceed to the point where it joins London Road at its intersection with Fairfield Street. *(The walk can be extended from here to include Ardwick, see p.271).* The new **vehicular entrance to Piccadilly Station** *(15)* is visible across the road. Turn left and walk down London Road in the direction of Piccadilly until the old **Police and Fire Station** (1904-1906) is reached. It was described on the opening day as "the finest fire station in this whole round world", and it is certainly composed of an eclectic mixture of Edwardian Baroque. This magnificent triangular structure is built round an internal courtyard, once used for drills and cleaning the fire appliances. The thirty-four firemen's married quarters were accessed by the verandas.

The complex also contained a police station, ambulance station, bank, gas testing station (!), and a **Coroner's Court**, for inquests into suspicious or sudden deaths. The frontage is a mixture of brick and brown glazed terracotta, now very much the worse for wear. Since the firemen moved out, the place has a semi-derelict and deserted air. A shopping centre development has been proposed, but nothing much has yet been done.

The Vimto sculpture

The Technology Arch

Piccadilly Station

Piccadilly Station lies across the road. It originated in 1842, as the terminus of the Manchester and Birmingham Railway, a line that joined the Grand Junction railway at Crewe, offering a direct route to Birmingham and the capital in about twelve hours. The station was shared (to limit expense) with the Sheffield, Ashton, and Manchester Railway, famous for the notorious Woodhead tunnel. It later became the joint station of the London and North Western and Manchester, Sheffield, and Lincolnshire (later Great Central) companies, and the restored **goods office frontage** of the former concern are a noteworthy feature. Cross the road and enter the **undercroft** by the entrance to the left of the tram tracks *(16)*. As the railways approached the terminus upon a viaduct, the station is placed over a large crypt-like area that was used as a goods station (reached by means of a hydraulic wagon hoist). Part of this is now used as a Metrolink station. Notice the **stone arches** immediately to the left in this gloomy passage. You are standing in Birmingham Street, a highway lost when the station was extended. The arches were a pedestrian entrance to the original building. The passage emerges on to the Metrolink platform, but ascend by the lift or escalators to the station concourse.

The new **concourse** can only be an improvement on the old one, a dreadful sixties creation erected in place of a far superior late Victorian building. It comprises a split-level shopping mall in addition to the usual railway facilities. Somewhere, one hopes that the original **Manchester and Birmingham Railway plaque** will have pride of place. The late-**19th-century train shed** has recently been completely refurbished, but the wrought iron railing (which divided the parts owned by the two companies) disappeared some time ago. A newly installed **'travelator'** transports

Piccadilly Station approach from across London Road

passengers to a **lounge area** above the platforms at the Fairfield Street end. We leave the station by the approach entrance, and pass the easily missed **flight of steps down into Store Street**. **Gateway House** (Richard Siefert, 1969) runs alongside the station approach. The range of shops contains the ***Ian Allan Bookshop***, a must for all transport enthusiasts. The approach deposits the visitor at the junction of Piccadilly and Ducie Street. The ***Piccadilly Indian Restaurant*** may be glimpsed to the left – a rare survival of the original buildings on this road out of Manchester.

You can now return to Piccadilly by walking directly ahead down London Road. Or you can embark on the next walk as an optional extension.

The Ashton Canal at Redhill (formerly Union) Street

8 Alternative Manchester (2): Ancoats

Start: Foot of Piccadilly Station Approach

Estimated time of walk: 1 hour

Highlights: A canal aqueduct, the oldest mill complex in Manchester, 'model' workers' housing, a glimpse of Old China, a secret printing press, and where the modern printing presses roared.

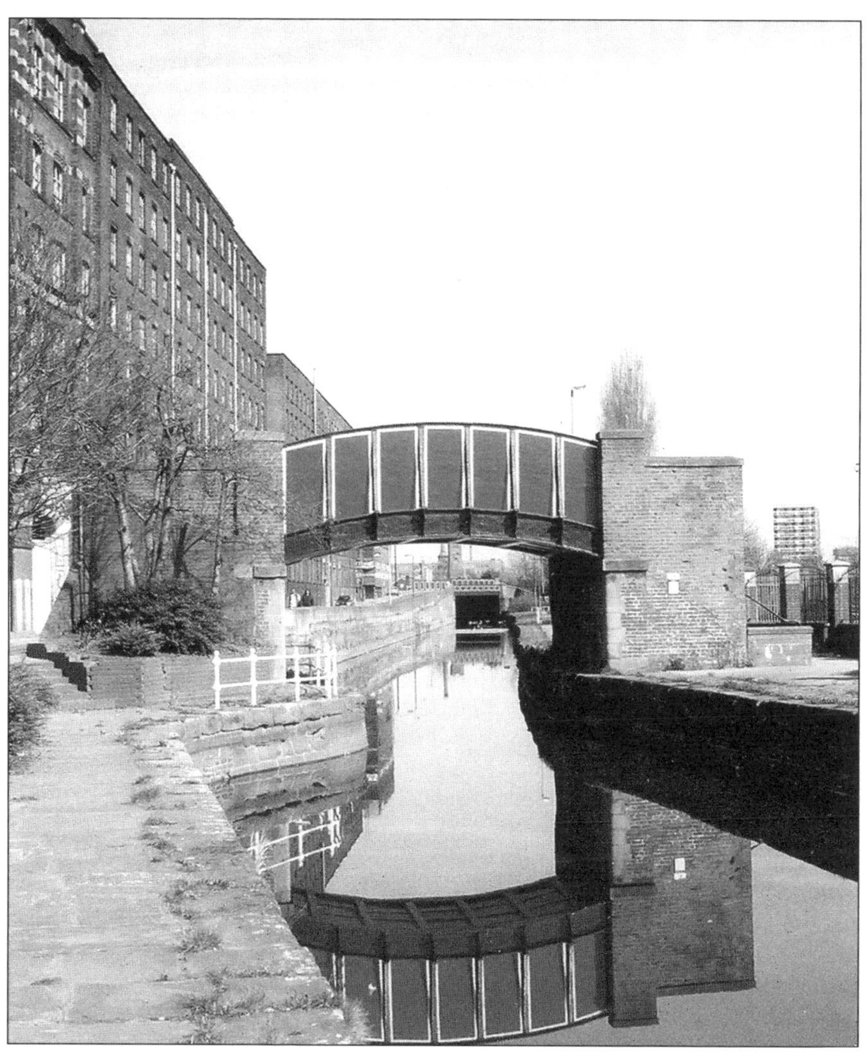

This walk takes you to Ancoats, the **world's first industrial suburb**. Visitors came in the early nineteenth century to gaze with a horrified fascination at the evidences of a new industrial civilisation. For why, one of Disraeli's characters asked, should he go to Athens? "The age of ruins is passed. Have you seen Manchester? Manchester is as great a human exploit as Athens." Vast wealth was created in the midst of a slum. Ancoats became one of the city's problem districts, but the residents began to disappear in the post-war prosperity, the mills closed, and it seemed that the entire area might become a wasteland of dereliction. However, a large part of Ancoats is now a conservation area, the canal system has been revitalised, and the transformation and regeneration of the district is now taking place at almost breakneck speed – it has been necessary to re-write most of this section since the last edition. Some of the major ongoing projects will be described in the course of the walk. Of course, the denizens of Piccadilly Village are now spilling over into Ancoats proper, and there are fears that the consequent gentrification will destroy whatever remains of the character of the old place. Only time will tell.

Ducie Street

Go to the right at the foot of the station approach. Ducie Street intersects all that remains of a great **canal terminal and complex**, at the junction of the Rochdale and Ashton Canals, and once as important as Castlefield (p.169). The Rochdale Canal opened in 1804, the Committee sailing to Manchester in two boats accompanied by the band of the Manchester and Salford Volunteers. It owned a large part of this canal basin, a useful transhipment point halfway between Liverpool and Yorkshire. The waterway was re-opened throughout on 1 July, 2002, by Fred Dibnah, a well-known local personality. The city centre section of the Rochdale Canal (linking this point to Castlefield) remains an important part of the 'Cheshire Ring'. (p.172)

The Ashton Canal not only offered an alternative Trans-Pennine route, but also linked with the canal network to the Midlands and the South. This canal also accessed (beyond Ashton) the Huddersfield 'Narrow' Canal, re-opened in May, 2001.Thus it is now possible to sail the 'Pennine Ring', going outward by either canal and returning via the Leeds and Liverpool and the Bridgewater canals – or vice versa.

The **large brick warehouse** on the right, built by the Manchester, Sheffield, and Lincolnshire Railway, provided the facility of goods transfer to and from the canal system. It now houses *The Palace*, an apartment hotel (served by a wall climbing lift), with offices and retail on the ground floor. We pass a curious round structure just beyond the building (framing the entrance to an underground car park) before passing the **Ducie Wharf** development. Notice that the Ashton Canal flows under part of this complex as it exits the Dale Street Basin *(1)*.

On the opposite side of the road is a low wall with a view over **Dale Street Canal Basin** *(2)*. The battlemented entrance is round the corner in Dale Street itself, adjacent to the **Rochdale Canal Warehouse**. This can be glimpsed over the wall on the left side of the basin. The structure dates from 1806 (constructed in millstone grit and looking as if it would stand until the crack of doom), and once straddled a canal arm with the 'shipping holes' clearly visible. The goods were loaded and unloaded by attic hoists powered by a water wheel. It is scheduled for conversion into offices.

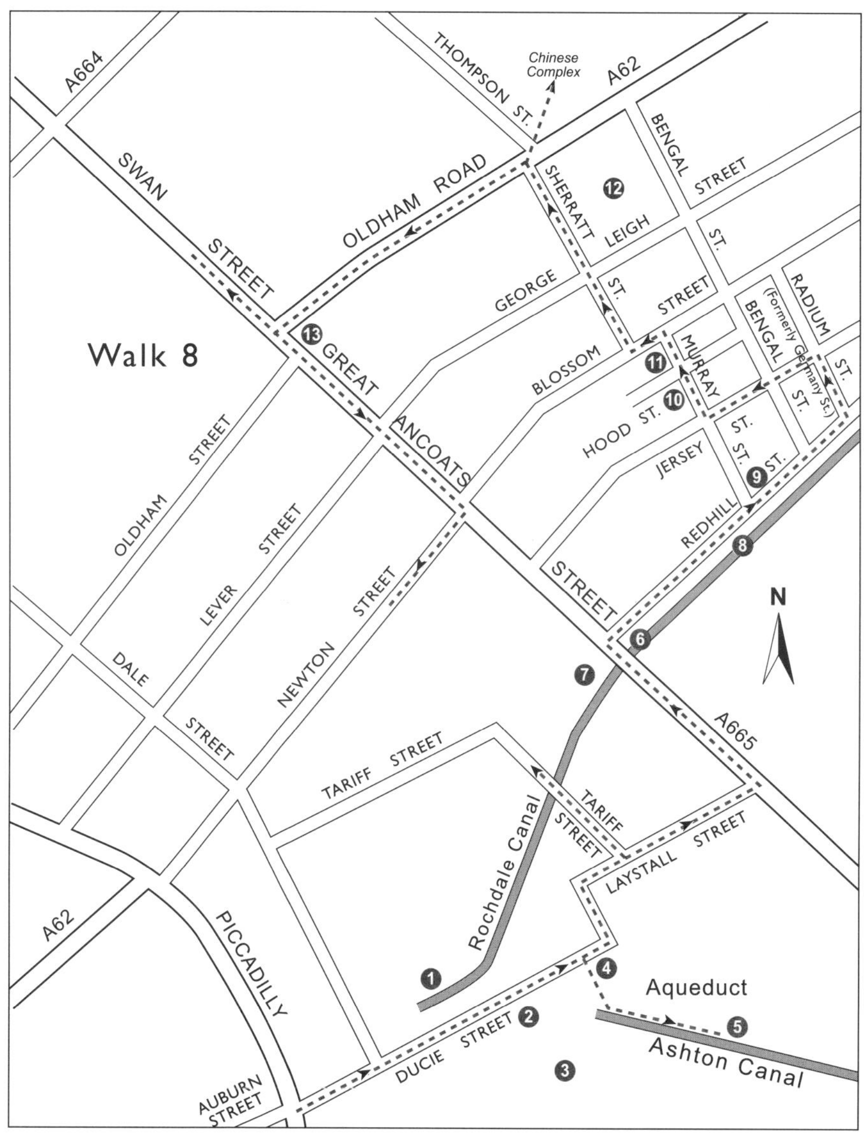

The basin is currently undergoing redevelopment, and will eventually be surrounded by office development. In the meantime, there is still a panoramic view of the canal junction. The Rochdale Canal exits the basin under Tariff Street, on the extreme right.

Recross the road to the commencement of Jutland Street, the **steepest street in Manchester***(3)*. L.S. Lowry (p.243) painted it. Some decades ago, an old gentleman became the terror of the taxi drivers. After coming into some money, his pleasure in life was simple – an afternoon's drinking, and home by cab, via a run down Jutland Street at top speed! Directly ahead is an entrance to **Paradise Wharf** *(4)* – keep the brick wall on the left and the small basin (once spanned by a warehouse) on the right, and admire the **traditional painted sign** on the side of Junction Works. Turn right towards the **restored crane** and the **wooden bridge**. Two short detours suggest themselves. You can cross the bridge and follow the towpath under Jutland Street (access steps) for a view of the (partly) restored basin in front of the brick warehouse, before returning. Or you can follow the towpath round to the left along the canal as it heads towards Ancoats and reach the stone **aqueduct** (5), which carries the Ashton Canal across Store Street (interesting view). The towpath runs through **Piccadilly Village** (1990-94), a prestigious canal-side development. Some of the new owners tried to have the towpath closed, since a public footpath past their windows was not included in the publicity! So we will not disturb them and retrace our footsteps back to Ducie Street.

Great Ancoats Street

Linda's Pantry, on the corner of Peak Street, is an excellent 'greasy spoon' café, and will perhaps prove useful if the new inhabitants begin to tire of dèsigner food. The road leads round into Laystall Street. The ***Jolly Angler*** lies at the bottom of Pigeon Street, on the right, a traditional pub that is off the beaten track but well thought of. But we can make a short diversion down Tariff Street on the left, as far as the **canal bridge**. The view to the left is over **Vantage Quay**, a restored canal basin intended to be the centrepiece for a residential development. The new build makes an interesting use of wood in the design, but pick out the (restored) **brick warehouse dating to 1836**. Back on Laystall Street notice, also, the impressive **warehouse in the popular Venetian style**.

We now reach Great Ancoats Street, a grand name dating from 1788. Prior to that, it was just Ancoats Lane. The name is thought to be Saxon in origin, meaning "gifted cottages or enclosures." It was situated in a rural area, the roadway being used by cattle drovers to avoid the narrow streets leading to the 'shambles'. However, some drovers took their cattle southwards, and the lane connected with a drovers' highway now known as Ashton Old Road. Then something happened. To appreciate the magnitude of the change, cross the road, turn left, cross the canal bridge, and pause in the area by the lock at the corner of Redhill Street*(6)*.

The first water-powered cotton mills were established in country districts. Richard Arkwright (p.189) installed a steam engine at a mill near the present C.I.S. building (p.247) in 1782, but this only pumped water to power the wheel. However, the Watt steam engine was soon adapted to power the machinery, and cotton manufacture became an urban phenomenon. There were two mills in and around the town in 1782. This had increased to fifty-two only ten years later. Many of these were established in the green field site of Ancoats, particularly after the first section of the Rochdale Canal had been cut in 1799.

Redhill Street

Brownsfield Mill *(7)* is situated across the road, opposite Redhill Street. A.V. Roe (p.200) used an upper floor as his first aircraft factory.

The **view alongside the canal in Redhill Street** (formerly Union Street) is a classic one *(8)*, and the famous illustration found in most books about the industrial revolution shows that the scene is still essentially the same. They are now undergoing restoration and conversion to apartments and retail units. James McConnel and John Kennedy erected the first large mill that we come across. Hailing from Scotland, they started in the manufacture of textile machinery (employing clockmakers, which Lancashire then had in such an abundance), but soon turned to cotton manufacture. They erected Old Mill in 1799, as the date stone proudly recalls, though the mill was entirely rebuilt in 1912. It was re-christened **Royal Mill**, to celebrate a wartime visit by King George V1 in 1942. Kennedy resided at Ardwick Hall, and was one of the principal promoters of the Liverpool and Manchester Railway.

Another pair of Scots, Adam and George Murray, erected a complex of four buildings around a yard between 1798 and 1806. The six storey **Old Mill** *(9)*, fronting Redhill Street, opened in 1798. It is the earliest surviving structure of its kind in the city, and is still very much in its original condition – perhaps the oldest steam powered cotton mill in existence. The Decker Mill dates from 1802; the six storey New Mill, on the Jersey Street side of the yard, 1804; and the rest of the complex was intended as warehousing. The central yard became a reservoir after the opening of the Rochdale Canal, with which it communicated by a tunnel under Redhill Street. Coal was later shipped in containers by barge through the tunnel, which is now blocked up. By 1818, the Murrays masterminded a commercial empire employing 1,300 workers. (A workforce of fifty signified a large concern at the time.) The complex has been secured for preservation, and is being restored to a mixed leisure, retail, and accommodation use, complete with the central water feature!

The Heart of Ancoats

St Peter's Church, Ancoats

The recently restored Doubling Mill, also known as Waulk Mill (1842), lies beyond Bengal Street. It currently (2004) contains a **Visitor Centre** (daily, 2.00-4.30), with a model of the New Islington development (currently under construction) on the opposite side of the canal, stretching from there as far as Pollard Street. When complete, this will provide an interesting diversion, and a new starting point for the Ashton excursion (see below). A new bridge will span the canal near this point, leading to a central spine alongside a new canal basin linking the Rochdale and Ashton Canals (intended as the focus for a complex of marinas and mooring places). The spine intersects a pedestrianised Mill Street (intended as a market and event area, and containing the old

Ardwick and Ancoats Dispensary building), and will eventually enable the visitor to access the (proposed) Holt Town Metrolink Station. The development itself is a mixture of retail, housing, and office accommodation, including low rent property for the local people.

Notice the canal bridge directly ahead. Here, the towpath changes sides, and the horses crossed by a small iron parallel bridge. To avoid a tangle with the ropes, 'dobbin' descended by means of the curious spiral ramp. **(This walk can be prolonged by the excursion to Eastlands and Ashton, described on p. 253)** Now turn left down Radium Street (formerly Germany Street, the name being changed in the First World War). A bump in the road, beyond the Jersey Street intersection, indicates a bridge over yet another long forgotten canal arm, evidence of how extensive this system once was. But we turn left into Jersey Street. Look out for **Beehive Mill**, on the right, with its name carved on a stone, and dating from 1820. One day, all the historic mills in the area may be restored to this standard. It currently houses a number of organisations working for the conservation of the area – together with a recording studio and *Sankey's Soap!* The latter is a venue for a variety of bands and performers from time to time, and takes its name from a (restored) painted advertisement, (probably executed in the 1920s) on the side of the water tower.

Jactin House *(10)*, set back beyond the car park at the corner of Murray Street, was the Male Methodist Mission (1903-5) and is being redeveloped. If you didn't mind the preaching, good beds might be had for a pittance. If you had no money … well, a bit of labouring work in an adjacent yard earned the right to a bed and a hot meal. Proceed down Murray Street to Blossom Street, and stand in front of **St. Peter's Church***(11)*. Although Ancoats was a poor district, the Bishop insisted that the necessary economy should be combined with some grandeur, hence the odd combination of a medieval 'romanesque' design in brick, married to a cast iron internal structure. It was consecrated in 1859, but fell out of use in the 1960s. Fortunately, it has been saved from demolition, and the first phase of restoration has concentrated on the tower. Additional funding has been obtained for the next phase.

The area in front of the church is intended for redevelopment as an open space. The original plan proposed an Italian style 'piazza', though this may be in some doubt. Indeed, a glance to the left, down Blossom Street, will reveal the Ice Plant, which serviced the needs of the original local ice cream vendors. Ancoats was (in some cases, still is) the home of Manchester's Italian Community. The sight of the men of the religious fraternity carrying the great statue of the Madonna, accompanied by the girls in colourful national dress, is familiar to generations of Mancunians at the Whit walks. (p.197)

Victoria Square

Go straight ahead, along Sherratt Street. The entire area to the right is earmarked for a core development, mainly residential, but including other uses. This, it is thought, might prove the catalyst in the regeneration of the area. Glance right at the point where George Leigh Street crosses, to see the **old elementary school building** (1912). It was necessary to place the boy's playground on the roof in such a crowded district. George Leigh Street is named after the original owner of the land in the area. It was largely sold to Thomas Bound, a builder, who commenced erecting cheap houses as early as 1775. The man made a fortune.

The great forbidding bulk of **Victoria Square** (12) looms on the right. This housing complex, intended to benefit the 'working classes', was erected in a vague Queen Ann style round a large courtyard in 1889. The corner towers contained laundries and drying rooms. The architect seems to have thought that he was building for an alien race – wooden skirting boards were not provided, since these might be ripped out and burned! The 'model' workers' housing (1898-9) on the left are in the form of much kinder terraces. However, the city fathers celebrated their progressive ways in the street names. This was all very well, but everyone (certainly by the 1960s) was too posh to live in Sanitary Street! The council dropped some letters to change the name to Anita Street.

Oldham Road

We have now reached Oldham Road, originally known as Newton Lane. Somewhere near this point stood a cottage – moreover, a place that played a humble part in English history. The puritans (who, at this stage, had the reform of the state church as their objective) had been forced underground in the later years of Queen Elizabeth's reign. They hit back by attacking the bishops, their principal enemies, in a series of scurrilous (but very amusing) pamphlets. The 'Martin Marprelate' tracts "printed in Almayne (Germany), over the sea, five leagues from a bouncing priest," were very much a home grown product. In 1588, when London became too hot, Robert Waldegrave (the printer and publisher) removed the press to the cottage on Newton Lane. He had just completed a batch of the latest installment, entitled "Ha' ye any more work for the Cooper?" (A pun on a bishop's name, using the street cry of barrel makers!) Lord Derby, then residing at Chetham's College, sallied forth and raided the premises. Waldegrave escaped, but the press was destroyed. The irony was that, in the year of the Armada, the puritans were amongst the Queen's most loyal subjects. But she could not conceive of a state church without those inconvenient Bishops. Interestingly enough, in changed times, our hero became printer to King James, Elizabeth's successor.

Opposite Victoria Square, across Oldham Road, is a part of the **Forbidden City of Old Peking!** The ancient Chinese Roof and the Pagoda at the street corner betoken a new development by Wing Ip, a very large Chinese supermarket. (Members of the public are cordially invited to join the restaurant proprietors laying in their weekly provisions.) Although there is a very useful cash machine on the Oldham Road side, entrance to this mysterious and blank-walled domain is obtained by the path from the corner of Thomson Street, skirting the **Fire Station** and Brigade Training School (notice the **Lancashire and Yorkshire railway memorial** on the left, all that remains of the large goods yard that occupied this site. The Wing Ip complex also contains a Chinese restaurant (what else!) rather curiously called ***'Glamorous'*** – perhaps something was lost in the translation.

Walk down Oldham Road towards the city centre. The wide junction with Great Ancoats Street is known as **New Cross**. The long vanished 'New Cross' (presumably to distinguish it from the 'old' Market Cross) was placed here in the eighteenth century. Perhaps someone wanted to start a rival market. It replaced the earlier 'Barlow's Cross' about which little is known. The site must have had some significance, since the bodies of suicides were buried there, one in 1753 with "a stake driven through the body." Human remains were discovered in the course of road works in 1846. In 1812, a group of starving labourers intercepted a cart en route to Shudehill here and appropriated fourteen sacks of oatmeal and other grains for 'distribution' to the crowd. New Cross is, by tradition, one of the three places in Manchester where the accession of a new monarch is proclaimed.

Swan Street

A brief detour down Swan Street, to the right, is recommended. The left side of this street once fringed **Smithfield Market**, which accounts for the surviving number of pubs. The area beside Shudehill had long been used as a provision market. Land was purchased in 1804 and the Manorial rights relating to markets were purchased by the Corporation in 1845. The Market (with an area of 26,212 square yards) became the most extensive in the country. However, it was later seen as an inconveniently placed traffic nuisance, and was removed to a new home in Gorton in the 1970s. A few of the old buildings survive, adapted to other uses. After reading the interesting inscription on the **Swan Street market building**, take a look at the area behind it, scheduled for a redevelopment package, including the historic fish Market. (A description of part of this area is given on p.163.) It will, it is said. constitute Britain's "first sustainable neighbourhood within a city". Swan Street also contains the ***Band on the Wall***, for those who appreciate jazz and blues.

Return to the **'Crown and Kettle'** (13), on the corner of Oldham Street and Great Ancoats Street. This stands on the site of an earlier pub, with the odd name of 'Iron Dish and Cob of Coal'. The 'Crown and Kettle' is a strange building, with neo-gothic windows and good quality stonework. One story suggests that it was intended as a Court House for magistrates sessions, but was found surplus to requirements. The old pub was a haunt of the Daily Express print workers, with its statue of Churchill

Jazz in the city – at Band on the Wall, Swan Street

and a fireplace surround made from the timbers of the R101 airship. It is to be hoped that these features will again be on view if and when the place reopens. (The building is currently in the possession of English Heritage.)

We now resume the walk along Great Ancoats Street. The **arTzu Gallery** (Tues-Sat, 11-5.30, Sun 12-4, free admission) is a new private gallery, offering affordable (from £300) paintings in a variety of styles. The **Daily Express Building** (Sir Owen Williams, 1939) is an almost exact copy of his building on Fleet Street. It makes a stunning use of glass and black 'vitrolite' for, under the energetic leadership of Lord Beaverbrook, the Express was then a power in the land, and a very progressive undertaking. At one time, it was possible to see the great printing presses behind the glass sheeting, but the whole complex now has a strange deserted

The restored Express building in Great Ancoats Street

aspect. After the preliminary refurbishment, the usual flats are proposed, together with a restaurant. After passing a **strange little building** (with a 'mock tudor' attic) we reach the commencement of Jersey Street. Notice **Coates School** (with plaque), a short distance down Jersey Street on the right, together with the **two 1920s houses** (built for electricity workers, next to the substation) almost opposite. Cross Great Ancoats Street to Newton Street, which eventually leads back to Piccadilly.

The police station in Newton Street, now housing the Police Museum

9 Alternative Manchester (3): The Northern Quarter

Start: Piccadilly/Newton Street

Estimated time of walk: 1½ hours

Highlights: A police museum, the Craft Village, curry heaven, quirky sculptures, and 'alternative' shopping.

This walk again starts in Piccadilly, which you should leave by Newton Street. (If you are joining it from the Ancoats walk, remember that Newton Street will be entered from the opposite end, so the following description up to the entry to Stevenson Square should be taken in reverse order.) It now contains **Fan Boy 3**, a new shop specialising in games, both electronic and traditional.

Newton Street

We are again in the land of warehouses, but with a difference – many of them are occupied by small businesses involved in wholesale clothing, known as the 'rag trade'. The rather solid mid-Victorian **warehouse at the junction with Port Street** *(1)* includes grime-coated stone. At one time, all the stone surfaces in Manchester looked like this, but a series of post-war smokeless zones (the city pioneered this approach), made it possible to clean stonework without risking further discoloration.

Take a detour to the right, down Hilton Street. Here, many of the **original buildings have been preserved and restored**. The same is true of Port Street, entered by a left turn. The 'Cobden Coffee House' stood somewhere in the vicinity, and its clientele (including Ernest Jones, the Chartist) made it a sounding board for contemporary social and economic questions – a kind of 19th-century 'think tank'. Victorian luminaries such as John Stuart Mill and Lord Shaftesbury visited it. We pass the ***Cuba Café***, a noted Salsa centre (tuition available), before turning left into Faraday Street.

Regaining Newton Street, we see the large **Post Office Building** across the road to the right. It is mainly Edwardian, but incorporates a (disused?) hideous sorting office annexe (1965-8) on the Lever Street side.

To the left of the Post Office may be found the interesting **Police Museum**. (Open Tuesdays 10.30-3.30, other times by appointment, telephone 0161 856 3278. Ring bell for admission.) The museum is housed in a former police station *(2)* erected in 1879 to serve 'A' Division (covering most of the city centre). We see the reconstructed **charge room**, with its desk and fireplace, before exploring the corridor with its **cells**. Note the Victorian beds with their wooden 'pillows'. This part of the old building is sometimes used for filming purposes. The stairs lead to the main gallery. The first police in Britain were the creation of Sir Robert Peel (p.93) when he was Home Secretary (and thus had direct responsibility for the maintenance of law and order in the capital). They were thus called 'peelers' or 'bobbies'. Despite early opposition to an 'un-English' continental institution, the idea was soon copied in towns and cities throughout the country. It should be noted that Britain has never had a national police force – the majority of the police forces remain the responsibility of the local authorities, although the number has been reduced by amalgamation.

The first 'bobbies' appeared on the streets of Manchester in 1839, and the **displays** illustrate the history of the police forces in Greater Manchester, including such matters as uniforms, equipment, the development of forensic science, and transport. Look out for the **relics relating to the career of Jerome Caminada**, Manchester's great Victorian detective. A small room contains **souvenirs of police forces from around the world**, and the old **police doctor's room** survives. The museum also houses a photographic collection and an extensive archive, which

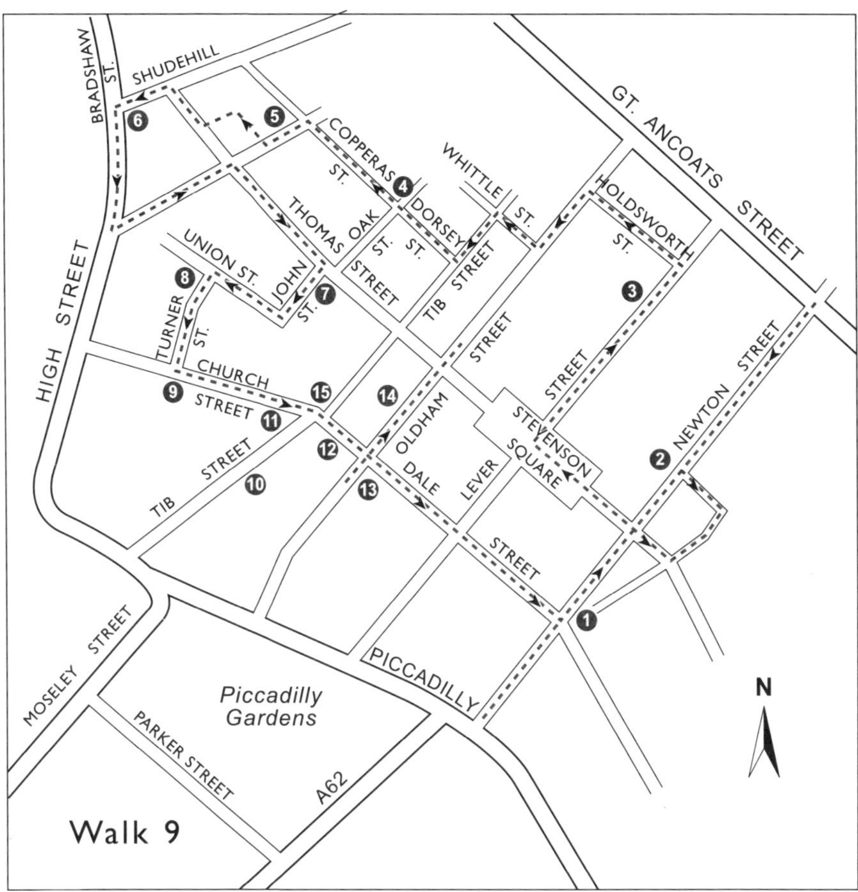

can be consulted by appointment. It is sometimes useful for those whose ancestors were either a local policeman or a crook.

Stevenson Square

Turn right beyond the museum and proceed by way of another section of Hilton Street into Stevenson Square, named after William Stevenson. He purchased a large part of the Lever estate and made a fortune from property development in the area. The Square is completely surrounded by warehouses, the majority of which are still occupied by textile businesses. In the 19th century, the Square was famous for its radical political meetings and demonstrations, but older people remember it as the scene (in comic song) of the depredations of Benjamin Von Gherkin, the notorious 'German Clockwinder'.

> He met a young woman in Stevenson Square,
> And she said as her clock were in need of repair.
> They ran upstairs, and she squealed with delight,
> For within ten minutes, he'd set her clock right!

As the district was transformed into a fashionable 18th-century residential area, the Reverend Edward Smyth indulged in some speculative activity of his own. He built his own church, anticipating a tidy income from the pew rents. St Clement's opened in 1793 on the corner of Stevenson Square and Lever Street, but did not prosper. Since Smyth owned the land, the Church of England only licensed it for ordinary services – such money-spinners as fashionable weddings and baptisms were forbidden.

> And the Church holds that Truth be told,
> Except the Place it be preach'd in be wholly freehold…

His speculative activities in another place had equally come to naught and he had no less than two churches left on his hands. In 1817, Smyth was reduced to advertising. "Two churches to be sold in Manchester; and, if not, a curate wanted. Address post paid…." The building fell out of use and was later demolished. *(The walk can be extended by the excursion to Eastlands and Ashton, described on p.257, by catching a bus to Ashton from here.)*

Lever Street

Turn right into Lever Street, and walk past the former Bus Station. Pause at the **row of restored house fronts**, dating to 1787 *(3)*. The cellars were used by the tradesmen who lived here as their place of business, the workmen residing in artisans' dwellings to the rear. Turn to the left, down Houldsworth Street, and take some time out to examine the interesting rear of the row (**plaque**). Upon reaching Oldham Street, note that ***The City*** pub has some excellent plasterwork decoration. There are some **interesting shops** at this end of the street – *Hang Fong* (Chinese Porcelain), *Moon Walk Collectables* (Star Trek items etc.), *Anything Theatrical* (costumes and masks), and *New Aeon Books* (occult).

A short distance in the Piccadilly direction, and the way now lies to the right, down Whittle Street, to reach Tib Street. The latter runs over a stream of the same name, now completely covered over. It was the centre of the pet trade in the last century, with a weekend bird market, but only one pet shop is left. They seem to have

Entrance to The Craft Village, Ancoats

been replaced by a number of rather seedy sex shops in this part of the street, though a number of the **original frontages** (complete with loom shop windows) have been recently restored. Other parts of the street, towards Market Street, have **ceramic tile poetry** inserted into the pavement.

The matching ceramic street names are particularly noticeable. This indicates that we are entering the heart of the **Northern Quarter**, an area devoted to alternative lifestyles and shopping. It is also an area in the course of transition as old property is refurbished, and is increasingly decorated with a number of outdoor works of art. A right turn into Dorsey Street leads through some 1970s housing (one of the first attempts to repopulate the city centre) to the ***Craft Village***, one of the quarter's principal attractions *(4)*. The official title is the 'Manchester Craft and Design Centre'. A former Smithfield Market building now contains a number of craft shop and workshop units on two levels – it is sometimes possible to see the craftsmen and women at work. The range includes ceramics and mosaics, silverware, jewellery, textiles, and furniture. A ground floor café incorporates some of the old market signs, and a piano is available for those who can play! The Centre is usually open Monday-Saturday, but note that most of the unit owners are absent on Mondays. (However, it is often possible to arrange a purchase if a unit is closed.)

Exit the Craft Village, and by a left, followed by a right turn, walk along Copperas Street. New buildings intrude on both sides, that on the right being **Design House** – containing one and two bedroom apartments, with retail at street level. It is part of the new Smithfield Market development. (p.157) We now reach the cobbled portion of High Street (sometimes the venue of a farmer's market) introducing the façade of the **Old Fish Market.** Note the **friezes illustrating a fisherman's life** in the gable ends.(5) The façade now fronts a new development of the usual offices and studio apartments, the iron gates opening onto a **pleasant courtyard** (complete

One of the friezes preserved as part of the Northern Quarter development

with the iron columns that once supported the roof) that is accessible at all hours. Walk through to Salmon Street, turn left, and arrive at Thomas Street. (If the gates are shut, go to the left and turn right, down Thomas Street.)

A short detour to the left leads to the entrance to the new **Chinese Arts Centre** (Mon-Sat 10.00am – 6.00pm, Sun 11.00am-5.00pm, free admission). Enter, but don't expect Ming vases or willow pattern plate – the Centre is intended to be a showcase for modern Chinese arts and craft, portrayed in a series of changing exhibitions. Nevertheless, traditional crafts (such as calligraphy) are taught in the downstairs education centre. There is an excellent shop, but the principal attraction is undoubtedly a **reconstruction of a 1930s Shanghai Tea Shop.** Cups of delicious tea are usually available, and boxes of different varieties can be purchased. Follow Thomas Street to arrive at Shudehill.

Shudehill

We pass to the left, along Shudehill. The name first appeared in 1554, and is something of a mystery. It can be translated as 'the hill of the husking of oats', but what that really means is anybody's guess. A large bus and Metrolink interchange is being developed on the area of open land to the right. ***Spy World*** is situated on the left, near the corner of Thomas Street, so if you have ever wanted to bug someone ... now is your chance!

Stand at the corner of Nicholas Croft *(6)*, where the tram lines cross. Withingreave Hall stood somewhere hereabouts, the town residence of the Hulme family. William Hulme (died 1691) left some property to maintain "four of the poorest sort of bachelors of arts taking such degrees in Brazenose College in Oxford". Parliament later authorised the trustees of the charity to grant building leases. As the town expanded and property prices escalated, Hulme's charity became a goldmine. Unfortunately, the clergymen who ran it tended to use it to provide jobs for other clergy! This scandalous state of affairs ended with the reorganisation of the charity in 1881. The remaining proceeds were sufficient to create and endow grammar schools in Manchester, Bury, and Oldham, together with a hall of residence at Owen's College (p.61). One of the outhouses of the old hall remained until modern times, for, adjacent to Nicholas Croft, stood the 'Rover's Return', a half-timbered building said to date to the mediaeval period. After a varied career as a pub, dining room, and curio shop, it was demolished in the 1950s. This event must have dispossessed the resident ghost, a Scottish highlander left behind in the course of the 1745 Jacobite Rebellion. Perhaps he haunts the city planning department.

Bradshaw Hall lay across Shudehill, almost alongside the tram lines. John Bradshaw became High Sheriff of Lancashire in 1753, an elevation which resulted in an episode of high drama at his front gate. The harvest failed. On 6th June, 1757, a party of starving men seized the corn from the mills at Clayton and marched to Manchester with the intention of taking the potatoes at the Shudehill market. They encountered a party of soldiers, ordered out by Bradshaw. Faced with a hail of stones, the soldiers opened fire and killed five of the crowd, wounding fifteen. The crowd was so desperate that this was not the end of the matter. They attacked local corn mills and later attempted to free an imprisoned rioter from the Salford Bridge lock up. The authorities, clearly having lost control of events, freed the prisoner, and everything subsided like a summer storm. The event is known in history as 'Shudehill Fight'.

The point commands a view directly along Withy Grove. The 'withies' or willows disappeared long ago, but a **range of 19th-century frontages** survives. The 'Seven Stars', once thought to be the oldest licensed public house in the country, was in this street. It bore a painted legend that the original license was granted in 1356, which was no mean feat – the licensing system did not exist at that date! The earliest record of it as a pub can be dated to 1551. Many other stories connected with the old building (including mysterious secret passages) were equally groundless. The one exception was very sad indeed. At some point in the 18th century, on a market day, a farm labourer was leading a horse that had cast a shoe down Withy Grove to the blacksmith. A 'press gang', lying in wait for such country boys that might come to market, grabbed him for service in the navy. The poor youth asked the landlord to nail the horseshoe to the stair post, vowing to reclaim it when he came back from the wars. He never did, and the rusting shoe remained as an accusation for nearly two hundred years. Like much else, this picturesque pub (which featured in local postcards) fell to the demolition hammer in the inter-war period.

The Curry Quarter

Nicholas Croft itself once had a flourishing second-hand book market, but all this disappeared with road widening. The remaining stalls transferred to Church Street. The walk continues to the left along Nicholas Croft, before turning left again into High Street. This part of Manchester is developing into a **'curry quarter'**, with a variety of restaurants and balti houses, usually much cheaper than the famous 'curry mile' in Rusholme. A right turn into Thomas Street reveals more restored **18th-century frontages**. A giant **Brush and Dustpan** *(7)* marks the corner of John Street. Walk a little further along this street and then look up. The collection of **birds** perched upon the warehouse brackets will not fly away – they are stuffed!

Manchester Buddhist Centre *(see next page)*

Follow the roadway round into Union Street, which continues past some **18th-century frontages** (with cellar entrances) to the **Manchester Buddhist Centre** *(8)*. There is a help desk, library, shop, and a small café. The friendly staff will show you the two upstairs meditation rooms if they are not in use – the largest contains an impressive carved image of the Lord Buddha, which is worth seeing. Naturally, the Centre is situated above a **vegetarian cafeteria**. Double back and turn right into Turner Street to reach Church Street, emerging adjacent to the old British Telecom offices. The place where people once argued over their 'phone bills has now been turned into **Conran-designed luxury penthouse apartments**. The ***market stalls*** – with strangely camera-shy assistants – are across Church Street, a pale reflection of what once was. They still include a second-hand bookstall and a dealer in tapes and cassettes.

Church Street

The 'interesting musical sculpture'

Theadjacent building once housed the **Coliseum Shopping Centre**, an alternative retail outlet intended to accommodate the stalls dispossessed from the old Corn Exchange by the IRA bomb. It appears to be the usual story of a property developer wanting higher rents after a proposed refurbishment. As the plaque states, the first Methodist meeting house in Manchester was established in Birchin Lane, to the rear of the present structure. Wesley preached here on Easter Day, 1751: "The world is my parish". The congregation later moved to new premises on Oldham Street.

Continue along Church Street, noticing the stalls of the ***Fruit and Vegetable Market*** on the left. ***Sacha's Hotel*** *(10)* can be seen across the car park on the right. The Former 'C and A' Store was turned into a hotel in the 1980s, when it was thought that a studied 'over the top' design style would attract a trendy clientele. This is evident from the outside, although the interior has been toned down over the years (the stuffed polar bear is no longer with us). The surviving corner of a demolished warehouse has been turned into an interesting **musical sculpture** *(11)*.

Affleck's Palace

We now come to the art nouveau exterior lamps that denote ***Affleck's Palace*** *(12)* and enter it to the right. *Affleck's* was the first 'alternative' shopping venture in Manchester, created by Urban Splash (see below), and perhaps the genesis of the 'Northern Quarter'. Go up the stairs to level one, passing under the straw camel to an assortment of clothing and fashion, including fashionable club and dance scene creations, leatherwear, lingerie, tee shirts, and 'vintage' garments. Other stalls sell jewellery, posters, and records. A number of ancient slot machines litter the place as decoration. The grand staircase leads to *Rubber Plantation*, a 'designer condom' retailer with a line in sex toys. The top floor has a number of stalls selling antiques, vintage clothing, shoes, records, and incense. There is also an unusual outlet for henna skin designs.

The street, created in 1772, is named after Adam Oldham, a parish constable and wealthy businessman (and a member of Birchin Lane Chapel). The Birchin Lane congregation moved to a new chapel directly opposite *Affleck's* in 1784. John Wesley himself presided at the first service in the new premises. "The whole congregation behaved with the utmost seriousness," he recorded. "I trust much good will be done in this place." Wesley, the son of a clergyman, was repelled by what he saw of the 18th-century Anglican (state) church – it was corrupt, distant, and seemingly had little to do with the lives of ordinary people. At university, Wesley and his group attempted to get closer to God by a timetabled round of disciplined bible study and prayer, which called forth the epithet 'Methodist'. All was to no avail until he suddenly experienced a very vivid religious experience, in which he felt the grace and power of God. Wesley then embarked upon a wide national preaching tour, in which numbers were converted at great outdoor meetings. A major religious movement developed that split from the Anglican Church after Wesley's death. The Methodist movement had a profound impact upon the new working class. In addition to religious faith, it offered people a complete alternative community. There were social clubs, schools, savings banks, insurance schemes, sports teams, and holiday excursions. It can also be seen as the cradle of

Welcome to Affleck's Palace!

radical politics and the Labour party. The present **Central Hall** *(13)* replaced the original Oldham Street Chapel in 1883. The Central Mission still carries on the good work, particularly amongst the homeless.

Urban Splash

The walk continues to the left along Oldham Street. **Smithfield Building** (Stephenson Bell, 1989), on the left-hand side beyond Church Street *(14)*, represents an important landmark in the renaissance of the city centre. It was a £10m development by Urban Splash, which took the Affleck and Brown building, together with other semi-derelict property (nine buildings in all) that surrounded an open courtyard. The court became an atrium, a winter garden overlooked by eighty loft apartments accessed by internal galleries. It communicates with the multi-storey car park alongside Church Street by an overhead walkway. (If you explore this section of Tib Street, round the back *(15)*, look out for the **blue and white ceramic decoration** on the car park wall, and the **war memorials** from the former warehouse that stood here.) The Oldham Street frontage has a number of specialist shops at ground floor level, including *Forbidden Planet* (for cult sci-fi items). 'Urban Splash' was the 1987 brainchild of Tom Bloxham, a student at the (then) Polytechnic. From a desire to obtain a cheap site for his money-making sideline (a poster shop) came the process by which he bought up increasing amounts of neglected property, turning them into bars, cafés, and 'alternative shopping' venues.

This end of Oldham Street has a number of clubs and bars. ***Dry 201*** (Ben Kelly, 1989) pioneered the 'minimalist' interior. ***Matt and Phred's Jazz Club*** attracts aficionados from far afield. Double back and turn left into Dale Street. As you walk along this road, notice the **18th-century houses** in Lever Street, to the right, and more frontages of the same date (with cellar entrances) further along Dale Street itself. We now arrive at Newton Street, where this section of the walk began.

The reconstructed North Gate of the Roman Fort

10 Castlefield

Start: Pioneer Quay (Bottom of Deansgate)

Estimated time of walk: 1½ hours

Interiors: Add 2 hours if combined with Walk 11

Highlights: The first canal terminus, the Roman Fort, the world's first railway station, and 'Coronation Street'.

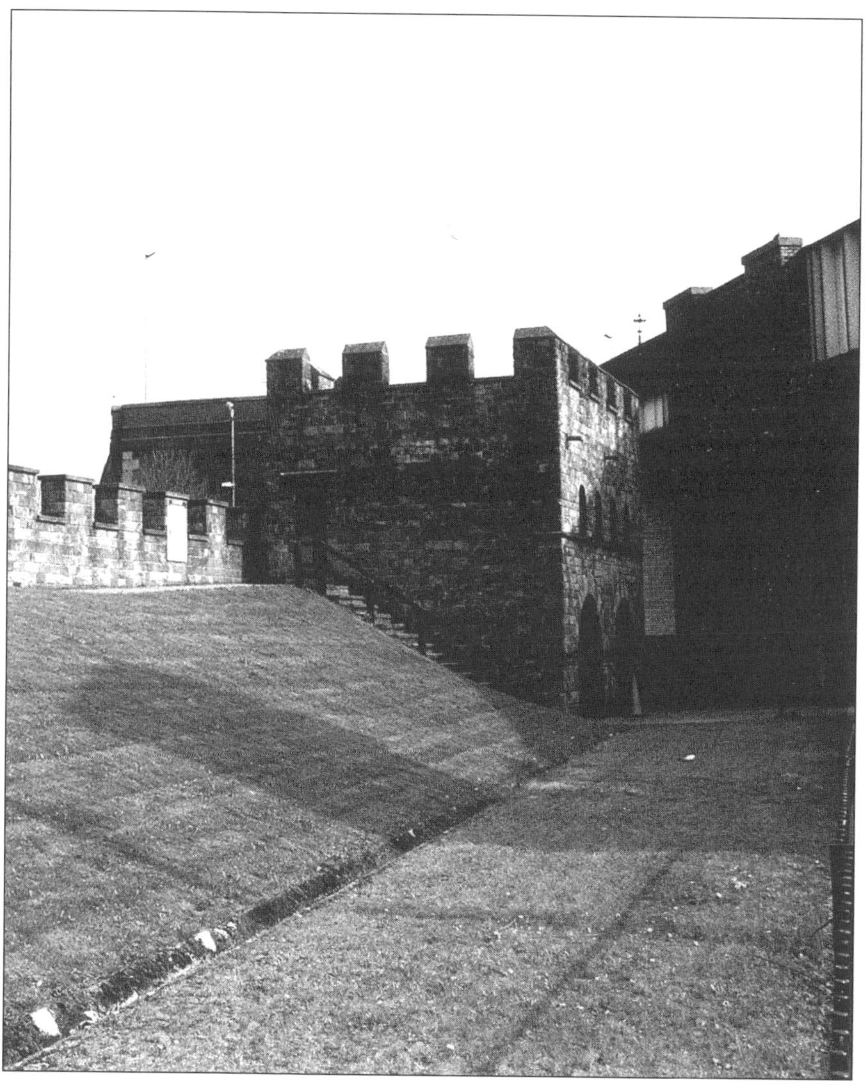

Several of the previous walks have either passed or terminated in the vicinity of Castlefield. The reason is simple. Castlefield is Manchester's top tourist attraction, a location that has pride of place in all the publicity. So, as you stand at Pioneer Quay *(1)* at the bottom of Deansgate, it is well to wonder why this should be so.

Castlefield history

The name, of course, means 'castle in the field', and refers to the Roman Fort – abandoned at some stage in the Saxon era, visible for many centuries in the countryside outside the small market town, and utilised as a quarry for building materials until it almost disappeared. Nothing much happened after that until Francis Egerton came on the scene. As the third Duke of Bridgewater, he was already heir to a sizeable inheritance when (so the story goes) our hero was crossed in love. He turned his back on the amusements of society and decided to develop the resources of his estate, which, in this case, comprised the colliery at Worsley. It was difficult to transport the coal overland to Manchester, but Francis and John Gilbert, his agent, thought they had the answer – a canal. Improved rivers (known as 'navigations') were then quite common, but they decided to employ a continental invention in the form of an artificial waterway or 'cut'. Fortunately, they had the services of James Brindley, an unconventional engineer of genius from a very humble background. When parliament proved sceptical about the principle of the proposed aqueduct over the Irwell at Barton, Brindley made a hurried model out of the only material to hand – cheese! Construction started in 1759, and the barges arrived at Castlefield in 1764. The work was undertaken by a new kind of labourer, who got the name 'navigators' or 'navvies' for short.

> That's the song of the bold navigators,
> For we are jovial banksmen all.

Castlefield was chosen for the Manchester terminus because the Medlock could be used as a feeder for the canal and the terminal basin. Thus, Castlefield "had become a sort of Maratime *(sic)* town, or Dutch Seaport". The canal produced coal in such cheap quantities in Manchester that it was a key factor in the critical mass that produced the first industrial revolution in the history of the world. Over 35,000 tons of coal was carried between 1773 and 1775 alone. The good Duke made an even greater fortune, but some accounts say that he was never happier than when dressed in old clothes, drinking, swearing, and smoking pipes with Gilbert, Brindley, and the navvies.

As the national canal system expanded, Castlefield became a major transportation centre, full of wharves and warehouses. It proved the means of supplying the growing manufacturing town with fuel, foodstuffs, potatoes, salt, 'Baltic' timber, stone, slate, lime, and raw cotton. This was why Castlefield was finally chosen as the terminus of the Liverpool and Manchester Railway, which opened in 1830. This was the first public railway in the world, with scheduled locomotive hauled passenger and goods trains.

By the mid-19th century, the last open fields had disappeared, and the area became full of labourers, warehousemen, watermen, and all manner of transients. This end of Deansgate, and parts of Castlefield, were also noted for wretched housing (including cellar dwellings), crowded lodging houses, rowdy drinking dens, and all manner of vice, drunkenness, and disorder. (Cholera and typhus were also

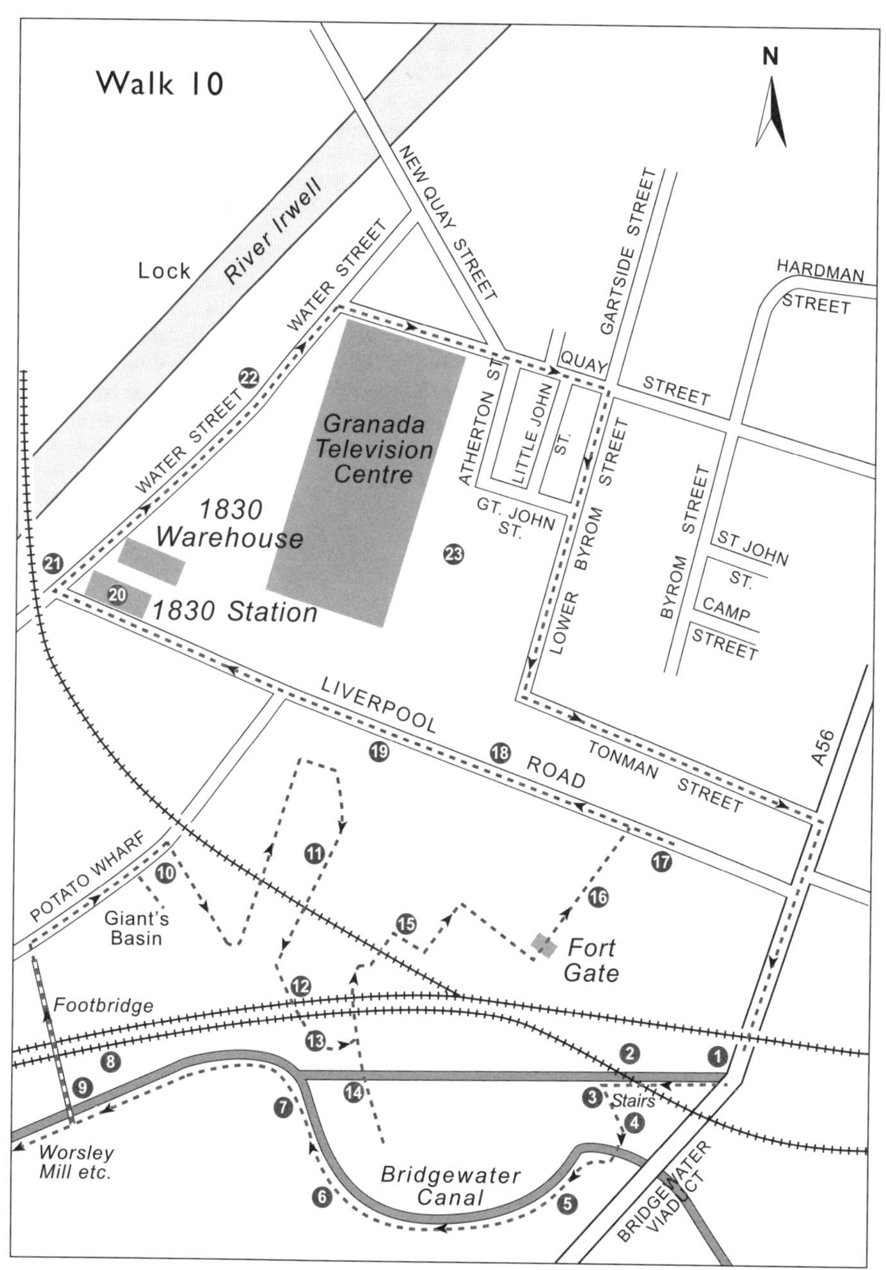

not unknown in the area.) Most of this was swept away by railway developments, particularly from the 1870s onwards. Eventually, the focus of Manchester goods traffic began to move away, although Castlefield remained important as a transport centre. But the decline of the area accelerated in the 20th century, and by the 1960s there was a lot of derelict land and run-down buildings.

Four things proved to be Castlefield's salvation. Firstly, the revival of the canals as a leisure facility, particularly the reopening of the **'Cheshire Ring'** in the 1960s, brought an increasing number of pleasure boaters through the area. The 'ring' constituted a regional circuit of canals that enabled boaters to embark on a cruising holiday without repeating any of the mileage sailed. Next, excavations on the Roman Fort site in 1972 and 1979 resulted in some exciting discoveries, and suggested that a reconstruction of the North Gate might prove a useful exercise. The release of a lot of derelict railway land for development purposes (including the 1830 station) happened at about the same time. Lastly, the celebration of 'Rocket 150' (the anniversary of the opening of the Liverpool and Manchester Railway) in 1980 was instrumental in the decision to resite the then 'Greater Manchester Museum of Science and Industry' in the old railway complex. The result has been the creation of **"Britain's first urban history park,"** and Castlefield is now the jewel in Manchester's tourism crown. However, it has not been all plain sailing, as aspects of the walk will reveal.

Pioneer Quay

We start the walk at the grassy area known as **Pioneer Quay**, a name chosen by a local radio competition in 1987 *(1)*. There is a view over the Rochdale Canal (p.154). The canal here was once in a tunnel cut through the very visible sandstone, but this was opened out in 1848-49 when the railway viaduct (p.129) was built. An **old railway structure**, which once supported a signal box, completes the picture. (The Quay area is scheduled for redevelopment.) Turn right into Castle Street, for a glimpse of a **canal arm** disappearing into a tunnel under the Central Station approach viaduct *(2)*. This was an extension of the arm that served the Grocers' Warehouse from the Bridgewater Basin (see below), and formerly terminated under a coal yard. It was cut through by the new Rochdale canal construction and, as the two canals are at different levels, it is flooded almost to the roof of the original tunnel.

After passing under the **railway bridge** (two magnificent skewed iron spans, battlemented in honour of the fort) we come to **Eastgate Building**, formerly Lamb's Furniture Manufactory, on the right, and incorporating some modern features in its recent restoration. However, the site of the **Grocers' Warehouse**, opposite, commands an **impressive view** over the Bridgewater Basin *(3)*. The new Canal Basin had a disadvantage in the form of a steep slope to the street level. Consequently, a short tunnel was constructed into the sandstone cliff so that the coal could be hoisted up a 47ft (14m) shaft to Castle Street (the subsequent extension of this tunnel has already been noticed). The original coal barges were long, thin, and low, and contained the coal in three removable boxes which could be hoisted out by crane (powered by water wheel), an early form of containerisation. The system went out of use with the advent of the Rochdale Canal in 1805.

The area at the tunnel entrance was extended, and a warehouse (designed by Brindley) built over the beginning of the canal arm in the 1770s. It was owned by the Manchester Grocers' Company from 1811 to 1836, and was used for the storage of dry goods. Although demolished in 1960, the lower level survives. You are standing on the restored **street level floor**, complete with the original **loading hatches**. Descend the **flight of steps** *(4)* from the here to the basin. The lower level of the

The YMCA, 'Y' hotel and leisure centre in the Staffordshire Basin

warehouse is clearly visible from a landing and from the bridge (see below) across the barge entrance – you might be able to make out the **waterwheel** that powered the hoist.

Bridgewater Basin

Take in the view from the quayside at the bottom of the steps. For the convenience of the visitor, a number of reproduction bridges have been installed in the **Bridgewater Basin**. That in front of the Grocers' Warehouse is a **'drawbridge'**, very Dutch in style, but completely out of place in the central Manchester area. The iron 'hump-backed' bridges are, by contrast, modelled on the originals. Proceed to the opposite side of the basin by way of the **iron bridge**, but do not omit looking to the left as you cross. Here is the **entrance of the feed water** to the canal from the Medlock beyond the Bridgewater Viaduct. The overflow was diverted into a tunnel. The remains of a Roman burial ground and bath house have been found in the vicinity.

Note also, to the left, the **Congregational Chapel** with its distinctive tower. Built in 1843, in the 'Italian Romanesque' style (by the architect of the Free Trade Hall), it has since been a recording studio (owned by Pete Waterman) and is now the home of the *Box Bar*. So, with the ghostly strains of Kylie Minogue echoing in our ears, we descend onto the opposite side of the Basin, turn right, and pass the ***Quay Bar*** (Stephenson Bell, 1998). The Bar's angled glass panels are derived from the design of a nautilus shell.

It is one of the few new Manchester bars built as a contemporary building, and sits on steel beams across Brindley's tunnel, into which is directed water from the overflow sluice at the water's edge *(5)*.

There is a good view from here of the old **coal and mineral wharf** across the Basin, constructed by cutting into the sandstone bank. The eye can trace the slope running up to Castle Street and the adjacent brick **weigh house** at the top (the weighing machine is still in position). The wharf was last used for freight in the 1970s. The traces of the ticket office and waiting room of the **Packet Station** can be seen in the retaining wall to the left of the Grocers' Warehouse. (A passenger 'fly boat' operated to Runcorn in competition with the river service.) **Gail House** is situated in the background. Once the site of an iron works, later a packing warehouse, this typical example of 1860s industrial premises has been sympathetically transformed into an office block. It is worth turning round to look at the rear of a solitary Georgian residence that fronts Chester Road, formerly the **wharfinger's house** (the man in charge of the operations in the basin).

The basin itself is now used as a **marina** for pleasure craft, and is a fine sight in the summer. Some are small cabin cruisers, but the majority of the vessels are reproductions of the **traditional canal narrow boat** as it evolved in the 19th century. The design has been adapted to provide modern accommodation, but the traditional **canal art and decoration** of 'roses and castles' is still an important feature that extends to ornamental buckets and other items. A number of these boats are privately owned, but many are hired. Continue to the second **'Dutch' bridge** that crosses a restored canal arm *(6)*. This leads to **Middle Warehouse**, built in 1831, and now called Castle Quay. Apartments, offices, a café, and the **headquarters of *Key 103* radio**, currently occupy the warehouse.

Dukes Canal

Turn to the right. The **Dukes canal**, or 'cut', starts here by bending to the right, beyond the Basin. (The Bridgewater canal proper starts at Waters Meeting, near Patricroft.) There is a fine view of the barge entrances to the **Merchants' Warehouse** on the right, the oldest surviving canal warehouse in the city. It was built of handmade bricks and timber beams in the traditional way in 1827-28 (the round headed windows are typical), though (strangely) at a time when iron girder and brick fireproof floors were being installed in local cotton mills. The goods were lifted in and out of the barges by a hoist. Although part of the building was damaged by fire in 1971, it was purchased by Jim Ramsbottom (a local bookmaker turned property developer) for the scrap price of the bricks in 1983. Jim had a vision for the area when few people paid it any notice, and was prepared to play a waiting game. In this case, funding (some of it from the European Union) was not obtained until 1996, when the warehouse was restored and converted into office accommodation.

This short stretch of the 'cut' leads to a **fine viewpoint** *(7)*, with the junction with the Rochdale Canal to the right, and Catalan Square and the entrance to the Staffordshire Basin directly ahead. The Square is accessed by the unusual new **Merchants' Bridge** (RHW Architects, 1996), something of a shock in these surroundings, yet perhaps in keeping with the great tradition of civil engineering. Continue along the cobbled towpath round the bend to the left. It is easy to imagine the noise of the hooves as the barges were towed along. Although steam traction was introduced in the second half of the 19th century, horses continued in service until the 1950s. A final **'Dutch' lifting bridge** crosses a restored arm serving **Slate Wharf**. This housing development stands on the site of New Warehouse, and comprises

Egerton Boats marina from Potato Wharf. The remaining 'working boats' moor here.

Bridgewater House and Irwell House. The restored basin was no doubt partly intended as an amenity for the new tenants' boats. Unfortunately, experience has shown that the residents of Castlefield (and elsewhere in the city centre) are usually birds of passage – an average tenancy of five years is the norm in these parts. They may form a community of sorts, but not the kind that invests in pleasure boating.

The source of the real boating market can be observed across the canal, nestling under the railway viaducts in the form of ***Egerton Narrow Boats***. This little marina *(8)* offers services to passing boaters (fuel, water, a chandlers shop, and chemical toilet disposal), but also hires out pleasure craft for canal cruising holidays. Before crossing the canal by the iron bridge, make a short detour by continuing along the towpath to the (restored) **Worsley Mill**. Dating from 1896, this former brick flour mill is distinctive, with a fine tower, gables of a differing size and the original portal served by the canal arm (spanned by an iron bridge) clearly visible. It contains apartments, accessed by a gap in the wall on the left, leading (by a passage) to Egerton Street. The **headquarters of the Manchester Civic Society** are to be found in Blantyre Street, to the rear of the building. Our way lies under the **Egerton Street Road Bridge**, rebuilt and widened to accommodate the new inner ring road. Ascend the steps to Egerton Street itself, and walk towards **St George's Church**. This fine neo-gothic structure was designed by Francis Goodwin, a London architect, and consecrated in 1828. It was the garrison church for the now vanished Hulme Cavalry Barracks, but is now converted into flats.

Somewhere near here was the site of Hulme Hall. The owners supported the wrong side in the English Civil war, and buried a large amount of 'treasure' in the grounds. Unfortunately, after the restoration, no-one could remember its location.

But don't try looking for it – one version of the legend says that the finder will be cursed, while another states that the treasure is guarded by demons!

The towpath continues alongside a large canal side development by Urban Splash (p.168). Notice the art-deco influenced **Box Works**. Modern apartments continue as far as the canal arm, with the original Britannia Mills beyond the iron towpath bridge. Retrace your footsteps, cross over the (reproduction) **iron bridge** *(9)* and pass under the viaducts to inspect the craft in the marina. You may be able to spot the last two working boats on the Duke's 'cut' that sometimes put in here. The pathway exits (by a right turn) into **Potato Wharf**, the point where the principal food of the Manchester workers during the industrial revolution was unloaded in the basins now used for the marina.

Another right turn leads to a footbridge over the **Giant's Basin** *(10)*, a large circular overflow sluice, which diverts floodwater into the Medlock (here situated in an underground culvert. It dates from the 1800s and replaces a clover-leaf shaped sluice constructed by Brindley. The bridge leads to ***Sustainability Northwest***, housed in an unusual but attractive building incorporating sustainable energy features. This cross-sector agency is concerned with such environmental issues as sustainable economic growth and the reclamation of derelict land. Retrace your footsteps back over the bridge, turn right and then right again to reach the large modern ***Youth Hostel***, (Halliday Meecham, 1995), perhaps the best low budget accommodation in the city. It offers a range of Scandinavian pine furnished rooms and dormitories, including family facilities. Members of the public may use the cafeteria.

Follow the path as it curves sharply around the corner of the hostel and pass under the brick viaduct (very narrow clearance at this point, so don't fall in!) to enter the **Staffordshire Basin**. Two inlets on the right, shaped rather like a tuning fork, mark the site of the (blitzed and demolished) Staffordshire Warehouse. Look across to the slope on the opposite side of the open space, with the **battlemented fort wall** on the top. It is all that remains of the original river cliff. The basin was used by the Trent and Mersey Canal, which served the Potteries and connected with the Grand Union Canal to London. The ***Bridgewater Packet Company*** operates a trip boat to Cornbrook on summer weekends from here, where their boats are usually moored. A larger vessel, with restaurant facilities, can be chartered for trips to the Lowry (p.245) by way of the new Hulme lock.

Castlefield Arena

The YMCA has opened the rather grand ***Castlefield Hotel*** (entrance at street level up the steps) on the left. It is a hotel, not the traditional hostel, and is sometimes used by artists working at the Granada TV studios. At this level, it contains the ***Y Club*** (operated as a separate enterprise). This sporting and physical fitness centre is one of the cheapest in Manchester (usually with a long waiting list) and, in addition to YMCA members, is mainly used by office workers and hotel residents (who have use of the facilities during their stay). These embrace state-of-the-art multi-gyms, squash courts, a sports hall with a mezzanine-level running track, and a **swimming pool** (observable through windows alongside the path). However, true to its traditions, the YMCA organises sessions for underprivileged children and schools deficient in sporting facilities. We turn right by the flight of steps leading to Liverpool

Road and another right turn leads to the **Castlefield Arena** *(11)*. The slope makes a perfect seating area, and it is equipped with all the necessary lighting and sound apparatus. The paved performance area was intended, in addition to performances, to be used for markets and a multitude of other functions.

Here, it may be worthwhile to sit and reflect. Although Castlefield is, in many ways, a tourism success story, something is missing. People! There are lots of weekend visitors to its attractions, lunchtime visits by office workers to the bars, and an evening crowd in search of entertainment. However (unlike the Albert Dock in Liverpool, or the Brindley Basin in Birmingham), it seems at times as if parts of the area are almost deserted. There are certainly not enough weekday visitors to sustain a daily pleasure-boat. Why? The original plan called for a balance between attractions, leisure, housing, offices and retail, but the actual development has been lopsided. This is only recently being addressed. More shopping and leisure facilities, together with regular daytime events and concerts in the Arena, will hopefully feature in the immediate future.

Leave the Arena by walking alongside the canal arm, pass under the brick MSJA viaduct of 1849 (p.129), and cross the iron bridge over the **Kenworthy arm** *(12)*. Note the **remains of the Kenworthy Warehouse** to the left, destroyed in the last war. Look up, and see that **great iron viaducts** span the entire area, built by the Cheshire Lines railway between 1873 and 1877. One is now used by the Metrolink trams, punctuating the usual quietness with a frequent whizzing noise. We next pass under the brick MSJA viaduct for the Altrincham branch, parallel with the ironwork, but at a lower level.

The pathway emerges into **Catalan Square** *(13)*, which is also the springing point for the pedestrian bridge. ***Barca***, a fashionable bar partly owned by Mick Hucknall, is accommodated in the railway arches, but also look for the **ceramic sun sculpture** (which tends to collect rainwater!). A right turn leads to the **stone canal bridge** *(14)*, commanding an excellent view – particularly when a barge is negotiating the **lock** to enter from the Rochdale Canal. Look out for the mason's marks on the stonework. After noting the **Lock Keeper's Cottage**, which was also used for levying tolls on barges entering the canal, cross the bridge to take a look at ***Dukes 92*** (it is by the ninety second lock). *Dukes*, like many buildings in the area, is one of Jim Ramsbottom's projects. The popular bar is situated in the former Merchants' Warehouse stables with a yard turned into an **outdoor performance area**, fully equipped with a stage. It has seen everything from rock to Shakespeare, and has a resident theatrical company.

We retrace our steps back over the bridge, bear to the right, and pass under a **sequence of viaducts** in which the two sections of the MSJA brick viaduct form a junction under the overall high level iron viaducts in a scene worthy of Piranesi.

The Roman Fort

Directly ahead is a **tableau of the archaeological section** *(15)* of the **Roman Fort**. The Roman general Agricola marched northwards in 79AD to subdue the tribal confederation of the Brigantes, and built a fort on a sandstone rise at the confluence of the Irwell and Medlock to guard his line of communications. This was a temporary affair, but soon became a permanent structure of earthen ramparts and wooden walls, about five acres in extent. A third fort was constructed in stone in the third century. What was it guarding? It stood to the north of the important road (along Deansgate) between the legionary bases of Chester and York, and near a ford on the Irwell that led northwards (via Ribchester) to Hadrian's wall, and southwards (via Watling Street) to London and the rest of the empire. Like all Roman forts, it consisted of a rectangular fortification with gates on each side, the starting points of streets that intersected in the centre. Here, the headquarters building and the commander's house would be located. Each quarter contained barracks, stables, and granaries.

Contrary to popular belief, the only Roman legionaries to be seen would be those companies or cohorts that sometimes marched through. The mixed garrison of about 1000 cavalry and infantry would be composed of auxiliary troops, sporting round shields and usually in their native dress. Evidence from tombstones suggest that it was at one point the home of a "regiment of Raetians and Noricans", recruited in what is currently Eastern Switzerland and Austria – so they might be used to our weather and the cold! (Roman legionaries were issued with breeches for service in Britannia.) To the left, the **reconstructed battlemented wall** can be viewed from the **double ditches** (imagine trying to run up and down these under fire), or ascend the rampart to have a fine view over the Staffordshire Basin. In either case, notice the **circular brick sculpture** of a Roman brooch found in the vicinity. To the rear of the wall are stones marking the **foundations of granaries** discovered in the dig. Stone pillars, slits, and dwarf walls would have ensured that the raised floor would be clear of rodents and damp. Most of the Roman taxes and tributes were paid in grain, and each member of the garrison would receive their weekly ration of it in a cup called a 'modius'. The superior legionaries would have some of their pay in salt (the origin of our modern 'salary').

Representation of a Roman brooch

We now leave the fort by walking along Beaufort Street, noticing the **stairs and lift** to the G-Mex Metrolink Station on the right. The unusual **mill building** opposite was once used for the storage of cotton waste. The street leads to the **North Gate** of the fort, the first portion to be reconstructed. Of course, only traces of the original foundations remained to be discovered, so the design of the gate is based on surviving examples on the continent. Walk through the archway and observe the entrance side, particularly the **plaque**. The inscription is based on whatever archaeological and historical evidence exists relating to the fort in this period. The second **base stone** to the left from the archways is considered genuinely Roman in origin.

Now turn round. There is a **fork in the road**. Ahead lies York, and the left-hand path is thought to be the start of the road to Wigan, not the first place that springs to mind as a Roman settlement. Outside the walls, and alongside the main road, are stones marking the **foundations of the Vicus**, a civilian settlement of perhaps 2000 inhabitants. (Timber structures were erected on stone foundations.) An inn, shops, and other 'facilities', tenanted by a mixture of native Celts and retired military personnel, catered to the wants of both the garrison and passing travellers. Beyond the foundations (to the left) is a **'Roman garden'** of plants introduced by the colonists. Evidence of metal-working has been found in the Vicus (settlement or village) area, and there would also have been a bath house and a cemetery. A Mithreum was discovered, some time in the early 19th century, in Hulme. The cult of Mithras, a Persian mystery religion, with its initiation rites and codes of honour, can be said to have been the freemasonry of the Roman army.

It is interesting to note that a **portion of wall** (not currently on view) under a railway arch to the rear of this area (described by A.J.P. Taylor as "the least interesting Roman remain in England") comprised all that existed of the Roman Fort until the results of the recent excavations. Now we have all that you see. The most precious find of all, an **early Christian 'word square'** (p.218), is proof that the Fort and Vicus in Manchester was a centre of the early Christian church. Before leaving the area, look to the right for the sculpture of **'Sheep'** *(16)*, by Ted Roocroft, attracting young children like a magnet.

Liverpool Road

Liverpool Road, with the ***White Lion*** on the corner, is now reached. The **terrace** *(17)* between this pub and Barton Street repays a short detour to the right. The large **top floor windows** indicate usage as a loom shop, tenanted by a handloom weaver. It was probably built in the 1790s, when the thoroughfare was called Priestnor Street, commencing at Humphrey's Gardens (a popular resort for the purchase of flowers and salads) on the corner of Deansgate, where Free Library building now stands, and leading to 'Lady's Walk', which ran towards the river. The street became Liverpool Road in the early 19th century, when it was extended through to the river as the result of the opening of a new bridge.

The area directly opposite the terrace was once open land, used for the hay market and witnessing at least four fairs a year. The old Acresfield Fair was transferred to here in 1823. A pleasure fair had, in fact, been held every Easter Week since 1760, attracting a variety of sideshows, freakshows, and menageries, including the celebrated Wombwell's Circus, with its elephants and lions. A regular market in old clothes and boots developed for the mill workers and factory hands in the 19th century. It seems an odd place to put a church, but Charles Barry designed one for the Church Commissioners (who were disbursing government funds to erect churches in the new industrial districts) identical to All Saints Stand, but with a tapering spire. (This early essay in Gothic stood him in good stead, for he went on later to design the Houses of Parliament.) It was consecrated in 1825, and largely catered to what was the rough end of town. As in other cases, the congregation declined as the residents moved out, and the church was closed in 1950 and demolished the following year. **Castlefield House** now stands on the site. This office block was in a rather bad state some years ago and many hoped that it too would be knocked down. Unfortunately, someone decided to refurbish it instead.

Meanwhile, the Knott Mill Fair was attracting a great deal of criticism with accusations of drunkenness and disorderly conduct. The city council abolished it in 1876, and took the opportunity to erect a greatly needed market building on part of the site. Retrace your footsteps and continue along Liverpool Road to see it on the right. The Lower Campfield Market, a fine iron framed market hall, opened in 1880. It later became the 'City Exhibition Hall', but was almost derelict by the 1970s. Manchester City Council restored the building and opened an Air and Space Museum in 1983, which later became the **Air and Space Hall** of the Museum of Science and Industry. The contents can be inspected through the plate glass windows at any time, but notice the **blue-painted pillar box** (this used to signify that it was used for air mail).

The ***Oxnoble*** is opposite, a pub named after a popular 18th -century variety of potato. The name appeared in the 1840s, when the place was obviously the watering hole for the labourers from 'potato wharf', but the building is earlier. Unfortunately, the exterior has recently received the attentions of a designer whose grasp of history is deficient (his design work leaves much to be desired as well). The building behind the pub, facing Bridgewater Street, was the **'Lock Hospital'**, relocated here in 1873. It was a charitable foundation for the treatment of venereal disease. Some of its first inmates were 'ladies of the town', temporarily detained there by the town's magistrates. Surprisingly, there is no plaque to commemorate this interesting aspect of our local heritage. **St Matthew's Sunday School** is just beyond the pub. This school building was probably designed by Barry and erected in 1827 (inscription), and is now a very pleasant open plan office area. The church operated a day school, a Sunday school, adult evening classes, and used the building for a variety of socials and entertainments. It must have been the heart and soul of this poor district.

Museum of Science and Industry

The **Museum of Science and Industry in Manchester** (including the Air and Space Hall, open daily 10.00-5.00, admission free, but charges for special exhibitions) is distinguished by its **three-dimensional sign** *(18)* on the corner of Liverpool Road. Atop two columns from Sebastian de Ferranti's Deptford Power Station (the world's first high voltage generating station, opened in 1889) is a three dimensional cogwheel. (Ferranti opened a factory near Oldham in 1897.) The **'Reflections'** art installation on the paved area outside the entrance in Lower Byrom Street, to the right, always attracts attention. Distorted images on the ground are reflected in a polished steel inverted cone, making a perfectly proportioned picture in the process. The Museum is largely created from the remains of a large railway complex, which only closed in 1975. It is the largest technology museum in Europe, and at least two hours should be devoted to a visit. (A descriptive tour may be found in Walk Eleven.)

The Museum occupies the whole right-hand side of Liverpool Road from this point, starting with the **Power Hall**. A water wheel and the Newcomen steam engine may be glimpsed through a **large plate window** on the Lower Byrom Street corner. It covers the former cart entrance. There is also another view of the locomotives and veteran cars a short distance down Liverpool Road, through a **window** on the right. The **Goods Office** and the **carriage ramp** follow on, with a **gateway** (no entrance to the museum) affording a glimpse of the **Gas Gallery**.

Liverpool Road Station

Cross Liverpool Road to the former **Castlefield Visitor Centre** *(19)*. (This facility appears to have closed.) It lies by the side of the steps leading down to the Staffordshire Basin. Looking back across the road, there is a fine view from here of the **mural by Walter Kershaw**, with the Grape Street Warehouse peeping above it. Continue down Liverpool Road, looking to the right.

The mecca for many visitors to Castlefield is undoubtedly the frontage of the **Oldest Railway Station in the World** *(20)*. The merchants and businessmen of both Liverpool and Manchester were enthused by the successful opening of the Stockton and Darlington Railway in 1825. Although this line has been claimed as the first British railway, only a few coal trains were actually hauled by steam locomotives. Indeed, private horse drawn wagons could be placed on it by payment of a toll, and there were certainly no proper timetabled services. Joseph Sandars, a rich Liverpool corn merchant, and John Kennedy, the largest mill owner in Manchester, had something more ambitious in mind. They thought in terms of a major trunk route, operating scheduled steam-hauled goods (and possibly passenger) services between their two towns. This concept had been popularised by William James, a land surveyor who advocated a national net-

The old Liverpool Road Station

work of railways in the 1820s. In fact, James made the first survey of the line before being imprisoned for debt (his enthusiasm had bankrupted him).

Only then was George Stephenson called in to complete the work. Stephenson, the great Victorian hero, was a mechanical and civil engineer of genius. But he was practically illiterate, relying on his son Robert for this part of the business. Unfortunately, Robert had gone to South America at this point in time, and there was no-one to check the calculations of George's surveyors. He consequently became a laughing stock, pilloried by opponents of the railway in parliamentary committee when the gross nature of the many errors became known. But George had supporters amongst the 'provisional committee' of the railway project, and was able to bounce back and complete a third and final survey of the line.

It was intended to terminate the line in Salford, for a bridge appeared out of the question. The Mersey and Irwell Navigation, a powerful opponent, owned the bank of the river. A change of heart resulted in last-minute alterations, and everything that you see here was built in the space of less than nine months! The Liverpool and Manchester Railway was opened by the Duke of Wellington on 15th September, 1830. Unfortunately, the 'Rocket' locomotive ran over William Huskisson MP at Parkside, and the delay only made matters worse as far as the expectant crowd was concerned (the Duke was not exactly popular in Manchester). He consequently arrived to a riot and a rain shower.

The station range incorporates a house on the corner of Water Street, built in 1808 and tenanted by James Rothwell, a partner in a nearby dye works. This was converted into the **Station Agent's House** and is now the Museum office. The actual **Station Building,** next to it, is quite small. The **main door** was used by first class passengers and is surmounted by an equally grand window and a **sundial**! The latter is a curious feature to be associated with a new form of transport, but it could be read from inside the waiting room. The **second door**, positioned to the right, was for the use of second class passengers. There is something very odd about this building. The frontage was arranged to create some sense of grandeur, with a parapet concealing the hipped slate roof, and a stucco rendering scored to give the impression of stonework. However the windows are, perhaps, too large, and it has been suggested that both they and the stone surrounds may have come from a building materials sale (the sundial presumably being thrown in for good measure). Peep through the windows to the left of the main entrance to see the **diorama in the restored booking hall**.

The remaining building to the right was constructed in 1831, in front of the viaduct. (The modern restoration revealed that it had been built in a hurry using poor materials.) The ground floor level was intended as shops, but the nature of the area (which could not remotely be described as fashionable) precluded this development. They became railway offices, though the section next to the station building probably opened as the **booking office of the Grand Junction Railway** in 1837. This conveyed passengers from a mid-point on the Liverpool and Manchester line to Birmingham, and so can be described as the first stage in the national railway system. Passengers could travel to London in through carriages the following year – the journey took about twelve hours, which was an improvement on two days by the fastest stage coach. The upstairs is a curtain wall for the **Carriage Shed**.

The importance of the growing passenger traffic surprised the company, who

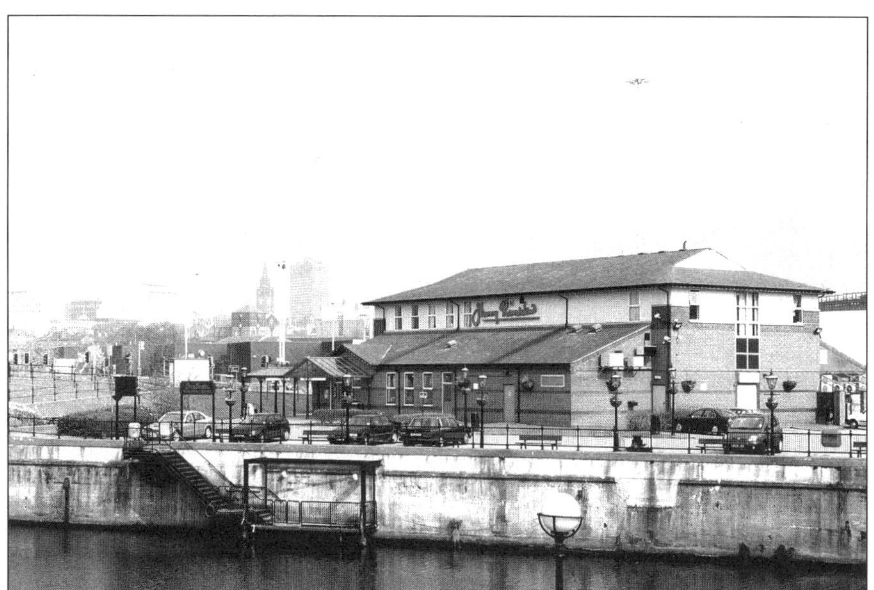

Harry Ramsden's Fish and Chip Emporium, Water Street and the embarkation point for river cruises on the River Irwell

realised that the site was too distant from the town centre. Not surprisingly, passenger traffic ceased when Victoria Station opened in 1844. The structure became goods offices, and thus the original station was preserved like an insect in amber. (A full description of the interior of these buildings, together with details of their operation, may be found on page 200.)

Water Street

We now stand at the corner of Water Street. To the left is the MSJA viaduct (p.129), with a distant glimpse of ***Harry Ramsden's*** Fish and Chip Emporium. Cruises along the Irwell and the Ship Canal sometimes commence from the adjacent quay. To the right is the **Water Street Railway Bridge**. The last minute extension meant that the levels of the viaduct would not permit a brick arch of the width demanded by the highway authority. Consequently, Water Street would have to be spanned by rigid iron girders – something never before attempted. Fortunately, the development of fire-proof floors in local cotton mills had resulted in the appearance of a 'T' section girder, and William Fairbairn, demonstrated by experiment that such could be used to bridge a wide area. This unique bridge was replaced by the present one in 1905. A view may be had of the arched **Irwell Bridge** *(21)*, to the left of the road bridge, prior to its junction with the viaduct. It contained a road for the exclusive use of the Navigation Company, approached by a ramp. (Not the visible one, which led from the pig platform to the abattoir.) The original ramp was a grand affair, topped by a water tank that was disguised as a triumphal arch! Remember the eleven workmen who drowned on 24th April, 1830, when their boat overturned during the construction of this bridge.

Passing under the Water Street Bridge, there is view of the **low-level yard** and the **1830 warehouse** to the right. Notice that it is built on a slight curve. Opposite was the site of Rothwell and Barnes' dye works. Mr Rothwell must have been a gallant gentleman, for he invited a party of ladies to view the opening of the railway and the arrival of the Duke of Wellington, going so far as to remove some of the slates so they could poke their heads above the rafters! To cope with the increasing traffic after 1837, an Arrival Station was built on the site.

Granada Studio Tours

Beyond the second **iron bridge**, built in the 1860s to access the Grape Street Warehouse, was the entrance to **Granada Studio Tours** to the right. Constant requests to visit the 'Coronation Street' set and tour the studios, together with the apparent success of film studio tours in America, resulted in this venture. The opportunity of providing a public tour, isolated from the main work of the studios, resulted from the availability of a lot of derelict railway land. However, the 'tour' complex incorporated two actual sets – **'Coronation Street'**, the most famous (and oldest) British TV soap opera, and the **Sherlock Holmes' Baker Street set** (the largest for television in this country). To these were added a set of the House of Commons (from a dramatised Jeffrey Archer book) and other attractions. As the greater part of the tour involved timed parties, there were always large numbers of waiting people to keep occupied and entertained. Unfortunately, the project experienced a crisis of identity, and began to lose its way. The peripheral attractions began to take over, and the fatal decision was taken to develop part of the site into a mini theme park, despite its size. A controversial attempt to install a 'white knuckle' ride failed (with passengers sometimes stranded in mid air), and the attraction was closed for a 'rethink'. It never reopened.

Cross Water Street to the car park for a good view of the **Grape Street Warehouse**. This was constructed by the London and North Western Railway from 1867 to 1869, and must be the first three-way iron frame building in the country. The great mass is 200ft (61m) long, by 100ft (30m) wide, and has five floors and a basement. The fortress-like appearance is deliberate, for the fine period sign proclaims it as a 'bonded' warehouse, a place where perfume, alcohol, and tobacco would be stored until duty was paid. When it was restored in 1982-3, the walls were repaired with matching bricks and treated with soot, to make it suitable for filming work! A little further on the car park side of the road is the garden setting for a **restored lock** *(22)*, indicating the portal of an **Underground Canal.** It opened in 1839, connecting the River Irwell with the Rochdale Canal by a 499 yard tunnel. The construction of the Great Northern Warehouse (p.58) cut it in two, though it was connected to the new building by a hoist. This traffic finally ceased in 1936, after which it was used as air raid shelters. It still exists, and it was seriously suggested that an electrically powered gondola service should be instituted between here and the 'Great Northern' leisure complex!

The Victoria and Albert Warehouse lies behind the lock, probably dating from around 1840 but perhaps incorporating elements of an earlier building. It stands on the site of the open quay and warehouses opened by the Old Quay Company in 1735. The Mersey had always been navigable as far as Warrington, and an Act was obtained in 1720 to 'improve' the Irwell as far as Manchester by locks, dredging, and cutting across bends. Traffic lay in the hands of the Old Quay Company and was carried in 'flats' – broad-beamed boats of a shallow draught, towed by horses. But, beyond Runcorn, the horse was dispensed with, keel boards lowered to forestall capsizing, and the sail raised for the journey across the estuary to the barge dock at Liverpool. The quay flats traded along other regional rivers and navigations and could also put to sea for coastal trade.

> The Old Quay Flats were my delight,
> I sailed in them both day and night.
> And now I lie grounded, with so many of our fleet,
> But hope to rise, and take a morning tide,
> My Admiral, Christ, to meet.

The old company was challenged by the formation of the New Quay Company in 1822. They planned a new fleet of barges. The launch of one of these, in 1828, turned out to be a disaster of epic proportions. The 'Emma' capsized, and a large number of leading citizens were drowned.

The building is now transformed into the luxurious five-star ***Victoria and Albert Hotel***. Each room is decorated with pictures and relics from a Granada Television production, and three suites are 'themed'. The 'Moll Flanders Suite', for example, has a late 17th-century decor complete with a period four poster bed. One interesting feature is a separate section for female guests staying alone, which is approached by an overhead gangway in full view of the front desk.

Quay Street

Turn right, down Quay Street. Here are the **Granada Television Studios**. Commercial television was introduced in Britain in the 1950s, and the founder of this company named it after a happy pre-war holiday in Spain. The two-storey building on Quay Street itself was Manchester's first post-war commercial building, designed in 1956 by Ralph Tubbs (the architect of the 'Dome of Discovery' at the 1951 Festival of Britain). The next phase comprised the eight-storey Granada House, and the Atherton Street frontage clearly dates from the 1960s. Granada is perhaps the most successful of the commercial television companies, famed for its factual programmes as well as drama and entertainment. Some of its more recent history has not been happy. However, it may have sloughed off the malign influence of assorted bean counters and men in suits (a bit like the recent history of the BBC, really), and become its old self again.

A right turn leads into Lower Byrom Street, past St John's Gardens (p.60). There is a **view of the back of 'Coronation Street'** to the right *(23)*, but notice how the **Accumulator Tower** has been incorporated into part of the studio complex. It contained the tank supplying the hydraulic machinery within the former goods yard. By the side of the Air and Space Gallery, to the left, is a pedestrian walk leading to Tonman Street. A rift in the management of the Mechanics Institute (p.142) led to the more radical members seceding. They largely believed in the 'scientific socialism' of Robert Owen (p.29). They obtained a site in this street for the establishment of a 'Hall of Science', and the foundation stone was laid by the great man himself in 1839. The building became known as 'Carpenters Hall', as the wooden frame and fittings were erected and fitted by the free labour of the carpenters and joiners of the town. The place was greatly used by the Chartist movement (p.66). Fergus O'Connor spoke here, advocating the purchase of shares in the ill-fated Chartist Land Company.

Unfortunately, the Hall did not prosper in later years, though the building soon had another use. Manchester was probably the first municipality to utilise the Free Libraries Act of 1850, when it purchased the building for library use. The Free library opened in 1852 in the presence of Dickens, Thackeray, and other important Victorian literary luminaries. It was condemned as unsafe in 1877, and demolished shortly after. Fortunately, there was a redundant Town Hall on King Street to move the library to.

Tonman Street passes the **Upper Campfield Market** on the right, similar in design to Lower Campfield Market and opening in 1882. Although renovated, it is currently out of use. It was once suggested as another gallery for the National Museum of Labour History, perhaps in the form of a 'People's Palace' of dioramas of social history and everyday working class life. This was rejected, and the future remains unsure. We emerge onto Deansgate, so turn right and inspect the front of the **Free Library Building**. Although the main library had been relocated, there was still scope for a branch library. A joint scheme of the Library and Markets Committees of the City Council planned a building that would improve the approach to the Upper Campfield Market. This fine structure has the **city arms** carved in a pediment, together with **figures** of 'commerce', 'peace', 'industry', and 'trade'. It was fitted with double windows on the Deansgate side to reduce the noise, while the lower floor was let as shops. A **central passage** leads to an entrance to the market building, intersecting an **arcade** running between Tonman Street and Liverpool Road. The building and library opened in 1882 but eventually fell into disuse. The restoration has resulted in a number of new enterprises, including *Jowata*, an African restaurant. However, the main occupant is the *Instituto Cervantes*, an official Spanish cultural organisation that offers language tuition.

You can reach Pioneer Quay, the starting point of the walk, by proceeding straight ahead. It is then quite easy to return to Piccadilly – the shortest way is to go to the left, along Whitworth Street West, then left into Lower Mosley Street, and keep walking until you hit Piccadilly.

The Reflection installation at the entrance to the Museum of Science and Industry.
(Photograph by Jean Mostall, reproduced with permission)

11 The Museum of Science and Industry

Start: Main Museum Entrance

Estimated time of walk: At least 2 hours

Highlights: Too many to mention!

This museum is said to be the largest of its kind in Europe, and, as such, deserves a chapter of its own. Manchester was the cradle of the industrial revolution, the first industrial society in the world. Consequently, the museum addresses, through artefacts, not only the process of industrialisation itself, but also the society it created. The main part of the museum ought to be regarded as a time machine in brick. We start at the last quarter of the Victorian era, and go back through time as we proceed in the direction of Water Street, arriving at the 1830 Station, and eventually at a building that existed before the railway arrived. (The museum itself is open daily 10.00-5.00, admission free.)

The new **entrance building** contains a ticket office and a well-stocked shop. Tickets are usually needed for entrance to special exhibitions, and visitors need to be 'counted'. We enter the entrance hall on the ground floor of the **'Great Western Warehouse'** of 1880, perhaps the only one in Manchester used by this company. Here, G.W.R. stood for 'Great Way Round', for their passenger and goods trains from the Midlands reached the city via Shrewsbury and Chester. There are **toilets**, lockers, an **information desk**, and a **gallery for temporary exhibitions**, but the most outstanding feature is a **pedestrian ramp** that connects with the first and second floors (cutting through the structural girders at some points). Our way lies down another ramp that leads to the side entrance, noting the display of **historic printing presses** on the left.

Textiles

We don't exit just yet, but proceed directly ahead through the entrance to the **David Alliance Gallery**, telling the story of textile fibres and **Manchester's cotton heritage**. Walk along the wooden platform and see Manchester as a major distribution and exporting centre, dominated by massive warehouses. Bright printed fabrics are exported to Africa and India. Pick up a phone in the **cotton merchant's office** and hear the latest news from the Royal Exchange. There is a **fine model of the S and J Watts warehouse** (p.120), together with a **model of a typical multi-storied spinning mill**, with the engine house to the rear, and the twin water towers. Listen to the **voices** of the different people attracted to Manchester by the textile boom – ranging from Nathan Rothschild to John Doherty, the union organiser.

At the end wall are two almost **identical dresses**. One is a silk creation, and the other is made from cotton. There is little to tell them apart – for mass-produced printed cloth allowed ordinary people for the first time to dress in imitation of the rich. Consequently, by the end of the 18th century, we are gravely told that husbands sometimes mistook the maid for the wife. (Well, that was their excuse!) The lower area to the left of the central platform is an **activity area based on fibre technology** (aimed mainly at children), but also contains a **jacquard loom**. This weaves patterned cloth by utilising several shuttles (each loaded with a different coloured yarn) stored in a 'drop box', activated by a continuous loop of punched card. It was the first programmed machine, and an important step on the road that ultimately produced the computer.

Turn round and retrace your steps back along the platform. A **handloom and a spinning wheel** give an impression of the pre-industrial era in textiles. A handloom weaver could only cope with cloth as wide as his reach – 'broadcloth' took two men to weave. The invention of the **'flying (or automatic) shuttle'** solved the problem, but created another, for spinners could not keep up with the increased productivity of the weavers. The result was a rash of inventions, and one of these is shown.

Arkwright's **Water Frame** was of crucial importance in the industrial revolution – it was the first spinning machine that could be installed in a mill powered by a water wheel. This resulted in the birth of the factory system. Richard Arkwright was the Bill Gates of his day. This Preston barber became the master of a new technology, developed the factory system in the North West and Midlands, and built a massive business empire. (A contemporary joke suggested that his secret ambition was to pay off the national debt single-handedly.) He erected one of his first mills in Manchester.

There follows an illustration of the **process of cotton manufacture**. On the lowest floors of the mill, men feed the contents of the bales into a series of machines that break down the lumps, mix the fibres, and beat out dirt and seed remains. This last operation is performed by a **'scutcher'**. This was a word familiar to past generations of Lancashire children. "Ah'll scutch t' living daylights out of thee if tha doan't behave!" On the middle floors, women operate **carding engines and drawing frames** to produce a continuous rope of cotton fibre. We turn left across the gangway to reach a portion of the **original warehouse staging**, used for loading and unloading the railway wagons.

Spinning and weaving

Spinning was usually performed by male 'mule spinners', on the top floors of the mill. The machine is called a **'mule'** because it is a cross between Arkwright's 'water frame', and Hargreave's 'spinning jenny', and was invented by Samuel Crompton of Bolton (much good it did him, for he died in poverty). This is a later version. If the machine is in motion, note how the **moving carriage** on the rails draws out the thread. The spinner would be continually moving back and forth, trying to keep out of the way of the carriage, and probably working barefoot (at least in the early days) to get a better grip on the oily floor. Indeed, the oil could spurt up at crotch level. (Cancer of the scrotum was a mule spinner's disease.) Later, they were issued with white canvas 'ducks' in some mills, which made them look like cricketers. Women were employed as 'doffers', replacing the bobbins.

Power looms usually only operated in one- or two-storey weaving sheds. It was a woman's occupation, save for the men who 'tackled' the loom when it required mechanical attention. For some reason, they had a reputation for gullibility, and comic 'tackler's tales' are legion. Threading the shuttle required sucking the end of the yarn through the hole – **'kissing the shuttle'** was the most common form of tuberculosis infection at one time. The noise of a weaving shed was terrible, and most weavers soon learned to lip-read.

Working conditions in the early mills were atrocious. In addition to long hours of mind numbing work, there was the danger of being amongst crude unprotected moving machinery. Indeed, the 'little piecers', often children as young as seven or eight, were required to crawl underneath the spinning machines and tie up broken threads. The atmosphere was unbearably hot (the humidity made the cotton easier to work), so the majority of the (mainly female) labour force worked with the few items of clothing that decency required. It is perhaps a comment on the morality of the time that the Victorian middle classes were more concerned about the spectacle of mill girls in their 'shifts' than child labour or industrial accidents. "The scenes daily enacted in our cotton mills would put to blush the pagoda girls of India, or the harem of the most voluptuous Ottoman."

Walk back down the other side of the platform. **Pattern printing**, using blocks, and then rollers, is illustrated, and the **evolution of dyestuffs** from vegetable to chemical forms is explained. (Notice that there is a **textile designer in residence**.) A fabric tent contains a **selection of videos** (including scenes in a mill), and we go behind the scenes of a **mail order warehouse**. It has long been a tradition in the north-west to purchase clothing from a catalogue. Lastly, do not forget that **recycled rags** are an important source of textile fibres.

The **first-floor** space of the warehouse contains **'Manchester Science'**, a new gallery illustrating the importance of scientific enquiry in the city and its region through the achievements of famous scientists associated with it. We enter a corridor, the right hand wall display setting the context by a collage of newspaper cuttings, exhibits, and descriptive material, all relating to the theme of **science and the media**, and working our way backwards in time. Note the current preoccupation with GM crops, the **molecular model of DNA,** and the **equipment used in the first successful IVF conception –** Louise Brown was the first 'test tube' baby and another Manchester 'scientific first'. The calculating machine – **Hartree's Differential Analyser** – hints at Manchester's role in the birth of the computer. Further back in time, one notices an **1882 Swan light bulb.** Electricity was the harbinger of the second industrial revolution in the last quarter of the nineteenth century, but for a variety of reasons, the technological initiative largely passed to Germany and America. This is in contrast to the period half a century earlier when Britain was the 'workshop of the world', and the **souvenirs of the Liverpool and Manchester Railway** and the **Davy Lamp** remind us of this fact. A number of items of historic lab equipment are displayed on the opposite side of the corridor, including a **1901 lab bench from the old Technical College** (which became UMIST, recently joined with Manchester University).

The main display area lies round the corner. The right hand displays are the reverse of the previous 'science and the media', and include some of the previous exhibits. Other items include a variety of **locally manufactured scientific instruments**. Children will inevitably be drawn to the **holographic tableaux** on the opposite side, in which the miniature figures re-enact scenes from Manchester's scientific history. Here you can see John Dalton on the bowling green of the 'Dog and Partridge'; the man himself addressing the Literary and Philosophical Society; James Joule inspired by the action of steam engines; Ernest Rutherford and his assistants; Rutherford attending an international conference; Bernard Lovell working on wartime radar; and Jodrell Bank tracking 'sputnik'.

Entrances along this side lead to rooms dedicated to individual scientists, each incorporating an audio-visual display to the rear. **John Dalton** (p.46) is represented by displays that include personal items (including his beloved **umbrella** and supposed **cradle**). Note the **thermometer** from the outer wall of his Faulkner Street home – he recorded the reading until the day he died. You can build your own molecular models or operate the **display illustrating the absorption of gas into water**. The **James Joule** (p. 235) room contains the kind of industrial **precision measuring instruments** that were so useful in this Salford brewer's investigations, together with a **reconstruction of his 'paddle wheel' experiment**. It is interesting to note that the scientific press of the day ignored this 'mechanic', and his first results were published in the 'Manchester Courier'! The **Ernest Rutherford** displays incorporate the **balance used in his work on atomic weights**, a replica of the **apparatus**

used to split the atom, and a **demonstration of his 'gold leaf' experiment.** The last room deals with the work of **Bernard Lovell**, the pioneer of radio astronomy. Note the **old crystal sets**, similar to those built by the boy radio enthusiast, the section concerning **radio telescopes**, and the **large model of 'sputnik'**. This was the first satellite, launched in 1957, and tracked by Jodrell Bank.

We leave the gallery by way of a display entitled **'Manchester Science Today and Tomorrow'**, which includes an interesting **robotic hand**.

Nearby are **demonstration classrooms** for school parties, and a fully equipped **Conference Centre**, with a large auditorium. **'Xperiment'** may be found on the **second floor**. This is a 'hands on experience' area for children, full of simple apparatus arranged around the themes of 'sense', 'energy', and 'light', including a special area for 'under fives'. This is an excellent way for harassed parents to take a break. (There is also an excellent **overview of 'Coronation Street'** from the windows of the 'Xperiment'.) Access to **online computers** is available in a nearby centre. The **Museum Restaurant**, offering a wide range of menus, is adjacent. The **basement** of the warehouse is used to accommodate the **library and archive**, and the **Collection Centre**. Here, in the latter, the visitor can 'go behind the scenes' and inspect 'materials in store', items from the museum collection that are not normally on display. There is much more space in the warehouse, used for **temporary exhibitions**.

The Power Hall

Exit by way of the side door on the ground floor, and proceed to the entrance to the Power Hall, noticing the **overhead crane** on the way. The **Power Hall** was the transit shed for the unloading of perishable goods such as foodstuffs, and was probably built around 1855 to replace an earlier wooden shed of 1831. We enter opposite a typical example of a **'Lancashire Boiler'** (built at Knott Mill) which has been cut away to reveal the double flue that increased the heating surface and thus produced steam at a faster rate. Turn left and go up the stairs. The first area illustrates pre-steam age sources of power, starting with a large **horse 'gin'** or winding engine.

The early mills in Lancashire, and elsewhere, were water powered by a **water wheel** such as the one displayed. Contrary to popular assumptions about the industrial revolution, they were located in rural areas where fast flowing streams could be found. So where did the labour come from? Mill settlements were created and cartloads of pauper orphan children shipped in from all over the country, as evidenced at Styal. Just beyond the water wheel, notice the **glassed over door** at the Liverpool Road corner. Then turn round to face the interior of the shed. Carts entered here to access the cobbled roadway that ran alongside the **central wooden staging** the length of the building. The railway tracks lay on the opposite side. This arrangement has been largely preserved.

Steam

A right turn brings us face to face with the **first steam engine**, or rather a one-third-size working model of the one that Thomas Newcomen installed at Dudley in 1712, to pump water out of a coal pit. (The real size of this type of engine can be gathered from the **cast iron piston** displayed at the side of the model.) This was an 'atmospheric engine' – the single power stroke resulted from the action of normal air pressure (the top of the cylinder was open) on a vacuum created below the piston by condensing low-pressure steam with a jet of cold water. One side of a

The Power Hall, inside The Museum of Science and Industry.
(photograph by Jean Mostall, reproduced with permission)

beam was pulled down, raising the working part of a pump deep below in the mine, and gravity caused it to descend again. The descending weight lifted the piston to the top of the cylinder for the next stroke. This was the only way that low-pressure steam (all that boiler technology could then produce) was able to operate a piston. The modern model would not work at first. Then, a computer calculated the point of balance on the beam, and all was well. Newcomen, a Cornish tinsmith, glazier and Baptist preacher, did not have such assistance.

Round the corner is an improved version as invented by James Watt, a canny Scotsman. A beautiful **cutaway brass model** illustrates the principles of the Watt engine. (Press the button to see it in motion.) Watt realised that the efficiency of the Newcomen machine could be improved by a separate condenser (saving the repeated heating and cooling of the cylinder). But how could he get the steam out of the cylinder to the condenser? Watt had his brainwave on a now famous walk to his local golf links in 1769. He would create a vacuum in the condenser, which would attract the steam to it! A simple air pump, operated by an eccentric rod from the beam, sufficed to do this. The next step was logical. Watt closed off the cylinder, and used the action of low-pressure steam acting on the vacuum in the cylinder, instead of the atmosphere. This also enabled the process to be reversed, with two power strokes, one from either end of the cylinder. Such a 'reciprocating' engine could be used to power a wheel, and, by 1784, Watt engines could be used to power machinery. Thus was a lumbering mine pump converted into a means of powering factories and mills.

The full size **Watt engine**, in its reconstructed engine house, dates from the period 1820-30, though it may incorporate earlier parts. The classical features almost make it a work of art! It is worth noting that the small **model engine** was used by John Dalton in his scientific lectures (p.46). Watt protected his investment with cast-iron patents, and the consequent royalties actually delayed their installation in many industrial concerns for many years. Nevertheless, the low-pressure steam engine, in a variety of forms, powered the Lancashire mills. There are a number of **later horizontal mill engines**, one with a grooved wheel to transmit the power by ropes to the mill machinery.

The lower area to the right, with its railway lines, is a natural arena for the **locomotive collection**. After Watt, Richard Trevithick developed the high-pressure steam engine (taking advantage of improving boiler technology), and applied it to producing vehicular movement in an experiment on the Pen-y-Daren tramway in 1804. (In order to win a bet for his iron master employer!) The steam locomotive is derived from this historic instance.

'Pender', built by Beyer Peacock of Gorton, operated on a narrow-gauge railway in the Isle of Man, and has been sectioned to show how steam locomotives worked. 'Pender' has a multi-tubular boiler to create steam quickly, an invention ascribed to Robert Stephenson (but probably suggested by Henry Booth, a director of the Liverpool and Manchester Railway). This can be contrasted with the reproduction of **'Novelty'**, a contender in the 'Rainhill Trials' of 1829. To increase the heating surface, a single flue was twisted back and forth so many times that it resembled a trombone. The hot gasses could only be drawn through the flue by bellows, activated by chain drive from the wheels. It worked, but breakdowns were frequent. The 'Rocket', entered by Robert Stephenson (with a tubular boiler), easily won.

It may be possible to see two other locomotives of this pioneer era. **'Planet'** is a working replica of the second generation of Liverpool and Manchester locomotives, from around 1832. **'Lion'** (if it has not returned to Liverpool) was built in 1838 to haul goods trains on the same railway, and shows the rapid advance of locomotive technology in the space of a few years. It is still sometimes steamed. 'Lion' had a starring role in the Ealing Comedy 'The Titfield Thunderbolt'. ('Lion' is on temporary loan from the Liverpool Museums Service.)

The **classic steam locomotive** design is represented by an engine built in 1911 by the Vulcan Foundry for the North Western Railways of India, at a time when Lancashire exported railway engines all over the world. Notice the broad gauge of 5ft 6in (1.7m) — the same as Ireland, for many Indian railways were built by Irish engineers. The modern traction era is symbolised by **'Ariadne'**, a DC pantograph electric locomotive. The London and North Eastern Railway decided to electrify the Manchester and Sheffield line (via the Woodhead tunnel) just before the last war, but only managed to complete a prototype locomotive before the war intervened. This locomotive was shipped to the Netherlands in 1945 to assist in the revival of the railways there (electrified on the same system as the LNER envisioned), and the Dutch railwaymen called it 'Tommy'. When British Railways took over and implemented the project in the early fifties, the whole post-war class was known by that name. When the Woodhead line was scandalously run down in the 1960s, Netherlands Railways were more than happy to purchase these engines. This is why 'Ariadne' is preserved in her Dutch colours. Do not neglect the contrasting examples of carriages – a magnificent (and rare) first class **carriage of the Manchester and Birmingham Railway**, built in 1842, and a **Lancashire and Yorkshire Railway carriage**, constructed before the First World War and adapted as an ambulance carriage in 1917.

The left-hand side of the hall is mainly devoted to the development of the internal combustion engine, from gas to petrol and diesel. A large **Mirlees diesel engine**, powering a generator, is displayed near the steam engines. This introduces a fine collection of **road vehicles**, from horse-drawn to veteran and vintage cars. The central gangway is part of the original staging, containing a display of **historic cycles and motorcycles**, early **Whitworth machine tools**, and **the cab (showing the control systems)** of another 'Tommy'. Be sure to inspect the massive **Beyer-Garret locomotive** before leaving the Power Hall. It was built for South African Railways in 1938 to overcome the problem of operating very powerful engines on narrow gauge light track. This problem was resolved by employing what are, in effect, two separate locomotives – the two power units distribute the weight, and are linked by a central articulated section supporting the large boiler. Beyer Peacock (of 'Gorton Tank' works) exported this successful engine design all over the world, and there is a collection of **photographs from their archives** on the wall behind the engine.

Exit the Power Hall by the door by this locomotive. The **Goods Office**, on the left, was built in 1859 and is connected with an unsubstantiated story concerning Karl Marx. Friedrich Engels tried to obtain him a position as a railway goods clerk in Manchester with the London and North Western Railway (the owners of the site at that time). Unfortunately, Marx's handwriting, in an age before the typewriter, was too bad. One wonders if the course of world history had been any different if he had worked here. We are now at the start of the **original brick viaduct** (Liverpool Road slopes down to the river bank). Rides are available from the nearby platform when the train is running.

A little further on, the way lies down a **ramp to street level**. This modern structure is built on the site of a ramp used to load and unload gentlemen's carriages in the days of the Liverpool and Manchester. (It was possible to travel in your own carriage, which was secured to a flat wagon.) Turn right through the **archway**, noticing the stones on either side. These protected the brickwork from the iron rims of cart wheels. The arch leads to a **low-level yard**, which is partly cut out of the slope of the hill. There is a good view of the **iron viaduct** constructed by the LNWR in 1867, which eventually accessed the Great Western warehouse. Items from the reserve collection are displayed in glassed-in sections of the viaduct. Walter Kershaw, a local artist, executed the large **mural** (illustrating the industrial history of the area) above the viaduct.

Electricity

Enter the **Electricity Gallery**, following the illuminated entrance sign. This is situated in a (very altered) part of the **1830 warehouse**. We descend through the midst of a **condenser** from Back o' th' Bank Power Station, near Bolton. The exhausted steam was fed into it from the turbines, and condensed by cold water flowing through the myriad small pipes. Demonstrations of 'what is electricity' follow, and early devices such as a **'wimshurst machine'** and **'leyden jars'** (for storage of static electricity) are shown. The next gallery tells the story of the infant industry, illustrated by a **blade from a Parson's turbine** (the first to be invented) and a section of a Brush **steam turbine**. The **switchboard from the Mansion House in London**, with its white marble and polished teak (it was the Lord Mayor's residence, after all!), is of particular interest. It was manufactured locally in 1891.

The story continues **upstairs**. The development of electricity supply in the Manchester area is shown on an **animated map**, and a **video** tells the story of the National Grid. However, the most interesting area is concerned with electricity in the home. Two wonderful sets of **'show' living rooms and kitchens**, from the 1930s and the 1950s, attract a great deal of attention. Other examples of electric devices are on display – look for the **Baird Television** (with its rotating scanner) and the early **'crystal set' radio**. The **pre-war advertising** films are amusing, particularly the one in which a woman's cooking (and marriage!) is saved by the purchase of an electric cooker. You can see how much physical energy (using a bicycle) is needed to generate enough power to operate a vacuum cleaner in a **display about using and saving electricity**.

Another **flight of stairs** leads to the 'pièce de résistance', a reconstruction of part of the **Turbine Hall** from 'Back o'th' Bank. (There were six similar generating sets, installed in 1923.) This one was dismantled and re-erected here, a task that involved removing the roof and floors of the warehouse. The massive base plate was lowered into place by a giant crane on a very still day. A cut away section shows the turbine blades, which operate a shaft connected to the large AC Generator. The overhead crane was used for maintenance purposes.

Computing

The rest of the floor is devoted to the **history of computing**, with particular emphasis on Manchester's role in its development. The display (subject to rearrangement) begins with a variety of **calculating aids** and mechanical devices. Notice the Victorian **'calculating engine'**, invented by Charles Babbage, a genius who failed to build a full size version that was to be powered by a steam engine! This can be compared to **'Hartree's Differential Analyser'**, a mechanical device developed at Manchester

University in the 1930s for scientific calculations. Note how computer programming originated with **punched cards**, in turn derived from the jacquard loom.

Alan Turing was, without doubt, the theoretical inventor of the computer (p.145), devising the earliest form of 'software'. A **display** tells the story of his work, starting with the 'Bomb', a wartime code-breaking machine at Bletchley, which imitated the workings of the German 'enigma' code machine. After the war, he participated in the work of a brilliant team at Manchester University, where the first proper computer was developed in 1949. This led to the 'Ferranti Mark One', the first commercially available computer, in 1951. A **Pegasus Computer** of 1957, used by Vickers Armstrong, is displayed.

A final set of stairs accesses the **top floor**, which is mainly given over to the theme of **alternative and renewable sources of energy**, the problems of **nuclear power**, and the issue of the **'greenhouse effect'**.

Gas

Exit the gallery and return to the foot of the ramp. The **figure of a lamplighter** indicates the entrance to the **National Gas Gallery**. A variety of **gas lamps** line each side of a viaduct arch, with a **recreation of an 18th-century experiment** (heating coal in a kettle to produce gas) situated at the end of it. A flight of stairs descends into a display of the **early history of the industry**, including the establishment of the first municipal gasworks at Manchester. Primitive **gas mantles** blaze, illustrating how crude (by modern standards) some of this new technology could be. In a striking tableau, a gas worker stokes a **retort,** and a **video** presentation depicts life in one of Britain's last coal fed gasworks. Models of **gas meters**, that great Victorian invention, are followed by a wonderful array of historic **domestic gas appliances** (including a rather scary looking hair dryer). Some are displayed in the window of a **gas showroom**, circa 1900. To the right of the showroom display window is a gallery devoted to the present day, particularly the production and distribution of natural gas – with a **model of a North Sea drilling rig**.

Water supply

At the bottom of the ramp again, enter the door at the end of the **1831 Shop Range** and descend the stairs leading to **Underground Manchester** in the old cellars. An infant is buried in a **churchyard** – the victim of unsanitary conditions in the late 18th and early 19th centuries in the new industrial districts. The Romans, of course, were past masters in matters of public water supply and sanitation. In a **reconstructed Roman latrine** (possibly in the fort across the road) a soldier holds a 'gomph stick' (used instead of toilet paper and kept in the bucket of water). The waste is flushed away by a continuously flowing culvert. Some of these principles were utilised by Mediaeval monasteries, as is shown, but town life up to the 18th and 19th centuries could be fairly squalid. **Wooden pipes** supplying water from the conduit in Spring Gardens and an 18th-century **chamber pot** (whose contents were thrown into the street gutter) are shown.

The water supply of the growing city was a major Victorian achievement, illustrated by the **model of Longdendale Reservoir**. The following section, dedicated to sewers and waste disposal, is the delight of young children. Listen to the **ballad of the great flood of 1872** when the Medlock swept away part of a cemetery, and coffins were lassoed from bridges. Only larger and better sewers and storm drains could forestall such things. Different types of **sewer section** are displayed. Note that the oval shape increases the velocity of the water flow. We now walk through a full-size **reconstruction of a sewer**, using materials from the 1830s. (Perhaps the stuffed rat will eventually be restored to a position of honour!) Not everyone had flush toilets, of course, and the contents of the cess pits were collected in **'honey carts'** as illustrated by the model. The contents were mixed up with animal waste from the markets, abattoirs, and municipal stables, dried, bagged, and exported to farmers all over the country as fertiliser (thereby defraying the cost of sanitation to the ratepayers). All manner of **lavatories** are displayed, including a fine **earthenware 'self-flushing' model** with a tip-up basin in continuous action.

Few working class homes had proper facilities for washing clothes, and the council provided a number of public laundries. It was the custom for everyone to help each other, and such places were real community centres for the local women, and a hive of gossip. Part of **Moss Street Public Wash House** has been reconstructed, complete with the sliding racks of the drying cabinets. Finally, the 'water cycle' is demonstrated in an animated diagram and **'Planet Water'** deals with contemporary issues.

The 'Making of Manchester'

The exit stairs lead to the end of the 'Making of Manchester' Gallery, but it is better to walk through to the entrance to the warehouse, which lies under the viaduct arch (noticing the reconstruction of a **'blind eye' sewer shaft** on the way). The entrance hall, which can also be accessed from the low-level yard, is a fine introduction to the **1830 Warehouse**. The timber construction of the floors, and the great brick walls are clearly visible, redolent of canal warehouse architecture, but strangely obsolete in an era of fireproof mills incorporating iron pillars and girders. Everything that you see was built in the space of five months! On one side of the entrance hall is **'Warehouse to the World'**, a particularly recommended audio-visual recreation in the 'son et lumière' style of the life and times of the warehouse and early 19th-century Manchester.

The rest of the warehouse is undergoing major development, and the following galleries may shortly be available. **'Food for the City'** will deal with the feeding of a growing urban population in the course of the industrial revolution. **'Communications'** (occupying the top two floors) will concentrate upon how people communicate with each other, and the skills and technologies involved, including writing, paper-making, printing, telecommunications, radio, and the internet. It will include a full-size reproduction of the **'Baby'**, the world's first computer, a great Manchester 'first'.

Return to the 'Making of Manchester' Gallery and walk back through the display to try to catch a showing of the **'Making of Manchester' presentation** in the little theatre area to the left. The content is perhaps a little too bland for some tastes, but it does point out the important role of water in the area's history.

The **'Making of Manchester'** gallery begins at the ramp entrance to the building and proceeds through the former railway offices of the 1831 structure, which supported the carriage shed above. Roman Manchester is represented by a few **finds from the Castlefield dig**, including locally worked iron nails. It is interesting to note the **table of descent of the Lords of the Manor**, and then realise that this form of local administration staggered on until 1838. A legal apparatus familiar to a follower of William the Conqueror ruled an industrial town of clattering machines. The **weights and measures** of 1754 indicate Manchester's importance as a market town, but the most precious exhibit is an **embroidered cap worn by Humphrey Chetham** (p.24). The case also contains the **uniform of a 'bluecoat boy'**.

Cloth working may have been established in the area as long ago as the middle ages, but it was a cottage industry until the end of the 18th century. A **room in a textile worker's cottage** has a spinning wheel and other items among the ordinary household furniture. The first phase of industrialisation involved the establishment of water-powered spinning mills in the surrounding countryside and the **model of the mill at Mellor** has a 'lodge' (reservoir) and 'goit' (mill race). Banck's **plan of Manchester in 1831** shows the new station in Castlefield. (The original owner pencilled in later railway proposals, some of which were never built.) Nearby are some **relics of John Dalton**, including his spectacles and 'thinking cap'! (p.46)

Listen to the **description of the 'Peterloo Massacre'** (p.131). "The wicked have drawn forth the sword: they have cut down the poor and needy, and such as be of upright conversation." The incident was a catalyst in bringing about municipal incorporation, and the embossing stamp of the **seal of the new Corporation** is displayed. Take a copy of the six points of the **'People's Charter'**. Most of the points are now part of our democratic way of life, but all had to be fought for (p.66). The Chartist movement was widely supported in Lancashire, particularly by working class nonconformist groups preaching "Christ and a fair wage, Christ and the full belly, Christ and the People's Charter!"

Peer through the windows at the **poor working class interiors**, the wretched hovels and cellar dwellings to be found in Lombard Street, and other lost areas of Deansgate. The mood changes with the onset of mid-Victorian prosperity. An improving standard of living, combined with the idea of an 'age of progress' through 'free trade', gave rise to a burst of confidence and the belief that poverty would eventually disappear. The displays illustrate a rash of **public buildings**, growing city pride, great exhibitions, and major projects such as the **Manchester Ship Canal**.

The harsh realities of the **20th century**, two world wars and an inter-war depression, follow. A **video of the blitz of 1940** reveals the terrible extent of the damage inflicted on the city centre. Do not neglect the **video of a 'Whit Walk'.** These processions of the churches and chapels with their Sunday Schools were a highlight of the Manchester calendar. Every child had to have a new suit or dress (even if it meant a visit to the pawn shop), and they were paraded around friends and neighbours in their new finery. "Eh love, are thi walkin' with t' scholars?" The question was usually accompanied with a few coppers (coins) to fill a new pocket. Wholesale demolition of the inner-city parishes resulted in a decline in numbers, but the tradition still exists. The gallery concludes with displays on the regeneration of the city in the last two decades, including the **model used by the Development Corporation.**

The 1830 Station

We now arrive at the **Second Class Booking Office** of the **1830 Station**. The railway did not carry third class passengers at all in the early years! (A descriptive account of the Station Buildings, together with the origins of the Liverpool and Manchester Railway, may be found on p.183.) There is an **entrance door** from Liverpool Road and an **original fireplace**, though the stairs, which communicated with the Waiting Room upstairs, disappeared a long time ago.

'Oldest in the World' is an accurate **audio-visual presentation of the history of the Liverpool and Manchester Railway**. An actual **paper ticket** can be seen in the display case, along with a number of **commercial souvenir items of the opening**, which created a stir throughout the whole country. The **station bell** hangs on the wall (no-one knows its original position). The lovely **Ackerman prints** of the railway repay close inspection, but do not miss the cartoon of the **"Effects of the Railroads on the Brute Creation"**. After the trains have supplanted horse-drawn transport, the poor beasts are reduced to begging for corn, busking with a fiddle, or running off to join the army! Of course, the reverse happened, for the railways created a boom in short-haul road transport, in connection with the expanding national system.

Pass through the (later) door into the **First Class Booking Office**. The re-creation, and the **tableaux of figures**, is impressive, but rather tongue in cheek, since it is impossible to know what the original booking hall looked like. The company's main concern was freight, which dictated a terminus at Castlefield, but the directors were soon to discover that passenger traffic was just as important, and that they had a station on what was then the outskirts of town. Consequently, the intending passengers booked their tickets at a variety of taverns and inns in the town centre. These establishments were used to booking passengers for stagecoaches, so stagecoach practice was followed. The tickets were hand-written, and included the passenger's name, and specified the destination and particular train.

A special omnibus performed the journey to the station door, and there were several routes traversing the principal streets. Of course, out of town passengers arrived directly at the station, and, with the growth of traffic, the first railway hotel and a coffee-house opened nearby. On passing through the **entrance door**, into the Booking Hall, the ticket was handed to the clerk. The passenger retained one portion of the ticket (rather in the manner of an airline boarding pass) and the booking clerk kept the rest. Information abstracted from the collected ticket portions was incorporated in a waybill, which was given to the train guard. Thus, the guard had a list of all his passengers and their respective destinations. This was then the only check against fraud, and the invention of the numbered railway ticket must have been a real godsend. **Outdoor porters** (one is seen in the tableaux), licensed by the company to tout for custom using a scale of charges, dealt with the luggage. They handed it over to 'indoor porters' (company employees) who duly strapped it onto the roofs of carriages very much like stagecoach bodies on railway wagon frames.

In the meantime, the passengers made their way up the **stairs** (the central portion of the banister is believed to be original) to the **First Class Waiting Room**. They could study the **sundial**, visible through the large triple light window. This area now contains a **display of scientific instruments**, many having been manufactured in the locality. **The Second Class Waiting Room**, next door, is now devoted to the **history of photography**, with particular emphasis upon Manchester. When the train was ready, the station bell was rung and the doors were unlocked, so let us follow the passengers out onto the platform.

The **platform** is rather low, more like a pavement, a tradition followed by railways on the continent to this day. Unfortunately, for some unfathomable reason, the original platform surface was removed during the restoration. The rear of the **Station Agents House** prefaces a view of the rail level of the **Water Street Bridge**. Near the Waiting Room door may be found the remains of the original **wooden housing** for the Station Clock, illuminated by a gas mantle (the **bracket and protect-**

ing iron hoop remain). Before the railways, every British town and city set their watches and clocks to their own time. But railway operations required a uniform time zone all along the line, usually set to Greenwich time (telegraphed to them at certain times of the day). This became convenient for everyone – the railway system created a common time zone for the whole country.

The carriage doors were locked after the passengers had boarded. (The railway directors were worried about people trying to alight from a new form of transport with speeds of up to thirty miles per hour!) The station bell was rung again immediately before the time of departure, and the guard (perched on a seat level with the roof of the brake carriage) gave the signal to the driver with a coaching horn. The journey to Liverpool, inclusive of a stop to take on water at Parkside, generally took about two hours.

Notice the **angle of the wall** at the end of the 1830 station building (the original stone flagged platform was cut off at the same angle here). This was to accommodate the sidings entering the **1831 Carriage Shed**, which has been restored to its 1860s condition (when it was used as a carpenter's shop), complete with planked floor! It would be nice if someone would rectify this in the not-to-distant future, and not only restore the shed to its proper appearance, but fill it with some suitable reproduction first and second class carriages. Nevertheless, it is worth a close inspection. The **door on the right,** just beyond the entrance, may have been used by Grand Junction Railway Passengers between 1837 and 1842, en route to Birmingham and, after 1839, London. The wooden roof trusses are supported on the left-hand side by a **row of iron columns**. Look closely at these, for they are placed at unequal distances to each other. They are hollow and were meant to act as drains for the guttering, a typical feature of industrial and warehouse architecture at the time. It is said that, in an attempt to economise, the London and North Western Railway re-used some guttering in the last quarter of the 19th century. The (inevitably!) Irish foreman moved the columns to fit the existing holes! Some types of humour never change. The shed was meant to hold up to 20 carriages, which were only 25–30ft (7.6–9m) in length.

There is a good view of the exterior of the **1830 Warehouse**, opposite. Wagons were turned (by small turntables or 'turnplates') on to transverse tracks that led into the stone arched loading bays at viaduct level. This is something that really ought to be re-created in at least one instance. (It would also be nice to see the return of some of the hydraulic shunting capstans, which also disappeared during the restoration.) Beyond the end of the warehouse is a good view of the **LNWR** viaduct and the **Walter Kershaw mural**.

Before leaving the main site, mention should be made of short **steam-hauled trips**, which are usually given at weekends. The 'Planet' replica is often used, together with reproduction Liverpool and Manchester second class coaches.

Air and Space

The visit is continued across Lower Byrom Street in the **Air and Space Hall.** (The antecedents of this fine building are given on p.182.) On coming through the door, the first sight is a visual contrast. To the right is an **English Electric P1A** experimental aircraft, the prototype of a new range of supersonic jet fighters that became known as 'Lightnings'. The aircraft was built at Preston in 1954 and was the first British jet to break the sound barrier. In contrast, the aircraft to the left goes back to

The frontage of the Air and Space Hall from Liverpool Road

the earliest days of aviation. Alliot Verdon Roe was a Manchester pioneer and built this **triplane** (powered by a Crossley four horse-power limousine engine) in 1909. It was the first all British aircraft. (This replica is the work of Avro apprentices.)

We follow the path round in a clockwise direction, turning right at the first fork, and passing a number of aircraft. The **Avro Avian biplane** dates from the 1920s, when a great deal of civil aviation was still a rich man's hobby. This example was the first aircraft to land at Barton, Manchester's pioneer airport. The **Avro 504K** was perhaps one of the most successful British designs. It first flew in 1913, was used in some of the first air operations in 1914, and later became a successful training aircraft. It was still being produced decades later, and this example can be dated to 1930. A magnificent **De Havilland Dragon Rapide**, with passengers embarking circa 1935, illustrates the pioneer era of civil air traffic. The famous **Supermarine Spitfire**, the plane forever associated with the Battle of Britain in 1940, can be seen opposite. The aircraft first flew in 1936, and developed in a series of marks throughout the war. This is a reconnaissance version of 1945, powered with a Rolls Royce Griffon engine, not the original Merlin.

The path now is to the left, past the **flight simulator**, for a fine view of the **Avro Shackleton**. A number of long-range strategic bombers were in at the planning stage when war broke out, but they only started to come on stream in 1942. The Avro company produced an unsuccessful design called the 'Manchester' and decided to add another two engines to produce the 'Lancaster' – one of the most successful bombers of the war. Large numbers of Lancasters were produced locally, and the City Council wanted one of the few remaining ones as a centrepiece for the new museum. One was found in an aviation museum store and the agreement almost concluded, but the maintenance staff at the location lobbied furiously to keep it there. They even attempted to gain publicity in the media against the move by circulating a rumour to the effect that it was haunted! So what you see is a 1950s development of the Lancaster, the Avro Shackleton. This aircraft fulfilled the post-war role of observation at sea and submarine attack, before a number were fitted with radar for advanced warning of aircraft and missiles. This particular aircraft operated in this role until the squadron was re-equipped by American AWACS in the 1980s.

A partly sectioned **Hawker Hunter** is adjacent, Britain's second generation jet fighter. It first flew in 1951, and this example went into service in 1954. The first British helicopter is displayed, a **Bristol Sycamore** developed in 1947. This 1957 example operated in Cyprus on 'search and rescue' duties, and is shown engaged in a medical evacuation. The twin-bladed **Bristol Belvedere Helicopter** saw service in the 1960s and could carry eighteen soldiers or three tons of equipment. The Avro company experimented a great deal with delta-wing designs after the war, and an **experimental aircraft** of 1953 is shown. The most famous design was the Avro Vulcan nuclear bomber.

Do not overlook the Japanese **'Okha' suicide aircraft**, part and parcel of the infamous Kamikaze assault upon the allied fleet. This rocket-propelled flying bomb was built in 1945, and captured by American forces. It was slung under a Nakajima bomber and released, allowing the suicide pilot to guide it to his target. Fortunately, the control system left a great deal to be desired, and many crashed harmlessly into the sea. 'Okha' means 'Cherry Blossom'. It is a flower that dies and then falls from the tree at the moment of its highest perfection. The allies found this attitude of life incomprehensible and disgusting, proof that such an enemy would not listen to reason until two atomic bombs had been dropped.

A flight of steps by the Belvedere leads to the gallery, which should be traversed in a clockwise direction. Here are **relics of Alcock and Brown** (including their mascots), two Mancunians who were the first to fly across the Atlantic in 1919 in a twin-engined Vickers Vimy bomber. Notice the **enormous wooden wheel**, taken in 1919 from an uncompleted experimental ten-engined (!) German triplane bomber. As we proceed through the paraphernalia of **passenger flight** over the years, look at the **painting of Ringway (Manchester) Airport in wartime** (including all the types of planes and activities), and explore the **cockpit interior of a Trident jet airliner**.

The **Air and Space display** includes some children's favourites, including a **Dalek** and a **Cyberman** from Dr. Who, together with his **police box**. A Bakelite radio churns out Orson Welles' notorious **'War of the Worlds' broadcast**. A **Gemini Paraglider** of the 1960s is displayed. It was part of an experiment to see if the capsule could make a ground landing. Look out for the **NASA Space suit**, which is easily missed. The remainder of the gallery is in the course of reorganisation, and will eventually contain displays relating to the **role of aviation in North West England**.

Oxford Street and the Refuge building, now the Palace Hotel, in the direction of St Peter's Square

12 Oxford Road and the Education Precinct

Start: Corner of Oxford St/Portland St

Estimated time of walk: 2 hours

Interiors: Manchester Museum – 1 hour; Whitworth Gallery – ½ hour

Highlights: Theatreland, the lost suburb, Manchester University, Eqyptian mummies, Tyrannosaurus Rex, the birthplace of the women's movement, and the Whitworth Gallery.

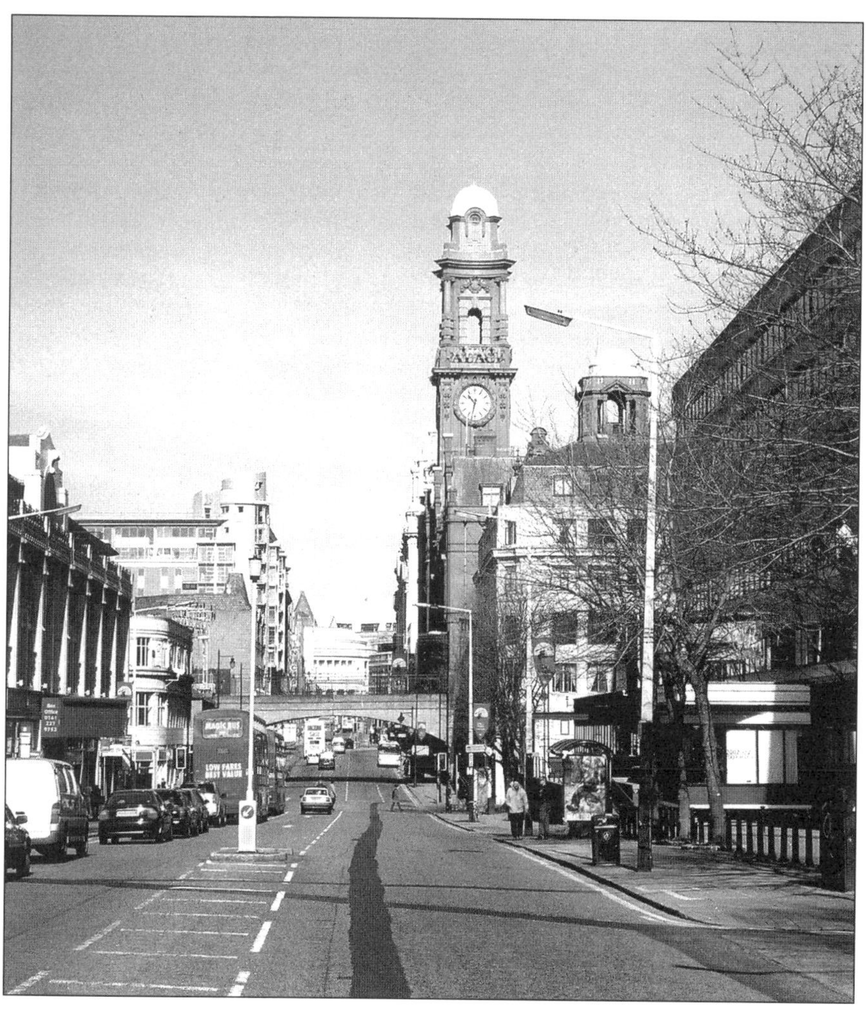

Unlike the other walks in the book, this one is mostly straight as a die, running southwards from the city centre through the heart of the Education Precinct. It can be combined with the Piccadilly to St Peter's Square or the Piccadilly to Knott Mill walks, or taken as an independent walk to do the museums justice. Whatever the case, the walk starts at the junction of Oxford Street with Chepstow Street and Portland Street *(1)*, a short distance along the latter from Piccadilly. (The portion of Oxford Street between St Peter's Square and the starting point is described on p.126.) If you decide to make a full afternoon or day of it, the walk may be prolonged into one of two interesting excursions by making use of a frequent service of buses.

As noted in a previous walk, a new road to the south of the town was constructed in 1790. The wealthy wanted to get out of the smoke of the new industrial developments and started to migrate to Broughton and Pendleton, or southwards to Ardwick, Chorlton, and Rusholme. At that time, there was only one route in the latter direction, along London Road to Ardwick Green and beyond. To serve the needs of this increasing population, the new thoroughfare cut across green fields from St Peter's Square to a point near Booth Street, where it joined an existing country lane to Rusholme and Wilmslow. The section as far as the River Medlock became known as Oxford Street, and the remainder Oxford Road.

Oxford Street

Oxford Street became an adjunct of Peter Street, in that the theatres and music halls spread along it, though these were elbowed by a sufficient number of increasingly grander offices and warehouses. Apart from a failed property speculation around All Saints, Oxford Road was far more nondescript. That is to say, until two universities and other academic institutions began to expand. It comes as a surprise to many that Manchester now has possibly the largest student population in Europe. There are over 70,000 at the main universities, and over 100,000 in the Greater Manchester area. (About 5% of this student population are foreign.) The majority of the Manchester higher education buildings are concentrated along Oxford Road in an Education Precinct, a wise planning decision made long ago in the 1960s.

From the starting point *(1)*, we proceed between *McDonald's* and the corner warehouse opposite (p.126). Beyond *McDonald's* the Gaumont Cinema stood to the right; 'South Pacific' ran here for over two years, as did 'The Sound of Music'. The former cinema is also remembered for the infamous 'Long Bar', situated in the basement. This place (genuinely claiming to have the longest bar in the country) was the haunt of American servicemen in the last war and shortly after. They generally hailed from the large base at Burtonwood, near Warrington, and were prepared to part with their money in return for a good time. Many of the local tarts got rich. One was able to retire and open a pub, and yet another actually married her paramour, a wealthy officer. She may still be a pillar of society in her American town.

The Gaumont itself was erected, in 1935, on the site of the Hippodrome. George Formby, a music hall comedian who made a successful transition to the cinema, began his career here. (A reproduction of the Hippodrome theatre arch was placed over his grave.) His persona was that of the 'gormless' Lancashire lad, constantly evading the screen censorship of the day by the double meanings in his ukelele-accompanied songs. As we walk down Oxford Street, it may be pleasant to think of the breezy young lad strolling along the promenade, attracting all the ladies with "his little stick of Blackpool rock!"

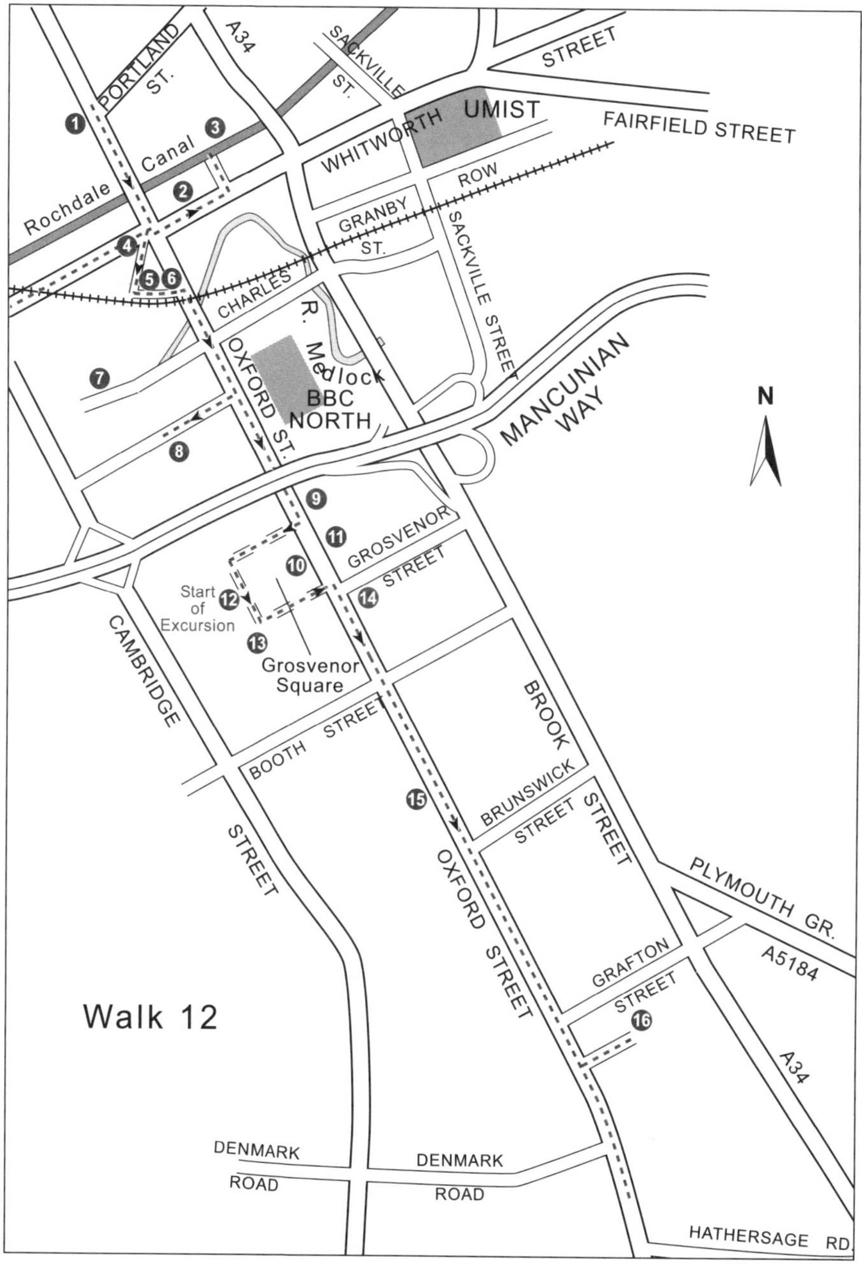

Pause at the corner of Bridgewater Street on the right. A disused underground gentlemen's lavatory (complete with wrought iron railings) is now the ***Temple of Convenience***, a small bar that also displays art from time to time. **Churchgate House** (Gibbon Sankey, 1898), beyond the street on the same side, was built as the headquarters of Messrs. Tootal Broadhurst, a major textile empire. This concern was interesting, for it controlled every aspect of the cotton process in an early example of 'vertical integration'. The façade is in the popular terracotta with Corinthian columns. (The artists of the design department exhibited their work in the ground floor windows.) It now contains, amongst much else, the offices of Marketing Manchester, the agency responsible for promoting economic regeneration in the area.

Opposite, **St James House**, an elaborate and bulky structure of Portland Stone in the Edwardian Baroque style, takes up the greater part of the street. Many of the features, including the central tower, owe their inspiration to Hawksmoor churches. Containing over 1000 rooms, it was built for the Calico Printers Association in 1912. An excellent hairdresser is included in the array of shops at street level. Notice that the building straddles the Rochdale Canal, which is visible opposite – just beyond Churchgate House.

The **Palace Theatre** is next door to St James House. The original opened in 1891, and was intended as a 'modern music hall'. Despite opposition from local Methodists and temperance organisations, it prospered, attracting a number of famous names – Little Tich, Vesta Tilly, Marie Lloyd, and Charles Chaplin (in 1903) all trod the boards. Then, after an extensive exterior rebuild (in the French neo-Grecian style), the Palace reopened as a theatre in 1913. Conventional 'society' drama and melodrama held sway for a long time. Although the façade was refaced in 1956, the theatre fell on hard times. After closure in 1978, it reopened after refurbishment in 1981. The theatre now specialises in high quality touring productions. If you attend a show here, inspect the beautiful (restored) 1891 auditorium in the interval. Note the **plaque** to Les Dawson, the much loved and sadly missed comedian. Les stood in the tradition of a long line of northern comedians, stretching back through Norman Evans and Frank Randle. Like Evans, he would adopt the persona of the northern housewife in her 'pinny' – gossipy but very shrewd.

The Palace Theatre, on the corner of Oxford Street and Whitworth Street

We have now reached the Whitworth Street intersection. Make a slight detour to the left as far as Atwood Street, passing **Bridgewater House** (1912) *(2)*. It is faced with self-cleaning white faïence tiles, which rather looks like Portland stone, and adorned with a bust of the 'Canal duke' over the door. The internal arrangements were revolutionary. Goods were unloaded from lorries at the rear, and left from the theatre end of the building – half the ground floor was devoted to goods movement, and 26 lorries could be dealt with at one time. **India House**, opposite, (1905-1906) was designed as a packing warehouse, an activity requiring plenty of light and a capacious basement for the presses, and good loading and unloading facilities. This was provided within a steel frame structure, fronted by a façade of brick, granite, and glazed sienna tiles and mouldings. H.S. Fairhurst was responsible for both buildings (it probably helped that he married into the family of the firm responsible for the India House commission).

The **Rochdale Canal** (p.154) is accessed *(3)* at the bottom of Atwood Street (it is also spanned by a footbridge leading to Linley House). The tall **chimney** marks the site of Bloom Street electricity works, an early example of energy conservation – exhaust steam and hot water was supplied to the office blocks in the vicinity. The towpath of the Rochdale Canal, from Castlefield to the Dale Street Basin (adjacent to Piccadilly Station), constitutes a strange walk through the back waters of Central Manchester.

The Cornerhouse

Retrace your footsteps to Oxford Street and cross over. The **Cornerhouse** (Tuesday-Saturday 11.00-6.00, Sunday 2.00-6.00), an arts centre opened in a former furniture showroom in 1985, marks the corner of Whitworth Street West. The box office, shop, and bar are on the ground floor, a restaurant occupies the first, which also acts as a gateway to two further floors of exhibition galleries. Small mini cinemas are installed in the basement. The art shows can be interesting, but the place is perhaps better known as an 'arthouse' cinema. The best thing about it was the hilarious visitors comments book, but the burden of being at the 'cutting edge' obviously means taking yourself very seriously, and the book is no more. The place can be frightfully 'politically correct'.

The main **Cornerhouse cinema** is established across the station approach *(4)*, in the old 'Tatler'. This rather odd place is located under part of the station, but is remarkably sound proof. It started its life in 1910 as the Kinemacolour Palace (an early colour film process), later becoming a 'news cinema' showing a continuous programme of newsreels, cartoons, and short comedies to people with time to kill. It became the 'Tatler Cinema Club' in 1969 (you became a 'member' within an hour), and offered a diet of allegedly 'erotic' films and visiting strippers. (An old chap who was obviously enjoying his retirement 'job' helped the ladies on and off the stage.) It became part of the Cornerhouse in 1985. A short detour down this street reveals the ***Greenroom***, situated an arch or two along the viaduct. An experimental theatre with a long history (founded in 1926), it was re-founded in 1983, and opened a 170 seat theatre here in 1987. In addition to some distinctive experimental drama, it is also a venue for jazz, comedy, and cabaret.

Turn round and espy the ***Ritz***, the last of the old time dancehalls. Established in 1927, the Ritz has seen it all. Ballroom dancing, swing, rock and roll, the regime of Jimmy Saville – how many Manchester marriages began here? In later years, it has catered to the disco scene. It was (maybe still is) famous for its 'grab a granny night'.

On the way back to Oxford Street, be sure to turn up the approach *(4)* to inspect **Oxford Road Station**. This was the principal station and headquarters of the Manchester South Junction and Altrincham Railway (p.129), still used by thousands of commuters. The original station was completely rebuilt in 1960, and is noted for the **curious design of its roof**. W.R. Headley, the regional architect for British Rail, roofed a rather difficult triangular site with three linked conical shells of nailed and glued timber, supported by laminated wooden arches. It looks impressive, but has proved difficult to maintain. However, as some have compared it to Sydney Opera House, the whole roof was restored in 1998.

Search out the long **flight of stairs** *(5)* on the other side of the odd metal podium. These lead down to a depressed cobbled area, below the level of the roadway. It would be known as a 'fold' in Lancashire, and is part of the valley of the (mostly culverted) Medlock stream. It is also all that is left of **'Little Ireland'** *(6)*. The Irish were drawn to Manchester during the industrial revolution, a process that accelerated after the potato famine. Although there were undoubtedly instances of discrimination and sectarianism, the immigrants were quickly assimilated – after all, Manchester was a very cosmopolitan place, and the Irish were one group amongst many. The people of Manchester, in general, were just as happy watching the Irish Roman Catholics in the Whit Walks (p.197) on Whit Friday, as they were watching the Protestants on Whit Monday – and a child in new clothes got a penny in their pocket on both days. However, in the early days, the Irish immigrants crowded into the cheapest accommodation that they could find. Here, it is reckoned that 4,000 people were crammed into 200 dilapidated cottages, constituting the worst slum in Manchester. Friedrich Engels came and described the scene in his 'Condition of the English Working Classes'. 'Little Ireland', was largely destroyed when the railway was built, and a good thing too. The ***Salisbury*** lies tucked away in the corner.

Upon regaining Oxford Street, the view is monopolised by the great bulk of the **Refuge Building (*Palace Hotel*)**. This, the largest Baroque revival building in the city, was built between 1891 and 1910 for the Refuge Assurance Company. The **section on the corner of Whitworth Street** was begun by Alfred Waterhouse, careful to select the right shade of brick and terracotta to create a tone of gravitas. It incorporates a corner tower, flanked by two gables, and terminates by a gable next to the clock tower. Notice that the buttresses between the windows sport the prows of small arks – no doubt symbolic of the worth of the company's policies! The **second half**, towards the bridge, dates from 1910, and was the work of Alfred's son. The central feature, linking both halves, is the impressive 220ft (67m) **clock tower**, surmounted by a dome. The whole thing was once described as "a tall young man in flannel trousers escorting two charming, but somewhat delicate old ladies dressed in lace". It now contains the *Palace Hotel*, a luxurious hostelry that makes full use of its palatial and fascinating interior.

Chorlton

After passing under the **railway bridge**, we cross the Medlock (visible through a **glazed panel** in the iron parapet on the left) and enter the old township of Chorlton. Oxford Road starts here. Shortly after the opening of this new road in 1790, the impecunious Roger Aytoun (p.140) sold the former Chorlton Hall estate to a syndicate headed by Samuel Marsland, a Stockport cotton manufacturer. Marsland and his associates carved it up into appropriately named streets and building plots aimed at a well-heeled clientele. As previously mentioned, the area rapidly filled with the middle class overspill from Manchester. However, a glance to the right, down Hulme Street *(7)*, reveals the considerable remains of **Chorlton Mills**, once the largest industrial complex in the region. Thus did cotton pursue the new middle class to the start of their new suburb. The other half of Hulme Street, across Oxford Road, leads to the *Lass O'Gowrie* and the UMIST Campus.

We pass, on the right, the **Dancehouse Theatre**, housed in a 1930 office and retail development that included the two Regal Cinemas (each with its own separate foyer) on the second floor. The Dancehouse is, of course, a temple of modern dance, the showcase of the Northern Ballet School. It contains a 430 seat auditorium, a café and bar (hosting jazz on some evenings) and a number of dance studios. A wide programme of dance performances is given throughout the year. The nondescript brick box of the **BBC building** is opposite. The BBC moved here from Piccadilly in the 1970s, and it functions as their northern headquarters, including local radio.

All Saints

We are now entering the All Saints campus of the **Manchester Metropolitan University**. In 1970, the Manchester College of Art and Design and the John Dalton College of Technology joined together to form Manchester Polytechnic, a Higher Education institution specialising in skills based and technical degrees. It absorbed a number of other educational institutions, and became the Manchester Metropolitan University in 1992. As Manchester's second university, it has certainly broadened its academic scope, but still offers a wide range of vocational oriented degrees. A short detour down Chester Street, on the right, reveals a **statue of John Dalton** (p.46), in front of the former college that bore his name *(8)*. It was removed here from Piccadilly Gardens, and a stone slab from his tomb in Ardwick Cemetery is placed by it. There is another view of the Chorlton Mill Complex, now largely converted into flats.

Follow the college building round the corner back onto Oxford Road, noticing the brick extension with odd linear windows. The **National Computing Centre** (Cruikshank and Seward, 1964) is opposite. It was conceived at a time when Harold Wilson had just made his 'white heat of technology' speech. One evening, the Prime Minister's aide phoned the architect. "The Prime Minister is announcing the opening of the NCC, can you do us a model for tomorrow?" The design was still only a hazy notion, but, within a few hours, the entire thing had been translated into a reality and an illustration – which graced the table at the press conference! The plans were then worked out from the picture, producing the white tiled structure, cantilevered out over the podium, that you see today. It has recently been refurbished, enclosing the pillared area with a glass screen. The NCC is an independent research organisation, dedicated to the dissemination of knowledge concerning computer technology and systems, with a wide range of individual, academic institution, and corporate membership.

The walk now passes under **Mancunian Way**. When it opened, in the early sixties, this elevated super highway was to be the first of a new inner city network that would solve the city's traffic problems. It didn't work out that way, for the congestion was just displaced to somewhere else. In any case, the money ran out (one of the slip roads finishes in mid air, a moment caught in time). The policy is now to develop an outer 'box' of motorways (keeping through traffic in the outer suburbs), while traffic is actually being restricted in the city centre. The name of this highway resulted from a competition. Interestingly enough, the second choice was 'John F. Kennedy Way'.

The **All Saints Building** is now on the right (Gordon Taylor, 1978). It incorporates the Sir Kenneth Green Library, considered to be one of the finest arts libraries outside of London. The Students Union lies across the road in the **Nelson Mandela building**. Round the corner is a **plaque** *(9)* recording the fact that Thomas Wright lived in the vicinity. Wright came from a humble background, and his charitable labours earned him the title of 'the prisoner's friend'.

All Saints itself is marked by **Grosvenor Square**, a grassy oasis by the side of a very busy road *(10)*. It was intended as the communal garden for the houses in a fashionable square, after the London practice. However, by the close of the Napoleonic Wars, only one house stood on the site of the present Ormond Building (see below), and that was Samuel Marsland's own home. People facetiously referred to the garden as 'Marsland's Grove'. As he wondered why this part of his speculation had not taken off, an opportunity occurred – he was approached by the Reverend Charles Burton. The clergyman wanted to build a church and Marsland thought that this was a good deal. After all, a fashionable place of worship would attract fashionable people. The site was thus sold to Burton for £2000 in 1819. All Saints was consecrated by the Bishop of Chester the following year. It was erected in the Grecian style (a domed tower was added in 1835) and could accommodate 1,800 people.

Burton managed to fill it with the anticipated fashionable congregation, for he was no ordinary clergyman. An inspired preacher, he originated from a Methodist family. However, his principal claim to fame was his interest in millenary predictions (calculating the end of the world and the 'second coming' through a mixture of biblical references and mathematics). He published a pamphlet in 1841, predicting that the world would end in 1868. Unfortunately (or fortunately, depending how you look at it) he died in 1866. The fashionable had disappeared by the end of the

A summer's day in Grosvenor Square

19th century, and two later 20th-century clergy exhibited great sympathy towards their working class parishioners. Etienne Watts, in particular, scandalised many in the inter-war period. He allowed the hunger marchers to shelter in the church (he is said to have stood on the steps shouting "sanctuary, sanctuary!") and permitted the use of the building for a theatrical performance. The 'respectable' church folk schemed behind his back to sell the site for a department store development. Unfortunately, All Saints was seriously damaged by bombing in the Second World War, and the gaunt smoke blackened structure lingered on until it was demolished in 1949.

It must be remembered that the gardens are also the landscaped site of the **churchyard** of All Saints. By the 1840s, it was clear that the income from the churchyard was far below expectations. Perhaps it could not compete with the new cemetery nearby. Whatever the reason, the churchwardens were worried. Consequently, a large part of the churchyard around the railings was assigned to pauper burials at a competitive rate. Mrs Gaskell, who lived in one of the nearby houses, describes such a funeral in the pages of 'Mary Barton'. The dead were placed in a large trench that was not closed up until deemed full – a (padlocked) hinged door covered the grave. Each day, a mockery of a painted tombstone and rectangular curb, manufactured from wood, was placed over the cavity, and the deceased were lowered in with whatever decorum could be mustered.

The stretch of Oxford Road facing Grosvenor Square consists of a **row of old properties** *(11)*, and includes two well-known Manchester places. ***On the Eighth Day,*** recently rebuilt, is a vegetarian/vegan café, operating as a co-operative. A customer once described the experience of eating there as similar to stepping into the pages of a novel by Malcolm Bradbury or David Lodge. ***Johnny Roadhouse*** is famous for second-hand musical instruments.

Make a tour of the Square in an anti-clockwise direction by turning down the side of the All Saints Building to reach the **Bellhouse Building** *(12)*. Older Mancunians remember the latter as the Ear, Nose, and Throat Hospital, but it is the solitary surviving house from the original Square development, dating from 1832. We pass **St Augustine's Catholic Church** (1968), containing a fine **ceramic mural** (by Robert Brumby) of the Risen Christ, to reach the Ormond Building.

Around Grosvenor Square

The growing problem of the poor in the new industrial society exercised the imagination in the early 19th century. Rich householders objected to the increasing poor rates, levied according to the value of property. Others, inspired by the writings of Malthus, saw the poor as drones, eating up scarce resources and thereby undermining society. The result was the 1834 Poor Law, which sought to reduce expense and reform the idle through the principle of 'less eligibility'. Anyone seeking assistance would have to enter a workhouse. Here, conditions were such that anyone with any initiative would leave as soon as possible. The diet was sufficient only to keep body and soul together, there was a regime of hard work (usually breaking stones or picking hemp), and families were separated. Parishes were joined together in 'unions' and each union maintained a workhouse.

Of course, the system could not be made to work properly – the workhouses could not possibly accommodate all the poor in the district. Eventually, only the severest cases (including the old, the sick, and the homeless) resorted to the workhouse. The others received financial assistance in their own homes, through a rigid application of the outdated rules and regulations that often caused a great deal of distress. The fear of going into the workhouse haunted generations of old people until the 1930s, when the last vestiges of the system were abolished. Fortunately, each workhouse was the responsibility of an elected Board of Guardians, and any local ratepayer (male or female) could stand for office. In the Manchester area, social reformers did eventually make an impact on the workhouse regime. Emmeline Pankhurst, the wife of such a Manchester barrister and radical, was elected to the Board of Guardians of the Chorlton Union (which met in the Ormond Building). Emmeline, along with her daughters, is better remembered for the creation of the Suffragette Movement (see below).

The **Ormond building**, built in 1881 in the Italianate style, contained the Chorlton Union's offices, used mainly for civil registration and applications for financial assistance. (By that time, most of the work was undertaken in hospitals, orphanages, and asylums in the suburbs.) It is now the offices of the University, but many of the original features still exist, including the mortuary (used at one point to store toilet rolls). Needless to say, it is said to be haunted.

A paved area *(13)* leads under an arch. *(This is the starting point for the excursion to Old Trafford described on p. 260.)* The **Righton Building** (1905), sporting a terracotta frontage, stands on the Cavendish Street corner. This former draper's shop, with a top-lit gallery supported by cast iron columns, retains the benches upon which cloth was once measured. The Department of History of Art and Design now uses it.

The way now lies to the left, down Cavendish Street. The **School of Art** originated from the teaching function of the Royal Institution (p.100). It successfully completed the transition to a fully fledged art school in the 1870s and moved here in 1881. The building is a Gothic revival sandstone structure, extended in 1898 (an inscription on the Ormond Street side records that the costs were defrayed by a £10,000 gift from the proceeds of the Royal Jubilee Exhibition). Adolph Valette taught here, his most famous pupil being L.S. Lowry. It now forms part of the Metropolitan University.

The adjacent handsome classical façade, with fluted Doric columns, is particularly noticeable. They belonged to **Chorlton Town Hall**, designed by Richard Lane (the architect of the Friend's Meeting House), and erected 1830-1831. The building was commissioned by the rudimentary local government organisation for the area, the Police Commissioners of Chorlton Roe (as the township was called), and contained a meeting room, offices for the poor law officials, and a dispensary (there had been a severe fever epidemic in 1825). The residents intended to preserve their administrative independence (to pay lower rates, presumably), but as the population rapidly increased, the demands placed upon the small organisation became unsustainable. Consequently, Chorlton township was absorbed by Manchester in 1842. The structure thus became a largely redundant hall, hired out for public meetings. Some of these were significant – a **plaque** records the fact that the Fifth Pan African Congress was held in the old Town Hall building in 1945. The participants included Kwame Nkrumah and Jomo Kenyatta. The dispensary was sold to the School of Art, and the original Town Hall now only exists as a façade.

Oxford Road is now regained. The old **Grosvenor Picture Palace** marks the corner of Grosvenor Street, now the *Footage and Firkin (sic.)*. Built in 1913-15, it marks the period when cinemas were becoming a permanent feature of the urban landscape, and were ostentatiously advertising themselves – hence the green and white faience and classy Baroque. Showing features such as Steve Reeves in 'Hercules Unchained', it eeked out a living until the 1960s, expiring in 1968. It is now a studenty pub. Take a look round the corner, at the former **Adult Deaf and Dumb Institute** *(14)* in Grosvenor Street, a Gothic building (1877) with interesting carvings (including that of a hand on a book, the badge worn by the deaf at that time).

We continue along Oxford Road. The elegant curving roof belongs to the new £32.2m **Manchester Aquatics Centre**, able to seat 2,500 spectators. Though this was intended as a key component of the Commonwealth Games, it remains as a facility for residents and visitors alike. It has **four pools**, including a 50m competition pool, a 25m diving pool, and over 200 square metres of **leisure pool**, complete with flumes and bubble pools. (The 50m training pool is in the basement.) The interior is usually visible through the window blinds.

Rusholme Road Cemetery was situated somewhere to the rear of the Centre. It was Manchester's first private cemetery, and along with Ardwick Cemetery constituted a Valhalla for Manchester's rich, great, and good. The site is now parkland. The **Humanities Building** (1994-1996), across Oxford Road, is a high 'energy efficient' concrete framed structure. The large atrium accesses three floors.

The intersection with Booth Street is now reached. The **Manchester School of Management (**1997-1998), a faculty of UMIST, occupies the left-hand corner, while the **Royal Northern College of Music** (Bickerdike, Allen, Rich, 1968) is on the opposite one. There is deck access at the first-storey level (you can see that it was once intended to extend to other buildings). The view through the glass on the Booth Street Side reveals a **statue of Frederic Chopin** (by Ludwika Nitschowa). It was presented by The Chopin Society of Warsaw in 1973 – the 125th anniversary of his concert in Manchester. The Royal College of Music dates from the late 19th century (Hallé was a founder member), and amalgamated with the Northern School of Music in 1973. It is one of the foremost centres of music education in the country, and, in addition to teaching, acts as an Arts Centre and a showcase for the many talents of its students. These public performances are given either in the **Concert Hall** (over 400 seats), or in the **Theatre** (over 600 seats). **Manchester Business School**, a part of Manchester University, is almost opposite the Music College, across Booth Street West.

The University of Manchester

The *Precinct Centre* straddles the roadway. As the letters indicate, it marks the entrance to the main **Manchester University Campus**. The ***Precinct Centre*** (originally the Phoenix Centre) was a bright idea of the 1970s when the University was expanding, apace and replacing a lot of derelict land and slum property (fortunately, brick was used to face the underlying concrete). For a time, it became a second Piccadilly Plaza – the upstairs mall was deserted, except for vandals, and the escalators were permanently out of order. Then things changed for the better. Now it comes alive at lunch-time, and there are a number of shops in residence, including the University Bookshop. So, go up the **escalator** and patronise the excellent lock up shop for fruit and sandwiches.

Exit by means of the **ramp**, and find yourself deposited at the start of **Waterloo Place**. As the name suggests, this is a row of Regency houses, mostly used as office accommodation. Some years ago, Mr McGill (a jovial and witty old Irish gentleman) had his second-hand bookshop here. He had one room full of unsorted material, which those in the know inspected in their old clothes, retrieving, as it were, blossoms from the dust.

The large brick box of the **Computer Building** (1972) is opposite. (The contribution of the University to the invention of the modern computer is told on p.197.) The first storey entrance is connected to the impressive approach ramp that is such a feature of the **Mathematics Building** (Scherrer and Hicks, 1968) next door, with its tall tower. When it first opened, a lady wrote to the local newspaper asking if students really needed a place that size "to do their sums".

Manchester Museum

We have now reached the **neo-Gothic complex** that constitutes the oldest part of Manchester University. The best plan is to inspect the interior of the **Manchester Museum** first. The great Thomas Huxley advised, in 1867, that Owen's College (p.61) ought to take over the collections of the Manchester Society of Natural History and the Manchester Geological and Mining Society. Consequently, the Museum is now the responsibility of Manchester University. It moved to this site in 1885. As the collections expanded, extensions were opened in 1912 and 1927. Over £12m was awarded by the Heritage Lottery Fund, and this, together with other grant aid, has resulted in the construction of a new wing and extensive refurbishment. (The museum is open Monday-Saturday 10.00-5.00, Sunday and Bank Holidays 11.00-4.00, admission free.)

Go through the first arch on the right *(15)* into a small landscaped courtyard. The main entrance is to the right in the new wing, and leads to a large **reception area**. A large and well-stocked **shop** (everything from classy reproductions to toy dinosaurs) is situated to the left, with a selection of carved stonework between it and the courtyard widows. These examples are from ancient Egyptian temples, and are fashioned from Aswan granite. The **column** depicts Ramesis II making offerings to the gods. It is interesting to note that the architecture of the temples was meant to represent the trees and plants growing in the mythical 'island of creation' from which all life sprang. A **case of stone and copper tools** indicates what a colossal task the carving of such pillars and blocks must have been.

An **information desk** is located to the right of the entrance, adjacent to the passage leading to the ***Café Muse*** (Daily 8-6, Sundays and Bank Holidays, 10-5, separate entrance from Oxford Road). Toilets may be found down the nearby flight of stairs. The remainder of the reception area contains a number of **cases designed to arouse the interest of younger visitors**. The contribution of Manchester's industrial pollution to the course of evolution is illustrated in 'Why Did the Moth Change its Spots?' Others deal with obtaining a cure for malaria from tree bark, constructing a bow from wood and animal materials, and (in the window) reassembling a four thousand year old pot from pieces like a jigsaw puzzle.

However, the principal attraction comprises the plaster casts of **Saxon Crosses** from Bewcastle (Cumbria) and Ruthwell (near Dumfries). They are carved in the Northumbrian style, and the depictions of saints and biblical figures have been painted according to the results of the most recent archaeological evidence. Crosses like these would have been erected at ancient religious sites, to claim them for the Christian faith, or marked places where preaching and missionary activity were periodically conducted.

Enter the **Discovery Centre**. Here natural history items can be examined in drawers, but staff will be on hand at times to demonstrate and answer questions – a wonderful 'hands on experience', absolutely ideal for children. You may be able to handle natural history specimens (including live ones!) from the Museum collections.

The **top of the stairs** accesses the **first ethnographical gallery.** A large **image of the Buddha** (from Southern Burma) first attracts our attention. It is not solid brass – merely a clever illusion by a master craftsman. The room should be negotiated in an anti-clockwise direction, starting with a curious display that includes a university 'mortarboard' cap and a Boddington's beer can. What conclusions would a visitor come to about us from this assemblage of artefacts? Yet scholars go into the most inaccessible parts of earth, as exemplified by where the **Mursi of Ethiopia** (all 6,000 of them!) dwell. But, since these items were collected, there are now roads, so this people defend themselves with semi-automatic weapons. That, presumably, is evidence of progress....

Pre-Columbian pottery hints at the civilisations destroyed by the Conquistadores, but all eyes will be drawn to the fine **suit of coconut armour**, worn by a 'champion' of the Gilbert Islands. **Basketry** follows (notice the rattan ball from the Phillipines), together with an assortment of (mainly African) **musical instruments**. Again, the eye wanders to a magnificent Maori **cloak of Kiwi feathers**.

The final two cases are intended as a counterpoint to those opposite. One is devoted to **collectors and collections** – with biographies of some of the principal museum benefactors and items from their collections. Finally, there is a case devoted to **contact and tourism**. The European as depicted in native carving is illustrated, together with native craftsmanship utilised to satisfy the modern demand for tourist souvenirs. Before leaving the room, observe the great **carved front of a Maori store house** or pataka, situated behind the Buddha image. These structures were placed on stilts, and contained the important treasures of the chiefs.

Pass into the **second ethnographical gallery** and continue an anti-clockwise traverse. There is a fine display of **African masks**, including some belonging to a woman's society initiating girls into womanhood. These ceremonies sometimes involved female circumcision. Notice the fine **carved tusk** from Benin, dedicated to an oba (ruler) of that place. **African pottery** can be compared to **Japanese pottery** – the latter display also shows the influence of this tradition upon British potters, including Bernard Leach.

The **Simon Archery Collection** may be found at the rear of the room. The origins and history of archery is depicted, including the legendary **English longbow**. It is thought that the use of this weapon became widespread after the Welsh wars of Edward I, and English archers distinguished themselves in the Hundred Years War, particularly at Agincourt. The best archers came from Lancashire and Cheshire.

> No warring guns were then in use,
> They dreamed of no such thing.
> Our Englishmen in fight did use,
> The gallant grey-goose wing.
> And with the gallant grey-goose wing,
> They made such a play,
> That caused the horses kick and fling,
> And down their riders lay.

The longbow can be contrasted with the **crossbow** – an effective weapon, but taking some time to load. There is a display of **weapons and shields** associated with the collection.

The cases on the opposite side of the room include **Native American Indian clothing**, including blankets; **bark cloth** from the pacific islands; and recent acquisitions. The central cases in the room house a variety of **African carving** and a superb collection of **Japanese artefacts** (including lacquer work) centring upon a superb set of **Japanese Samurai armour**.

We now proceed upstairs into the **Money Gallery**, around which one should move in a clockwise direction. It depicts the history of money from ancient times (**Roman and Greek coins**), in both Europe and the rest of the world. Visitors may wallow in nostalgia over the **British pre-decimal coinage and paper money**, but should not omit the **German 20 billion mark note** (a relic from the 1920s inflation) or the **token notes from Robert Owen's 'Labour Exchange'** (indicating value through the amount of work performed). Note the **historic medallions**, many commemorating local events. The centre cases include the **Prestwich Hoard**, unearthed by a mechanical digger in a school playground. It probably dates from the anarchy of the civil war between Stephen and Matilda in the twelth century when "men said openly that God and his saints slept".

The Money Gallery leads to a short passage containing a **display of reconstructed heads**. The university has an international reputation in this branch of forensics, in which tissue, muscle structure, and skin covering is built up on a skull to produce a facial reconstruction. The head of **Worsley Man** is shown, together with the original skull upon which it is based. The skull was discovered in the course of peat digging at Chat moss in 1958, and is thought to be the result of a ritual murder. The victim was in his twenties and underwent a 'triple death' – he was strangled, decapitated, and thrown into the water. It was probably some kind of sacrifice and may be linked to the Celtic cult of the head (crude stone heads are found all over the North west area). The **reconstruction process** is illustrated, and a number of **faces derived from Mycenean tombs** in Ancient Greece can be seen. (Other examples of facial reconstruction may be found in the Egyptology section.)

The display leads to the **Mediterranean Gallery**, which is a balcony affording views into Egyptology below. Everyone usually makes a beeline for the great reconstruction of a ship, suspended in space. This impressive one-third size **replica of a Greek trading ship** was sponsored by Delta Travel. The original dates to 300 BC, and was found off the coast of Cyprus, complete with the remains of its cargo of wine and almonds. The condition of the wreck suggested that the vessel may have been scuttled, after being plundered by pirates. In this region, where it cost as much to transport goods 75 miles by land as to sail from one end of the sea to another, the influence of sea travel was crucial.

The civilisations that developed around the rim of the sea were dependent, as many of the artefacts illustrate, upon two commodities – **wine and olive oil**. The themes of **Peoples, Man and the Sea**, and **Travellers' Tales**, incorporate items produced by the peoples of the Ancient Near East, Greece, Italy, and the Roman Empire. The depiction of the **invention of the alphabet and writing** is particularly interesting, and this can be followed up with the **papyrus from Fayoum Oasis** (written in Roman times) – business letters, a fragment of comic dialogue, and poetry.

However, it is the finds associated with Manchester that catch the imagination, the realisation that the place probably began as an offshoot of this world. Two **altars, erected by soldiers of the garrison at the Roman fort**, are displayed. A captain of the "regiment of Raetians and Noricans (present day eastern Switzerland and Austria) fulfils his vow" and a centurion of the Sixth Legion (did he hate being seconded to command auxiliaries?) erects his altar to "Fortune the Preserver". Nearby is something that is priceless – the **Christian Word Square**. This shard has ROTAS

OPERA TENET AREPOSATOR scratched on it (Arepo the sower guides the wheels with care). This apparently meaningless piece of gibberish has been found in only a handful of places throughout the Roman Empire (including Pompeii). However, the letters can be rearranged in the shape of a cross to read PATERNOSTER O (Our Father). The remaining letters (A and O) stand for alpha and omega, the first and last letters of the Greek alphabet, a description of God as the "beginning and end" of all creation. Thus had Christianity, as an underground religion, taken root in one of the most far-flung places of the Empire.

Descend the **stairs** to the **Egyptology Collection**, and make a nod in the direction of the **busts of Jessie and Amelia Howarth**. After taking an early retirement from the world of business, they fell in love with ancient Egypt (as a consequence of reading a book, and then taking a Nile cruise). They were able to finance a number of excavation seasons, conducted by the young (if a little eccentric) archaeological pioneer, William Finders Petrie. They amassed a large collection, which Jesse donated to the Museum, even paying for an extension to house it all. Consequently, Manchester Museum probably has the best Egyptology collection outside the British Museum.

As you gaze upon the magnificent **mummy case** that introduces the displays, reflect on the fact that a great deal of nonsense is spoken about the ancient Egyptians, usually by people who have all seen the same horror films. The Egyptians were eminently practical in everything that they did, and their religious beliefs and funerary practices were rooted in their concrete experience of this world. Egypt is truly the 'gift of the Nile'. Until modern times, the melting snows of East Africa resulted in an annual inundation that created fertile soil along the river banks. It was only after the kingdoms of Upper and Lower Egypt were unified under one king or Pharaoh, that the greatest possible advantage could be taken of this phenomenon. Only Pharaoh, his officers and civil servants, could mobilise the labour to fix the field boundaries and mastermind the irrigation system. The Pharaoh was the source of all life, or the giver of food at any rate. He was semi-divine, in consort with the gods to guarantee fertility. He presided over the great religious festivals.

Round the corner, to the right, is the **mummified body of the Lady Asru**. At some stage in Victorian times, it was unwrapped (apparently a popular after dinner entertainment at the time). The lady lived to a great age, as the **bust of her facial restoration** depicts. She was a "chantress of Amun", in the temple complex of Amun–Ra, an important state god at Thebes around 700 BC. The gods were propitiated at great festivals (in which the royal family took part). Thus, the god would take up residence in the temple, which constituted a link between the human world and the divine. Temple design recreated the layout of the Egyptian house. The shrine was the divine bedroom, offerings of food and drink would be made, and the god entertained by people like Asru, with music, singing, and dancing. Ordinary people did not take part in these rituals – they were forbidden entrance to the temple complex. The priests had other occupations. When not on duty in the temple, they would pursue the professions of law and medicine, act as administrators, and even run their own businesses.

The topic of **disease in ancient Egypt** is dealt with in nearby displays. Headed by Dr. Rosalie David, the Museum is a world centre for forensic investigation of mummies (including a tissue bank), work that also has significance for modern medicine.

The development of **funerary customs and rites** is illustrated in the cases along the right-hand side of the main gallery. In archaic times, only the Pharaoh had any hope of immortality. But, since he was the giver of life, his subjects might hope for a continued existence as his subjects after death — which no doubt accounts for the lavish tombs and pyramids. However, the great nobles, began to build their own tombs as they embraced other beliefs. (An **early wooden box coffin,** and a **variety of tomb goods,** are shown.) The 'ka', or spirit of the deceased, surely resided in the tomb. A magic 'false door' enabled the spirit to pop out from time to time, and partake of offerings of food and drink (presumably grumbling at what was on offer), and move around amongst the living – probably listening in on what people were saying about them. All in all, it does not sound like a great deal of fun.

The offerings were sometimes placed in pottery **soul houses**, which also give some indication of domestic architecture at the time. The concept developed, and the tomb became the 'house of the ka'. Like the temples, the tombs were modelled on the layout of a house, with a master bedroom, reception room, guestrooms, and even a harem and lavatory! The deceased was supplied with **models of servants** (including concubines and dancing girls!) and images painted on the walls of a variety of activities. Magic transformed them into reality, so that the afterlife was rather similar to life on earth.

These beliefs underwent a radical change at the end of the Old Kingdom with the development of the cult of Osiris. The legend stated that he had been a mortal, murdered by his brother Seth. However, he was brought back to life, and his resurrection promises resurrection and immortality to his followers. This curiously prefigures Christian theology. Indeed, there was actually a form of judgement in which the heart of the deceased was weighed in the balance. The ka now had other possibilities. It could sail (by **magic model boats**) to the Fields of Osiris in the West. Again, the afterlife was like the life on earth, since the fields had to be worked. But the magic servant figures could do this for you. Soon, anyone who could afford it opted for mummification, and followed the spells and practices laid down in the Book of the Dead.

There is a fine **display of mummies**, from a number of periods, on the opposite side of the gallery. Since the ka inhabited the body at times, it was necessary to preserve it by the process of mummification. The internal organs were removed and placed in canopic jars. (The brain, considered of no importance, was extracted through the nostrils by a metal hook.) The cadaver was then packed in natron, a form of salt, dehydrating it by absorbing all the moisture. Finally, the body was wrapped in bandages and placed in an inner casing (which was, in turn, placed in an outer casing or box). Care was taken to paint in a magic doorway.

The complete contents from the **Tomb of the Two Brothers**, excavated by Petrie in 1905, are displayed in the middle of the gallery. Nekht Ank and Khnum Nakht must have been half brothers, for one has Nubian or negroid features. The **mummy cases** are in exceptionally fine condition, and are displayed with the accompanying **tomb chests** and **canopic jars**. The tomb goods include **figures of servants** and **model boats**. The **skeleton** of one of the occupants exhibits excessive curvature of the spine, probably resulting from arthritis.

Do not leave without examining the **later mummies**, dating from Roman times. Some superb (and rare) **examples of portraiture**, employing coloured wax on board, are on view. Nearby are displayed examples of facial reconstruction, including the **head of mummy 1770**. The fate of this young girl is something of a mystery. At some stage, the body had been in water for a period, and the loss of part of a lower limb suggested that it had received the attention of crocodiles. Curiously, the embalming took place a long time after the immersion. Although it was obviously someone of great importance, the embalmers did not know the sex – both artificial nipples and a penis were provided, in addition to padding out a complete limb. Did the discoverers think that the ka would haunt them, without a proper home?

We now proceed into a **second gallery**. In contrast to the first, this deals with **everyday life in ancient Egypt**. Most objects are from contrasting sites excavated by Petrie in the Fayoum Oasis – two sides, as it were, of the same coin. Kahun was a town housing workmen employed on the construction of the pyramid of Sesostris III. Notice the **workmen's tools**. Gurob could not have been more different. It was a palace harem, used as a base by the pharaoh for hunting and fishing expeditions. **Cosmetics and jewellery** take pride of place here.

The most intriguing display must surely be **finds from Amarna, the capital of Akhenatan**, the 'heretic' pharaoh. Akhenaton attempted a religious revolution, introducing the worship of the life force in the form of a solar disk. This did not please the temple priests, who controlled immense estates, and Akhenaton eventually failed. There is a **relief of the Pharaoh and Nefertiti**, his wife, making offerings to the solar disk. Although it is a replica, take a look at the **bust of Nefertiti**, one of the great masterpieces of Egyptian art.

Retrace your steps, and pass out of the Egyptology galleries by the **bridge** (with a waiting area). A walk through **model of a magnified cell**, the basis of all life, is available on the right. We now enter the **Natural History Gallery**, a veritable monument to the art of the taxidermist. The **springing tiger** and the **polar bear** are impressive, but children are usually drawn to the **skeleton of Maharaja**. This elephant was purchased at a circus auction in Scotland, and walked all the way to its new home at Belle Vue Zoo, in Manchester. (A small painting shows the keeper arguing the toll at a toll-gate on a turnpike road.) The beast got a little temperamental in her old age, so her tusks were blunted. It is worth seeking out the **oldest specimen**, one of the last of the old breed of English cow, the work of the Manchester Society of Natural History. A **skeleton of a whale** hangs from the roof.

The **flight of steps** leads to a balcony, replete with **birds** in glass cases and **insects** in desk-like boxes (lift the lids to view). The gallery communicates with the **Vivarium**, where the specimens are, at least, alive. Spike, the **Savannah Monitor** spends most of its time sleeping in an artificial desert, complete with cacti. The large **snakes** are popular, and the **chameleon** is lively, but the small blue **poison dart frogs** prove to be the favourite of many visitors.

The **uppermost gallery** contains **Science for Life**. Here is a variety of interactive displays about the human body, largely appealing to children and budding hypochondriacs.

Retrace your steps to the Natural History Gallery, and continue further in a downward direction. **Meteorites** occupy the mezzanine level, and there is a view of a **model of the solar system** from the balcony. Back on the ground floor, we arrive at the **Mineralogy Gallery**. The museum has one of the finest collections of mineral specimens in the country, including regional specialities, such as kidney-shaped **hematite** from Cumbria, or **Derbyshire Blue John**.

By now, small children will be chafing at the bit, for we enter the **Geology Gallery**, and the kingdom of the **dinosaurs**. It is presided over by the skeleton of Tyrannosaurus Rex, the largest and most dangerous of the predatory meat eaters. 'Stan', as he is affectionately known, is a cast of a specimen in the Black Hills Institute, Dakota – at forty feet long and twelve feet high, he is about average size for the species. The recently acquired **skeleton of a Tenontosaurus** (from Montana) is genuine. A predator surprised this plant-eating creature, for teeth marks were found in the neck bones. The skeleton is complete – volcanic ash covered it shortly afterwards. The fossilised **remains of its last meal** (and the stones swallowed to aid the digestion process) are also displayed. Some life-size models of dinosaurs are nearby, along with **fossilised footprints**. Other life-size models of a **Plesiosaur** and an **Icthyosaur** are suspended over their fossilised remains. (This specimen may be absent for conservation purposes.) The skeleton of a **prehistoric bison** represents a more recent prehistoric period. Fossilised plants should not be neglected. Indeed, one cannot miss the lower part of a **giant carboniferous tree fern**, the twisting roots indicating the swampy conditions in what would become the coal measures. If you have the time, the gallery is a fascinating introduction to palaeontology, dealing with the origin and development of life on earth.

University buildings

The Museum is part of the original **Manchester University Building**. Owens College (p.61) moved to this site in 1873. The rapid development of the institution led to demands for university status, but this could only be achieved by the creation of the Victoria University in 1880 – a federation of Colleges in Manchester, Liverpool, and Leeds. Manchester always strained at the leash, and independence was obtained in 1903, when all three Colleges became separate universities. Manchester became a progressive place – women had been admitted as early as 1883. Alfred Jevons laid the foundations for the academic study of economics. Britain's first public health laboratory was established. And Ernest Rutherford carried out the work that later led to the splitting of the atom (recorded in a **plaque**). Since 1906, the university has produced 20 Nobel prize winners. (Its role in the invention of the computer is described on p.197.) Professor Bernard Lovell pioneered radio astronomy, being responsible for the large radio telescope at Jodrell Bank. It opened in time to track Sputnik.

Back on Oxford Road, the old University building is best viewed from the **second arch** on the right (where there is a small **visitor centre**). The **original structure** of 1873 stands to the rear of the courtyard, which contains a **'glacial erratic'** (carried down in the Ice Age from Cumbria). The courtyard is fronted along Oxford Road by an impressive neo-Gothic façade with a tower, incorporating the **Whitworth Hall**, where degrees are awarded. The whole complex was masterminded by Alfred Waterhouse, and completed by 1898.

Brunswick Street, to the left, leads past a number of buildings, chiefly devoted to science and engineering, which date from the first period of post war expansion in the fifties and sixties. Opposite, on the right, development has turned the former Burlington Street into a private roadway leading to the **John Rylands University Library** (the comparatively recent extension is seen). The **Student Refectory**, on the corner is sixties trash, with an odd corrugated appearance that some might say corresponds to some of the food on offer. (The **tower** behind is a student residence.) Notice the fine **row of 19th-century houses** across Oxford Road, all converted to other uses.

Pass the (neo-classical?) front of the **Students Union** (1953-56) on the right, and come to Lime Grove, another vanished street. It leads into a **grassy court**, with the brick of the old library building (1935 – 1937) in the background. The Arts building, to the left, dates from 1958. Return to Oxford Road, pause, and turn your eyes towards the great stone bulk of the Roman Catholic church of the **Holy Name**. It was designed by Joseph Aloysius Hansom, and was mainly erected between 1869 and

The older buildings of Manchester University

1871. Hansom is now remembered for the invention of the famous horse-drawn cab that bears his name (the 'gondola of London'). He apparently sold his rights to the design for £10,000, but never received the money. The church is a reworking of 13th-century French Gothic in stone, but the intended spire and tower never materialised. The rather plain West tower was added in 1926 –1928 as a memorial to Father Bernard Vaughan S.J. If you have time, cross over and explore the **interior**, noticing the fine terracotta decoration. (The same firm was also responsible for the Natural History Museum in London.)

The plain, grey, brick box of the **Medical School** (1972-1974) is next door, across the side street. Look in the direction of the car park, on the right side of Oxford Road, for a glimpse of the **Contact Theatre**. The exterior of this remarkable building looks as if someone has shot it, and the design is expiring like an animal, shaking four feet in the air. Although part of the University complex, the Contact has its own repertory company, specialising in new (and often controversial) work.

Turn left at Nelson Street, for a short diversion. Towards the bottom of the street is a row of Victorian houses. One of these was, just before the First World War, the home of the Pankhurst family *(16)*. It now houses the **Pankhurst Centre** (open 12.00 – 4.00, Tuesday, Wednesday, and Friday, although the public rooms may be shown at other times if politely requested.) Please note that the rest of the house operates as a women's advice centre, from which men are excluded. Richard Pankhurst was a barrister, a man of progressive social and political views. His wife Emeline, and daughters Sylvia and Christabel, resided here from time to time. Their role in obtaining the vote for women through the agency of the 'suffragette movement' is well known. However, both Emeline and Christabel had rather conservative political views. Sylvia, on the other hand, sympathised with working women, and became a socialist. (She often worked in partnership with Annie Kenny, who had started life as a local mill girl.) The first room is largely dedicated to Sylvia, her life and work. The other room is a **reconstruction of the parlour of the house** as it would have appeared on 10th October, 1903 – the scene of the founding act of the Women's Social and Political Union (the suffragettes).

We retrace our footsteps, back towards the **early 19th-century house** across

Manchester Royal Infirmary

Oxford Road, now used by the University student accommodation service. The **Royal Eye Hospital** (erected 1884) is on the left-hand corner, but this side of the remainder of Oxford Road is the preserve of the original building of the **Manchester Royal Infirmary**. (The early history of this important Manchester institution is given on p.90) The present structure was erected between 1905 and 1908 in the 'Baroque Revival, style, a pleasing pattern of red brick and white stone. There is an interesting **plaque** affixed to the lodge gates.

The Whitworth Gallery

It now only remains to cross the road and visit the **Whitworth Gallery and Park.** (Gallery open Monday-Saturday 10.00-5.00, Sunday 2.00-5.00, admission free.) Sir Joseph Whitworth, the Stockport born engineer, had an illustrious career – later in association with Sir William Armstrong. Whitworth was a pioneer in precision engineering and machine tools, and made a fortune. Most of this was left in the hands of trustees for the benefit of his native city. Part was expended upon the new Technical School (now UMIST), and the remainder was used to purchase Potter's Field. This became the present public park, and the adjacent Grove House housed the Whitworth Institute that opened in 1890. Like other Victorians, Whitworth's trustees wanted to create a public institution that would improve the state of industrial design. However, the collection policy soon strayed into the realms of fine art. A **new frontage** (designed by J.W. Beaumont), in Ruabon brick and terracotta, was added in 1908 when the place was enlarged. From that time on, it has been known as the Whitworth Gallery. The University took it over in 1958, and embarked on a thorough modernisation of the interior – very sixties 'Scandinavian' design by John Bickerdyke. A new modernisation programme is underway.

The current policy of the gallery appears to be always to show something new.

The Whitworth Gallery

Most of the material displayed is ever changing, and this applies to both the permanent collection and visiting exhibitions, so this description will necessarily be limited. We pass the **shop and the bistro** to enter the long **Textiles Gallery**, which cuts across. As was appropriate for Manchester at that time, the Institute acquired Sir Charles Robinson's collection of textiles in 1891. However, the first object of interest is nothing of the sort – nothing less than the great stone sculpture of **Genesis** (1929-1931) by Jacob Epstein. This is intended to portray a pregnant woman as the 'mother of all races', but the subject matter and its abstract treatment caused outrage when first exhibited. Nobody seemed to want the thing, and it was actually exhibited for a time in a side-show on the 'Golden Mile' at Blackpool!

The first case of textiles, to the left, contains an absolute gem. Hannah Smith, who one imagines as a very precocious but lonely little girl, made a very fine (and rare) **embroidered casket** in 1657. She also left a note about where and when it was made (also displayed), discovered in our own time, in a secret drawer ("I have written this to fortify myself & those that shall inquire about it...."). We do not know who Hannah was, or what became of her – the childish note is all that has been passed down to posterity. An interesting display of richly embroidered **church vestments** follows. Another case is devoted to the **Arts and Crafts movement**, with work associated with William Morris. Examples of **contemporary knitting** (including sixties fashion) contrast strangely with items of **folk dress**. The examples of **patchwork and quilting** indicate a tradition that has now become a feminist icon.

An interesting selection of fabrics manufactured in Manchester as **African exports** is shown. Great attention was paid to local taste in colour and patterns. Africa is also represented in two other cases. Post-pharaonic **Coptic textiles**, from the period before the Islamic conquest, have miraculously survived from excavated shallow graves. In contrast, the **West African** textiles are modern.

Qashqai textiles and carpets, produced by an Iranian nomadic tribe presage a superb display of **Chinese mandarin robes**. (The mandarins constituted the state civil service, recruited by a series of competitive examinations based on the Confucian classics.) Lastly, do not omit the case of **Indian brocades**. The Manchester cotton exports effectively destroyed Indian textiles, a point emphasised by Gandhi. (Though this did not stop the northern mill girls taking him to their hearts, when he paid a brief visit in the thirties.) The spinning wheel remains a potent emblem on the Indian national flag.

A changing selection of watercolours, from the permanent collection, usually graces the **Central Gallery** beyond. The **Watercolour collection** includes fifty by **Turner**, seven sketch books used by **Cozens**, a selection of work by **Girtin** (including his only surviving sketchbook), works by **Constable, Cox**, and **Gainsborough**, not forgetting **Pre-Raphaelite sketches**. The **print collection** has examples by **Durer, Mantegna**, **Rembrandt**, and over 300 **Japanese prints**. The work of **Picasso, Van Gogh**, **Degas, Matisse, Hockney**, and (of course!) **Blake** distinguishes the modern collection.

The **South Gallery** is to the left, with a fine view of the park, and illustrating the original height of the rooms before the sixties alterations. A selection from the collection of larger **modern paintings** is consequently displayed, the trend favouring abstract expressionism. The modern collection continues in the **Staircase Gallery**, to the right of the Central Gallery, with **smaller paintings and prints**. A **Temporary Exhibition Gallery** is located to the rear of the ground floor.

Ascend the staircase to a **mezzanine level**, created in the sixties. The so-called **Landing Gallery** (with a view down into the South Gallery) is used to display items from the large collection of **prints**. Access may be obtained to the **Mezzanine Court**, created by the first phase of the new refurbishment, and opened in 1995. Notice the brick rear wall of Beaumont's front. It is presently used for temporary exhibitions. We retrace our steps and go right, past the lecture hall to the **North Mezzanine Gallery**. Again, it is largely used for temporary exhibitions. Pass down the staircase, noticing the examples of **Burne-Jones stained glass** at the foot. The way now leads into the Textile Gallery and the entrance.

We emerge into the daylight once more – just the time for a turn around the park. There is a **statue of Edward VII**. He spent most of his life waiting for his long lived mother to die, becoming king in 1901 and then dying himself in 1910. His mother never really thought him capable of much, and gave him no real responsibility. He thus passed his time with gambling, race horses, chorus girls (his 'incognito' visits to Paris were legendary) and a string of mistresses. (He passed away in the company of both his wife and his last mistress!) Yet, the great British public was always ready to forgive, for he was clearly, under all the royal flummery, one of them. He did much to enable a political alliance with France to come about, and was known by everyone as 'Edward the Peacemaker'. *(The walk ends here, but it can be continued to Didsbury Village by the excursion described on p.263.)*

Salford Cathedral

13 The City of Salford

Start: Blackfriars Bridge

Estimated time of walk: 1 hour

Interiors: Salford Museum and Art Gallery – 45 min

Highlights: Salford's historic centre, its cathedral, and a walk back into the past times by way of a magic street

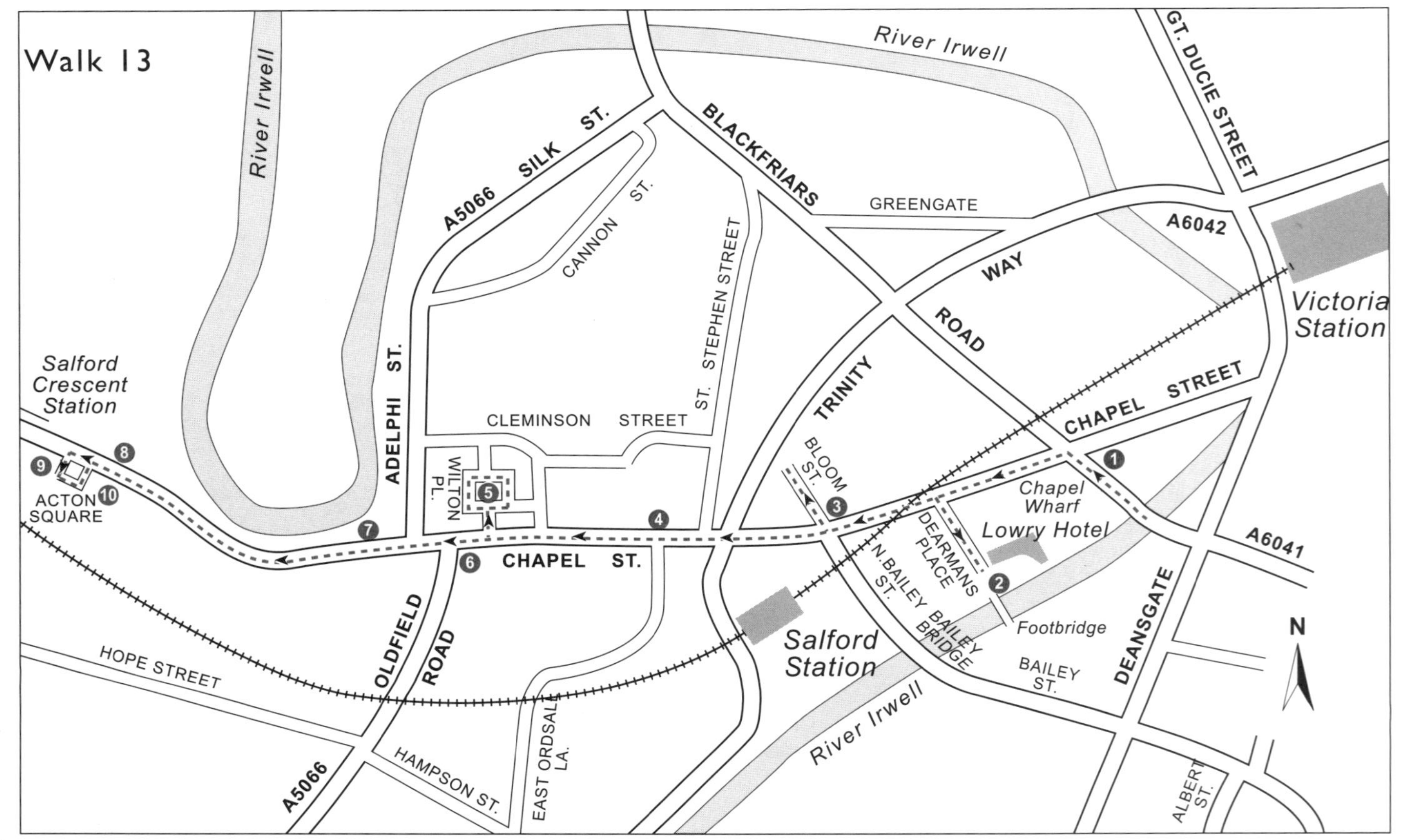
Walk 13
River Irwell
GT. DUCIE STREET
River Irwell
A5066 SILK ST.
BLACKFRIARS
GREENGATE
CANNON ST.
ST. STEPHEN STREET
A6042
WAY
ROAD
Victoria Station
Salford Crescent Station
ADELPHI ST.
CLEMINSON STREET
TRINITY
CHAPEL STREET
BLOOM ST.
WILTON PL.
ACTON SQUARE
Chapel Wharf
Lowry Hotel
DEARMANS PLACE
A6041
CHAPEL ST.
N.BAILEY ST.
BAILEY BRIDGE
Footbridge
DEANSGATE
BAILEY ST.
Salford Station
N
HOPE STREET
OLDFIELD ROAD
River Irwell
A5066
HAMPSON ST.
EAST ORDSALL LA.
ALBERT ST.
1
2
3
4
5
6
7
8
9
10

This section deals with the district on the far bank of the River Irwell called Salford. The word is carefully chosen. Although Salford is a city in its own right, most visitors regard it as an extension of central Manchester. It was ever thus. Daniel Defoe, in the course of his famous 'Tour' described the Manchester of 1726 as "One of the greatest, if not the greatest meer *(sic)* Village in England ... and, including the Suburb, or that part of the Town called ... over the Bridge; it is said to contain about fifty thousand people". Defoe obviously meant to find out the name of this "suburb", but left without actually getting round to it.

But it could have been so very different. The ancient royal manor of Salford (held by Edward the Confessor) gave its name to the Hundred of the Shire County in which the township of Manchester was situated. The name of the future borough and the city must surely, then, be Salford. However, one of the clerks of the Norman feudal lords made a slip with his pen. Two separate charters had to be issued to the mediaeval burgesses, and Manchester and Salford townships were divorced forever. Manchester, with the church and market, became the dominant partner from the first. The rapid growth of the town in the industrial revolution left Salford far behind.

Because of its mighty neighbour, Salford never really developed a proper town centre. The shops in Chapel Street could never hope to compete with those across the river. In more recent times, industrial decline hit Salford very badly, since there was not the compensating growth in the service sector that Manchester experienced. And, it must be admitted, some of the wounds were self-inflicted. Throughout the seventies and eighties, it almost seemed that the Council had a death wish. Chapel Street was allowed to decay, and property was demolished without any particular reason – it was the classic example of 'planning blight', in which schemes came and went while the fate of buildings remained in limbo.

Our first Salford walk is along Chapel Street to Salford University. Here you can see the process of urban renewal in action before your very eyes, with a variety of schemes completed or under way.

The heart of the city

We start the walk at Blackfriars Bridge (p.70), easily reached by Market Street from Piccadilly, or Deansgate from Exchange Square. Cross the bridge, and come to the intersection of Chapel Street and Blackfriars Road, the old mediaeval heart of the township *(1)*. Here stood the cross, where a market was held. The whole area was transformed by the construction of the railway in the 19th century, but the ancient church remains.

Sacred Trinity has its origin in the generosity of Humphrey Booth (p.17). Salford born, and a churchwarden of the Collegiate Church, it saddened him to see his neighbours having to walk into Manchester to attend divine service. He hit upon the idea of erecting a 'chapel of ease' (a convenient church for ordinary services, but reserving the lucrative right to baptise and marry to the old parish church). The original chapel was consecrated in 1635, and remains the only church in Britain with this particular dedication. It was elevated to the full dignity of a parish church in 1650.

The present structure largely dates from the extensive rebuilding in 1753, undertaken at the behest of Dr. John Clayton, a vigorous champion of the established church. In 1747, he forbade John Wesley to preach within the precincts of his building. Wesley adjourned to Salford Cross, where some of the more unruly elements of the parson's congregation broke up the meeting with the threat of making use of the local fire engine, which doesn't seem a very Christian thing to do. The church was restored in Victorian times, when the present West Window was inserted. It narrowly escaped demolition in 1904, when the railway viaduct was enlarged.

Because of its shape, the area at the east end of the church was known as the 'Flat Iron Market'. It specialised in the hawking of old clothes and shoes and the surviving photographs show that it must have been the very picture of poverty. Some of the old churchyard gravestones survive, particularly at the east and west ends.

When I was young I ventured life and blood,
Both for my King and for my country's good.
In later years my chief care was to be,
Soldier to him who shed his blood for me.

Unfortunately, the church is usually locked, and can only be entered by arrangement. The interior is very 18th century in feel, with three **galleries** mounted on Tuscan columns. The timber **roof** is Victorian. The most interesting object is **Humphrey Booth's tombstone**, brought here in 1894 after discovery (in an upside down position) during building work at the cathedral. He, "whose Piety lives in Trinity Chapel at Salford," died shortly after receiving communion for the first time in his new place of worship. The church has a **communion flagon** dated 1691.

Notice the **row of original buildings** opposite the church, an indication of what Chapel Street must once have been like, before proceeding in the direction of the iron girder railway bridge. Turn left down Dearman's Place to inspect **Chapel Wharf** *(2)*, the home of the five-star ***Lowry Hotel***. The spectacular **bridge**, that connects it with the Manchester side, is visible directly ahead. It has opened up this new waterside development (which is described on p.68).

Continue under the **railway bridge**. The structure crosses the road at an oblique angle, and almost masks the entrance to the **Deva Centre** on the right. The old brewery has been turned into an 'urban business village environment' (the mind truly boggles!), retaining the old **central tower** with its multi-coloured brickwork and the legend "Threlfall's Brewery Company". The impressively named ***Hang 'em and Bang 'em*** picture framers is passed before reaching the **Independent Chapel** *(3)*. This nonconformist group traces its origins to the English Civil War, and is now known (after a series of modern amalgamations) as the United Reformed Church. The **datestone** indicates that the chapel was built in 1819. The plain brick frontage is pierced by two entrance doors, divided by a charming **stone balustrade**. Interestingly enough, the chapel does not conform to the modern building line.

A short excursion into Bloom Street, round the corner, leads to the **Salford Model Lodging House**, with the municipal **coat of arms** in terracotta. To counteract the vile lodging houses that infested late-Victorian Salford (believed to be the haunt of criminal elements), the council decided to provide cheap accommodation for transient workmen. As Salford House, the building has been transformed into thirty-nine luxury apartments. One wonders what the original inmates would have thought. The old **Gas Office** (1880) is next door, sporting a fine brick tower in the Scottish Baronial style. Seven years after this building opened, both the chief executive and the superintendent went missing, along with most of the gas receipts!

Salford Station

Back on Chapel Street, take a look down New Bailey Street, across the road, leading to the Albert Bridge. It is spanned by a series of fine iron **railway bridges**, including one with Grecian patterns in cast iron. Here is located **Salford Station**. Nowadays, it only comes alive for the commuters in rush hour, but it was originally the terminus of the oddly named (considering the location) Manchester and Bolton Railway, which opened in 1838. The line was extended, via the bridges and the Chapel Street Bridge, to Victoria Station in 1844. Prior to the First World war, an elite group of Manchester businessmen repaired to this station at four in the afternoon (it was the most convenient for the offices and warehouses in the Deansgate area), to catch the 'Blackpool Club Train' home to their seaside residences on the Fylde coast. The luxurious private carriages were chartered from the Lancashire and Yorkshire Railway by what was, in effect, a travelling gentlemen's club. In addition to the first class fare, the members paid an annual subscription and the bills for the drinks and snacks served by the steward. And, of course, one had to be proposed for membership and approved by a secret ballot! Another train conveyed businessmen to their hideaways in the Yorkshire Dales, but that was open to anyone with a ticket.

The old Salford Cinema

We continue down Chapel Street, crossing Trinity Way, and passing the **Salford Cinema** (with a date of 1912 clearly visible) on the right, one of the first generation of cinemas in this country. An eclectic mixture of styles, including Queen Anne windows and a **Moorish tower**, it is now used by an evangelical church. Trinity Way, a new by-pass road, cuts across Chapel Street, connecting with Irwell Street and Ordsall Lane.

A short distance beyond, **Bexley Square** *(4)* opens on the right. The rather lovely little paved area, populated by four mature trees, is flanked by rebuilt regency style house frontages, used as offices.

These frame a view of the **Old Salford Town Hall**. The classical façade of fluted columns and pilasters, with a wreathed entablature, was the first important commission undertaken by Richard Lane (architect of the Friends Meeting House and Chorlton Town Hall), undertaken in 1825-1827. It was erected for the ad-hoc organisation that provided municipal services before Salford was incorporated. Now it contains the Magistrates Courts. To the left is a fine pair of wrought-iron **gates**, framed by a stone screen, which connects the old Town Hall with a brick 19th-century extension.

Back on Chapel Street, note the ***Church Inn*** in Ford Street, with an unchanged early 19th-century exterior. The honey-coloured terracotta of the **Salford Education Offices** really stands out, particularly as the façade is in an unusual Jacobean Renaissance style, aping the fashion of the early 17th century. It is a positive riot of moulded ornamentation, including the heads on the door pillars. There is a good wrought iron balcony over the entrance, and a flight of oriel windows at one end. It was opened in 1896 as the Salford School Board Offices.

Salford Cathedral

We have now reached **Salford Cathedral**. Prior to 1848, Roman Catholics in Salford had to trudge across the Irwell to such chapels as the 'Hidden Gem'. Dr. James Sharples, a provisional bishop for the area, inspired a movement to create a place of worship in Salford. Land had been purchased near Hunt's Bank, but the railway wanted that. Fortunately, the company paid a good price, enough to buy the Chapel Street site. Two businessmen donated £1,000 each, an immense sum in those days, and the foundation stone was laid with much ceremony in 1844. Construction took four years at a cost of £18,000 (it took the parishioners forty years to pay off the debt). In 1850, two years after the consecration, it became the cathedral church of the newly created Roman Catholic diocese of Salford.

One Matthew Ellison Hadfield produced the design of the building, a man who greatly admired the Gothic style of architecture. It was the first modern Roman Catholic church in England to be built in a cruciform shape. The **West front** (with statues of St Peter and St Paul, and a Madonna and Child at the window point) is inspired by Howden church in Yorkshire. The **choir and sanctuary** imitates Selby Abbey; the **lofty spire** a copy of that at St Mary Magdalene, Newark; and the **decorated groined roof** was suggested by St James at Liege.

The cathedral is usually open to visitors from 8.00 to 12.30. At all other times, enquire in the adjacent cathedral bookshop.

St Philip's

After noticing the rather solid façade of the former **Manchester and Salford Savings Bank** (1885), we make an excursion to the right to view **St Philip's Church** *(5)*. At the conclusion of the Napoleonic wars, a patriotic fund was set up by the government as a thanksgiving for the victory of Waterloo – the intention was to finance a host of new churches. There was an ulterior motive. The establishment was still afraid of the radical ideas of the French Revolution, and thought that they would rapidly spread in the new industrial districts. The 'Waterloo churches' were intended as an antidote to this possibility. However, the scheme was hijacked for their own purposes by elements of the newly emerging business elite. In particular, it was found that a government sponsored church made the ideal centrepiece for a fashionable residential property development.

And so it proved with St Philip's. The architect engaged was none other than the young Sir Robert Smirke, who went on to design the Bank of England and the British Museum. Although the classical style was starting to go out of fashion, as far as churches were concerned, Smirke insisted upon it. His employers, in return, insisted that he place his grand colonnaded porch and circular tower in the centre of the south wall, to create an imposing prospect from the main approach, instead of at the west end. Curiously, the consecration took place on St Matthew's day, 1825. Another church at Castlefield was to be consecrated to St Matthew the following weekend. Possibly, the bishop decided that he would not have two churches of the same dedication, and the Salford one lost out. It became St Philip's instead. This

St Philip's Church, Salford

The Old Pint Pot beside the River Irwell

must have nonplussed the clergyman – halfway through the ceremony, he found that the prayer book had a page missing, and his mind went blank as to what came next. In modern times, the church was the scene of the labours of Canon Peter Green, a greatly admired evangelical preacher and writer.

The church is often locked these days, but a polite enquiry at the nearby rectory may yield results. The interior is rather austere, with three **galleries** supported by Greek Doric columns and a rather ponderous frieze. A good copy of **Da Vinci's 'Last Supper'** surmounts the communion table.

The **County Court**, a typical Victorian public building, is located behind the church, opposite a fine **row of houses** dating from the 1830s. Upon returning to Chapel Street, look out for the **'Angel'** on the right-hand corner. This healthy living initiative offers classes in everything from reflexology to anger management at an affordable cost to local residents. The centre was opened by a survivor of the bombing of the nearby hospital, and is dedicated to the nurses who lost their lives in the incident.

Indeed, the former **Salford Royal Hospital** is only a short distance away towards the end of Chapel Street. It owes its origin to the Salford and Pendleton Royal Dispensary, a charity institution opened on an adjacent site in 1827. The present brick building dates from 1896. As already mentioned, one wing was destroyed by a bomb in an air raid in 1941. The fourteen nurses who died are listed in the **commemorative plaque**. The hospital, now surplus to requirements, recently closed. It is now transformed into the almost inevitable apartments. At the junction of Oldfield Road, almost opposite *(6)*, is a **Boer War Memorial** unveiled by Edward VII and Queen Alexandra in 1905.

Adelphi House – an elegant Georgian house, now a library

The Crescent

The superbly restored **Adelphi House** *(7)*, a fine brick Georgian habitation, marks the start of The Crescent. The Salford University International Media Centre is based here. The ***Old Pint Pot*** shares the grounds, and is easily overlooked – though not by the staff and the students. **The Crescent** was once the glory of Salford. As the rich moved out of the city centre, many fine residential areas were created for them. In Salford, the villages of Pendleton and Broughton were transformed, and a stretch of road bordering a picturesque bend in the river suggested a fine crescent similar to those at Bath. (The river is no longer visible, since the road was widened in the 1960s.) The houses were erected in the 1820s, and were much sought after. A short distance from the heart of Manchester "the fair mansions of The Crescent were famous for the abundance and excellence of their fruits, the orchards were crowded with peaches, nectarines, magnum bonum plums, cherries, pears etc". Little remains, save some surviving **original brick frontages**. Later buildings, now mainly belonging to the University, and including a **Graduate Centre** and a **Conference Centre**, occupy the site of former terraces.

The new residents availed themselves of a service provided by John Greenwood. His 'omnibus', between Pendleton Church and Manchester, was perhaps the second such service in the country. An employee later invented a retractable guide wheel, which ran along a grooved central rail and kept the bus wheels on smooth metal plates laid along part of the route. The plates often worked loose, and the invention was not popular with other road users. Consequently, the 'perambulator' was abandoned, though a local saying "as useless as a five-wheeled bus" was current for a number of years afterwards.

Salford University

We now come to the main campus area of **Salford University** to the right. The Royal Technical Institution was founded on the site in 1896, and later metamorphosed into the Royal Technical College and the Royal College of Advanced Technology, the latter awarding degrees. It also obtained an excellent reputation for its practical and innovative teaching methods, and an involvement with both the local community and industry (the institution pioneered 'sandwich' degrees with one year industrial placements). The University was granted its royal charter in 1967. The curriculum has broadened beyond purely scientific and technical subjects, but there is still a healthy bias in this direction.

Just before the **Maxwell Building** (a tower block that has 'sixties' written all over it) is an easily missed sign indicating the **start of the Irwell Valley Way**. Although by no means complete in its entirety, it is possible to follow the course of the river from here to its source – a spring in a field just north of Bacup, in Rossendale.

Peel Park

The walk has now reached the entrance to **Peel Park** *(8)*. Lark Hill, a house in the midst of extensive grounds, was purchased by public subscription in 1846. The open space became a public park, named in honour of the hero of the hour, Sir Robert Peel (p.93). Although the greater part of the park lay behind the mansion, it was provided with an elaborate entrance from The Crescent, in the form of an archway with adjacent statues. (Lord Ducie later donated a set of 'Italian' gates, from the demolished Strangeways Hall.) Salford at last had a place fit to receive royalty, and that is what happened in 1857, when the Queen and Prince Albert visited the Art Treasures Exhibition at Old Trafford. They received the greetings of 82,000 children assembled in Peel Park, and the Queen was visibly moved.

Time has not been so kind to the grand entrance. The 'Italian Gates' disappeared for scrap in the Second World War. The ornate arch was demolished shortly afterwards. The saga of the statue of poor old Joseph Brotherton has been recounted elsewhere (p.67). But the statues of **Queen Victoria** and **Prince Albert** still remain, an echo of that sunny and triumphant day, when all ahead seemed continuous progress and improvement.

The house was significantly altered and extended to accommodate a municipal museum and library, both opening in 1850. The library is believed to have been the first free municipal library in the country. The building still contains the **Salford Museum and Art Gallery** (open Monday-Friday 10.00-5.00, weekends 1.00-5.00, admission free), but the library is now represented by the **Local History Library** (open Tuesday, Thursday, and Friday 10.00-5.00, Wednesday 10.00-8.00) which, amongst other things, is useful for family history. The right-hand entrance is closed, so enter by the left. Since the greater part of the Lowry collection has been removed to the new centre, the vacated space has been filled with **'Life Times'**, a series of changing exhibitions about Salford and its people. The **interactive local history** centre is noteworthy.

Lark Hill Place

However, the museum is famous for something else. **Lark Hill Place** is a recreation of historical aspects of once typical Salford streets. Inspired by the pioneering work undertaken by the York Castle Museum, the first part of the 'street' opened in 1955. Visitors can inspect a wide range of historic interiors. A **17th-century panelled room** can be contrasted with a **Georgian interior**. The **Victorian parlour** (with a view into the park) is readied for tea. And a **working class cottage**, simple, but homely, awaits the family returning from work. The shops, including the classic **'corner shop'**, are a veritable treasure trove of long forgotten products. Do not omit the **blacksmith's forge**, or, for that matter, the **cloggers**. Remember that the majority of Lancashire workers wore this wooden soled, iron shod, footwear within living memory. Those who carry on the local dancing tradition still do. The **Victorian Gallery**, upstairs, is the only other part of the museum unlikely to change. The paintings are not particularly notable, but they create a fair impression of the artistic tastes of the increasing middle class in Victorian Britain.

If there is time, do have a stroll in the **park** behind the museum. A major face lift is planned, and it should soon be restored to its former glory. Notice the original Technical College building on the right, as you walk back towards The Crescent. Take great care in crossing the very busy road, and make for **Acton Square** *(9)*, another prestigious early 19th-century property development. The left-hand corner is the site of **Joule House**, once the residence of James Prescott Joule. The son of a Salford brewer, Joule was a self-educated boy who later obtained tuition from John Dalton. After giving up the idea of building a 'perpetual motion machine', he turned his attention to investigations into friction, energy, and heat. He became a pioneer physicist, suggesting theories on which later developments in electricity and heat mechanics were based. Indeed, his name was given to a unit of measurement. (He also has a moon crater named after him.)

Jubilee House is on the opposite corner. This charming mock Tudor structure was opened as a Nurses Home in 1901. It now houses the **Working Class Movement Library** (open Tuesday to Friday, and alternate Sundays), originating from the collection of Eddie and Ruth Frow. When their house was eventually bulging at the seams, it was re-housed at the present site in the form of a charitable trust. The collection includes the records of political organisations and trade unions, and a vast number of pamphlets, posters, and leaflets, many of which are extremely rare.

As in similar developments, the vista of Acton Square was once closed with a church. However, the former Christ Church was no property developer's gambit – it was, instead, a tribute to the power and influence of Hugh Stowell. He arrived in Salford to take up the position of curate of St Stephen's Church in 1826, and his preaching soon filled the church to 'standing room only'. There must have been many tempting offers in the offing, for a group of the townsfolk decided that the only way to keep him in Salford was to build him his own church. Fortunately, parliament had passed an Act stating that anyone who built a new church had the right of appointing the minister. The clergy of the old Collegiate Church fought this right tooth and nail, but Stowell's sponsors went to the trouble of obtaining their own Act (just to make sure!), and Christ Church was consecrated in 1831. Thomas Wright designed the edifice in the classical manner, and a 'wedding cake' spire was later added in 1843.

Stowell went from strength to strength, a veritable power-house of energy. Four new churches were eventually created out of Stowell's parish, not to mention the schools and other institutions that he helped set up. But he would brook no contradiction. An evangelical Protestant at a time when the established church was increasingly influenced by 'ritualism', he made many enemies. He was also intolerant of Roman Catholicism. Nevertheless, the bishop led over 200 clergy at the head of a mile-long procession at his funeral, in 1865. The church was sadly neglected in later years, and its condition resulted in demolition in 1958.

We now return along the Crescent to reach **Albion Place** *(10)*. The **Cenotaph** commemorates the soldiers of the Salford territorial units (part-time volunteers) and the 'Salford Pals' battalions (p.122) who lost their lives in the First World War. The majority served with the Lancashire Fusiliers (the regimental badge incorporates a sphinx). The memorial also records similar services in the Second World War. The old **Central Fire Station** is located at the rear of the square. It has recently been turned into a number of retail units, and it is rumoured that Harold Riley, the Salford Artist, has taken one for a gallery.

Here the walk ends. However, you may wish to walk to the nearby **Salford Crescent Station**, and catch a train back to Oxford Road or Piccadilly Stations. Part of the line is on a viaduct, and there are interesting views, particularly of Castlefield.

Salford Quays, with a view of the Designer Outlet

14 Salford Quays

Start: Piccadilly Station Metrolink (or any Central Manchester Stops)

Estimated time of walk: 2 hours (including tram ride)

Interiors: Ordsall Hall – ½ hour; Lowry Centre – 1 hour; Imperial War Museum North – 1 hour

Highlights: A dockland reborn, an ancient hall, meeting Mr Lowry, and wartime nostalgia.

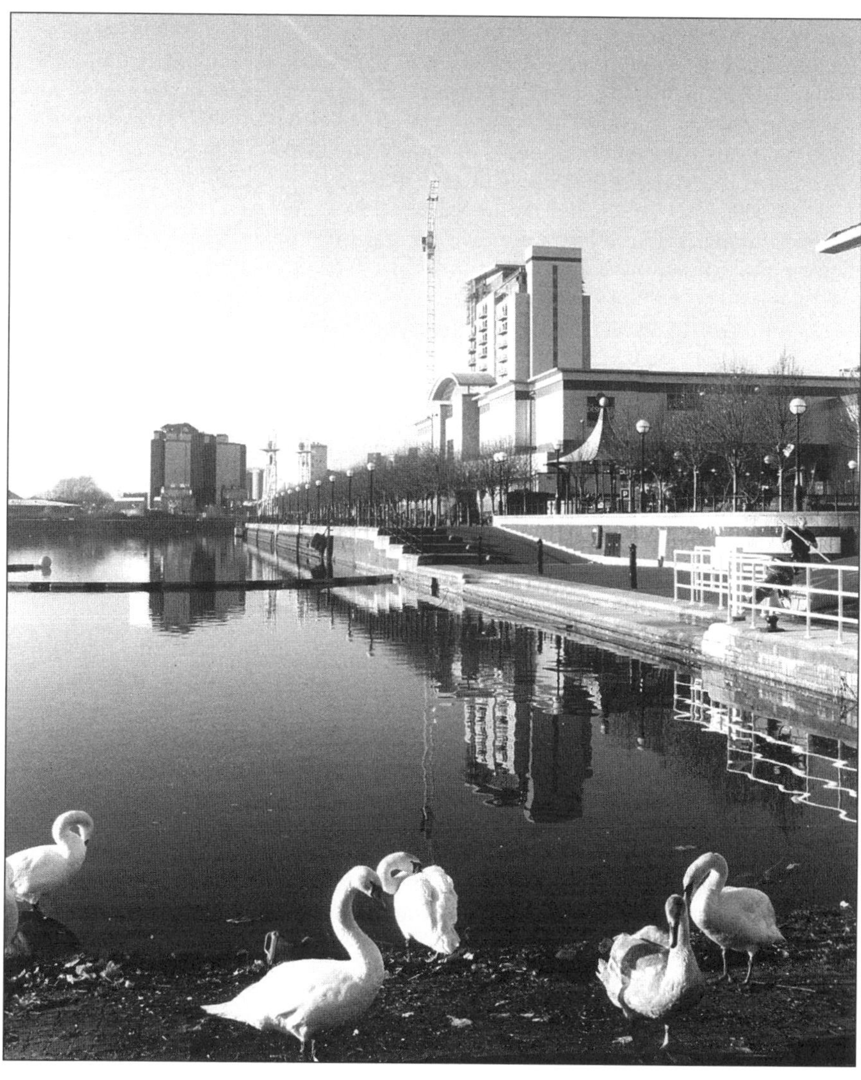

On this walk, we take an excursion by Metrolink tram through the second Salford success story – Salford Quays. Note that there is plenty of parking at the *Designer Outlet* in the quays area if you plan to arrive by car.

The 1870s and 1880s were decades of industrial depression. Perceptive observers realised that it was not just a matter of the operation of the trade cycle. There must be underlying structural causes. In Manchester, the culprit was identified as the 'Liverpool toll bar' – the handling charges and dues charged by the Mersey Docks and Harbour Board made Manchester goods uncompetitive. The answer seemed to be the construction of a ship canal that would turn Manchester into an inland port. The initiative in this bold venture is usually ascribed to Daniel Adamson, but a whole cohort of local businessmen held similar views. The canal project became a crusade in which several organisations were involved, embracing all sections of the community including the trade unions. After a great deal of opposition from a variety of vested interests, an Act of Parliament was obtained in 1885. Over 16,000 navvies (assisted by steam shovels) laboured six years to dig the 35-mile long waterway. At one point, the project almost collapsed through lack of funding, but Manchester City council stepped in and saved the day. Queen Victoria eventually opened the **Manchester Ship Canal** in 1894.

The docks were established on the Salford side. Pomona catered for coastal vessels and the remaining sailing ships. The large Salford Docks dealt with ships from all over the world, including transatlantic traders. It was home to Manchester Liners, which operated to America and Canada. The De Trafford family sold their estate, a former deer park, for conversion into Britain's first large-scale industrial estate. Westinghouse was one of the first occupants, erecting a reproduction of their American head offices. Metropolitan Vickers, and other famous companies of the time, followed.

Economic historians have calculated that the canal did indeed revive Manchester's fortunes before the First World War. It went on to play an important part in the economic life of the city until the advent of the container revolution. The new ships were just too large, and the docks and headwaters were closed to all except small boats in 1982. (But there is still a ship repair business visible from the Lowry!) The canal was acquired by Peel Holdings, a property development company, anxious to exploit the opportunities along its banks.

Salford City Council purchased the derelict Salford Docks in 1983, and the redevelopment of the area began in 1985. **Salford Quays** is often compared with London Docklands, but there are important differences. In the first place, it is a distinct area, with no enclaves or parts not included within the project. No local people were displaced or even affected by the development. Secondly, the decision was taken to rebuild the docks completely. Consequently, there are no rats. The water is constantly purified, and bathing or water sports are forbidden for periods following the opening of the gates to the basins (in connection with boat movements). A danger flag is flown until the water is considered pure again. The council developed the infrastructure, and this provided the ideal setting for private developers. The Quays are a sought-after address, both for businesses and house or flat hunters, and are now seen as a symbol of Salford's regeneration.

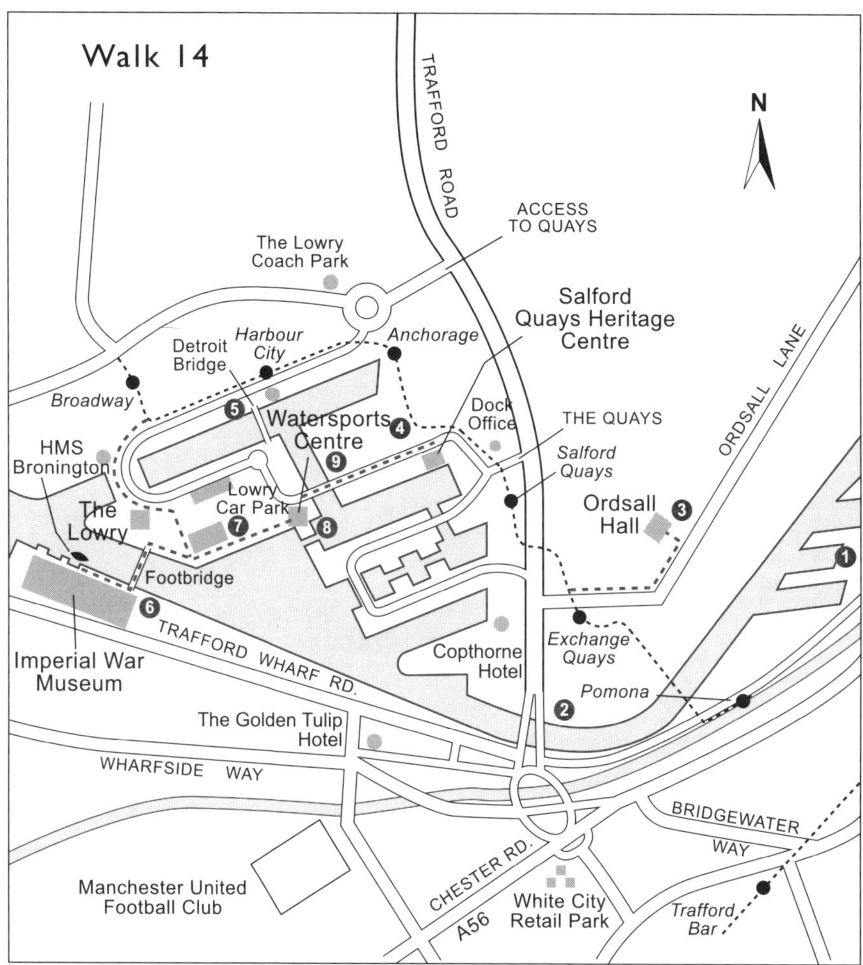

Manchester to Salford

Our excursion to Salford Quays is performed by an Eccles-bound Metrolink tram. We leave Piccadilly Station undercroft, cross London Road, and travel up Aytoun Street to reach Piccadilly Gardens. The tram then continues by way of Mosley Street and St Peter's Square, before climbing the incline in Lower Mosley Street alongside the G-Mex Centre. It then turns a sharp right, following the old station viaduct alongside Whitworth Street West with views of the Great Northern Development to the right.

Beyond Deansgate, there are excellent views of Castlefield through the girders of the high-level viaduct to the left. We follow the **Duke's Canal** on the left, with a glimpse of St George's church in the distance at the newly widened Egerton Street. Several of the warehouses here are being developed by Urban Splash. The railway lines on the lower viaduct are rising to our level. The Duke's Canal turns under the viaducts and is temporarily lost from sight.

There is a good view of the **Irwell**, which around here becomes the Ship Canal, on the right. Notice the **names along the brick wall,** which refer to the vanished streets in the neighbourhood. Woden's Den refers to a lost cave (built over in Victorian times) that was considered holy, and full of mysterious Norse carvings.

Cornbrook Station is the interchange point for the Altrincham and Eccles services (there is no pedestrian entrance or exit at the moment). A quick glance to the left reveals an odd little **entrance arch** in the middle of a traffic island. It comes from an old confectionery factory that stood in the area, and marks the boundary of the borough of Trafford. The tram now follows the railway line in passing over the Altrincham route, before parting company with the trains to cross the Duke's Canal. The way now lies along a newly built **viaduct between two canals**, the Duke's on the left, and the Ship Canal on the right.

You may be able to spot the remains of **Pomona Docks** *(1)* on this side, although they are scheduled for a property development. The name comes from Pomona Gardens, a Victorian pleasure resort that they replaced, a place frequented by (as the locals would say) "mucky women".

T'was down in Albert Square, I never shall forget,
The day it was fine, but the evening, it was wet.
She hid behind a veil, but seemed a real flash rover,
So we rode at night in the pale moonlight,
Way down to Pomona!

Of course, when the 'lady' removes her veil, it turns out to be his wife – intent on stopping his "mashing!"

The next station has revived the old name. It will be the junction for the intended line to the Trafford Centre, and part of the configuration is already in position. In the distance may be seen the **White City Arch** and the **Trafford Park Mural**, an evocation of the heyday of the great industrial estate, painted on the end wall of a 1932 warehouse by Walter Kershaw. The tram swings sharp right and crosses the Ship Canal, with a fine view up the Canal and Irwell towards Manchester. (Perhaps best seen on the return journey.) The **Swing Bridge** *(2)* is to the left, erected in 1893, but now fixed in position with the new road bridge alongside it. It formerly divided Pomona Docks from the main Salford Docks (now Salford Quays). Plunging down a ramp like a roller coaster, we pass between the **Colgate-Palmolive plant** to the right and the maze of glass office blocks, constituting **Exchange Quay**, to the left.

Ordsall Hall

It is a good idea to leave the tram at **Exchange Quay Station** for a short while, and turn right down Ordsall Lane. Just an ordinary road down a housing estate, and then we turn a corner, to find an ancient manor house in the shape of **Ordsall Hall** (open Monday-Friday 10.00-4.00, Sunday 1.00-4.00, admission free). The Hall *(3)* was the home of the Radcliffe family. Like many of the gentry and nobility in the north of England, they adhered to the old faith after the Reformation. There is a legend that Guy Faulkes hatched the 'gunpowder plot' while staying here, but this is very unlikely, for the Radcliffes were 'occasional conformists' – they attended the Collegiate Church as required by law (still maintaining a chapel there), but kept a 'massing priest' in the Hall. In fact, they were particularly loyal, serving in the Elizabethan Irish campaigns and supporting Charles I in the Civil War.

The house was given up as a residence at an early date, becoming a farmhouse, a

Ordsall Hall

Victorian mansion, and (in the heyday of the docks) a working men's club! This curious history preserved the building from major structural change, and it again stands in an open setting in something approaching its original condition. The next development stage involves the recreation of part of the moat.

Enter by means of the **screened passage**, between the hall and the kitchens (a typical mediaeval arrangement). The **Great Hall** probably dates from the early 16th century, though it includes some mediaeval timbers. The Lord and his family sat at the high table on the dais, and members of the household in the body of the Hall. Note that, at this period of history, the fire was in the middle of the floor. The little **oriel window** is quite charming, but do not miss the small **minstrels' gallery**, above. A door leads to the **Star Chamber**, which may be older than the Hall. This would be the Lord's 'solar', the only private room in the house. It is restored and furnished to its 17th-century condition, complete with a carved four poster bed. The brick **Kitchens** are much later than the rest of the house, and have been restored to their original Victorian condition. Some other rooms are usually used for temporary exhibitions.

Ordsall Hall has two other interesting features. Firstly, there are a number of 'living history' performers who are 'in residence' from time to time. Secondly, a 'white lady' is said to haunt the house. A **special video camera** transmits continuous coverage on the Hall's internet website, just in case she decides to put in an appearance!

Salford Quays

Beyond Exchange Quay Station, the tram curves to the left on a **section of grass track**, crosses Trafford Road, and enters **Salford Quays**. It immediately turns right and calls at **Salford Quays Station**. **St Peter's Basin**, one of three created from a former dock is glimpsed to the left – the other basins are St Louis and St Francis. A whole **range of eating places** – *Hanrahan's, Frankie and Benny's, Chiquito*, and

Ontario Basin

Arbuckles – slides past on the right, indicating certain assumptions as to the (transatlantic?) culture of the people who work around here.

We continue past the end of the **Ontario Basin**, with a number of forlorn **cranes** (moved here from elsewhere in the dock area). Cotton was once unloaded in this dock. To the right, adjacent to Trafford Road, is a large white building, the old **Dock Office** (1927). Dock work was a casual occupation – the men were hired to help load or unload particular ships. The dockers would congregate here, and the list of work available was chalked on a slate in one of the ground floor windows.

The tram curves to the left near the Heritage centre and begins to ascend to a short viaduct section *(4)*. You might catch a glimpse of the 32ft (9.7m) **totem pole**, in front of the large **Furness House** (1969) on the right. This was formerly the headquarters of Manchester Liners, and the building is designed to create the impression of a ship's bridge. The totem pole was carved by a Kwakiutle Indian at the request of the then company chairman, and is meant to mark the long trading association with Canada.

Descending from the short viaduct, the tram now pauses at **Anchorage Station**. The great bulky **Anchorage Building** is perfectly hideous, seemingly designed by the team responsible for Ceaucescu's palace. And it is little better round the other side, the part facing Eerie Basin (though this is distinguished by an interesting sculpture, executed by Wendy Taylor, of an enormous **anchor**). Over 2000 people work in this monstrosity.

The way now lies to the left, along a **grassy reservation** alongside the main roadway. Here is a good view on the left of the **Eerie Basin**, once used for the discharge of grain in bulk. We pause at **Harbour City Station**, to the rear of the great building of that name. Look out for the **Detroit Bridge**, a little beyond it *(5)*. This was a railway swing bridge, once situated near the Trafford Road Swing Bridge (the stone column supporting the pivot is still visible), allowing rail traffic access to Trafford Park and Trafford Wharf from the Salford direction. Replacing an earlier single track bridge, it was built by Dorman Long in 1942. The bridge was removed to its present position in 1988, an operation requiring its flotation on pontoons down a section of the Canal. For this, bureaucracy required that it be registered as a ship! It now divides the Eerie basin from the **Huron Basin**.

There are good views of the Lowry and the surrounding area in the distance. A single track Metrolink branch to the Lowry is projected (the junction, it will be noticed, is already fabricated), but the tram turns sharp right on to a private right of way, and calls at **Broadway Station**. Alight here, retrace the route to the road, and turn right, following the curving road to the Lowry. The end of the Huron Basin is passed, a popular spot for model boaters. Adjacent to the multi-storey car park, on the left, may be found the **Digital World Centre**, a facility for businesses (with an internet café).

The impressive entrance to the Lowry Centre

The Lowry

The **Lowry**, designed by Michael Wilford, is a major new arts complex – comprising an art gallery, two theatres, an interactive exhibition, a restaurant, corporate hospitality suite, a bookshop, publishing house, and study centre. It cost £94m, of which £64.3m came from the National Lottery. The building is perhaps best seen from the opposite bank of the Ship Canal, and at sunset, when the light catches the glass and polished metal. Otherwise, it seems a mass of sharp geometric forms, cones, cubes, and circles. The tall drum tower (housing the archive and study centre) is meant to reflect Salford's industrial past. The Lowry has been compared with the Guggenheim in Bilbao. (The galleries are open Sunday-Wednesday, 11.00-5.00, Thursday-Saturday, 11.00-8.00, admission free, except special exhibitions.)

Walk through the **foyer** to the right and ascend the escalator to the **galleries**. Before looking at the paintings, view the excellent video in the **'Meet Mr Lowry'** display. L.S. Lowry is much misunderstood. He was not from the working class, as his family was quite well off (he worked, for a time, as a rent collector). Nor was he a genuine 'primitive'. He had art lessons at the Art School at All Saints, where he was taught by (amongst others) Adolphe Valette. He lived a curious, almost solitary, life. He was mother fixated and never married. As is clear from the words you will hear, he never developed a rational philosophy of life or art. His paintings were a mere extension of his own complex personality and its inner demons.

Most people think of his 'matchstick figures', and in the **Lowry Galleries** you will find them in profusion. But his paintings are much more complex. They reveal an obsession with loneliness, and spiritual and physical deformity. The face with the staring red eyes is quite terrifying. Most of the pictures here originated in the Salford museum collection. Interestingly enough, Manchester City Art Gallery has the contents of his studio and sitting room, removed from the modest terraced house that he occupied at the time of his death. These rooms were recreated for a short period at the Art Gallery, and became one of its most popular attractions. There are no plans to reconstitute the exhibit in the new display areas, so it might be a nice idea if they came here.

Temporary exhibitions are to be found in the other galleries, for which an admission might be charged. We now follow a display area around the side of the building in an anti-clockwise direction, past the café. This brings us to **'Artworks'**, an interactive exhibition popular with young children. (Open Monday-Friday 10.00-3.00, weekends 10.00-4.00, admission charge. Enter through Hexagon Shop by lift.) Here you can be the artist, painting a digital mural or conducting an orchestra, before exploring the **giant head**. The Lowry has two theatres. The **Lyric Theatre**, with 1,750 seats, has the largest stage outside London. The **Quays Theatre**, with 460 seats, offers the intimacy of smaller venue.

Back outside, turn right and walk onto the **Lowry Lifting Bridge** *(6)*. This marvellous new pedestrian bridge was designed by Casado of Madrid, and fabricated by Parkman's of Salford. The view from it is impressive. Downstream are the **Mode Wheel Locks**, the first on the Ship Canal system, and powered from the red brick hydraulic tower to the right. You might see a ship in the **graving dock**, undergoing repair. The view upstream runs to the Swing Bridge in the distance, with the Quays to the left and Trafford Wharf to the right. The *Samuel Platt* public house is visible at the end of the latter, named after one of the pioneers of the Canal saga (his steam yacht, 'The Norseman', headed the opening day procession).

The Imperial War Museum North

Cross the bridge, noting the shining glass of the **Peel Estates** offices directly in front, turning right to reach the **Imperial War Museum North** (open daily, 10-6, admission free). This is an outstation of the Imperial War Museum in London, open to the public from July 2002. The building is designed by Daniel Libeskind, and is intended to represent a world shattered by conflict. It consists of a 29 metre high **'air shard'** (with spectacular views across Manchester from the top), a domed 'earth shard', and a 'water shard' with views across the Canal to the Lowry.

There is no access from the waterfront, so follow the path to the left of this frontage round the opposite side to the main entrance. In this area, a lift ascends **the tower** (comprising the 'air shard'), from which there is a particularly fine view. The entrance itself leads to a **ground floor area** comprising an information point, a cloakroom, cafeteria, toilets, and an exceptionally well-stocked shop. A **canal side restaurant** is located in the 'water shard' part of the building.

Lifts ascend to the **upper floor**, but it is best to ascend a flight of stairs to the landing on the main level.

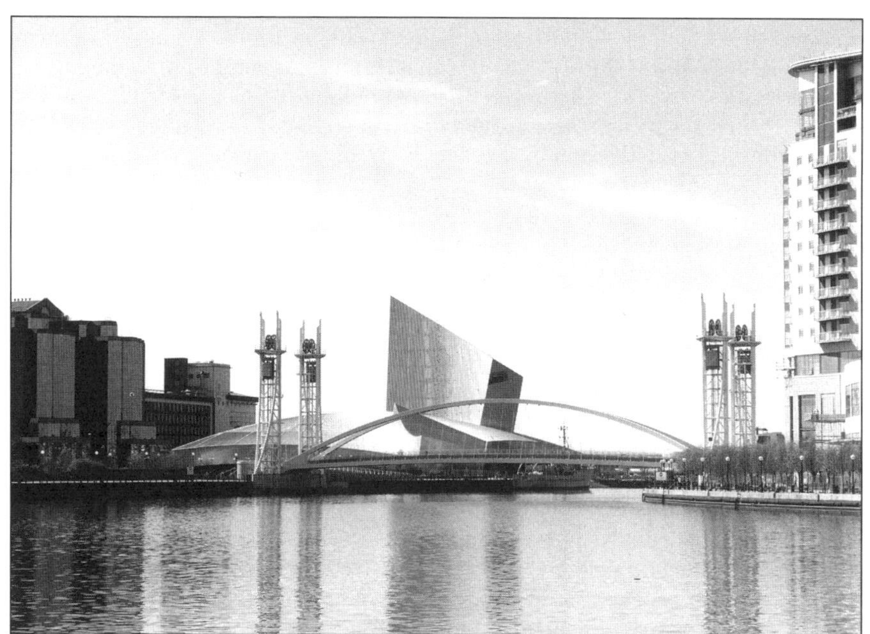

Imperial War Museum North

The entrance to the right accesses a **Special Exhibitions Gallery**, but most visitors go straight through into the main exhibition area – where they come face to face with a **Harrier V.T.O.L. 'Jump Jet'**, seemingly mounted just like a model. This highly successful fighter and ground attack aircraft entered service in 1969, fitted with an unusual engine that could be 'vectored' into a downward thrust mode. This meant that it could vertically take off and land in a confined space, yet still perform as a normal jet aircraft. (It could also engage in some pretty unorthodox moves in a dogfight too, even avoiding missiles!) Its flexibility proved a godsend in the Falklands War, and it remains the only British military aircraft purchased for use with the American armed forces.

We now traverse the displays in a clockwise direction, starting with the wall to the left of the entrance. Here is the **pageantry of war before 1914**, characterised by the **ceremonial helmets** only slightly disturbed by the **khaki** adopted for the guerrilla conflict against the Boers. All is utterly changed around the corner, where displays illustrate the **'Great War'**. Search out the **'hardtack'** biscuit and read the comment inscribed on it, for the exhibits depict **life in the trenches**. Linger in front of the **video of the Battle of the Somme**. Some of the scenes are posed in training areas, such as the wild rush 'over the top', but others are authentic. The wounded man being carried down the trench died a few minutes after the cameraman finished filming. Other aspects of the conflict are shown. Notice **the tail of a shot down German albatross fighter**, no doubt kept like a sporting souvenir. And it is clear that the campaign on the **Eastern front** was every bit as horrible as that in Flanders. Of course, everyone expected a great **naval** battle, but the German high seas fleet only once ventured out in force. The result was the inconclusive battle of Jutland, marked by the **ship's bell from HMS *Iron Duke***, the British flagship.

The scene changes, with the new angle of wall, to life and times on the **home front in Britain**. It was the first war in which Britain was bombed from the air, and there are relics of the great hydrogen filled **Zeppelin airships** (the Manchester area was twice attacked by the 'gasbags') and the twin-engined **Gotha bombers**. There is a **computerised casualty database** where you can trace ancestors who laid down their lives for king and country.

An enclosed area, the **first of the 'silos'** is situated in the angle of the walls. It is devoted to the theme of the **experience of war**, and contains a curious display in the manner of a **series of filing cabinets of personal effects and letters**. There are mementoes of the recruits in both wars and the period of 'national service'; **badges of the 'pals battalions'** (p.122); and a most poignant exhibit – a **letter from a nine year old boy to Lord Kitchener**, pleading to be allowed to enlist and take part in the game that older boys looked forward to. Other material relates to the **experiences of prisoners** (including those in Japanese camps); **internees**; and **evacuees** who were labelled like luggage. The **ship's bell of the Lusitania** is exhibited. This liner, sunk by a U-Boat off Ireland in 1915, had a dramatic effect upon public opinion in America.

The next set of displays, enclosing Silo two, is devoted to the **inter-war period**. The relics of the **Spanish Civil War**, in which many local men fought as volunteers in the International Brigade, are noteworthy. A **1932 German ballot paper** reminds us that the majority of the German people did not vote for Hitler – he was invited to form a government by the leaders of other right-wing parties, in an arrangement that they thought they could control ...Video film illustrates such charming activities as organising **boycotts of Jewish shops** and **book burning.** "Where one burns books, one later burns men."

Silo Two contains displays about women and war. Contrasting **videos** reveal all manner of **participation by women in armed conflict** and a variety of **female peace campaigns**. Look for the **pair of wire cutters** used at the Greenham Common protest.

Next comes a long section about a variety of aspects of **World War Two**. A **sea mine** is surrounded by a display concerning the **war at sea**. There is an army **'bren' gun**; a **'mickey mouse' gas mask** intended for children; and a **target map of Hamburg** (the centre was destroyed by a fire storm created by allied bombing). Of course, this was seen at the time as Nazi Germany "reaping the whirlwind" of what they had sown. Indeed, the **video film** of the **Battle of Britain** and the **'Christmas Blitz'** on Manchester are worth a glance.

Other sections deal with the **Desert** and **Jungle** wars. The former was a rather unique affair. The Eighth Army and the Afrika Korps fought each other in a harsh landscape almost completely bereft of 'civilians'. It was thus a 'soldiers war' – each side respected the other, and thought of themselves as a group of professionals who just happened to be in a position where they had to kill each other. It was one of the few instances (perhaps the only one) where a degree of chivalry prevailed. Both sides tuned in to Belgrade radio to hear Lale Anderson sing Lilly Marlene, and, sadly, sometimes advanced into battle against each other singing this song. The Eight Army did not adopt any form of conventional dress code, as might be seen in **Jon's cartoon of 'Two Types'!**

Explore **Silo Three** before continuing with the wall displays. This Silo deals with **impressions of war – myths, propaganda, and children's war toys**. The material relating to the **liberation of the concentration camps** (which created a profound impression in Britain at the time) is real enough, though, and introduces the displays about the post-war world. Inevitably, various episodes of the **'cold war'** are dealt with, including the **Cuban missile crisis** (which brought the world to the closest point it has ever been to a nuclear war), the **invasion of Czechoslovakia in 1968**, and the **implosion of the Soviet Empire** in the 1980s – notice the **piece of the Berlin Wall**.

In perusing this display, we pass a **Russian T34 tank**. The allied nations contributed in a variety of ways to the defeat of the Nazis. The Soviets tied down a large part of the Nazi land forces and more or less ripped the heart out of the elite Panzer (tank) regiments at the Battle of Kursk in 1943. The principal instrument of victory was the T34, simply designed, rugged, and manufactured in enormous quantities by emergency factories set up beyond the Urals, out of range of the German bomber force. Fortunately, drivers and mechanics could be recruited from the former inmates of the machine tractor stations, set up under the auspices of the Five Year Plan.

Silo Four looks at the **contribution of the Commonwealth** in the last war. The video of the almost forgotten **exploits of the East African troops** in Burma is particularly interesting. **Silo Five** considers the **role of science and technology in modern war**. Look for the **'Protect and survive' leaflets** issued by the Thatcher government in the 1980s. These were mercilessly satirised at the time and feature in 'When the Wind Blows' (a cartoon book and film) by Raymond Briggs. The final wall display deals with the **post cold war era**, and features the **break up of Yugoslavia**. The **last silo** concludes with **the effects and impacts of war**. It is all summed up by the **three-wheeled invalid carriage**, but the **1945 plan to rebuild Manchester** is interesting. Of course, there was no money to carry it out – and a good thing too, for the place would have ended up looking like downtown East Berlin.

The **main exhibition space** contains three exhibits. Most people are drawn to the ubiquitous **'25 pounder' field gun**, but do not neglect the **fire brigade pump trailer** and the **Trabant Car**. The former saw great service in the 'blitz' – there was such a shortage of proper fire appliances that many of these pumps were towed by requisitioned taxicabs. The latter remains, of course, the icon of the collapse of the Berlin Wall – a two stroke fibreglass bodied chariot of freedom. Last, but not least, search out the **'time stack'** situated in the rear wall of Silo One. Here, a kind of dumb waiter arrangement summons a selection of artefacts that can be personally handled and inspected.

You are in the midst of a large arena. In the course of your progress around the displays, concentration will have been interrupted at least once by an audio-visual presentation. The **'Big Picture Show'** utilises most of the wall space in the arena, using sixty projectors. The shows are usually given at hourly intervals and last around fifteen minutes. Current subjects are 'Why War?'; 'Weapons of War'; and 'Children and War'. Please be advised that these **shows contain loud noises and flashing lights**, so you should retreat into a Silo or leave this area when a show is announced if you feel it will affect a medical condition or frighten small children.

Go back across the bridge and descend the steps on the right, leading to **Centenary Walkway**, opened by Princess Anne in 1994, and celebrating the anniversary of the opening of the Manchester Ship Canal by Queen Victoria. Look out for a series of **embedded steel discs** – these are engraved with words and pictures emoting the history of the docks and the area. **'Waterside @ the Lowry'**, a large new apartment block, is situated on the left, together with ***The Designer Outlet @ the Lowry***, a two-storey shopping centre *(7)*. It contains such 'names' as *Karen Millen*,

The 'Lifting Bridge' and the final stages of construction of the new apartment block at Salford Quays

Molton Brown, *Whistles*, and *Flannels*, and eateries such as *Limes* restaurant. In some of the designer outlets, a minimum of 30% is discounted from the ordinary shop price. The upper floor contains a ***Warner Village Mutiplex Cinema***. At **Salford Wharf Park,** there is a good view across the widest stretch of water, used by ocean-going ships for turning movements. We have now come to Welland Lock, the entry point from the Canal to three enclosed docks. Adjacent to the lock is the **Watersports Centre** *(8)*, offering courses in canoeing, kayaking, sailing, and wind-surfing at a variety of levels.

Pause on the footbridge *(9)* over the new **Mariners Canal** (intended for small boat owners), which cuts through the housing development to the Eerie Basin. The Canal is centred on the frontage of **Harbour City**, another piece of Bucharest transplanted to Salford. One can almost imagine the dictator fleeing in his helicopter – but it actually grows on you, and you end up feeling that it is an impressive vista (and thousands of postcards can't be wrong).

The way now lies alongside **Ontario Basin**, past a ***Beefeater Inn*** and a ***Travel Inn*** to the **Four Corners Sculpture**. This work of art (by Noah Rose) echoes the shapes of propellers, hulls, and sails, whilst the weather vane represents Pomona and Salford Docks. **Salford Quays Heritage Centre** (open Monday-Friday, 9.00-4.30, admission free) is located towards the end of the Walkway. The Centre has permanent and temporary displays, a resource centre, and a variety of literature about the docks and the quays.

From here, it is a short walk to Salford Quays Metrolink station for the return journey to Manchester. *(The walk can also be extended by the excursion to Eccles and the Trafford Centre, described on p.265, by catching an Eccles tram from Salford Quays or Broadway Metrolink stations.)*

15 Excursions from Manchester

A number of excursions are listed in this chapter. These may be undertaken in connection with certain of the walks (the starting points are listed in the text), particularly when the walk occurs in the morning, or at a time that allows the excursion to be 'added on'.

Bury and the East Lancashire Railway

Start: Corporation Street

Estimated time of walk: An afternoon

Highlights: The Jewish Museum, a collection of buses, the largest municipal park in Britain, old-fashioned trams, the legend of 'Fair Ellen', and a ride on a steam train.

The CIS building from Great Ancoats Street

This excursion starts with a short walk into Cheetham Hill, commencing at the end of Corporation Street. The great 400ft, 25-storey **CIS (Co-operative Insurance) Building** (Sir John Burnett Tate and Partners, 1962) towers skywards on the right. The concrete service core is covered with fourteen million mosaic pieces. It is actually part of a larger complex, with a smaller block in the foreground and **New Century Hall** (not seen from this point) in between the two. At the time of its opening, the great tower was the tallest building in Europe. The hall is used for a variety of functions, including the December exhibition of the Manchester Model Railway Society. A rather splendid office block, now used as a hotel, closes off the vista at the end of the street.

Cross the **Ducie Railway Bridge**, virtually in its 1901 condition, at the east end of Victoria Station. An opening at the opposite end of the bridge, on the right, is easily missed – so stand at the top of the stairs for a view over the **valley of the Irk** stream. Much is still industrial wasteland, but a start has been made with landscaping. The area of Red Bank and Angel Meadow, perhaps the worst slums in Manchester, were in the valley, but no-one lives here now.

Cheetham Hill

We now walk up Cheetham Hill Road, which leads to what is still called Cheetham Village. Once a very fashionable area, it was rapidly turning into a working class district by the end of the 19th century. **St Chad's Roman Catholic Church** is a prominent landmark, but notice the elegant **old Town Hall** (across the road), dating from 1856, and the former **'Free Library'** building. The tall chimney tower of **Strangeways Prison** presides over the view to the left. (The prison was practically rebuilt a few years ago, after the interior was destroyed in a notorious riot.)

There has been a Jewish community in Manchester since at least the 18th century. The great industrial metropolis attracted many German and West European Jews, and this group made an important contribution to the life of the city (the cultural life in particular). Later, large numbers of Jews fled pogroms and poverty in Russia in the last quarter of the 19th century. Many of these settled in Cheetham Hill, which became something of an unofficial ghetto. The increasing prosperity of the community led to its dispersal, largely to the leafy suburbs of Prestwich and Whitefield further to the north. Assimilation into the mainstream of British society accomplished the rest of the transformation. A few former synagogues are left, and one of these (on the right) now contains the **Manchester Jewish Museum** (open Monday-Thursday 10.30-4.00, and Sunday 10.30-5.00, closed Jewish holidays, admission free). Edward Salomans designed this rather fine building in the Moorish style in 1873 for the Sephardic community of Spanish and Portuguese Jews. The historical collections are worth a visit, and advertised 'heritage tours' start from the museum.

As we continue our walk, the tower of a church lies ahead. A rather misguided attempt at redevelopment has left **St Luke's Church**, consecrated in 1836, an accusatory ruin (in its heyday, Mendelssohn once played a recital on the organ here). Behind the church, in Boyle Street, may be found the **Museum of Transport** (open Wednesday, Saturday, Sunday, and Bank Holidays, 10.00-5.00, admission charge). Located in Manchester's first bus garage, the museum rather appropriately contains a large collection of historic buses, once operated by the local authorities (and a few private operators) in the Greater Manchester area. Pride of place is given to a **rare Victorian horse bus**, but do not neglect the displays about the evolution of public transport in the Manchester area, which include such things as ticket machines and items of uniform.

After leaving the museum, the walk continues along Cardinal Street to terminate at **Woodlands Road Metrolink Station**. Catch a Bury bound tram from here, purchasing a Metrolink Day Rover ticket (about the same cost as a Bury return fare, but permitting unlimited travel on the entire Metrolink system for the day).

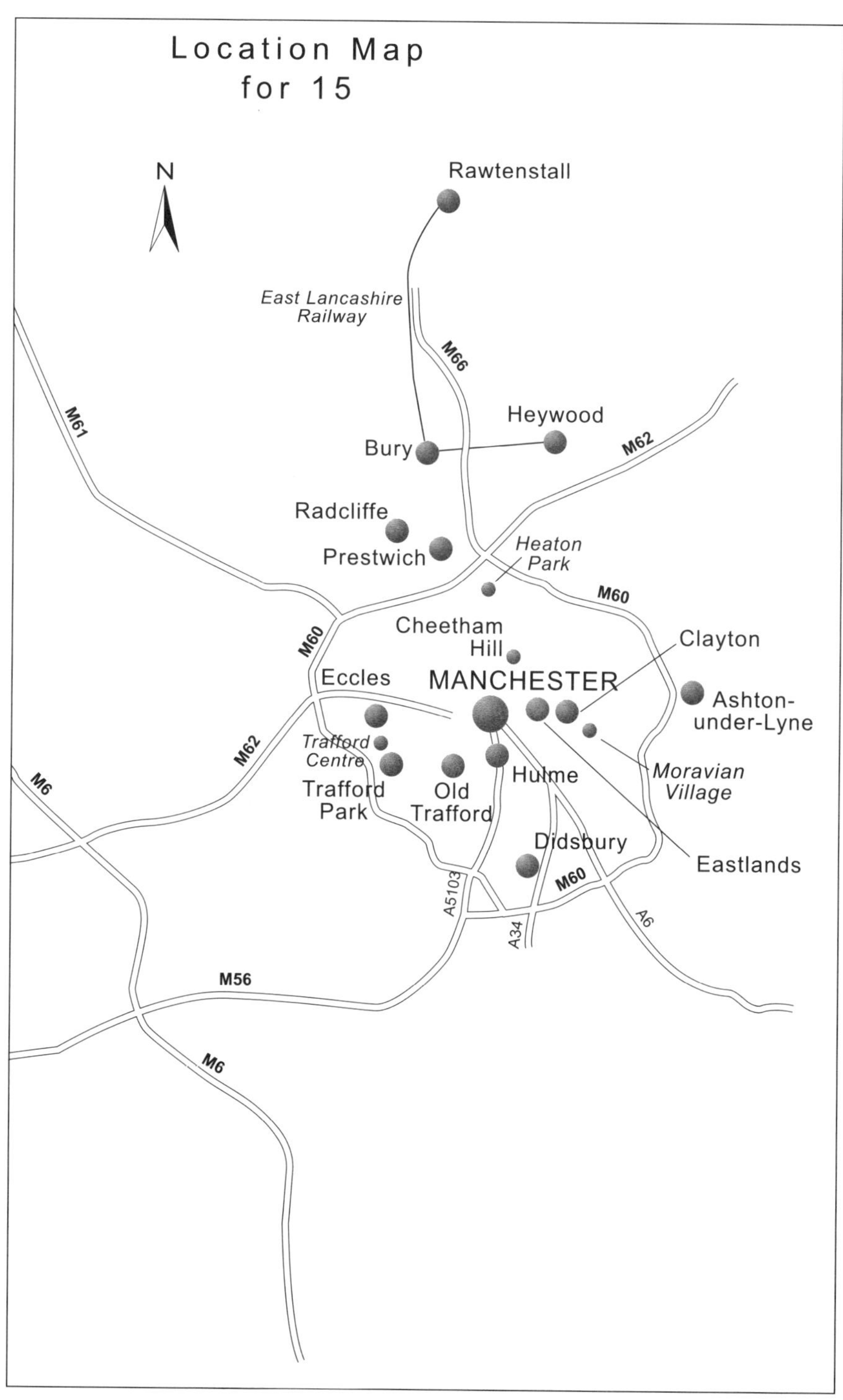
Location Map
for 15
N
Rawtenstall
East Lancashire
Railway
M66
M61
Heywood
M62
Bury
Radcliffe
Prestwich
Heaton
Park
M60
M60
Cheetham
Hill
Clayton
Eccles
MANCHESTER
Ashton-
under-Lyne
M62
Trafford
Centre
Moravian
Village
M6
Trafford
Park
Old
Trafford
Hulme
Didsbury
Eastlands
M60
A5103
A34
A6
M56
M6

Heaton Park

A branch of the prolific Egerton family, ennobled as the Earls of Wilton, once resided at **Heaton Park**. In 1902, Manchester City Council purchased both the house and the extensive 640 acre parkland setting (which the family had originally intended to be sold off as building lots), thus acquiring what is still the largest municipal park in the country. You can catch a **glimpse of the house** to the right, near Bowker Vale Station. The long **Heaton Park Tunnel** was built at the insistence of Lord Wilton, so that his view might not be spoilt! Alight at **Heaton Park Station**, and enter the **park** by the gates across Bury Old Road (open daily until 9.45p.m.).

You could spend all day here, but if time is pressing, the following itinerary is suggested. Take the right-hand path at the fork beyond the gate, noticing the **Papal Monument** to the right. This stone marks the spot where Pope John Paul celebrated mass during his visit to Britain. The pathway leads to the intersection of the main drive and the roadway to the **lake**. Follow the latter, and admire the **frontage of the original Town Hall**, that forms a backdrop to the sheet of water. (Rowing boats can be hired.) The terminus of the **Heaton Park Tramway** is situated a little further on. The trams once had a short terminal siding in the Park (complete with waiting and tea room) at the Middleton Road entrance. The building was converted into a tramway museum some years ago, and the tracks were extended to the lakeside. (A further extension, to the house and the Bury Old Road gate, is projected.) Enthusiastic volunteers operate the trams, and they are always ready to answer questions. The ticket includes admission to the **museum**, so hop on board! You may be lucky enough to ride on 765, the beautiful single deck Manchester car. Other, double deck vehicles, are in the restoration pipeline, but will have to wait for the new depot to be built. The trams usually operate on Sundays and Bank Holidays, 1.30 to 5.30 (and a limited service on Wednesdays in June and July), from Easter to September.

We now retrace our steps, turn right, and follow the main drive towards the house. The **paddock** on the left can contain anything, from horses to highland cattle, and is followed by the **children's zoo** (with ducks, goats, rabbits etc.), presided over by some very vain peacocks. The drive terminates near the original home farm of the estate. This is now a **children's farm**, with cows, pigs, and (upstairs) a hatchery for baby chickens.

However, the main attraction is the nearby **Heaton Hall**. (Open April-October, Wednesday-Sunday and Bank Holidays 10.00-5.30, admission free). The present structure is largely the creation of James Wyatt, added around a far older house after 1772. Sadly, the Council did not purchase the original contents of the house, but it has been re-furnished in the style of the period. Some of the rooms are impressive. The **Library** introduces the **Music Room**, with a fine Samuel Green **organ** (note the portrait of Handel) and the **original music stands**. The Noble Lord was very fond of music – he, and members of his family were talented musicians, and gave private concerts in this room. The **Dining Room** is also impressive, but the 'pièce de résistance' is upstairs. The Hall has one of the few surviving examples of an ephemeral fashion of the 18th century, an **Etruscan Room**.

Back on the Metrolink tram, we can also alight at **Prestwich** for a view of the fine **mediaeval parish church**, a potter round the antique (or junk?) shops, or a walk down the beautiful wooded **Prestwich Clough** in the Forest park. **Besses o' th' Barn** Station requires an explanation as to the name. 'Bessy' once kept the tollgate on the turnpike road here. In Lancashire, at that time, people did not use surnames, so the girl would be called after her occupation. To the German weavers in the locality, she was thus 'Bessy of the Bahn (road)'! **Whitefield** has a nice Waterloo **church**, and was the boyhood home of Robert Clive (of India fame).

Radcliffe

Leave the tram at **Radcliffe**. The town centre lies to the left of the station, but turn right, under the railway bridge, and follow the road to **Radcliffe Tower**. You are standing before the only **mediaeval stone fortification** in the Greater Manchester area. Not a lot of people know that, because it is not publicised very much. The old timber house is long gone, but the stonework remains – a pele tower, a place of refuge against Scottish raids, and unusual to find this far south. The tower is forever associated with the legend of **Fair Ellen**, the lovely daughter of the Lord of Radcliffe. Unfortunately, he had remarried, and the insanely jealous stepmother, Lady Isabel, plotted a most bizarre revenge on her rival. Poor Ellen was murdered and her remains were cooked in a pie, to be served to her father when he returned from hunting that night. The poor cook boy (who had worshipped her from afar) found out what was in the pie, and warned the father just in time (thereby inheriting the Lord's estate). The adjacent **mediaeval parish church** is also worth a look.

Bury

The tram at last arrives at **Bury Interchange Station**. The first sight that greets our eyes is the **Kay Monument**, commemorating John Kay, the local boy who invented the 'flying shuttle'. **Bury Market** is deservedly famous, especially the **black pudding stall**, and the landscaped foundations of **Bury Castle** (a grandly named manor house, fortified by Sir Richard Pilkington, a 'favourite' of Richard III) should be sought out. The **Museum and Art Gallery** (open Tuesday-Saturday, times vary, free admission) has the **Wrigley bequest**, one of the best provincial art collections in the country, including work by Constable, Cox, Turner, and De Wint. (Children will appreciate the good **local history displays** downstairs, including a large model railway.) The **Lancashire Fusiliers Museum** (with relics of General Wolfe) is a short bus ride away (open Monday, Tuesday, Thursday 9.30-4.30, admission free).

Of course, the principal attraction in the town is the **East Lancashire Railway**, extending to Rawtenstall. This former railway line is owned by a trust (including local authority representatives), but operated by a group of volunteer railway enthusiasts. The main station is located on Bolton Street. Ask if the adjacent **Bury Transport Museum** is open. The line operates at weekends and Bank Holiday Mondays throughout the year. (Ring 0161 764 7790 for train times.) The Saturday trains are usually a mixture of steam- and diesel-hauled, but Sundays and Bank Holiday Mondays are all steam! It has everything – cuttings, tunnels, bridges (including a viaduct), level crossings, and restored stations. The line follows a pleasant river valley, with views of moorland at the northern end, and an extension from Bury to Heywood in the opposite direction is now open.

At **Summerseat Station**, visit the ***Waterside Inn***, astride the river. The trains cross at **Ramsbottom Station**. It is worth spending an hour exploring this unspoiled traditional mill village, created by the famous Grant brothers, who appear as the 'Cheeryble Brothers' in 'Nicholas Nickleby'. Look out for the **'Grecian Urn' foun-**

East Lancashire Railway locomotive on the Brooksbottom Viaduct, Summerseat with Holcombe Tower on the horizon *(Picture kindly supplied by Mr A.E. Bayfield)*

tain, explore the specialist shops, and visit the **Heritage Centre**, run by the local residents (open on Summer Sundays). If you are energetic, follow the path up the steep 'rake', past Emmanuel Church to Holcombe village. From here, ascend Holcombe Hill to the **Peel Monument** (p.93). This is the highest spot in Greater Manchester, and, on a fine day, there is a view as far south as Staffordshire.

The little halt of **Irwell Vale** is frequented by railway photographers (tea is available in the Methodist Chapel on a Sunday). There is a picturesque walk along the valley of the River Ogden to Helmshore, where **Higher Mill Museum** is situated.

Rawtenstall

The train terminates at **Rawtenstall Station**. The little town has the last remaining ***Temperance Bar*** (known locally as the 'sass shop') in the North of England, with an interior unchanged since 1920. Sample such traditional delights as 'black beer and raisin', but remember that these were weapons in the fight against the scourge of the demon drink. The local heritage society has created a fine visitor centre in the historic **Weaver's Cottage**. Finally, the town Museum at **Whittaker Park** (also the location of the artificial ski slope) is a delightful example of what Victorian museums used to be like. Children will adore the tableaux of stuffed animals.

Eastlands and Ashton-under-Lyne

Start: Stevenson Square or Redhill Street

Estimated time of walk: An afternoon

Highlights: Manchester's New Stadium, Clayton Hall, a Moravian village, Manchester's own regiment, a museum of social history, and mediaeval stained glass.

This Northern Quarter excursion can be undertaken in connection with the Northern Quarter Walk, commencing either at Stevenson Square or at the indicated point in the Ancoats walk. In the latter case, proceed over the Rochdale Canal Bridge, following the road round to the right (by New Union, New Islington, and Weybridge Streets) to reach Mill Street. Here, there is a glimpse to the right of the old **Ancoats Hospital** building. But we turn to the left, walking as far as Beswick Street on the right. This street crosses the Ashton Canal and deposits us at the junction with Merill Street and Every Street, where a Metrolink station is intended. The great stadium dominates the view in the distance.

Eastlands

The Ashton bus (from the nearby stop) passes **Eastlands**, once a large area of derelict land which included a part of the old Bradford Gasworks (some **gasometers**, converted to storing North Sea gas, remain). The **City of Manchester Stadium**, the centrepiece of the XVII Commonwealth Games, cost £90m, most of the money coming from the Lottery Sports Fund. It was designed to hold 38,000 people for the Games, and up to 48,000 when used as a football stadium. The magnificent Opening Ceremony of the Commonwealth Games was broadcast from this stadium around the world. (It is now the home of Manchester City F.C., though used for other events from time to time.) There is a **training track** next to the stadium, and **Sportcity**, with its academy of excellence, indoor athletics hall, indoor tennis courts, and state of the art sports science and medical unit, is adjacent. It incorporates the **National Squash Centre**. Nearby is the **Velodrome** (cycling track) with an eye-catching roof. The whole

The City of Manchester Stadium *(copyright Manchester 2002 Ltd)*

will be linked with the city centre by the projected Metrolink line to Ashton, linking at this point (by means of an interchange station) with the old Ancoats Goods Loop railway line. However because of government procrastination, and a lack of co-ordination between a variety of bodies, the line was not available in time for the Games.

Clayton

The bus continues along Ashton New Road, and passes through Clayton. Clayton Park is situated within the angle of Ashton New Road and North Road. It is the location of **Clayton Hall** (not clearly visible from the main road), a moated manor house dating back to the 15th century. The hall was the ancestral home of the Byron family (related to the Byroms, see page 10). A small child, burnt to death at some unspecified period, haunts the place. It looks picturesque enough from the outside, but the interior has been extensively altered. It is now partly used as a private residence and the rest houses offices for the Council's Leisure Services Department. (Groups of visitors may inspect an information centre, and undertake a short tour, by prior arrangement.)

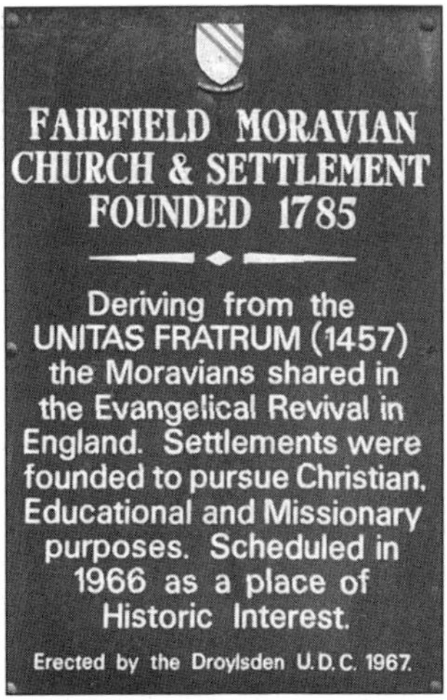

Beyond Clayton, the bus passes through Droylsden. Alight near the junction of Manchester Road with Scott Road and Buckley Street, proceeding down the latter before following the path over the Ashton Canal. This leads to **Fairfield Moravian Settlement**. The Moravians are the oldest Protestant denomination, tracing their origin to 1457 (predating the Reformation by sixty years) in Bohemia and Moravia (present-day Czech Republic). They were inspired by the teachings of Jan Hus (John Wyclif, the English reformer, influenced Hus.) A community settled here in 1785, in what was then open country. They were much respected, and it is said that Wesley was greatly inspired by the Moravian church. A religious community still exists, and everyone is welcome to services in the church. (Guided tours of the settlement and church buildings are available for parties of 20 or more, ring 0161 370 3461.)

FAIRFIELD MORAVIAN
CHURCH & SETTLEMENT
FOUNDED 1785
Deriving from the UNITAS FRATRUM (1457) the Moravians shared in the Evangelical Revival in England. Settlements were founded to pursue Christian, Educational and Missionary purposes. Scheduled in 1966 as a place of Historic Interest.
Erected by the Droylsden U.D.C. 1967.

The residential area, with its wide cobbled streets, 18th-century houses, and mature trees, is a nice place to live. The main pedestrian terrace forms a symmetrical frontage of the **Church**, flanked by a High School and College (the Moravians were educational pioneers, numbering Comenius amongst their thinkers.) The old **burial ground** has no headstones, just single plaques, with single men on one side and single women chastely on the other. (Only married couples could await the day of judgement together.)

Ashton-under-Lyne

We eventually arrive in **Ashton-under-Lyne** (the 'lyne' in question was the great fence surrounding the Royal Forest, high on the Pennine moors. The town is known for its market – there is a fine **Victorian Market Hall** (recently destroyed by fire and awaiting restoration). The old Town Hall, to one side of the Market Place, now houses the **Museum of the Manchester Regiment**. (Open Monday-Saturday

A cobbled street and cottages in Fairfield Moravian Settlement

10.00-4.00, admission free.) This regiment had its depot in Ashton, and was the only regiment in the British army to use a municipal coat of arms as its badge. Although a military museum, the displays emphasise the social context of the regiment's history and the impact of war on the locality. Alongside the medals and weapons, topics such as civil unrest in the industrial revolution, and the role of women on the home front in both World Wars, are dealt with. Do not miss the **reconstruction of a Flanders trench**.

The parish church of **St Michael and All Angels** is well worth a visit. (Open Wednesday-Saturday 10.00-4.00.) The Victorians 'improved' the old church by knocking it down and building a new one in the same style, but reinstalled the **unique mediaeval stained glass**. It is 15th century in origin, and tells the story of St Helena. Probably, this was the original dedication.

The **Portland Basin Museum** (open Tuesday-Sunday and Bank Holidays 10.00-5.00, admission free) is a new development at the Portland Canal Basin. Curiously, a genuine canal warehouse was all but demolished and a pastiche erected in its place. The museum is on two levels. Visitors enter on the upper level, and find themselves in a **representation of a 1920s street**, with the downstairs rooms of a typical terraced house, a school room, a fish and chip shop, and other tableaux. Downstairs, there are displays about **local industries**, particularly hatting, coal mining, and textiles. Look out for the **working transport models** of canals and railways. The **Portland Basin** is a former Canal Interchange, the junction of the Ashton and Peak Forest Canals, with links from the Macclesfield and Huddersfield Narrow Canals. An annual Waterways Festival is held here, and boat trips from the museum waterfront are usually available.

Ashton holds an annual **Black Knight Pageant** (known locally as 'riding the black lad'), meant to commemorate Sir Ralph, the infamous 'black knight'.

Old Trafford

Start: Grosvenor Square

Estimated time of walk: 2 hours

Interior: Manchester United Museum – 1 hour

Highlights: A reborn housing area, a UFO landing ground, and the 'Theatre of Dreams'.

This excursion starts at Grosvenor Square, All Saints, and may be combined with the Oxford Road Walk. Leave the Square by way of Cavendish Street, which has become a pedestrian walk under the arches formed by the Metropolitan University buildings. After passing through the courtyard of a Student residence, we cross Cambridge Street and find ourselves on Stretford Road. Directly ahead is the graceful **Hulme Arch** (Chris Wilkinson, 1997), a steel monument which bestrides the bridge over the Princess Road motorway at an oblique angle. A good spot for photographs. The arch symbolises the regeneration of the district of Hulme.

The old terraced working class housing was demolished in the 1960s and replaced by what was then the largest council estate in Europe. The centrepiece of this development was a series of enormous concrete crescents, supposedly inspired by Georgian Bath. They were, in fact, shoddily built monstrosities that nobody really wanted to live in. Hulme rapidly degenerated into a 'sink' estate, holding records for crime, drug abuse, and suicides. Hundreds of decent families had to put up with this social and planning disaster. And in the middle of it all was a plaque, stating that it had won an architectural award. The only possible solution was to rip the 'crescents' down, and start all over again. Present day Hulme is a success story, the result of a scheme in which the tenants were actually consulted. It is an interesting mix of public and private enterprise, and is now a sought after address.

Hulme

It is possible to walk to Old Trafford from here, but most people will want to catch a bus on the other side of the bridge (book to Warwick Road). The bus passes down Stretford Road, past some of the new housing. Opposite **Hulme Library** is the grassy enclave of **Hulme Park**, the first new public park in the city since the 19th century. Metal strips, inserted in stone cobbles, are etched with illustrations chosen by residents to represent the history and life of the area. The cobbles are rather special too. The park is positioned, it would appear, on the intersection of two ley lines, so the stone is heat resistant – just in case a UFO decides to land! The **Zion Centre**, next to the library, was a Methodist Hall, but now has a new lease of life as an 'arts and media space' for people under 25.

Stretford Road terminates at Trafford Bar, where the tollgate was situated on the turnpike road to Chester. There is then a glimpse on the right of the **Swing Bridge** and the **Trafford Park Mural**. You may also catch sight (on the left) of the **'skyhook'**, a rather amusing modern sculpture.

The **White City Gate**, on the left, marks the entrance to a business park, but has an interesting story to tell. The Botanical and Horticultural Society was formed in

The impressive Hulme Arch – now an established landmark

Manchester in 1827. They purchased this sixteen-acre site, laid out gardens and constructed a large glasshouse. The gardens proved a popular public attraction, but had declined by the turn of the century, prompting a company to step in and acquire the site for the 'White City Amusement Park'. Opening in 1907, this 'refined' attraction was not above advertising itself at night by 25,000 electric lights. The White City is remembered by older Mancunians in its final incarnation as a Greyhound Racing Stadium.

Manchester United

Alight from the bus at Warwick Road, with the **Lancashire County Cricket Ground** at the bottom of it. We, however, cross Chester Road and walk up Matt Busby Way.

The name inspires memories in a lot of people – and not just football fans. Manchester United is probably the most famous football team in the world. But the rise to a global position had very humble beginnings – an amateur side formed by the workers of the Lancashire and Yorkshire Railway Carriage and Wagon Works at Newton Heath, in 1878. (It was then known as 'Newton Heath'.) There is a charming story concerning the early years of the club. In 1901, the financial position was so desperate that a fund-raising bazaar was held. The team captain's St Bernard dog wandered the stalls with a collecting box tied to its neck. One day the dog seemingly

The 'Theatre of Dreams'

disappeared, but ended up in the hands of a rich brewer who sought out the owner. Interestingly enough, the brewer gave the team a donation that covered the deficit. The club became 'Manchester United' in 1902.

The glory days began with the fondly remembered Matt Busby. The 'busby babes' were an incomparable team, but many perished in the terrible Munich crash in 1958. United bounced back, and the rest is too well known to be repeated here. Curiously enough, the majority of supporters come from anywhere but Manchester! Ordinary Mancunians will often state a preference for Manchester City, the other local team. Indeed, it has been argued that United's super star status has removed it from its working class local roots. It is very difficult to obtain tickets at short notice, as every match tends to be sold out, and the cost of a season ticket (after joining a waiting list) might deter all but the most die-hard supporter, someone whose entire life revolves around the club. And there are many people like that.

The 67,000 seat **'Theatre of Dreams'** is on the left. It contains the **Manchester United Museum** (open daily, 9.30-5.00), which will even interest visitors who have little interest in the game. A visit may be combined with a (pre-booked) stadium tour, which includes the changing rooms, players lounge, and (wait for it!) a walk down the historic tunnel on to the sacred turf. (To book a tour, ring 0161 868 8631.) You can also eat in the ***Red Café*** while watching soccer highlights on a television 'wall'. Inevitably, there is also a huge souvenir shop. Gary Rhodes, the television chef, is a United supporter – one of the reasons he opened the nearby ***Rhodes and Co*** (and not as expensive as you might think).

You can return to the city centre by walking to Trafford Bar Metrolink Station and catching a tram. *(Alternatively, you can join the Salford Quays excursion by walking over the Swing Bridge to Exchange Quay Station.)*

Didsbury Village

Start: Whitworth Park

Estimated time of walk: 2 hours

Interior: Gallery of English Costume – ½ hour

Highlights: The 'Curry Mile', a museum of costume, a giant 'toastrack', and the 'trendiest village' in Manchester.

An excursion may be added on to the Oxford Road walk, commencing at Whitworth Park. Catch a bus going to Didsbury village, and pass along Wilmslow Road through the famous **'Curry Mile'**. On every side are virtually wall to wall curry houses, in all shapes, sizes and styles – balti, flock wallpaper, you name it, everything is there. This extends to a number of sweet houses, sari houses, and Asian jewellers. Not, perhaps, as inexpensive as it once was, but still a recommended experience.

To the left, behind the shops, **Victoria Park** is located. This legendary Victorian suburb, once the most exclusive address in Manchester, had its own gates and police force. Enough large houses remain to give an impression of what it must once have been like.

Platt Hall

Platt Hall may be found at the corner of Platt Lane, on the right. This 18th-century gentleman's house stands on the site of an earlier structure – once the home of the Worsley family. It is now famed for the **Gallery of English Costume** (open daily 10.00-4.00, 10.00-5.30 in summer, admission free) containing one of the finest collections of historic costume in the country, with some exhibits dating back to the 17th century. The remains of the surrounding estate was acquired by Manchester Council before the First World War, and turned into the pretty **Platt Fields** park. Local anglers (and optimistic small children!) fish the **lake** in the park, and the park itself is usually the venue for the annual Manchester Show.

Platt Chapel is just beyond the parkland, to the right. A small brick nonconformist place of worship, it was erected in about 1687, at a time when such places had to be some distance from the towns that they served. It is now the headquarters of the local photographic society. Hollings College, now part of Manchester Metropolitan University, is on the opposite side of the road. It is known in Manchester as **'the toast rack'**, because of the quirky very 1960s design. (Interestingly enough, it was largely built to train catering students.) The bus passes the **Owen's Park** complex, with its tower (a large Manchester University student village), and passes through what is left of Withington Village. Unfortunately, the local cinema appears to have closed. It was one of the last independent outlets in the Manchester area, and could be relied on for friendly service.

Didsbury

The bus now turns to the left, and soon enters **Didsbury Village.** This area is now populated with university staff and professional people. The profusion of cafés, bars, and restaurants, have earned it the reputation as 'the trendiest village in Man-

The cosmopolitan centre of Didsbury

chester'. The shops start by the site of the old station (the closed railway line is slated for a Metrolink route to Stockport). It is worth seeking out ***Morten's Bookshop***, a very reputable dealer in second-hand and rare books and prints. Past the university buildings, the road does a sharp left at the point of the old village centre. An **historic pub** marks the site of the old village green.

The parish church is nearby. A chapel was recorded in Didsbury in 1235, and may have stood on the site of a far earlier building. It was rebuilt as a stone church in 1620, though much extended and altered since. The present **St James's Church** owes its appearance to the last major rebuilding of 1855. It contains the **17th-century tomb of Sir Nicholas Mosley**. The adjacent 18th-century **rectory** was once tenanted by Alderman Fletcher Moss, an eccentric but public-spirited member of the city council. His strong antiquarian interests, together with a late flowering passion for the bicycle, produced a series of published works under the title 'Pilgrimages to Old Homes'. Sadly, the house is no longer open to the public, but the **beautiful gardens** are worth a visit. Didsbury also contains **'The Towers'**, perhaps the finest Victorian mansion in Manchester. It was the home of Daniel Adamson – the decision to proceed with the building of the Manchester Ship Canal was taken in the drawing room. (The house is private property.) East Didsbury railway station is but a short walk, so it is possible to return to the city centre by suburban train.

Eccles and the Trafford Centre

Start: Salford Quays

Estimated time of walk: 2 hours (an afternoon if including Trafford Centre shopping)

Highlights: An old church, a unique swing aqueduct, and a 'themed' shopping centre.

After visiting the Lowry, the excursion by Metrolink to Salford Quays can be prolonged by boarding an Eccles tram at Broadway or any of the other nearby stations. The tram runs through the streets for the rest of the journey, passing down Langworthy Road and turning left into Eccles New Road. Notice the former 1920s tram depot on the left, near **Weaste Station**. There is a section of original track still in situ in the cobbles of a side street. At the approach to Eccles, we dive under the major road junction in an underpass, and terminate adjacent to Regent Street.

Eccles

Eccles (the name is perhaps Saxon in origin, and probably indicates an early church) was a small weaving village in the 18th century, but was transformed – firstly by the opening of the Mersey and Irwell Navigation; then by the cutting of the Dukes Canal; and latterly by the construction of the Manchester Ship Canal and associated industrial premises. Now it is more or less a suburb of Salford. It is famous for **Eccles Cakes**, a flat cake of flaky pastry folded around a nest of moist currants, first baked in 1796. The original shop is no more, but *Parker Bradburn Bakers* are supposed to make them to the original secret recipe.

Be sure to seek out **St Mary's Church**, at the top of the pedestrianised Church Street. There is mention of a church here in 1120, but the present building is from a later mediaeval period. A **chapel** has been fitted out as a small museum, with a fine **Jacobean tomb**. However, the most interesting exhibits were recovered by archaeologists from the **Duke of Bridgewater's family vault**. Evidently, the good Duke thought that it might not see much future use, and assigned it to John Gilbert, his talented agent. The remains of John's coffin, and those of other family members are displayed. Elsewhere in the church, there is a **memorial** to the family that resided at Agecroft Hall. This venerable house was dismantled in the 1920s, shipped across the Atlantic, and re-erected in Virginia – where it is now a major tourist attraction. On a market day, you can sometimes obtain tea in the meeting centre at the church.

You should now catch a bus to the Trafford Centre. It passes out of the town, crosses the **Duke's Canal**, and turns left, to follow it to the Ship Canal. The canal bank is one long row of boats of all shapes and sizes. We cross the **Ship Canal Swing Bridge**, while the canal crosses the Ship Canal on the left. This was the site of James Brindley's stone aqueduct over the River Irwell, the feature that gave him so much trouble before the parliamentary committee (and led to the model hastily carved from cheese). The Ship Canal virtually obliterated the course of the old river, sweeping away the original aqueduct. But the Duke's Canal still had to cross at the same level without impeding the passage of ocean-going ships and the sailing ships that were still in use at the time. The solution was the unique **Barton Swing Aqueduct**. When it was required to open, gates sealed off each end, so that a box of water was swung clear of a passing ship. It is still operational, but rarely used these days.

The Trafford Centre

Like Kublai Khan's Pleasure Palace, the glittering glass domes of the **Trafford Centre** now come into view. Here Peel Estates decreed not a palace, but a major shopping centre. People get the wrong idea about the Trafford Centre. It is not an out-of-town hypermarket, for shopping in bulk. It is not even an ordinary mall, like the Metrocentre at Gateshead or Meadowhall at Sheffield. Instead, the company undertook a great deal of research into upmarket malls and shopping trends in the United States. Consequently, two things are apparent. With few exceptions, it is aimed at a customer interested in brands, labels, and more specialised shopping. And it is based on the assumption that a shopping mall can be turned into an attraction in its own right, with themed areas, leisure and entertainment facilities, and event based attractions.

Wander down the galleries, reminiscent of Brussels or Milan, tastefully decorated in the neo-classical manner. Explore the themed area, and compare the quality with other leisure attractions – this could not be remotely described as 'tacky'. Examine the attractions – the **giant fountain**, the singing teddy bears, the musical entertainment on offer. There are multi-screen cinemas, a bowling alley, a superb children's play area, and a 'festival village' of smaller retail outlets. (The leisure section and food court can be isolated from the shopping area, and remains open until long past midnight.) A branch of *Selfridges*, with a most excellent food hall, may be found amongst the shops. Take some time out to look at the exterior, with its columns and classical statuary.

Despite the large bus station, the centre is very much designed with the car in mind, and that is its current Achilles heel, for the congestion is sometimes quite horrendous. A Metrolink line is projected. Do not miss the view of the spectacular **viaduct** in the distance, carrying the M6 over the Ship Canal. You can return the way you came or catch a bus direct to the city centre.

Interior of the Trafford Centre *(with kind permission from the Trafford Centre)*

16 Further afield: Greater Manchester

Greater Manchester contains a number of towns and tourist attractions, many of which are well worth visiting. A number have already been dealt with, but this brief list may be of help in choosing a day or half day out.

Wigan

Wigan is, perhaps, the furthest town from Manchester, best reached by a frequent train service. Most people go there to visit **Wigan Pier.** (Open Monday-Thursday 10.00-5.00, weekends 11.00-5.00, joint admission charge available for all attractions.) The actual **'pier'** was a tip-up wagon hoist (since recreated) on the canal, a local joke popularised by George Formby. The present 'pier' is a major **heritage centre** with tableaux, 'living history', etc. The complex includes **Trencherfield Mill**, with its **working mill engines** and **Opies Museum of Memories**, devoted to the history of packaging and everyday design. Don't omit a **canal boat trip** before you leave. Wigan also has a fine shopping centre and market. **Haigh Park** (open all reasonable times, charges for some attractions) is at the opposite end of the town, and has a model village, miniature railway, and other attractions. On the way to it, notice **Mab's Cross**. The wife of a Crusader married someone else in his absence, thinking her first husband dead. Upon the return of her rightful lord and master, the poor woman had to walk barefoot to the cross every day as a penance.

Bolton

Bolton is also best reached by train. It has a fine **Town Hall** and two popular **markets** – one a restored Victorian market hall, the other a vibrant meat and fish market. The old **market place** is comparatively unspoiled, the scene of the execution of the Earl of Derby in the civil wars (he spent his last night in the nearby ***Man and Scythe***). The Victorian **parish church** has a small museum, with Saxon and mediaeval carved stones. The excellent **Municipal Museum** (open Monday-Saturday 10.00-5.00, admission free) contains a good Egyptology gallery – but do not neglect the aquarium in the basement.

Bolton has three historic houses in the vicinity. **Hall i' th' Wood** (open Tuesday-Saturday, 11.00-5.00, Sundays, 2.00-5.00, and Bank Holidays, April-September, admission free) is a picturesque 16th-century half-timbered building, with a 17th-century stone extension. When it was divided into tenements in the 18th century, one was the humble home of Samuel Crompton (p. 191). **Smithills Hall** (same opening times, admission free) is far older, dating from the 14th century. It is known as the **'house of the bloody footprint'**. George Marsh, the Protestant martyr, was condemned to death in the Great Hall. Upon leaving, he stamped his foot to emphasise his innocence of all crime, and the footprint has remained to this day (a reddish brown stain in the shape of a pointed shoe). Marsh was burnt at the stake in 1555. **Turton Tower** (open Monday-Thursday 10.00-12.00, 1.00-5.00, weekends 1.00-5.00, May-September, admission charge) is a lovely old house, built around a stone pele tower dating to 1420.

Middleton

Middleton is on the road to Rochdale, and is served by a frequent bus service. The remains of the old village green were obliterated by a dreadful shopping development in the sixties, but the old quarter is intact. The ***Old Boar's Head*** is a charming half-timbered 17th-century pub. **St Leonard's parish church** (Thursday and Friday, 11.00-3.00, Saturday, 12.00-3.00) dates from 1412, though the tower incorporates earlier stonework. In 1700 it was provided with a "wooden steeple for a stubborn people". Ralph Asseton rebuilt the church in 1513, in thanks for a safe return from Flodden Field. The **Flodden window** is unique – it depicts, with named figures the company of Middleton archers who distinguished themselves in the battle. The ghost of a cavalier haunts the nearby ***Ring o' Bells*** pub. Do not omit a visit to the **Old Grammar School** (open Tuesday-Saturday, 1.30-4.00), founded in 1572.

Rochdale

Rochdale is a few miles beyond Middleton, and can be reached by a direct train service (Metrolink line projected). An elegant Town Hall presides over the Esplanade, part of which is constructed over the River Roch, making it **the widest bridge in Britain**. An **Arts and Heritage Centre** may be found at one end of it. The fine mediaeval **St Chad's parish church** (Tuesday-Thursday, 2.00-4.00, May-August) is located at the top of a flight of steps – the original foundations were deposited there by 'building boggarts', a herd of spectral pigs. The 'baum rabbit' haunts the churchyard. The **Greater Manchester Fire Service Museum** may only be visited by appointment (ring 01706 900155). The co-operative movement began in Rochdale in 1844. The movement was inspired by the 'scientific socialism' of Rober Owen, but it had a practical motivation. Workers were often in thrall to unscrupulous shopkeepers who charged high prices for adulterated food. The option of owning the shop solved this problem. The little shop is now part of the **Rochdale Pioneers Museum** (open Tuesday-Saturday 10.00-4.00, Sunday 2.00-4.00).

Oldham

Oldham is usually visited (bus or train, Metrolink line projected) for the famous Tommyfield Market (antiques flea market on Wednesdays).

Stockport

Stockport (frequent suburban train service) is a town in a valley, dominated by an impressive railway viaduct. It is famous for its **market** (look out for Cheshire cheese), which is near the **parish church** – if it is open, inspect the mediaeval chancel with its effigy of a knight. **Hat Works** (open Monday-Saturday 10.00-5.00, Sunday 11.00-5.00) is Britain's only museum of hats, once a major industry in the town. The **Stockport Air Raid Shelters** (open Monday-Saturday 11.00-3.00, Sunday 1.00-5.00) are a new and unique attraction – sandstone caves used in World War Two for shelters, and restored to recreate life in the 'blitz'. In addition, the elegant **Memorial Art Gallery** (open Monday-Friday, except Wednesday, 11.00-5.00, Saturday 10.00-5.00, admission free) and the **Stockport Museum** (open daily, 1.00-7.00, November-March weekends only, admission free) are both worth a visit.

Two excellent houses are in the vicinity. **Bramhall Hall** (open Mon-

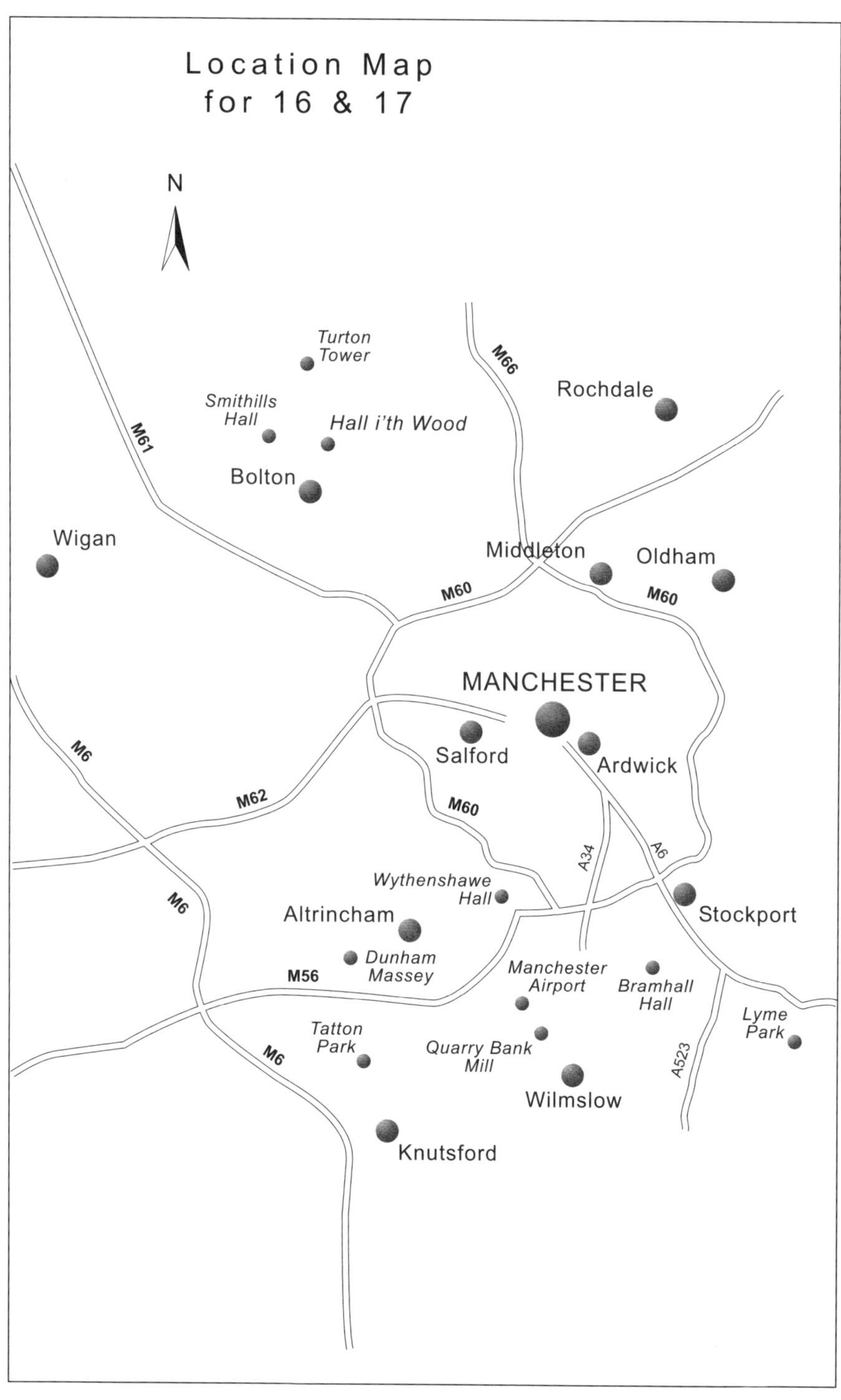
Location Map
for 16 & 17
N
Turton
Tower
Smithills
Hall
Hall i'th Wood
Bolton
Rochdale
M66
M61
Wigan
Middleton
Oldham
M60
M60
MANCHESTER
Salford
Ardwick
M6
M62
M60
A34
A6
Wythenshawe
Hall
Stockport
M6
Altrincham
Dunham
Massey
M56
Manchester
Airport
Bramhall
Hall
Lyme
Park
Tatton
Park
Quarry Bank
Mill
M6
A523
Wilmslow
Knutsford

day-Saturday, 1.00-5.00, Sundays and Bank holidays, 11.00-5.00, Easter to September, admission charge) can be reached by local bus. It is an ancient half-timbered mansion, with parts dating back to the 14th century (**rare wall paintings**). Travel by train to Disley Station for an energetic country walk to **Lyme Park** (National Trust, house open Monday, Tuesday, Friday-Sunday, 1.00pm-4.30pm, admission charge). You will recognise it from the television adaptation of 'Pride and Prejudice'. An extensive Elizabethan mansion has been altered and given neo-classical features in the 18th century. The deer park (with present herd) and the **'Cage'**, a hunting pavilion, are additional attractions.

Wythenshawe & Styal

Wythenshawe Hall (open Wednesday-Sunday 10.00-5.30, April-October, admission free) can be visited en route to the airport or Quarry Bank Mill. It is another 'magpie' half timbered old house, parts of which date back to 1540. It was besieged during the Civil War. Notice the **Cromwell statue**. **Manchester Airport** is connected with Manchester by a frequent and fast train service. It is considered a good day out by children and aviation enthusiasts, who throng the viewing terrace. The latter can be distinguished by their personal radios, tuned to air traffic control frequencies. **Quarry Bank Mill** (National Trust, open daily 11.00-6.00, April-September, Tuesday-Sunday, 11.00-5.00, October-March, admission charge includes all attractions), the only working water-powered textile mill still producing its own cotton cloth in Europe, can usually be accessed by a shuttle bus from the Airport. The mill, typical of its period, is in an attractive country setting. The complex includes the **Apprentice House** (where the pauper children lived) and the **workers' village** (the houses are now private property, please respect).

Altrincham and Dunham Massey

Altrincham, at the end of a Metrolink line, retains some historic buildings and has some interesting shops. It is a short bus ride from **Dunham Massey** (National Trust, house open Saturday-Wednesday, 12.00-5.00, admission charge), formerly the seat of the Earls of Stamford. The house is largely 18th century, but the interior reflects the appearance of a great country house on the eve of the First World War. The **gardens** are exceptional, and are surrounded by a well-stocked deer park.

Knutsford and Tatton

Although not situated in Greater Manchester, **Tatton Park** (one of the most popular National Trust properties) is a short distance from Altrincham and can be reached by a frequent direct train service (alight at Knutsford). **Knutsford** is a lovely little place, with a Georgian **coaching inn** and architectural curiosities and **follies** reminiscent of Portmerion. The main street terminates at the Grand Lodge of **Tatton Park**. (House open 1.00-4.00, Tuesday-Sunday, April-September, admission charge. Gardens open 10.30-5.00, included in admission. Parkland is free, open from 10.30am) The superb **house** is set in a magnificent deerpark, complete with a **lake**. The **gardens** (including a Japanese garden) are justly famed, and the **old Mediaeval hall** can also be visited. There is a **working farm**, with shire horses and a variety of animals.

17 Ardwick

The author takes leave of the reader on a slightly different note. The greater part of this book is intended to highlight the great work of regeneration that has taken place in recent decades in the City of Manchester. However, there have been defeats (particularly in the 1960s and 1970s) as well as victories. To show what we must guard against, take a short walk or excursion through **Ardwick**.

The name is Anglo-Saxon in origin, but the real claim to fame is as the first middle-class suburb, a development starting in the mid-18th century, the first place that the new industrial elite made for themselves well beyond the then bounds of the town.

Proceed from Piccadilly along London Road to **Ardwick Green**, once a private park (complete with pond) for the residents. It now contains a **cenotaph** commemorating the brave men of the 'Eighth Ardwicks', a territorial (part-time volunteer) battalion based in the nearby **drill hall**. (There is a **glacial boulder** in the children's park at the opposite end.) The Green was surrounded by fine Georgian houses, a few of which remain. Sir Robert Peel's father (p.93) resided at one time in one of them. But the back of the Green is now like a row of rotten teeth, with many gaps. **St Thomas's Church** still stands. Consecrated in 1741, as a 'chapel of ease', it is the third oldest church in the city. It was extended at various times, and received a tasteful **campanile tower** in the 1830s. The interior of the church was pure Georgian, with galleries, a Samuel Green organ, and a lovely east end graced with a 17th-century Italian painting of the nativity. To this must be added a memorial chapel to the 'Ardwicks', many of whom perished in 1915 at Gallipoli. All gone! The gutted interior is now a centre for voluntary community groups.

Apsley Cottage Inn, at Ardwick Green. It sounds so rural – a real 'local' pub that's popular with customers attending rock concerts at the nearby Apollo Theatre

Turn left at the far end of the park, and follow **Higher Ardwick** round to the right. The Regency terraces disappeared in the 1960s. Somewhere here was a house tenanted by a music teacher, who had married one of Charles Dickens's female relatives. Dickens visited and no doubt played with their disabled son, said to be the model for 'Tiny Tim'.

Go right at the railway bridge, down Devonshire Street. A stone plaque on the right marks the site of **Ardwick Cemetery**. The cemetery was Manchester's second oldest, and the most exclusive. Here were interred Thomas Potter, the first Mayor, John Dalton (p.46), and Ernest Jones, the Chartist. It was converted into playing fields in the sixties. **Nicholl's Hospital**, a charity institution founded in 1881, stands on the corner of Hyde Road. The gaunt brick building, with a tall central tower, is now the Ellen Wilkinson Comprehensive School. A glance to the left down Hyde Road reveals a railway bridge in the distance. It was the place where Sergeant Brett was murdered (p.39), and some older residents still call it the 'fenian arch' to this day.

Now turn right, down Hyde Road. Again, one sees a rather desolate part of the city. The old Hippodrome Music Hall (previously known as the Empire) stood on the right-hand corner, near the traffic island. We are now back at Ardwick Green.

As it is with liberty, the price of a civilised city is eternal vigilance.

Index

More Discoveries around Manchester:

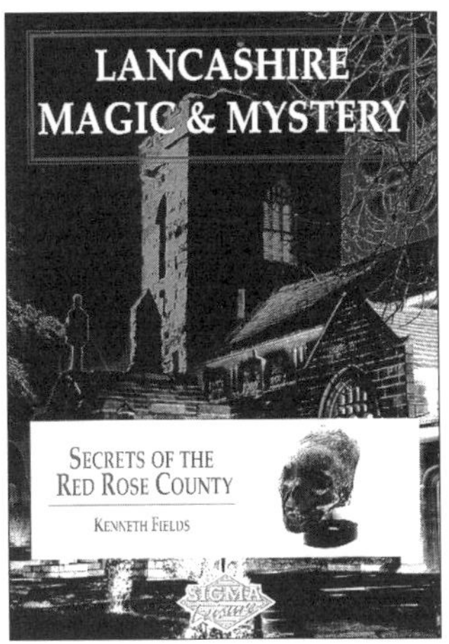

LANCASHIRE MAGIC & MYSTERY: Secrets of the Red Rose County

Kenneth Fields

Covering all of Lancashire, including Merseyside and Greater Manchester, Kenneth Fields's book guides you to places of mystery and curiosity. With tales of hauntings, witchcraft, religious relics, folklore and UFOs, this book is a must for anyone interested in the supernatural. Will appeal to visitors and residents, and armchair travellers who relish the secret history of the landscape. *£7.95*

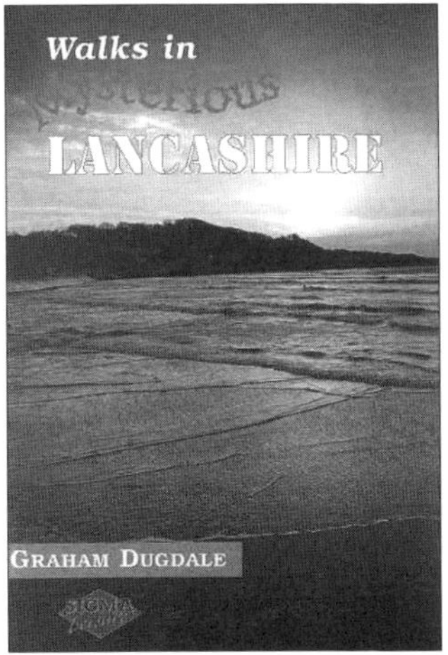

WALKS IN MYSTERIOUS LANCASHIRE

Graham Dugdale

Delving into a host of mysterious places throughout Lancashire, this unusual collection of 30 walks, suitable for all the family, will appeal to walkers with enquiring minds. From the enchanting follies of Lord Levenshulme of Bivington to the origins of the 'American Dream' in Worton, history and legend are inextricably linked in this succession of fine walks set in the superb Lancashire landscape. Lucid walking directions and the author's ornate, hand-drawn maps complement the entertaining commentary. *£6.95*

BY-WAY BIKING IN LANCASHIRE

Henry Tindell

From Morecambe Bay to Bolton and from Blackpool to Burnley, Henry Tindell reveals Lancashire's outstanding potential as a destination for mountain bikers. 27 routes explore a fine variety of off-road tracks in a wealth of countryside and villages all within easy reach of the large northern towns and cities. As well as routes for the hardened off-roader, Henry has included some safe riding and easy trails suitable for young and old. *£7.95*

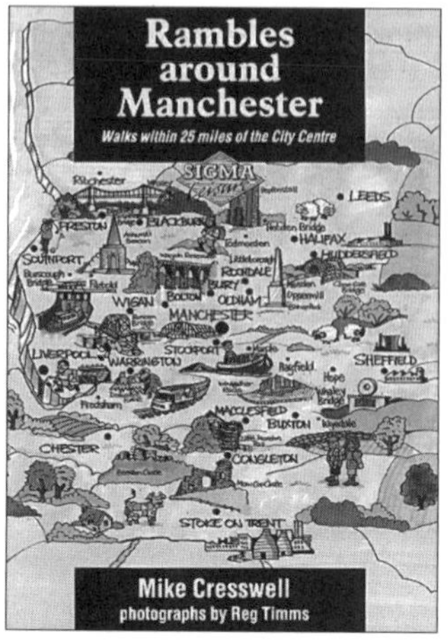

RAMBLES AROUND MANCHESTER

Mike Cresswell

Not along the city streets or down suburban roads, but out and about in the super scenery that is so easily accessible from the city by car or public transport. This book includes 16 circular routes which can be varied to give around 100 fabulous walks. The areas covered include the South Pennines, the Ribble Valley, West Lancashire, Delamere Forest, North Staffordshire, and the Peak District.The walks are illustrated with striking photographs from the camera of Reg Timms, a prize-winning Northern photographer. *£7.95 (updated edition due summer 2005)*

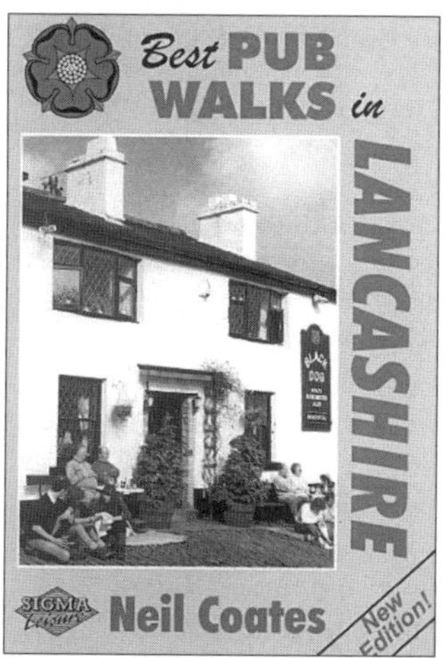

WEST PENNINE WALKS

Mike Cresswell

Bolton's Mike Cresswell is renowned for the accuracy of his instructions and his impish humour. In this second edition he has re-walked every single one of his routes exploring the countryside of the delightful West Pennine area. *£7.95*

BEST PUB WALKS IN LANCASHIRE

Neil Coates

Lancashire has a rich pub heritage and a surprising variety of countryside for invigorating walks. First published in 1991 and revised over the years, the book has been completely up-dated to reflect, in particular, changes in opening times, catering and beers available – which all contribute to the very best in pub walks! *£7.95*

BEST TEA SHOP WALKS IN CHESHIRE

Clive Price

"A winning blend of scenic strolls and tasty tea shops" – *Cheshire Life.* Discover the Cheshire countryside and its traditional tea shops where walkers get a warm welcome. The walks range are just long enough to work up an appetite for a traditional afternoon tea and locations range fromKettleshulme in Cheshire's hill country all the way to Parkgate on the Dee estuary. *£7.95*

(updated edition early 2005)